MW01260209

OXFORD CLASSICAL MONOGRAPHS

Published under the supervision of a Committee of the
Faculty of Classics in the University of Oxford

The aim of the Oxford Classical Monographs series (which replaces the Oxford Classical and Philosophical Monographs) is to publish books based on the best revised theses on Greek and Latin literature, ancient history, and ancient philosophy examined by the Faculty Board of Classics.

Late Roman Warlords

PENNY MacGEORGE

OXFORD
UNIVERSITY PRESS

OXFORD

UNIVERSITY PRESS

Great Clarendon Street, Oxford OX2 6DP

Oxford University Press is a department of the University of Oxford.
It furthers the University's objective of excellence in research, scholarship,
and education by publishing worldwide in

Oxford New York

Auckland Bangkok Buenos Aires Cape Town,
Chennai Dar es Salaam Delhi Hong Kong Istanbul Karachi
Kolkata Kuala Lumpur Madrid Melbourne Mexico City Mumbai Nairobi
São Paulo Shanghai Taipei Tokyo Toronto

Oxford is a registered trade mark of Oxford University Press
in the UK and certain other countries

Published in the United States
by Oxford University Press Inc., New York

British Library Cataloguing in Publication Data

Data available

Library of Congress Cataloging-in-Publication Data
MacGeorge, Penny.
Late Roman warlords / Penny MacGeorge.
p. cm.–(Oxford classical monographs)
Includes bibliographical references and index.
1. Generals–Rome–Biography. 2. Rome–History–Empire, 284–476. I. Title. II. Series.
DG312. M33 2002
937′.09′0922–dc21
2002070215

ISBN 0-19-925244-0

Typeset by Kolam Information Services Pvt Ltd, Pondicherry, India
Printed in Great Britain
on acid-free paper by
Biddles Ltd, Guildford & King's Lynn

PREFACE

This book was written as a result of research undertaken for a D.Phil. thesis at the University of Oxford from 1992 to 1996. Its focus, within the context of the fifth-century western Roman Empire, is an examination of some of the individual, non-imperial, leaders of that period, who, as their political importance was based on military power, have been described by some historians of the period as warlords. Although I am not totally happy with this description (nor, hence, the title of this book) it has proved difficult to find a more accurate and pleasing one that is also as succinct.

The translations from Latin are mine, with a few exceptions, as indicated in the footnotes. My translations of the panegyrics of Sidonius Apollinaris are strongly influenced by those of Anderson, but I have endeavoured to produce a version close to the basic meaning but modern in language, at the expense of poetic style. For entries from Hydatius' chronicle I use the numbering system from Burgess (1993). For all works written in Greek I have generally used and cited published translations in English. The translation of the fragments of Damascius is by John Matthews or Michael Whitby. Unlike the Latin texts, those in Greek are not given (with the exception of a few particularly important words). For the fragments from Priscus' history I use the numbering system from Blockley (1983). While contributions from many other people have been incorporated into this work, the mistakes and infelicities are, of course, all my own.

I thank all those who have helped me produce this book and the thesis that preceded it, especially my doctoral supervisor Bryan Ward-Perkins, of Trinity College, Oxford. I am grateful for his invaluable assistance, kindness, and encouragement, particularly for extensive proof-reading and polishing of my translations for the thesis and, more recently, for helping to ensure the survival of this book. I also want to express my gratitude to John Matthews for his advice and guidance, especially on the Greek sections, and to John Drinkwater, who first encouraged me into postgraduate study, and who has read drafts and given me so much advice and kindness over the years.

I must also thank all the other busy people who took time to assist me in my research and writing. This long list includes Roger Tomlin for his translation of the impenetrable Paulinus Petricordiensis; Michael Whitby and Michael Sharp for their advice on Greek; Neil Christie and the late John Lloyd for information on Italian archaeology; Peter Heather and Simon Loseby for their encouragement in my first year; David Lambert of Brasenose College and Alan Lawrence of Newfield School, Sheffield, for their generous assistance with German translations; Chris Howgego and Cathy King for their numismatics expertise; Margareta Steinby for answering my queries on Roman topography; Mark Humphries of St. Andrews University; Benedict Sallway; David Pritchard of Leeds Grammar School; Lucienne Drew of Newfield School, Sheffield; Hugh, Fiona, and Martin Jones for their help with ICT and many other things; and (for their assistance with research expenses) the Craven Committee, St. Anne's Travel Fund, Trinity College, my stepfather Gordon Anderson and both my late grandmother Hilda Heakin and my late mother Alma Houghton-Anderson (both greatly missed).

I am also very grateful to Madame Gisèle Lacam for giving me permission to use the photograph of the 'Ricimer' coin from the publication by her late husband Guy Lacam, *Ricimer, Leon I et Anthemius: le monnayage de Ricimer*; also J. P. C. Kent and Spink and Sons for permission to reproduce the Ricimer monogram from *Roman Imperial Coinage*, x; and the Museum of Berry in Bourges for their permission to use the photograph of the diptych of Aetius. My thanks also to the staff in the academic division of OUP for their help in turning a thesis into a book, and to the always helpful librarians at the Ashmolean and Bodleian Libraries

Last, but not least, I thank my husband Michael MacGeorge for the practical help and encouragement without which this book could not have been written, Caitlin for help with final checks, and both my daughters, Caitlin and Ellen, for putting up with 'Mummy's work' for so long.

P. MacGeorge

Isle of Wight, 2002

CONTENTS

ILLUSTRATIONS

PLATES

MAPS

FIGURES

ILLUSTRATIONS

PLATES

MAPS

FIGURES

ABBREVIATIONS

Standard abbreviations such as *Pan., Ep.*, and frag. and obvious contractions of names (such as Claud. for Claudian) used in the footnotes are not included.

AASS   *Acta Sanctorum*, ed. J. Bollandus *et al.* (Antwerp, Tongerloo, Paris, Brussels: 1643–1925)

CIL   *Corpus Inscriptionum Latinarum (Inscriptiones Latinae Antiquissimae)*, ed. Th. Mommsen *et al.* (Berlin: 1863–)

HE   *Historia Ecclesiastica*

ICUR   *Inscriptiones Christianae Urbis Romae*, ed. G. B. de Rossi (Rome: 1857–88)

ILCV   *Inscriptiones Latinae Christianae Veteres*, ed. E. Diehl (Berlin: 1925–31)

ILS   *Inscriptiones Latinae selectae*, ed. H. Dessau (Berlin: 1892–1916)

MGH   *Monumenta Germaniae Historica*

MGHAA   *MGH, Auctores antiquissimi*, 15 vols. (Berlin: 1877–1919)

MGHSRM   MGH, *Scriptores rerum Merovingicarum*, 7 vols. (Hannover: 1884–1920)

Nov.   *Novella* (followed by abbreviation of name of the legislating emperor)

Pat. Lat. J.-P. Migne, *Patrologiae cursus completus. Series Latina*, 217 vols. (Paris: 1844–55)

PLRE i   A. H. M. Jones, J. R. Martindale, and J. Morris (1971). *The Prosopography of the Later Roman Empire, i.* AD 260–395 (Cambridge)

PLRE ii   J. R. Martindale (1980). *The Prosopography of the Later Roman Empire, ii.* AD 395–527 (Cambridge)

RE   *Realencyclopädie der classischen Altertumswissenschaft*, ed. A. Pauly, G. Wissowa, W. Kroll, *et al.* (Stuttgart: 1893–)

CHRONOLOGY

(Only reasonably secure dates are included. All dates are AD.)

378   Defeat of Roman army at Adrianople.
395   Death of Theodosius the Great. Final division of empire into East and West.
406–7 Crossing of the frozen Rhine by barbarian tribes.
409   Assassination of patrician and *magister militum* Stilicho.
410   Sack of Rome by Goths under Alaric.
423   Death of western emperor Honorius.
425   Infant Valentinian III becomes western emperor.
429   The Vandals cross to North Africa.
433   Flavius Aetius becomes dominant in the West.
437   Marriage of Valentinian III and Eudoxia.
451   Defeat of Attila by Aetius and Visigoths in Gaul.
452   Attila attacks Italy, but retreats.
453   Death of Attila.
454   Assassination of Aetius by Valentinian III.
455   Assassination of Valentinian by Aetius' followers. Petronius Maximus emperor. Vandals under Gaiseric sack Rome. Petronius Maximus killed. Gallic senator Avitus proclaimed emperor at Arles and moves to Rome.
456   Ricimer defeats Vandals in or near Corsica. Avitus defeated at Placentia by Ricimer and Majorian, ordained bishop, (?) possibly assassinated.
457   Majorian formally installed as emperor. Ricimer made patrician.
460   Majorian's abortive campaign against the Vandals.
461   Majorian assassinated by Ricimer. Ricimer places Libius Severus on throne. In Gaul the *magister militum* Aegidius refuses to acknowledge him.
463   Battle of Orleans.

464	Marcellinus of Dalmatia fighting in Sicily. Alan attack on North Italy defeated by Ricimer.
465	Death of Aegidius in Gaul. Death of Libius Severus in Rome.
466	Euric takes Visigothic throne in southern Gaul.
467	Anthemius appointed western emperor. Marcellinus accompanies him to Italy. Ricimer marries Anthemius' daughter Alypia.
468	Joint expedition against Vandals defeated. Assassination of Marcellinus.
471	Failure of Anthemius' campaign against Euric.
472	Ricimer besieges Anthemius in Rome, proclaims Olybrius emperor. Rome sacked and Anthemius killed by Ricimer's Burgundian nephew Gundobad. Ricimer dies. Olybrius dies.
473	Gundobad made patrician, makes Glycerius emperor.
474	Glycerius deposed and flees Italy. Julius Nepos Marcellinus' nephew becomes emperor in Italy.
475	Julius Nepos overthrown by the *magister militum* Orestes and flees Italy. Orestes makes his son Romulus Augustulus emperor.
476	Odovacer kills Orestes and deposes Romulus Augustulus; becomes King of Italy. Traditional date of fall of Roman empire in the West.
480	Last legitimate emperor Julius Nepos assassinated in Dalmatia.
486	Aegidius' son Syagrius defeated at Soissons by Frankish king Clovis.

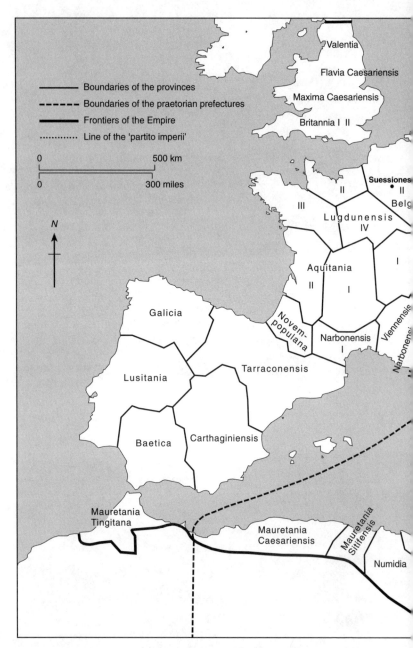

Map 1: Dioceses and provinces of the Late Roman Empire

Raetia I • II

Noricum Ripense • Noricum Mediterraneum

Pannonia I • Valeria

Venetia

Mediolanum

Emilia

Ravenna
Ariminum

Flaminia

Pannonia II

Savi

Etruria

Picenum

Salona

Dalmatia

Moesia I

Dacia Ripensis

Moesia II

Valeria

Rome
Roma

Samnium

Prevalitana

Dardania

Dacia Mediterranea

Thrace

Hemus

Europe

Corsica

Campania

Apulia

New Epirus
Old Epirus

Macedonia

Rhodope

Hellespontus

Sardinia

Lucania

Thessaly

Asia

Lydia

Consular

Agrigentum
Carthago

Sicily

Achaea

Caria

Crete

Introduction

There must have been real, long-lived individuals who, born in the security of the extensive, powerful, and eternal empire of the late fourth century, ended their lives in fledgling barbarian kingdoms, remembering the sacks of Rome and aware that a king not an emperor now sat there. Whether or not many strands of continuity remained, it would be patronizing to think that people of the time were not conscious of the political, social, and economic changes that had occurred in their lifetimes and which must, in many cases, have affected their own lives directly or indirectly. After all, although many aspects of the life of, say, a Ukrainian of the year AD 2000 might be similar to those of their birth in 1910, this would hardly lead us to assert that they had not experienced and survived shattering change, or that they were unaware of it. The ways in which people react to change, and find ways to adapt physically and mentally, and, if possible, to profit from it, are as interesting as the hows and whys of the change itself.

We can only very occasionally (for example with the Gallic aristocrat, poet, and historians' *bête noire* Sidonius Apollinaris) reach out to the people of the fifth century, and to ordinary people virtually never. For four groups—emperors, saints and Fathers of the Church, the aristocracy, and, lastly, the military élite—we have at least some extant evidence that can be synthesized and analysed. From the last group, this book will examine the careers of Marcellinus of Dalmatia, the general Aegidius and his son Syagrius, and the barbarian patrician Ricimer and his short-lived successors (down to the successful coup of Odovacer). All these men held high Roman military rank (although in the case of Syagrius this is probable rather than certain); and all exercised considerable political power, being the effective, if not the legitimate, rulers (even if temporarily) of areas of the old empire. These ranged in size from Ricimer's domination over Italy and what else remained of the Roman empire in its last decades to Syagrius' control of, perhaps, the territory of one unimportant Gallic city, or even merely the remnants of the Gallic field army when the last emperor had long fallen.

As the basis of their political power was military power, they, and other similar men, have often been referred to as warlords. Although there have been several studies of these warlords, there does seem to be a place for a new and thorough examin-ation based on primary sources, and including discussion of the historical debates and theories. Emphatically no attempt is made to fit all the warlords to one common format. This book does not try to describe the events of the end of the empire in the West, still less to explain them, but will reconstruct something of the lives and, if at all recoverable, the attitudes of a few men who shaped and were shaped by those events.

It is well known that the sources for this period are difficult, and one group of scholars sees them all as so unreliable that we might just as well pack up our historical bags and all go home. Nevertheless, I have, with great caution, used nearly all the available sources, even the fragmentary and problematic, to produce, as best as possible, old-fashioned narrative history. In each case the primary sources have been used to produce as complete a chronological account as is possible of each man's career. Nearly all the ancient written sources (including those which are admittedly unreliable and even verging on folklore) have been utilized, and many examined in detail. Where pos-sible, use has also been made of archaeological, numismatic, and place-name evidence. Writing narrative history for this period is, as has been said many times before, rather like trying to piece together a jigsaw with many missing and damaged pieces. In the writing it has sometimes seemed as though the commonest words in this book are 'possibly' and 'probably'; and perhaps the probables should all be read as possibles and the possibles as guesswork. At the end of the day I have simply tried to recon-struct as common sense dictates.

Following a brief overview of earlier warlords who were their predecessors, each of the three parts to this book is an 'in-depth' study of one, or more than one, warlord, but also necessarily of the regions with which they are chiefly associated. The first part looks at Dalmatia and Marcellinus, its ruler from the A D 450s to 468. He was of Roman origin and, as well as ruling Dalmatia, was involved in the wars against the Vandals and with the western emperor Anthemius. The second part concentrates on Gaul, primarily northern Gaul, the Gallic *magister militum per Gallias* Aegidius, and his son Syagrius, a regional ruler in north-eastern Gaul, probably based at Soissons. This covers the period *c.* A D 458 to 486 (the latter date being well after the formal end of the western empire).[1] The third part is on Italy, the Suevian-Gothic patrician Ricimer who ran the empire there from *c.* 458 to 472, and his two successors as patrician, the Burgundian Gundobad and the Roman Orestes; and, finally, Odovacer, who became the first barbarian King of Italy in A D 476. Each of these three parts is somewhat different in emphasis, organization, and the issues explored. The major theme of the first part is the question of the western or eastern affiliations of Marcellinus. The second part, to a large extent, examines the problem of the existence or non-existence of a 'kingdom of Soissons'. The third part includes a section on the character and motivation of Ricimer, particularly in relation to the emperors that he made and unmade, and how historians' assessments of these have altered over time.

A secondary objective has been to explore the possibility that what was happening in Italy and Dalmatia, and especially northern Gaul, and the activities of regional leaders might hint at what was happening in immediately post-Roman Britain. This is so well studied, and extensively written about in English (and so often misleadingly, and sometimes no doubt cynically, sold to the reading public as 'The Age of Arthur'), that it is easy to forget that it is almost entirely undocumented. Discussion of the possibilities of comparison is included in Part II. An appendix briefly explores the topic (relevant to Pts. I and III) of sea power in the Mediterranean during the fifth century A D.

Much has been written about the fall, or Fall, or absence of fall, of Rome in the fifth century (notoriously reinterpreted

---

[1] The material produced in connection with the (supposed) anniversary of Clovis' conversion, in 1996, which would be relevant to Pt. II, was only beginning to be published when this book was being completed and so it was not possible to incorporate it.

with each generation). We are, no doubt, still as far as ever from this distant transitional world and the real people who lived in it. Which is not to say that we should not attempt the journey.

I
Predecessors

By the early fifth century AD supreme military command was no longer exercised by the western emperor. The lack of military activity among fifth-century emperors, both eastern and western, was in stark contrast to that of emperors of the third and fourth centuries, who had led their armies in the field and cultivated the respect and loyalty of their men. This sea change gave high-ranking imperial officers opportunities to aggrandize their military and political roles, and one individual would usually become dominant in the West. This process lies behind the careers of the men discussed in this book, although by the later fifth century their power bases were increasingly regional.

In the fourth century AD the dominant military leader held the rank of *magister militum praesentalis*, either *equitum* or *peditum*, but in the fifth century he held the title of [*comes et*] *magister utriusque militum praesentalis*. Many of them also held the consulship one or more times. There was obviously no constitutional designation for a military leader who was also the power behind the imperial throne, but a sort of *de facto* title did develop. The style of *patricius* had been revived by Constantine I. It was not an office with particular duties and rights, but a high-status personal title or dignity, and held for life (the holder often being designated as the patrician 'of' a particular emperor). From the time of Flavius Constantius,[1] the combination of supreme military rank together with the title of 'patrician' came to mark the dominant figure in the West, and allowed his involvement in both military and civil matters.[2]

---

[1] Prosper, *Chron.* 1256 *s.a.* 415 and 1271 *s.a.* 419; *Cod. Theod.* XV, 14, 14; Hydatius, 52 (60) *s.a.* 416; etc.

[2] On the western patriciate see Baynes (1922: 227); Barnes (1975: 155–69); Demandt (1970: 631); O'Flynn (1983: 65–7, 85–7); Barnwell (1992: 43–7).

Others might hold the title of *patricius* but they were not *the* Patrician.[3]

In the later fourth century there had been ambitious imperial generals who exercised great power in the state when the ruling emperor was weak. Many of the causes of the decline of the western empire were inherent and perhaps inevitable; but one was not. That was the genetic accident that the sons of Valentinian I and, crucially, the sons and grandsons of Theodosius should prove to have characters and capabilities so very different from those of their fathers. It had been normal for ruling emperors to lead Rome's armies in the field, but neither Honorius or Arcadius did so. The only example of a ruling emperor in military action in the West during the fifth century is that of Majorian. It was largely this trend that allowed the separation of military power and, increasingly, political power from the imperial throne. In previous centuries such men would usually have disposed of their nominal master and made themselves emperor but, presumably because many were barbarian by birth, and perhaps because the imperial succession had become more monarchical and dynastic, they did not do so. They either continued to 'serve' the existing emperor or, if they got rid of him, set up a replacement, usually from the aristocracy.

Merobaudes, a German, possibly a Frank (in a position of power *c.* AD 375–88), was *magister peditum* under Valentinian I, and was instrumental in the proclamation of Valentinian II, but seems later to have transferred his allegiance to the usurper Magnus Maximus.[4] Bauto, a Frank (in a position of power *c.* AD 380–86/7), became *magister militum* in the reign of Valentinian II and exercised great influence in the West (perhaps the bravest thing he ever did was to stand up to Saint Ambrose).[5] His daughter Eudoxia may have married the Emperor

---

The view of some scholars (for instance Ensslin (1931: 497)) that it equated with the post of *magister utriusque militiae* is now rejected.

[3] When there were other patricians Aetius was addressed as *magnificus vir parens patriusque noster* rather than just *patricius noster* (*Nov. Val.* 36).

[4] Zosimus, IV, 17, 19; Ammianus, XXX, v–x; Prosper, *Chron.* 1183 *s.a.* 384. His suicide seems to have been connected to his transference of allegiance (Pacatus, *Pan. ad Theodosius, Pat. Lat.* III (XII), 28, 4).

[5] Zosimus, IV, 33; Ambrose, *Ep.* 57.

Arcadius.[6] After his death, another Frank, Arbogastes (in a position of power *c.* AD 388–94), perhaps related to Bauto,[7] became supreme *magister militum*, because, according to one source, of his military prowess and his popularity with the army (described as being controlled by Frankish mercenaries).[8] He intervened in civilian affairs, pursued personal vendettas against other Frankish leaders, slew members of Valentinian's council, bullied the emperor, and defied his attempt to dismiss him.[9] Not long afterwards Valentinian died in strange circumstances. Arbogastes set up a pagan academic, Eugenius, as emperor, but was defeated by Theodosius and fell on his sword.[10]

Of all the dominant *magistri* perhaps the most famous is Stilicho (in power AD 394–408), whose father was a Vandal cavalry officer. (His mother was Roman.)[11] A major difference between Stilicho and his predecessors and successors was that he came to power not as a result of a successful military career and control of the army, but mainly because of his relationship to the Emperor Honorius' father Theodosius I, whose adopted daughter, Serena, Stilicho married.[12] Stilicho was promoted by Theodosius, and by the time of the emperor's death in AD 395 was *magister utriusque militum praesentalis*.[13] He may have honestly believed that the dying Theodosius had entrusted to him the protection of both his sons, Honorius in the West and, more problematically, Arcadius in the East.

---

[6] Philostorgius, *HE* XI, 6. His testimony is usually accepted, but he is the only historian to report this (nor is it ever mentioned in relation to Arcadius' son Theodosius II). Arcadius marrying the daughter of a Frankish general is perhaps inherently improbable.

[7] John of Antioch (frag. 187) is alone in reporting that Arbogastes was Bauto's son.

[8] Zosimus, IV, 53; Greg. Tur. *Historiae* II, 9 (quoting from a history by Sulpicius Alexander).

[9] Greg. Tur. *Historiae* II, 9, 87; Zosimus, IV, 53; John Ant. frag. 1 (who has a wonderful description of him tearing up the rescript, roaring with rage, and storming out with a drawn sword).

[10] John Ant. frag. 187.

[11] Orosius, VII, 38; Claudian, *de Cons. Stil.* I, 35–9.

[12] Given Stilicho's social position, this was perhaps a love-match.

[13] For Stilicho's early official career and titles see *PLRE* i, 853–8, Fl. Stilicho.

It is not surprising that in the early years of Honorius' reign the real power lay with Stilicho, a grown man in control of the armed forces and supported by an inner circle of courtiers.[14] It is more surprising that Honorius did not meet an untimely end so that Stilicho could assume the purple. The reasons may have been Stilicho's loyalty to Theodosius' family combined with his Vandal ancestry (although there is really no logical reason why this had to debar him). Stilicho's stubborn belief in his right to concern himself in the eastern half of the empire deflected his energies, and he continually failed to deal decisively with Alaric,[15] causing his support in the senate and imperial court to evaporate. The situation was complicated by Stilicho's vicarious ambition for his son Eucherius (having failed to get a royal grandchild from the marriages of his daughters to Honorius). When the emperor finally turned openly against him in AD 408, Stilicho did little to resist and seems to have let himself be killed.[16]

A period of military and political confusion, and the Gothic sack of Rome, followed his death, but one of his subordinates, Flavius Constantius, took revenge on Stilicho's murderers, and gained supreme command of the armed forces as *magister utriusque militum* in AD 410/11.[17] He had some successes in containing and coming to terms with the Goths, and destroyed the usurper Constantine III in Gaul.[18] By AD 415 he held the title of *patricius*, and in AD 417 married Honorius' sister Galla Placidia, by whom he had two children, Valentinian and Honoria.[19] He dominated political life in the last years of Hon-

[14] Matthews (1975: 258).

[15] He never had the military edge over Alaric, perhaps because his forces were unreliable or understrength, because of bad personal generalship, or a propensity for containment and compromise. In the latter case he was following the policies of his mentor Theodosius, in which indeed he may have had no choice.

[16] The main source is Zosimus, V, 34–7.

[17] Olympiodorus, frags. 8, 39; Orosius, VII, 42; Prosper, *Chron.* 1247 *s.a.* 412; John Ant. frag. 197; etc.

[18] Orosius, VII, 42–3; Olympiodorus, frags. 1, 20, 22, 26; Prosper, *Chron.* 1243 *s.a.* 411; Hydatius, 42 (50) *s.a.* 411, 52 (60) *s.a.* 416, 61 (69) *s.a.* 418; etc.

[19] Olympiodorus, frags. 8, 20, 34; Prosper, *Chron.* 1259 *s.a.* 416, 1267 *s.a.* 418; Hydatius, 52 (60) *s.a.* 416, 54 (62) *s.a.* 416; etc.

orius' reign,[20] and was finally proclaimed co-Augustus in AD 421, but, most unfortunately for Rome, died seven months later.[21] After Constantius' death, a number of generals, including Asterius, Bonifatius, and Castinus, jockeyed for power; and Castinus may have been behind Ioannes' seizure of the purple on Honorius' death in AD 423.[22] Both men fell from power when an eastern army returned the infant Valentinian III and his mother to the western throne in AD 425.

This period, from the battle of Adrianople in AD 376 to the Vandal invasion of North Africa in AD 429, has been described as one of irreversible change for the worse for the western empire.[23] Within two generations, the separation of the eastern and western empires had become established, and several barbarian peoples had become settled in the western empire, where the imperial armies were no longer dominant. Increasingly, barbarians were recruited in groups or as individuals into temporary or semi-permanent federate units. Barbarians were also recruited as *bucellari*, bodyguards or companions similar to those in Germanic and Celtic societies. Close bonds were formed between commanders and *foederati*, and even more so with *bucellari*, and it may have been this, as well as, or rather than, the western military command structure,[24] that enabled the *magistri militiae* to take power.

It was against this background that Flavius Aetius fought his way to power in the AD 420s, and he stands, directly or indirectly, behind all those discussed in this book. Aetius was of Roman birth, his father a high-ranking army officer who had served under Stilicho, his mother an Italian noblewoman.[25] His early life was unusual; he had been held hostage by Alaric's Goths for three years, and later by the Huns.[26] It is likely that

---

[20] Sid. Apoll. *Pan.* VII, 210–11.

[21] Olympiodorus, frag. 34; Hydatius, 67 (75) *s.a.* 420, 68 (76) *s.a.* 421; John Ant. frag. 197; etc.

[22] Prosper, *Chron.* 1278 *s.a.* 422; John Ant. frag. 195; Hydatius, 74 (83) *s.a.* 424; etc.

[23] Williams and Friell (1994: 144).

[24] Varady (1961: 362); Liebeschuetz (1990: 467–8).

[25] Greg. Tur. *Historiae* II, 8; Zosimus, V, 36; Merobaudes, *Pan.* II, 110; etc.

[26] Greg. Tur. *Historiae*, II, 8; Merobaudes, *Pan.* II, 1–4, 127–43, *Carm.* IV, 42–6.

Plates 1 and 2: Ivory consular diptych of Flavius Aetius, courtesy of the Museum of Berry in Bourges

he gained useful knowledge of these cultures and personal contacts within them, even perhaps knowledge of their languages.[27]
Aetius held a court position under the western usurper Ioannes,
and was sent as an envoy to the Huns, returning with a Hunnish
force just too late to prevent Ioannes' deposition. However,
Aetius not only survived, but gained promotion to *magister
militum per Gallias*.[28]

In c. AD 425 Aetius began a long series of campaigns in Gaul,
against the Visigoths, Franks, and Burgundians, making use of
Hun cavalry. He was also engaged in a protracted power
struggle both with rival generals, including Felix and Bonifatius, and with Valentinian III's mother and regent Galla Placidia. This ended in c. AD 433, by which time both Felix and
Bonifatius were dead. Aetius became *magister utriusque militum*,
and shortly afterwards *patricius*.[29] He had not gained this position easily and had come close, on occasion, to defeat; at one
point having to flee to the Huns. From this date, however, we
know of no challenge to his position, and for the next twenty
years he led the Roman army and involved himself in political,

[27] Indeed, Stein (1959: i, 223) suggested that it was Aetius' barbarian
connections that enabled him to control the army. Several historians, including, most recently, Liebeschuetz (1993: 270–2), have stressed his reliance on
personal control of Hun forces.

[28] Prosper, *Chron.* 1288 and 1290 *s.a.* 425; *Chronica Gallica a 452*, 100 *s.a.*
425; Cassiodorus, *Chronica s.a.* 425; etc.

[29] The course of this power struggle is complicated and controversial. The
main sources for this and his campaigns are: Prosper, *Chron.* 1290 *s.a.* 425,
1303 *s.a.* 430, 1310 *s.a.* 432, 1322 *s.a.* 435, 1335 *s.a.* 439, etc; *Chronica
Gallica a 452*, 102 *s.a.* 427, 106 *s.a.* 430, 111 *s.a.* 432, 117 *s.a.* 435, 118 *s.a.*
436, 119 *s.a.* 437, etc.; John Ant. frags. 196, 201, 201 (3); Hydatius, 84 (94)
s.a. 430, 85 (95) *s.a.* 430, 89 (99) *s.a.* 430, 94 (103) *s.a.* 433, 104 (112) *s.a.* 437,
etc.; Sid. Apoll. *Pan.* VII, 210–18, 233–5; Procopius, *Wars* I, 3, 16–21;
Cassiodorus, *Chronica s.a.* 435, *s.a.* 451 and 454; Marcellinus *comes*, *s.a.*
432; *Annales Ravenna s.a.* 435; *Nov. Val.* 17 and 33; Greg. Tur. *Historiae*
II, 7; Merobaudes, *Pans.* I and II; *Vita Germanus*, 28.

diplomatic, financial, and ecclesiastical matters, and in the barbarian settlement.[30] He was considered by contemporaries to be the real ruler of the West.[31]

When, during the AD 440s, Attila established himself as supreme leader of the Huns, Aetius, rather than being reliant on Hun manpower, found himself defending first Gaul and then Italy against Attila. While he was victorious at the Battle of the Catalaunian Plains in Gaul (thanks to his alliance with the Visigoths), he was miserably unsuccessful in his attempt to defend Italy.[32] Aetius had probably always been resented by Valentinian, the changed situation with the Huns undermined his position, and the final provocation may have been his attempt to marry his son Gaudentius to one of Valentinian's daughters,[33] which was particularly significant because the emperor had no son. It is interesting that Stilicho and Aetius (and possibly Constantius and Ricimer), for political or personal reasons, appear to have had imperial ambitions not for themselves but for their sons.

In AD 454 Valentinian himself killed the unsuspecting Aetius, and in AD 455 two of Aetius' barbarian *bucellari* took revenge by killing Valentinian. The Vandal king Gaiseric typically took advantage of the chaos to mount a pillaging attack on Rome, carrying off, as well as huge amounts of loot, the widow

[30] Scholars have seen Aetius' connections with either the aristocracy in general or the Gallic aristocracy in particular as crucial to his personal success, and linked this to the fall of the western empire: see Stein (1959: i, 337–42); Moss (1973: 720–2, 731); Twyman (1970: 480–503). However, there is little evidence for Aetius in particular being significantly more 'allied' to the aristocracy than anyone else. This was perfectly natural support of his own class interests (as practised by all other similar figures). While it is true that, as Wormald (1976: 223) has pointed out, the ascendancy of the aristocracy and that of the dominant generals paralleled each other, this was due less to interaction than to the same set of external circumstances.

[31] For instance, Cassiodorus, *Variae* 1, 4, 11; Constantius, *Vita Germani* 28: 'qui tum rem publicam gubernabat'.

[32] *Contra* some historians, there is evidence that he did make an attempt to do so (Hydatius, 146 (154) *s.a.* 452–3).

[33] Prosper, *Chron.* 1373 *s.a.* 454.

and daughters of Valentinian and Aetius' son.[34] The combination of the death of the military and political leader of the West
and that of the last male of the Theodosian dynasty was to prove
disastrous. It is in this dark hour that the stories of Marcellinus,
Aegidius, and Ricimer begin.

[34] The main sources are: Hydatius, 152 (160) *s.a.* 453–4, 160 (167) *s.a.* 455;
Prosper, *Chron.* 1373 *s.a.* 454, 1375 *s.a.* 455; *Addit ad Prosp. Haun. s.a.* 454
and 455; *Annales Ravenna s.a.* 454; Sid. Apoll. *Pan.* v, 305–6; Procopius,
Wars I, iv, 24–8; John Ant. frags. 200 and 201; Marcellinus *comes, s.a.* 455;
Jordanes, *Getica* 235, *Romana* 334; Priscus, frag. 31; etc.

PART I

Marcellinus and Dalmatia

2

The Background and the Sources

DALMATIA AND SALONA

Throughout the centuries in which Dalmatia was a province of the Roman empire its physical geography influenced its development, and as the empire declined and disintegrated geography remained a factor in its fate. The province was composed of two regions: the rugged and sparsely populated interior with some fertile river valleys and mining areas,[1] and the coastal strip which, although narrow and broken, had been the site of flourishing cities from the pre-Roman period.

The factors that led to Dalmatia's comparative obscurity during the high empire granted a measure of safety in the later years of decline and danger, as its peripheral and littoral position in the Balkans and lack of rich agricultural resources made the province a low-priority target. This was especially true of the coastal area, which was protected by mountain ranges. The main lines of land communication between the eastern and western empires, especially important after the founding of Constantinople, ran to the north of Dalmatia through the Drave and Save valleys via Serdica and Sirmium; while communications south from the Danube frontier towards the Dalmatian coast were limited. The coastal area was naturally oriented to the Adriatic and Mediterranean, providing harbours important to imperial sea routes up the Adriatic and across to Italy.

Dalmatia lay between Rome and the western provinces and the richer, more developed Eastern Mediterranean world (Dalmatia's eastern border coinciding with the dividing line), and this location was to be significant in the fifth century AD. Under the Tetrarchy it was ruled by the eastern Caesars, but after the

---

[1] Iron, copper, and gold were mined. Dalmatian mines supplied the Balkan mints (Zaninovic (1977: 796)).

death of Constantine it passed to Constans as part of Illyricum, and was governed by a *praeses* in Salona.[2] From the third century A D onwards the archaeological record shows significant changes in material culture and infrastructure, reduction in trade, and quantitative and qualitative decline in urbanization and hence in Romanized character. Everywhere, except at Salona, there is a dramatic drop in the number of inscriptions.[3] Mining, however, probably continued in the interior into the fourth and fifth centuries.[4]

The end of the fourth century A D brought a period of disruption to the Balkans, following the permanent entry into the empire of Goths and other barbarian peoples. In A D 395 the Goths settled in the Balkans rebelled and sacked a number of Dalmatian cities, some groups reaching the Adriatic coast, although it is possible that the scale of the devastation has been exaggerated.[5] Even so, the gradual collapse of an effective Danube frontier from the early fifth century had serious repercussions. The Balkans were the scene of repeated indecisive fighting between Romans and barbarians in the first part of the fifth century, and the control of the eastern dioceses of Macedonia and Dacia became a political issue between the eastern and western governments in the years of Stilicho's regime.[6] In the Dalmatian interior unwalled cities and towns were abandoned.

---

[2] Wilkes (1969: 417).

[3] Ibid.

[4] There is archaeological evidence for the continued prosperity of the mining areas in the fourth century (Wilkes (1969: 417)). The *Praepositus Thesaurorum Salonitanorum Dalmatiae* (*Notitia Dignitatum*, Oc. XI, 23) may also have been connected to the mines. The mines administration was probably at Salona (Wilkes (1969: 423)). In the early sixth century Theoderic ordered an investigation into the iron-bearing areas in Dalmatia, but it is unclear whether the mines were still operational or not (Cassiodorus, *Variae* III, 25).

[5] Claudian, *In. Ruf.* II, 36–7. Jerome, who was born on the Dalmatian/ Pannonian border, writes in A D 407 of 'the entire province laid waste by barbarian enemies, private property ruined, flocks and herds driven off, slaves captured or butchered', but was later able to sell family property near his home town Stridon (supposedly destroyed by the Goths) for a substantial sum (Kelly (1975: 3)). Claudian writes that: 'All that tract of land lying between the stormy Euxine and the Adriatic is laid waste and plundered, no inhabitants dwell there.' Claudian is, however, describing destruction which he blames on Rufinus, enemy of his patron Stilicho.

[6] See Cameron (1970: 59–62), on Claudian's propaganda poems.

Some of the Dalmatian upper classes moved to Italy,[7] while refugees from Pannonia and inland Dalmatia took shelter in the coastal cities.[8]

Although Alaric and his people occupied areas close to Dalmatia,[9] and indeed proposed Dalmatia for official Gothic settlement,[10] this never happened. From the AD 420s the barbarian peoples settled to the north of Dalmatia came under Hun domination, cutting the province off to the north; but Hun attacks took place mainly to the east of Dalmatia and never touched the coastal areas. When Attila's empire disintegrated in AD 454, settlements of Ostrogoths, Sciri, Rugi, Alans, and others remained.[11] The coastal area of Dalmatia was increasingly isolated. The roads from the Adriatic to the Save valley had fallen into disuse,[12] although the coastal cities were able to maintain links with Italy and Constantinople by sea. From the AD 460s, however, a threat to littoral Dalmatia emerged with the consolidation of Vandal power in North Africa under Gaiseric, who made frequent and widespread raids across the Mediterranean. This was a most unwelcome development for the cities of the Dalmatian coast.

By far the most important of these was Salona, the provincial capital and the largest and most Romanized city of the province.[13] Its prosperity was based on trade and industry, and it had important harbour and port facilities. The city was situated in a well-sheltered bay, on a narrow but fertile coastal plain. The location was secure and defensible, encircled by the sea and by high ridges, with one, easily defended, pass four kilometres to the north giving access down to the city, guarded by the fortress of Klis.[14] Early in the fifth century major reconstruction and

---

[7] *Cod. Theod.* VI, 29, 12 mentions Dalmatian refugees in Italy.

[8] Wilkes (1969: 419) and (1972: 378).

[9] Sozomen, 9, 4, 2–4 (= Olympiodorus, frag. 1); Zosimus, V, 29.

[10] Zosimus, V, 48.

[11] See Jordanes, *Getica* 265.

[12] Wilkes (1969: 417).

[13] The city itself was larger than the other cities of Dalmatia, such as Narona or Scodra, as was its territory, which included the fertile islands of Brattia (Brac), Pharia (Hvar), and Issa (Vis) (Zaninovic (1977: 781)). Salona's population in the time of Diocletian is estimated at *c.* 60,000 (Dyggve (1951: 4); Praga (1993: 32)).

[14] Dyggve (1951: 4).

strengthening of the city's walls took place, with the addition of rectangular towers.[15] In the last twenty years archaeological evidence has also been uncovered for defensive activity in the late Roman period on the islands just off the coast from Salona.[16]

In AD 305 Diocletian had built a palace (or, more accurately, a palatial retirement residence-cum-fortress) on the coast at Split, three miles from Salona. Also situated in, or near, the city in the fourth century were a state *thesaurus* (for the collection of gold and silver), *baphium* (dyeing works), and *fabrica* (arms factory).[17] There is, however, no record of Salona having a mint.[18] After the collapse of the Danube frontier, Salona became the site of a *gynaecium* (clothing manufactory), previously situated in Bassiana in Pannonia II (the *Notitia* records a second *gynaecium* at Split, but this is probably the same establishment recorded twice).[19] The number of late Roman inscriptions and the large and impressive churches dating to the fourth, fifth, and sixth centuries AD testify to the city's comparative prosperity. Salona had been an early nucleus of Christianity,[20] but a late pagan community also existed.[21]

A number of developments increased Salona's importance in the late antique period: the deterioration of the inland routes between the East and West and the correspondingly greater importance of sea communications (for trade, diplomacy, war, and private travel); the increasing advantage of defensibility; and the rise of Ravenna (with which Salona had well-established

[15] Wilkes (1969: 360).

[16] Most of the fortifications are Justinianic, but there is indication of late Roman activity on some islands, for instance Palagruza and Svetac (Kirgan (1994: 37)). Cambi (1994: 29) suggests that this was to protect maritime routes from the south to the north Adriatic and to Italy, but the defence of Salona may also have been a factor.

[17] *Notitia Dignitatum*, Oc. XI, 23, 66; IX, 22. The *fabrica* is described only as *Salonitana armorum*, so the type of equipment being produced is unknown. Wozniak (1981: 357) speculates that it was a 'naval arsenal'.

[18] Hendy (1985: 405). (But see p. 42 for the theory that a mint did exist.)

[19] *Notitia Dignitatum*, Oc. XI, 46, and 48.

[20] Wilkes (1969: 233); Praga (1993: 33).

[21] Cambi (1994: 28).

links) as the 'capital' of Italy.[22] Twice late Salona was a vital
strategic target. In AD 424/5 the city was seized by the eastern
government on the death of Honorius;[23] and eastern seaborne
forces used Salona as their base in the subsequent campaign to
restore Valentinian III (while land forces marched via Sirmium). Valentinian and Galla Placidia wintered in the city
(perhaps the occasion of the defensive improvements recorded
on an inscription in the *Porta Caesarea*[24]). In the AD 530s
Salona was a major strategic target and crucial battlefield in the
Justinianic reconquest (the Ostrogoths having garrisoned the
city).[25]

It can be assumed that when Marcellinus ruled Dalmatia in
the third quarter of the fifth century he did so from Salona, but,
although he has been called 'Marcellinus of Salona', no ancient
source explicitly links him with the city. However, a Byzantine
geographer, Stephanus Byzantius, gives the meaning of the
term *Salonae* as 'a city in Dalmatia, the adjective from which
is *Saloneus*, according to Priscus in his sixth book'.[26] This may
have originated in a reference by the fifth-century historian
Priscus to Marcellinus, as inferred by Blockley, but this is not
certain. Marcellinus' nephew and successor Julius Nepos was
residing at a villa just outside the city when he was assassinated

[22] Dyggve (1951: 3) describes Salona and Ravenna as 'sister towns, the two
foci of an Adrio-Byzantine culture'.

[23] Philostorgius, 12, 13–14 (= Olympiodorus, frag. 43): 'accompanied by
Placidia and Valentinian they crossed Pannonia and Illyricum and stormed
Salona, a city of Dalmatia. From there Ardabur sailed with a force against the
usurper'. The eastern sources provide two accounts of the eastern seizure of
Salona. The first is that, as above, it was taken as the army moved westwards in
AD 424. The second, for which there is better evidence, is that the city was
secured immediately on Constantinople's awareness of Honorius' death (late
summer AD 423): 'Theodosius privately dispatched a military force to Salona a
city of Dalmatia, that in the event of any revolutionary movement in the west
there might be resources at hand to check it' (Socrates, VII, 32, 2). This may
have been on the initiative of Galla Placidia rather than of Theodosius II, as he
was then in Eudoxiopolis (Wilkes (1972: 388))).

[24] Wilkes (1972: 389).

[25] Procopius, *Wars* V, v, 2 and 11; V, vii, 1–10, 26–37; V, xvi, 8–16; etc.

[26] Blockley (1983: ii, 345). The *Ethnika*, compiled by Stephanos, was
a sort of gazeteer, giving brief explanations of geographical and ethnic
adjectives.

in AD 480.[27] This was almost certainly Diocletian's residence at Split, and it is possible that both men lived there.[28] Occupation of the huge, imposing, walled complex of buildings would not only be secure, but also prestigious, as it almost certainly retained some symbolic significance. Archaeological investigation has shown that in the stages postdating Diocletian the northern area was used for industrial and, possibly, military purposes, while the southern area continued to be residential.[29] The site remained, at least in part, intact in the fifth century AD, and it sheltered a large resident population in the sixth century, at the time of the Slav invasions.[30]

The recent archaeological investigations at Split have produced little definitely fifth-century material, but there are indications of continued and changing use. At some time in the fifth century AD the victory figure on the west gate was replaced by a cross, but the temple opposite the mausoleum and the mausoleum itself were not consecrated as Christian churches until the seventh century AD. It is likely that the mausoleum was intact well into the fifth century, as it is mentioned in a poem by Sidonius Apollinaris in the present tense.[31] The capital and arch in front of the rectangular temple (as well as outbuildings near the east gate) appear to be of fifth-century date.[32] There are also a number of capitals and two fragments of carved sarcophagi resembling work in Salona of the fifth or sixth century.[33] The demolition of the eastern baths seems to have taken place in the middle of the fifth century.[34]

There is good ceramic evidence for continuous fourth- and fifth-century occupation. Imported material (pottery and glass) is rare after the very early fifth century, but occasional objects

[27] Marcellinus *comes*, *s.a.* 480.
[28] What is usually referred to (technically, erroneously) as 'Diocletian's palace' is sometimes in ancient sources called a 'villa' (Wilkes (1986: 56 n. 150)).
[29] Marasovic (1982: 21).
[30] Wilkes (1986: 71).
[31] Sidonius, *Carm.* XXIII, 497.
[32] Marasovic (1982: 21). The additions to the temple are clearly likely to have been initiated by someone of pagan leanings.
[33] McNally (1975: 251).
[34] McNally (1975: 222).

continue until the mid seventh century.[35] In certain sectors several types of imported pottery were found, mainly African and Phocaean red slip-ware; also fifth-century lamps.[36] Most of the late Roman and post-Roman artefacts were found in a building with a mosaic courtyard in the residential sector near the east gate. Of post-Diocletian date, it seems to have been in use in the early fifth to sixth centuries.[37] The other sector in which late Roman material was found in quantity was the mausoleum area.[38] Of the late Roman coins found (mainly minted in the East) there were no identifiable fifth-century coins later than those of Honorius and Arcadius (although they may have been among the twenty-eight unidentifiable coins).[39]

Coin usage continued throughout Dalmatia into the early fifth century AD, but then declined drastically, and the number of late Roman coin finds in Dalmatia is tiny. Even in the southern Balkans as a whole, post-AD 408 coins are rare and finds are concentrated in small areas, mainly along the Siscia–Sirmium–Singidunum corridor.[40] The majority of the identifiable fifth-century coins in circulation in the southern Balkans came from the eastern Propontis mints.[41] Although Marcellinus was an independent ruler, like similar contemporary figures he does not seem to have minted coins in his own name. A theory has been advanced that the very rare group of *tremisses* of Julius Nepos includes coins struck at Salona,[42] or Split, possibly before he left for Italy and again after his return.[43] If correct, this would be further evidence for the late prominence of Salona and the unique position of Nepos and Marcellinus, but, unfortunately, the theory is not convincing in the current absence of

---

[35] McNally *et al.* (1972: 52).

[36] NcNally *et al.* (1972: 78 ff., 97).

[37] McNally *et al.* (1972: 210–22); McNally (1975: 11–12).

[38] McNally *et al.* (1979: 141).

[39] Clairmont, Auth, and Von Gonzenbach (1975: 90, 135–42).

[40] Duncan (1993: 58–9).

[41] Vasic (1988: 183); Duncan (1993: 72).

[42] Demo (1988: 255 n. 20). Demo accepts that there is no evidence for a mint at Salona, but considers that the presence of one is suggested by the existence of a *thesaurus* earlier in the century (attested by the *Notitia Dignitatum*).

[43] Lacam (1983: 596–607); and (in slightly amended form) Demo (1988: 247–70).

supporting evidence. The coins were probably struck by Odovacer in Italy.[44]

It is difficult to assess the Roman military presence in Dalmatia in the fifth century. There are units recorded in the lists of the *Notitia Dignitatum* for the diocese of Illyricum, but nothing specifically for Dalmatia. Although Dalmatia, like other Balkan provinces, was an important recruiting ground, in normal circumstances the military presence in the province would have been minimal. The diocese of Illyricum as a whole was assigned large numbers of imperial troops: 22 units of *comitatenses*[45] and 195 units of *limitanei*,[46] though in the fifth century there may have been fewer in reality. Of the 195 units, 171 were assigned to the Danube frontier, leaving only 24 units for the rest of the diocese, including Dalmatia. Although river units on the Danube are mentioned, the list of naval forces in the *Notitia Dignitatum* does not record any naval units at Salona or elsewhere in Dalmatia.

The *Distributio* section of the *Notitia Dignitatum* mentions a *comes Illyrici* (under whom the *comitatenses* are listed), while the chapters (and index) mention a *comes Italiae* (but with no *officium* or troops). This may reflect two command structures of different dates between AD 395 and the early 420s.[47] A command similar to that of the *comes Illyrici* mentioned in the *Notitia* was held by a *magister militum*, Generidus (in AD 409), according to Zosimus' *Historia Nova*.[48]

---

[44] Kent (1966: 146–50).

[45] *Notitia Dignitatum*, Oc. VII (*Distributio Numerorum*), 40–62. As no cavalry units are recorded, one can probably add federate cavalry units (Jones (1964: 1426)).

[46] *Notitia Dignitatum*, Oc. XXXII, 22–68, XXXIII, 24–74, XXXIV, 14–55. These units are listed in the commands of the *dux Pannoniae I et Norici Ripensis*, *dux Valeriae Ripensis*, and *dux Pannoniae II*.

[47] Jones (1964: 1422–3). The *Notitia* is a notoriously difficult document; its multi-layered structure no doubt reflects the invasion, response, retreat, regrouping, casualties, and breakdown of normal communication channels, creating both a commander's and a staff clerk's nightmare.

[48] Zosimus, V, 46. Generidus' command consisted of Dalmatia, Upper Pannonia, Noricum, and Raetia. Generidus was of barbarian birth and a pagan, and had therefore at one point fallen foul of regulations stating that western officers had to espouse Christianity. Zosimus describes him as being of noble character and above bribery.

Zosimus also noted that in A D 409 'the emperor decided that five units[49] from Dalmatia should leave their own base there and come to guard the city. These regiments comprised 6,000 men in all, whose daring and strength made them the top soldiers in the Roman army. Their commander was Valens.'[50]

From Zosimus' description, one would expect these units to be at least *comitatenses*, but this is not certain. If they were units that had been based in Dalmatia they were more likely *limitanei* (perhaps from Salona, the seat of the *praeses*). If they were field-army units, they could have been in Dalmatia following a general retreat from the Danube frontier and regrouping in Dalmatia,[51] a suitable area for recuperation and redeployment. However, these units may not have been from Dalmatia, but some of the cavalry *cunei* of 'Dalmatian horse' that are recorded in both the East and West in the *Notitia* (the name indicating the original recruitment ground, and perhaps type of unit, rather than their immediate location),[52] possibly stationed at Intercisa.[53] It has been proposed that remnants of the Danube army, withdrawn to Dalmatia, were the basis of Marcellinus' power,[54] but the probable time gap seems too great.

Zosimus does not give Valens' rank, but if the units were *limitanei* he was probably *Dux Dalmatiae*.[55] If these troops were part of a small field army, the rank of *comes rei militaris* is likely.[56] This is the basis for modern speculation that, at a later date, the latter was Marcellinus' title. It is possible that, in the first decade of the century, a specific command for Dalmatia

---

[49] Zosimus' Greek term is vague, and 'units' seems a more appropriate translation than Ridley's 'legions'. Here, and throughout Pt. I, I am very grateful to Professor John Matthews, Professor Michael Whitby, and Dr Michael Sharp for their advice on the Greek translations.

[50] Zosimus, v, 1–2 (Ridley's translation), not here using Eunapius or Olympiodorus as a source.

[51] As suggested by Dr Roger Tomlin.

[52] Varady (1961: 370–1). For the units see *Notitia Dignitatum*, Or. XLI, 15, 18, 19; Or. XLII, 17, 18; Oc. XXXII, 23, 28, 29, 31, 34, 36, 37; Oc. XXXIII, 25, 29, 32–5, 37, 39–43; Oc. XXXIV, 14, 18–20; etc.

[53] Varady (1961: 391).

[54] Musset (1995: 23).

[55] As he is referred to by the translator of Zosimus (Ridley (1982: 223 n. 161)).

[56] As suggested in *PLRE* ii, 1137, Valens 2.

existed (which may have disappeared by the AD 420s, when the *Distributio* lists a *comes Illyrici*).[57]

In conclusion, there is little scope for the existence of substantial bodies of troops in Dalmatia in the early fifth century. It is quite possible, however, that *limitanei* were stationed at key locations such as Salona, and in the mining areas.[58]

If the military situation in the early fifth century seems confusing and obscure, it is positively illuminating compared with our knowledge of developments in the rest of the century. The imperial military position generally deteriorated. The East continued to have adequate, if not ample, access to effective resources, which were augmented by subsidies and diplomacy. In the West there was limited recovery under Flavius Constantius and Aetius, but the financial base for army funding was being steadily undermined and forces becoming increasingly irregular. It seems, therefore, unlikely that any *comitatenses* remained in Illyricum by the mid century, and on the evidence of the *Life of Saint Severinus* any *limitanei* would gradually have disintegrated and disappeared by the AD 460s.[59]

The existence of Attila's empire to the north in the middle of the fifth century would have increased the need for defensive measures in Dalmatia. If the eastern government was in charge of the province at this time (see Ch. 3), it might have been able to spare troops to garrison the coastal cities, if only to secure the sea route to Italy. However, it is hard to see Aetius, hard pressed

---

[57] The relevance of this discussion will become apparent when the possible rank of Marcellinus is discussed.

[58] There is some limited epigraphic evidence possibly relevant to the late Roman military presence in Dalmatia, in three (undated) inscriptions from Salona. The first (*CIL* iii, supp. 1, 9538) refers to a *numero ata*, which may be the *Numerus Atacotti* mentioned in the *Notitia*, listed as a unit of the eastern army under the *Magister militum per Illyricum c.* AD 395, but subsequently it (or another unit of similar name) is listed under the western army in the *Distributio* as *intra Italiam* (early AD 420s). The second is a memorial inscription with a Christian symbol, *Saturnin . . . Militi Salonitano* (*CIL* iii, supp. 1, 9537). The third is an inscription, *Victor in . . . Maurorum F* (*CIL* iii, supp. 1, 9539); there are a number of units with this component in their name in both eastern and western armies (for instance *Equites Mauri Illyriciani* and *Equites Mauri Alites*). These inscriptions date to either the fourth or the fifth century AD (and may be the memorials of either serving or retired soldiers).

[59] Eugippius, *Vita Severini* XX, 20, 1.

in Gaul and then faced with Hun invasions of Gaul and Italy, sparing manpower in the AD 440s and early 450s. Coastal cities like Salona, that possessed walls and some financial viability, probably took autonomous measures to defend themselves against both possible attack from the north and Vandal sea raids, by hiring barbarians, or by local recruitment.[60]

After AD 424/5 we hear almost nothing of military or political developments in Dalmatia, until the sources record the emergence in the 460s of Marcellinus, an independent or semi-independent warlord with his power base in Dalmatia. It may be significant that this coincides both with the Vandal threat and attempts by East and West to meet it.

THE SOURCES FOR MARCELLINUS

Although the material on Marcellinus is limited, some of the sources are contemporary with Marcellinus and comparatively reliable. An important source is the contemporary western chronicle written by Hydatius, a native of Gallaecia (probably born in Lemica in the AD 390s), who became a bishop of a Gallaecian see (probably Aquae Flaviae, modern Chaves in northern Portugal).[61] He mentions Marcellinus in AD 464–5 fighting the Vandals in Sicily, in 465–6 in connection with the Emperor Anthemius, and in 468 participating in a joint eastern and western expedition against Gaiseric. Hydatius took an interest in events in the western Mediterranean as well as in Spain and, despite his remote geographical position, as a bishop he would have had access to religious and secular information via the ecclesiastical network.

Most news reached Hydatius as oral report, and in origin ranged from official notifications to unsubstantiated rumour, and was no doubt often out of date. Some of this information would have come from sailors and merchants in Spanish ports and from travelling clergy. Some originated from the envoys of

---

[60] The inscribed tombstone of Flavius Valerius, the *centenarius* of a *numerus* of archers, found in Salona, is thought to date to the sixth or late fifth century, on the basis of lettering style (*Bullettino di archaeologia e storia dalmata*, 33 (1910), ed. Fra. X. Balič, 59–60 no. 4122A). Wilkes (1969: 422) suggests he served under Marcellinus.

[61] Burgess (1993) 3–4; Muhlburger (1990) 196, 199.

both Roman and barbarian authorities who travelled between
centres of power, and who became of greater importance as
other long-distance communications ceased to operate.[62] Even
the embassies of barbarian kings may well have included Roman
clergy or translators, and their news would easily enter clerical
circles.[63] The AD 468 entry concerning Marcellinus falls into
this category; almost certainly coming from a Suevian embassy
returning from Constantinople.[64] Hydatius' entry on Marcellinus' earlier Sicilian victory over Vandals might have a similar
source, possibly from envoys sent by Aegidius from Gaul to
Gaiseric in North Africa in AD 464–5 calling into a Gallaecian
harbour on their return journey.[65] It is likely that such information was generally factually correct but, with the exception of
key events like accessions, it would have been difficult for
Hydatius to date all reported events precisely, and he would
therefore have placed some in the chronicle only in rough order
within a year.

Other western chronicle entries, Italian in origin, record only
Marcellinus' death: the sixth-century chronicle of Cassiodorus,[66] the *Paschale Campanum*,[67] and the *Fasti Vindobonenses*.[68] There is a reference to Marcellinus fighting the
Vandals in the *Consularia Constantinopolitana*, among the last
few brief entries added by a Spanish author (see p. 40 below).

Often used in reconstructing Marcellinus' career is a letter by
Sidonius Apollinaris, supposed to show that Marcellinus was
proposed as emperor by a group of Gallic nobles,[69] and sometimes that, hence, Marcellinus himself was from Gaul. Sidonius
refers to a 'Marcellan' conspiracy to 'seize the diadem' (almost
certainly shortly after Avitus' death). However, Mathisen has

---

[62] Muhlberger (1990: 211).

[63] For instance, Hydatius, 227 (231) *s.a.* 465–6, 'Reuersi legati Sueuorum
obisse nuntiant (Seuerum quarto) imperii sui anno', and Hydatius, 238 (244)
s.a. 466–7, 'Legati de rege Gothorum reuersi referunt portenta in Gallis'.

[64] Hydatius, 234 (238) *s.a.* 466–7.

[65] Hydatius, 220 (224) *s.a.* 464–5; see Pt. II, p. 94 for text. The fact that
Hydatius gives the months for the outward and return journeys suggests they
landed in Spain.

[66] Cassiodorus, *Chronica* 1285 *s.a.* 468: 'In Sicilia Marcellinus occiditur.'

[67] *Pasch. Camp. s.a.* 468: 'Marcellinus occiditur Sicilia'.

[68] *Fasti Vind. Prior. s.a.* 468: 'occisus est Marcellinus in Sicilia mense Aug'.

[69] Sidonius, *Ep.* I, ii, 6.

shown that the name is almost certainly 'Marcellus' rather than 'Marcellinus', and he was almost certainly Gallic.[70] A better candidate is the Marcellus, praetorian prefect in Gaul *c.* AD 441–3, who built a church at Narbonne and was probably connected with that city.[71] No real reason exists to connect the conspiracy with Marcellinus of Dalmatia.[72]

There are two references to Marcellinus in the eastern, annalistic chronicle, written by his namesake Marcellinus *comes*: a notice of Marcellinus' death, and a passing reference which describes the western emperor Julius Nepos as 'the son of the sister of Marcellinus, once patrician'.[73] Marcellinus *comes* was a *cancellarius* who wrote in Latin in Constantinople in *c.* AD 518/19, using primarily eastern sources. He was Illyrian,[74] and it is thought that he wrote, in part, for the Illyrian community in Constantinople,[75] who, it might be thought, would have had a particular remembrance of Marcellinus. Like another eastern source discussed below, and unlike all the western sources, Marcellinus *comes* records that Marcellinus of Dalmatia was a pagan. Jordanes[76] (who makes use of Marcellinus' chronicle) briefly mentions Marcellinus of Dalmatia in the *Getica*, in connection with Julius Nepos. Marcellinus *comes* and Jordanes are the only writers who give Marcellinus the title of *patricius*.

A number of later eastern works include information on Marcellinus deriving, in varying degrees, from his contemporary Priscus: a tenth-century Byzantine anthology, the *Excerpta de Legationibus Iussu Imperatoris* compiled by the Byzantine emperor Constantine Porphyrogenitus;[77] the eighth-century

---

[70] Mathisen (1979: 598–601).

[71] *PLRE* ii, 712, Marcellus 2.

[72] Mathisen (1979: 598–601); Max (1979: 226–9).

[73] Marcellinus *comes*, *s.a.* 474: 'Nepote Marcellini quondam patricii sororis filio'.

[74] For biographical details see Cassiodorus, *De Institutione Divinarum Litterarum* XVII; for his possible sources, Croke (1983: 86–90).

[75] Croke (1983: 86–7).

[76] Also eastern in his sources and viewpoint (Croke (1983: 101–2); Goffart (1988: 22)).

[77] The fragments preserved in the *Excerpta de Legationibus* (*Rom.* 10 and *Gent.* 14) are considered to be taken directly from Priscus' original text, with some slight condensation and omission, and are therefore referred to by Blockley and here as Priscus (frags. 38 (1) and 39 (1)).

Chronographia by Theophanes;[78] and three sixth-century works—the *History of the Vandal War* by Procopius,[79] Evagrius' *Historia Ecclesiastica*,[80] and Jordanes' *Romana*[81] (the last two references being brief).[82] The material in the *Excerpta de Legationibus* relates directly to Marcellinus, the others cover the campaign against the Vandals in AD 468 in which he took part, only Procopius mentioning Marcellinus by name. Priscus' invaluable history, of which only fragments are extant, was written in Greek in the eastern empire, and covered the years AD 434–74. Enough exists in the fragments, some of which are extensive, to show that it concentrated on the eastern empire, especially its foreign policy and diplomacy (in which context the extant material on Marcellinus appears).[83] It is generally thought to be a trustworthy source.[84] Its inadequacies, common in classical historiography, of imprecision and a stress on personality in causation, do not greatly affect what survives concerning Marcellinus.

The other major eastern source for Marcellinus is the *Life of Isidorus* or *The Philosophical History*, written in Greek by the pagan philosopher Damascius in the early AD 520s. Damascius was part of a sophisticated, pagan, and Neoplatonist circle, still influential, especially in Alexandria and Athens, and which included his teacher and patron Isidorus (the head of the Neoplatonists in Athens), Proclus (his predecessor and an important

---

[78] Theophanes, AM 5961, 5963. Theophanes compiled his work from earlier sources, including Malalas, and is closely paralleled by Evagrius (Heather (1991: 239)).

[79] Procopius, *Wars* III, vi, 1–27. The Procopius material relevant to Marcellinus is examined in detail in Ch. 4. As it is contained in a section derived mainly from Priscus, Procopius' history as a whole is not discussed here.

[80] Evagrius, *HE* II, 16.

[81] Jordanes, *Romana* 337.

[82] Both Theophanes and Evagrius cite Priscus as their source. Blockley assigns all the above to one fragment (53) of bk. 6. They will be referred to as Procopius, Evagrius, etc.

[83] It is clear from the surviving text that other information on Marcellinus has been lost.

[84] It has certain idiosyncrasies, such as the avoidance of the use of Latin ranks and titles (Blockley (1981–3: i, 52–3)), which explains why none is recorded for Marcellinus.

teacher), and leading pagans such as Agapius, Marinus, Nomus, Athenodorus, Pamprepius, and Severianus.

Although the *Philosophical History* was essentially a pagan tract, concerned with eastern Neoplatonism and its leading figures, it includes incidental historical material from both East and West.[85] In common with Priscus' history, *The Philosophical History* is no longer extant, and it has an even more tenuous and complex textual transmission. An epitome exists in the ninth-century *Bibliotheca* by Photius,[86] and short quotations from Damascius' work appear in the *Suda*.[87] From what can be made out from the fragmentary and condensed text, Marcellinus appeared because of his similar beliefs and interests and, especially, because of his association with Sallustius, a Cynic philosopher and colleague of Damascius and Isidore. This material (which is not, at the time of writing, available in English) has often been ignored in discussing Marcellinus and is at odds with the conventional portrayal of him.

Finally, some of the sources for Marcellinus' nephew Julius Nepos, who followed his uncle as ruler in Dalmatia, are of some interest. These consist of a number of brief notices of Nepos' short reign in Italy (AD 474–5),[88] and his assassination in Dalmatia in AD 480,[89] plus a section of the *Codex Justinianus*.[90]

---

[85] For instance, on Attila's invasion of the West (Damascius, *Vita Isidori*; Photius epitome, *Bibliotheca* (Cod. 242) 12).

[86] It consists of summaries of 386 books by pagan and Christian authors, plus biographical details and literary criticism. Photius was unable to make a simple summary of such a sophisticated work and merely copied out unconnected passages and discoursed on Damascius' eloquent language. It is impossible to reconstruct a coherent book from the fragments, but it is clear that it was much more than a biography of Isidore, and that digressions provided information on other men (Polymnia Athanassiadi, Oxford seminar, 1995)).

[87] The lexicon known as the *Suda* is thought to have been compiled in *c*. AD 1000, and is a 'compilation of compilations' (Kazhdan (1991: 1930)).

[88] *Anon. Val.* 7, 36; Marcellinus *comes*, *s.a.* 474 and 475; *Fasti Vind. Prior. s.a.* 474 and 475; John Malalas, 375; *Pasch. Camp. s.a.* 474.

[89] *Fast. Vind. Prior. s.a.* 480. The other notices are in Marcellinus *comes*, *s.a.* 480; *Auct. Prosp. Haun ordo prior. s.a.* 480; *Auct. Prosp. Haun. ordo post.* and *marg. s.a.* 480; and *Anon. Val.* 7, 36. Malchus (frag. 1) suggests that the assassination was initiated by Glycerius, then Bishop of Salona.

[90] *Codex Justinianus*, vi, 61, 5.

3
The Origins and Career of Marcellinus

In building up an outline of Marcellinus' career from the 450s to his death in A D 468, previous reconstructions have used as a starting-point the few lines on Marcellinus within Procopius' account of the expedition against the Vandals (see p. 65 below). It is on this basis that Marcellinus is considered by most historians to have been an officer of the western Roman army, in Dalmatia originally as an appointee of Aetius, and, sometimes, as a friend or colleague of Majorian. All the other evidence on Marcellinus, and indeed Dalmatia, has then tended to be interpreted in the light of these assumptions.[1] Here, a new approach will be taken, initially disregarding Procopius' information on Marcellinus and using the other sources to produce a reconstruction which will then be considered against the Procopius material.

Although modern accounts assume that Marcellinus was an appointee of the western government, there is a possibility that Dalmatia was, throughout the period in question, actually formally part of the eastern empire. The administrative background is quite complex. In A D 395 the prefecture of Illyricum (that is, the Balkan provinces and Pannonia) was split between Arcadius and Honorius, a division that had previously been

---

[1] For instance, *PLRE* ii, 708–10, Marcellinus 6 has Marcellinus as a friend of Aetius, probably *comes rei militaris in Dalmatia*, who rebelled against Valentinian, but returned to his allegiance under Majorian, who sent him to Sicily, probably as *magister militum*. See also Gordon (1960: 117–18) for Marcellinus as a 'pupil of Aetius and an advisor of Majorian'; O'Flynn (1983: 116–18) for Marcellinus as a former friend of Aetius, co-operating with Majorian but the bitter enemy of Ricimer; and Wozniak (1981: 353–61) for Marcellinus as *comes rei militaris Dalmatiae* rebelling against Valentinian III.

made by Gratian for reasons of military expediency[2] and with no particular geographical or cultural logic to it. The western half became the diocese of Illyricum (sometimes referred to as the diocese of Pannonia),[3] one of the three in the prefecture of Italy.[4] It consisted of the Diocletianic provinces of Dalmatia (almost exactly the earlier province of Illyricum),[5] Noricum *Ripense*, Noricum *Mediterraneum*, Pannonia I, Pannonia II, Savia, and Valeria.

Two dioceses of the Diocletianic prefecture of Illyricum, Dacia and Macedonia (earlier Moesia), passed to Constantinople.[6] These were normally part of the huge prefecture of Oriens, but, when military and political need arose,[7] the administrative structure would be temporarily reorganized and an eastern prefecture of Illyricum brought into existence.[8] In the later years of Stilicho's power, the West made an unsuccessful claim for Dacia and Macedonia.[9] However, the East had an equal, if not better, claim to the western part of the old prefecture of Illyricum, that is, the West's diocese of Illyricum (including Dalmatia), because the prefecture of Illyricum had in the fourth century been under eastern rather than western rulers.[10] Furthermore, Alan Cameron has suggested that on

[2] Hodgkin (1880a: 275–6 note c); Maenchen-Helfen (1973: 34–5). (The dioceses of Dacia and Macedonia were added to the praetorian prefecture of Oriens.)

[3] The diocese is named in the *Notitia Dignitatum*, and other sources, as Illyricum, but the *Laterculus Veronensis* calls it the diocese of Pannonia; presumably its title in the early fourth century.

[4] *Notitia Dignitatum*, Oc. II, 31.

[5] The old province of Dalmatia lost a small amount of territory in the south-east to the new province of Praevalitana, part of the eastern diocese of Dacia (Wilkes (1969: 418)).

[6] *Notitia Dignitatum*, Or. III, 19.

[7] For instance, when their possession was disputed by Stilicho.

[8] I am grateful to Professor John Matthews for information on this point. The prefecture of Illyricum also appears on modern maps of the empire as Illyrica or Illyria. In AD 395 it seems to have consisted of the dioceses of Dacia and Macedonia, but not Thracia, the diocese to the east of them, presumably because Thracia included Constantinople.

[9] See Zosimus, V, 26(2).

[10] The name Illyricum used for the area on the Adriatic between Istria and Epirus originated from the pre-Roman kingdom of Illyria. As if the official use

the death of Theodosius in AD 395 all Illyricum still belonged
to the East, and that western Illyricum was only ceded to the
West (in AD 396) on a temporary basis.[11]

There is evidence that in AD 437 the western diocese of Illyricum had been formally passed back into the administration of the
eastern empire. There are two sources for this.[12] The first is
Cassiodorus, referring to Galla Placidia:

it is known that the empire she ruled was shamefully reduced. In short,
she purchased herself a daughter-in-law by the loss of Illyricum.
A union between rulers was made by the deplorable division of the
provinces.[13]

of the term Illyricum for a fourth-century prefecture, a later, smaller, eastern
prefecture, and a western diocese, as well as it having been the name of the huge
Augustan province (which was divided *c.* AD 9 into Pannonia and Dalmatia) is
not confusing enough, it was also used in a looser, geographical, sense to
describe the southern Balkans as a whole.

    [11] Cameron (1970: 60). Cameron's argument is based on Claudian, *In. Ruf.*
II, 153 ff. (dating to AD 395), which lists the areas under Stilicho's domination and does not include Illyricum, and Claudian, *Pan. Theod.* 200 ff.,
of AD 399, which does list Illyricum with other western provinces. The list
of provinces in the panegyric celebrating Stilicho's consulship in AD 400
(Claudian, *Cons. Stil.* II 230 ff.) includes only Spain, Gaul, Britain, Africa,
and Italy, although earlier (192–207) Claudian refers to 'the peoples of Gaul,
Carthage, Pannonia, and Save', and also to Stilicho enabling the peasant
of Illyria to return to his fields and once more to pay tax (400). I am not
sure that Claudian can be used quite as precisely as Cameron does here, but
the impression is certainly one of ambiguity on ownership of western Illyricum.
    [12] I have come across Socrates cited as an authority for the cession (*HE* vii),
but he only records the wedding.
    [13] Cassiodorus, *Variae* XI, i, 9: 'administrat imperium indecenter cognis-
citur imminutum. Nurum denique sibi ammissione Illyrici comparavit, facta-
que est conjunctio regnantis divisio dolenda provinciis'. This was written
c. AD 534 to the Roman Senate. Why Cassiodorus was so critical of Galla
Placidia in this is uncertain, especially if, as suggested by Van Besselaar (1950:
32) quoted in O'Donnell (1979: 17 n. 10), Cassiodorus' family came to the
West in AD 424/5 with Valentinian and Galla Placidia. Wozniak (1981: 367–8)
suggests a connection with the strategic importance of the area to Theoderic.
A more likely explanation is that it is incidental, resulting from Cassiodorus'
need to contrast a well-known female ruler unfavourably with Amalasuntha,
whom, with other members of the Gothic royal family, he was at pains to
portray favourably. Cassiodorus' source of information here is presumably
Italian.

The second is Jordanes:

the emperor Valentinian travelled from Rome to Constantinople to take in marriage Eudoxia, daughter of the emperor Theodosius and, in order to repay his father-in-law, surrendered the whole of Illyricum.[14]

Given the context and Cassiodorus' position and access to official files, it is unlikely that his statement is without any factual basis. Jordanes' source might have been Cassiodorus' lost Gothic history (this was the basis of his *Getica*, and he worked on the *Romana* at the same time), or an independent source, possibly Priscus' history (which he also used for the *Getica*).[15]

There is other indirect evidence. First, on several occasions, in negotiation with barbarians, eastern emperors acted as if they held legal title in the supposedly western diocese of Illyricum: for instance, the eastern emperor Marcian (AD 450–7) granted lands in Pannonia to Gepids, Huns, Goths, and other tribes.[16]

Second, Polemius Silvius, a western writer who had served in the imperial palace,[17] listed the provinces in Illyricum in AD 448 as Dalmatia, Pannonia I, Pannonia II, Valeria, Prevalis, Misia, Epirus *uetus*, Epirus *nova*, Noricus *ripensis*, Noricus *mediterranea*, Savia, Dardania, Haemimontus, Dacia, Scitia, Creta *insula*, Achaia, Macedonia, and Thessalia.[18] Mommsen was of the opinion that he was using out-of-date and inaccurate material for Illyricum,[19] but, in fact, this list would be broadly correct for an eastern prefecture of Illyricum in *c.* AD 448, if the

[14] Jordanes, *Romana* 329: 'Valentinianus imperator a Roma Constantinopolim ob suscipiendam in matrimonio Eudoxiam Theodosii principis filiam venit. Datamque pro munere soceri sui totam Illyricum'.

[15] Jordanes also used Marcellinus *comes*' chronicle for the *Romana*, but this says nothing on this subject (surprisingly, given his Illyrian connection). Croke (1983: 91) suggests that Jordanes and Marcellinus used a shared written source, now lost. This might be a lost history by Symmachus (Ensslin (1948) quoted in Croke (1983: 92)), or a common eastern source (Croke (1983: 93–109)). Either might have been Jordanes' source for Illyricum.

[16] Jordanes, *Getica* 263–5. See also Blockley (1992: 71): 'In Pannonia, which the East Romans regarded as within their sphere at this juncture'.

[17] *Chronica Gallica of 452*, 121 *s.a.* 438.

[18] *Laterculus Polemii Siluii*, V, ed. Seeck (1962: 257).

[19] Mommsen (1909: vii, 657–67).

western diocese of Illyricum had been transferred in its entirety and merged with the eastern prefecture of Illyricum.

Third, Sidonius Apollinaris portrayed the figure of Rome saying to the eastern empire in AD 467: 'I see you extending your rule to Illyricum and the land of the Macedonians',[20] and when listing lands under western authority mentioned only Noricum, Gaul, and Sicily.[21]

Fourth, in December AD 437 a letter was sent from Pope Sixtus to the bishops of all Illyricum, concerned with maintaining Roman ecclesiastical jurisdiction over Illyricum. He enjoined the bishops to submit to Anastasius of Thessalonica (who was subject to Rome), and to pay no attention to the decrees of eastern synods, except on matters of faith that had his own approval. The context of the letter is not clear, but may be confusion over ecclesiastical boundaries caused by secular administrative reorganization in that year.[22]

It is usually assumed that any territorial concession was agreed at the time of the betrothal of Valentinian III and Eudoxia in AD 424 and took place on their marriage in AD 437.[23] Galla Placidia desperately needed Theodosius' help

---

[20] Sidonius, *Pan.* II, 468–9: 'In Illyricum specto te mittere iura ac Macetum terras'. This is in among a number of territories yielded by Rome to Constantinople. Unfortunately one cannot be certain exactly what lands Sidonius means by 'Illyricum'; and Dalmatia (then in Marcellinus' control) is not mentioned.

[21] Sidonius, *Pan.* II, 377–8.

[22] Sixtus, *Ep.* x, *Ad Totius Illyrici Episcopos*: 'Nec his vos ... constitutis, quae praeter nostra pracepta Orientalis synodus decernere voluit, credatis teneri, praeter id quidem quod de fide consentientibus judicavit'. Sixtus, *Ep.* ix, *Ad Proclum Constantinopolitanum Episcopum*, dating to Dec. AD 437, and Sixtus, *Ep.* viii, *Ad Synodum Thessalonicae Congregandam*, dating to July AD 435, may be related.

[23] This chronology is given by numerous writers, but the rationale is never explicit; the basis seems to be the statement of Cassiodorus that Galla Placidia gained a daughter-in-law, and the reference to the transfer in Jordanes immediately following his record of the wedding. Although it is logical to assume that Galla Placidia had to make some concessions to gain eastern support in AD 424, there is no reason why the transfer should not have been agreed at a later date as part of the wedding arrangements, or indeed why some transfer of territory should not have taken place at the earlier date. The wedding is mentioned by a number of eastern sources but, surprisingly, among western sources only by Prosper (*Chron.* 1328 *s.a.* 437), but with no mention of territorial concession.

to restore her young son in the West, and it must have seemed an acceptable price to pay. Constantinople may have seen it as a way of offsetting the expenses of the campaign of restoration. It may have hoped that in the future a son of Valentinian and Eudoxia would rule an undivided empire,[24] as Galla Placidia's father had done only thirty years before.

The historical evidence for Dalmatia being in western hands during the mid-fifth century is in Procopius' *Wars*. His material on Marcellinus includes the following information: 'there was in Dalmatia a certain Marcellinus, one of Aetius' acquaintances . . . When Aetius died . . . he refused to obey the emperor any longer'; which implies that Dalmatia was part of the western empire. This passage is given in full and discussed in more detail in Chapter 4.

Also, a geographical passage Procopius wrote in the late sixth century records that 'the first inhabitants are Greeks called Epirotes as far as the city of Epidamnus (Dyrrhachium) and adjoining this is the land of Precalis, beyond which is . . . Dalmatia, all of which is counted as part of the Western Empire'.[25] However, this refers to the mid sixth century, when Dalmatia was ruled by the Ostrogoths.

There is therefore a contradiction between the evidence that Illyricum was, in the mid fifth century, ruled from Constantinople and that of Procopius, that Dalmatia at least was part of the western empire and Marcellinus a western appointee. The most usual method of dealing with this problem has been to ignore it. However, Wozniak attempted to get round it by suggesting that:

Between 437, when all of Illyricum passed to the East, and 454, Salona and coastal Dalmatia seem to have reverted to or remained under West Roman administrative control, while formally under East Roman sovereignty . . . While Dalmatia was ceded formally to the East as part of the general cession of West Roman rights in Illyricum (437), administrative control of coastal Dalmatia appears to have remained in the hands of the government at Ravenna. While only occasionally exercised, the legal sovereignty of Constantinople over Dalmatia was held in reserve as a right to be resurrected when necessary.[26]

---

[24] Oost (1968: 245).   [25] Procopius, *Wars* v, xv, 25–6.
[26] Wozniak (1981: 354–5).

The only reason for proposing this odd and complicated political and administrative situation is the need to reconcile the
evidence for the transfer of Illyricum with Procopius' statement
on Marcellinus. One doubts that the eastern government would
have accepted such an arrangement, and why should Constantinople have given up control of a strategically important, rela-
tively secure, area while retaining others that offered less
advantage (see p. 39)?

Another theory is that Galla Placidia gave up not territory but
the West's claim to the eastern provinces of Illyricum, which
had been pressed in Honorius' reign.[27] However, it is hard to
reconcile this with the clear statements of Cassiodorus and
Jordanes and the evidence for eastern activity in some parts of
the western diocese. Nor would such cession have been any
inducement to Theodosius, who was in by far the stronger
position; Constantinople had been in clear possession of eastern
Illyricum for decades (see Ch. 2). A more plausible explanation
is that, contrary to the statement of Jordanes, only *part* of the
diocese of Illyricum was formally ceded in the AD 430s. This
has been suggested by a number of writers, but there is no
consensus on exactly what the division was.[28]

There is very strong evidence that Noricum (often administered with transpadane Italy) remained in western control. For
instance, Priscus records meeting an embassy of West Romans,
which included Promotus the Governor of Noricum, in
AD 449,[29] and in the AD 460s remaining *limitanei* in Noricum
ripensis were expecting to be paid from Italy.[30] Also, Sidonius

[27] Stein (1914: 344–77) and (1925: 354–8). He suggested that Sirmium was
also transferred.

[28] See, for instance, the quotation from Wozniak above; Barnwell (1992:
147 n. 3), suggesting that 'part' of the diocese was transferred; Demougeot
(1951: 502 n. 39) and Móscy (1974: 349) for the ceding of 'the Sirmium area';
Barker (1911: 412) for the 'final cession by the western empire of part of
Dalmatia'; Zeiller (1967: 6) for the transfer of 'les provinces pannoniennes,
sinon les noriciennes'; Bury (1923: 225): 'a considerable part of the diocese of
Illyricum, Dalmatia, Valeria and eastern Pannonia certainly were transferred';
Praga (1993: 32) on the fact that the 'cession of western Illyricum ... did not
affect Dalmatia'; and Wilkes (1969: 419) on a substantial part of western
Illyricum being transferred to the east, including most, if not all, of Dalmatia.

[29] Priscus, frag. 11 (2).

[30] Eugippius, *Vita Severini* XX, 20, 1.

refers to Noricum as still under Rome's rule (see above). The clearest case for transference from West to East is Pannonia II, containing the important city of Sirmium situated on its eastern border, and the Save and Drave valleys, areas in which Constantinople long retained a strategic interest.[31] Sirmium was, in AD 441, the seat of the eastern praetorian prefect of Illyricum, Apraeemius (who fled to Thessalonica when Sirmium was attacked by the Huns in that year).[32] Whichever parts of the diocese of Illyricum did pass into the control of the eastern government would have come under the administration of the prefect.

For much of the diocese of Illyricum any change in administrative status would have been purely theoretical. Large areas of the diocese were completely out of imperial control (although the authorities may well have expected, especially in the AD 420s, that this would be rectified). Parts of Pannonia, Valeria, and Savia had been settled by groups of Alans, Goths, and Huns, and possibly Marcomanni, from as early as the AD 370s, and other Germanic tribes followed in later decades; and from the 420s the Huns were expanding westward into the region.

In the case of the province of Dalmatia, the East would have had an interest in the coastal cities, especially Salona, particularly at those times in which it was intervening politically or militarily in the West (as under Leo or Justinian). In AD 424–5, Salona was seized by eastern forces as a priority target. In fact it would have made strategic and political sense for Constantinople to retain possession of Salona after AD 425 by agreement with Galla Placidia. There is also a possibility that Salona was under eastern administration slightly earlier, *c.* AD 414/15; two official inscriptions are dated by eastern consuls only, one of whom was never recognized in the West.[33]

---

[31] See Menander Protector, 12, 6; 25, 1 and 2.

[32] *Nov. Just.* 11, 1: 'cum enim in antiquis temporibus Sirmii praefectura fuerat constituta ibique omne fuerat Illyrici fastigium ... Postea autem Attilanis temporibus ejusdem locis devastatis Apraeemius praefectus praetori de Simitana civitate in Thessalonica profugus venerat'. Thessalonica had previously, in the fourth century, been the seat of the prefecture of Illyricum, which must have transferred to Sirmium at some date prior to AD 441, perhaps 437.

[33] Wilkes (1972: 388), citing *Bullettino di archaeologia e storia dalmata*, 7 (1873), 98 n. 50.

Whatever the formal status of Dalmatia, by the AD 450s Marcellinus had established himself as an independent ruler there. We have no direct evidence as to Marcellinus' origins, nor the position or rank that he held in Dalmatia before then. Those writers who believe that Marcellinus was an officer of the western imperial army suggest that he was *comes* (*rei militaris*), which is considered to be an appropriate rank for a military command in Dalmatia, but there is no direct evidence for such a post existing at the time (see pp. 25–6). Marcellinus is often thought to have held, at some point, one of the regular ranks and titles of *magister militum praesentalis* (*equitum* or *peditum*) in the western Roman army, under Majorian or Anthemius or both. While this is quite possible, the only military rank ascribed to him by ancient writers is that of *dux*, technically the commander of a force of *limitanei*. The Spanish author of the *Consularia Constantinopolitana* records: 'A great army with [or, 'under'] *dux* Marcellinus was sent against the Vandals.'[34] While it is conceivable that Marcellinus was *dux* before gaining a more prestigious rank, it is more likely that *dux* here simply designates the leader of a military force in the field (Hydatius uses it in this manner).[35]

Marcellinus' main title may have been *magister militum Dalmatiae*. Julius Nepos was known by this title after Marcellinus' death, when he held power in Dalmatia before becoming emperor. It appears in a ruling in the *Codex Justinianus*, dating to AD 473,[36] in a section on matrimonial law, concerning a family dispute over an inheritance. This suggests that this office, although military in origin, was held by someone who also had a

---

[34] *Consularia Constantinopolitana*, *s.a.* 468(a): 'Aduersum Wandalos grandis exercitus cum Marcellino duce dirigitur'. This refers to the joint eastern and western attack under Leo and Anthemius. For the author and the dating see Burgess (1993: 199–207, 245).

[35] Barnwell (1992: 39–40).

[36] *Codex Justinianus*, vi, 61, 5, addressed to *Nepoti Magistro Militum Dalmatiae*. If this dates to AD 473 (see below) it can only be from the eastern empire, as in that year the short-lived puppet emperors Olybrius and Glycerius, unrecognized by Leo, held the title of emperor in Italy, and it is inconceivable that Nepos would have gone to them for a legal ruling. There is a conflict between the date given at the end of the ruling, *D. K. iun. Leone A. V. Cons.* (AD 473), and the note at the beginning, *idem A. A.*, which suggests that the same emperors were ruling as at the date of the previous ruling (given as Leo

civil and legal role.[37] Also significant is the fact that Nepos was quite routinely requesting a ruling on a Dalmatian matter from the eastern emperor, through the established administrative procedure of *suggestio*. It shows that Nepos, even if acting as a *de facto* ruler, preserved a formal relationship with the eastern emperor, accepting him as the supreme legal authority over Dalmatia. As the ruling dates from approximately five years after Marcellinus' death, and Nepos, an undistinguished character, had gained his position in Dalmatia on the strength of his relationship to Marcellinus, it seems likely that it was originally held by Marcellinus, perhaps assumed by analogy with the powerful military figures of the time in both the eastern and western empires. Its use in the *Codex* shows that, at least by his nephew's time, it was acceptable to the administration in Constantinople.

Linked to the conventional idea that Marcellinus was a western army officer is the assumption that he seized power on the strength of his control of substantial military forces in Dalmatia. If Marcellinus commanded imperial forces at the time of his coup, they are unlikely to have been permanently stationed in the province (as shown above, pp. 24–7); nor is it likely, given the military and financial pressures on both governments, that such forces would have been sent into Dalmatia in the AD 450s. This is particularly the case for the western government, which could not even defend Italy. We have no direct evidence for the forces under Marcellinus' command when he took power, but when Marcellinus was in Sicily *c.* AD 461 his men were mainly 'Scythians' (see p. 46), meaning either Huns or other tribesmen from beyond the Danube.[38] They could have originated in either the western or eastern army, or, as

and Anthemius), which is dated to the (eastern) consulship of Fl. Marcianus (AD 472). The *idem A. A.* is probably mere carelessness and the date at the bottom, of AD 473, will be the correct date. (Even if AD 472 were correct, it is improbable that Nepos would have applied to Anthemius, who died in that July and spent the previous months besieged in Rome.) I am grateful for Professor John Matthew's advice on the dating here.

[37] This is not, of course, unique; other *magistri* took on non-military functions, for instance Aetius and Ricimer.

[38] Blockley (1981–3: ii, 395 n. 147) and Demandt (1989: 173) suggest they were Ostrogoths from Pannonia.

seems more likely, have been recruited by Marcellinus himself, before or after gaining power. An alternative scenario is that Marcellinus was not a western army commander posted to Dalmatia, but came to rule in Dalmatia from a regional (civil, or civil and military) power base. It is possible that Marcellinus was a member of an important Dalmatian family, perhaps from Salona.[39] The isolation of the coastal area would have encouraged a long-term increase in the power and autonomy of local landowners and city élites.

There is important eastern evidence on Marcellinus' background in the fragments of Damascius' work copied in the *Suda* (and repeated in briefer fashion by the Photius epitome of Damascius' work).[40] The entry on Marcellinus in the *Suda* reads:

Marcellinus, a virtuous [or, 'capable'] and noble man, ruled Dalmatia, a district in Epirus inhabited by Illyrians [or, 'ruled Dalmatia and the Illyrians who dwelt in Epirus'].[41] He was educated in Roman culture and was very skilled in prophecy and in all other respects a man of extreme learning. He held his rule in freedom, subservient neither to the Roman emperor nor to any other ruler of the nations, but was independent and governed his subjects with justice. He possessed an adequate judgement of civil government and remarkable courage, and

[39] Epigraphic evidence from Dalmatia suggests that there may have been a prominent family in Dalmatia called Nepos, the name of Marcellinus' nephew. At least four memorial inscriptions incorporating the name have been found in the province: Aelia Nepotes (*CIL* iii, supp. 1, 9850); Aelia Nepos (*CIL* iii, supp. 1, 13984); Julius Nepos (*CIL* iii, supp. 1, 10040); and Nepotes (*CIL* iii, supp. 1, 9527). The name also possibly appears in an inscription in the apse of the basilica in Salona, recording money given for work on the church, dating perhaps to *c.* AD 405–20 (Dyggve (1951: 41 n. 27, citing *Bullettino di archaeologia e storia dalmata*, 27 (1904), 25). Since writing this I have discovered that Praga (writing in the 1950s) suggested that Marcellinus 'came from one of the most respected families of decurians in Dalmatia' (1993: 34). Unfortunately, he neither gives any evidence for this nor cites any source.

[40] In this section of Pt. I in particular I am very grateful to Professor John Matthews for his translations from the Greek, his advice on the Neoplatonists, and his direction to the enlightening Oxford seminar and the article in the 1993 *Journal of Hellenic Studies*, both by Polymnia Athanassiadi, on the Neoplatonists.

[41] Whitby suggests that the text may be unreliable here, and gives this alternative translation.

was practised in war. A companion [or, 'associate'] of his was Sallustius the philosopher.[42]

Sallustius was born in Emesa in the first quarter of the fifth century, where he began the studies continued in Alexandria and Athens. At a later date, probably the late A D 470s, Sallustius accompanied Isidorus from Athens to Alexandria.[43] He is described by Damascius as a Cynic philosopher and wit.[44]

There are also two *Suda* entries in which snippets of Damascius' material on Marcellinus are used to illustrate a word or phrase. One reads: 'The army following Marcellinus was distinguished [or, 'more distinguished'] for the preparedness [or, 'good order'] of its equipment.'[45] This passage does not agree with the one other reference to his forces by Priscus in the *Excerpta de Legationibus* (see p. 46), which shows those in Sicily to have been composed mainly of mercenaries, and disloyal ones at that. Damascius may be referring to a different body of soldiers, perhaps Marcellinus' *bucellarii* in Dalmatia.

The other passage refers to some unknown persons having great hopes of Marcellinus, probably the Neoplatonists: 'To such an extent did the reliability [or, 'honesty'] of Marcellinus in sacred matters inspire firm hope in them'.[46]

The Photius epitome (sect. 91) includes an anecdote describing Gaiseric's reaction to Marcellinus' death:

The king of the Carthaginians, hearing that the Romans had treacherously, and against their oaths, done away with Marcellinus, their ally against him, was elated by his hopes of victory, and is reported to have uttered words more fitting to a Roman emperor than a Carthaginian; for what he said was that the Romans had cut their right hand off with

[42] *Suda*, M 202 (= Damascius, frags. 158, 155, 159) (Matthews' translation with Whitby's alternative translations).

[43] Damascius, frag. 138 (= *Suda* σ 62).

[44] Damascius, frag. 138 (= *Suda* σ 62); Damascius, frag. 159 (= *Suda* μ 202); Damascius, frag. 147 (= *Suda* σ 63); Damascius, *Vita Isidori*, Photius epitome, *Bibliotheca* (Cod. 242) 89.

[45] *Suda* II, 473 (= Damascius, frag. 156) (Matthews' translation with Whitby's alternative translations).

[46] *Suda* IV, 136, 15 (= Damascius, frag. 157) (Whitby's translation).

their left. Marcellinus was independent ruler of Dalmatia, and was a Hellene in his beliefs.[47]

In the original work this passage may have appeared in a chapter mainly on Sallustius. Section 89 of the epitome gives his philosophic views; section 90 concerns the praiseworthy character of an unnamed person in public life (possibly Marcellinus, the subject of the following section, and, if so, paralleling his description in the *Suda*);[48] section 92 describes how Sallustius, 'looking into the eyes of those he met, used to foretell the violent manner of death to befall each one';[49] and section 93 refers to Sallustius and Isidorus.

Damascius' information in both the *Suda* and Photius' epitome confirms Marcellinus *comes*' statement that Marcellinus was a pagan. He was probably Neoplatonist by education and leaning. It would be natural to assume that he had been educated at either Alexandria or Athens. The proportion of the eastern population that remained pagan in the fifth century is debatable, but certainly included an educated and influential minority, often referred to as Hellenes (as is Marcellinus in the epitome). In the East, paganism was not a completely spent force in the fifth century, as the anti-pagan legislation and literature shows, and those who adhered to the old religion believed fervently.[50] There were still important centres of pagan learning, especially Athens and Alexandria. Leading pagans played a part in political events as late as AD 484.[51]

---

[47] Damascius, *Vita Isidore*, Photius epitome, *Bibliotheca* (Cod. 242) 91 (Matthews' translation).

[48] Photius, ed. Henry (1971: 27 n. 3). The ancient writers all give Marcellinus favourable or neutral treatment, and Damascius especially gives the impression that Marcellinus had good standing as a ruler and military leader, as well as a personal reputation for justice and learning. This is particularly impressive because Damascius was critical of many people, pagan or not. He was narrowly moralistic, a social reformer, and generally reserved his admiration for the holy, simple, and mystic (Athanassiadi, Oxford seminar, 1995). It is perhaps surprising that no Christian anti-pagan-biased views of a more adverse kind have come down to us.

[49] It is possible that in the original there was some connection between this passage and Marcellinus, who himself met a violent end.

[50] Kaegi (1968: 59–98).

[51] Chuvin (1990: 95–6). Examples of politically active pagans include Severianus (*PLRE* ii, 998) in the AD 450s and 60s, and Pamprepius (*PLRE*

That Marcellinus had links with this Neoplatonist circle is confirmed by his personal association with the philosopher Sallustius. The Greek term *hoi sunen* is vague, but implies that Sallustius was in some way with Marcellinus. This might mean that Marcellinus had spent time in Athens at the same time as Sallustius, and (or alternatively) that Sallustius visited him in Dalmatia.[52] There is a hint in Damascius' material on Sallustius in Photius' epitome (unfortunately very cryptic) that Sallustius travelled widely; he is described as journeying the world with bare feet.[53]

The *Suda* entry and the Photius epitome of Damascius both describe Marcellinus as an independent ruler, which tallies with Priscus' account. The reference to the 'Roman emperor' could apply to either the western or eastern emperor, although, as Damascius was an easterner, the use of 'Roman emperor' without further qualification seems more likely to have referred to the eastern emperor. If so, then 'any other ruler of the nations' might refer to Ricimer, perhaps reflecting the irregular nature of his power.

The statement connecting Dalmatia with Epirus is puzzling; most especially if Marcellinus had taken the province over from the western government. Epirus was, of course, to the south-east of Dalmatia and, at that time, in the diocese of Macedonia, and, as such, a clear part of the eastern empire (see also the Procopius passage on p. 37). This may be a factual error by Damascius, or more likely by the *Suda* editor (many of the confusions in the *Suda* are a result of the condensation of the original texts).[54]

ii, 825), who was involved in the revolt of Illus in AD 484–8. But Cameron (1982: 217–89) has argued that official tolerance was limited.

[52] The context of the information suggests the latter. Hodgkin (1880b: 446) imagines Marcellinus 'holding long conversations with Sallustius who dwelt in his palace'.

[53] Damascius, *Vita Isidori*, Photius epitome, *Bibliotheca* (Cod. 242) 251.

[54] I have considered the possibility that Dalmatia and Epirus were connected administratively at the time that the *Suda* was compiled c. AD 1000, but have found no evidence for this. Epirus was part of the theme of Dyrrachion and Nikopolis created in the ninth century, fragmenting later into smaller units; Dalmatia was either under foreign control or independent until the 860s. When it came back under Byzantine control, it became a theme in its own right (parts of southern Dalmatia were linked to Serbia in the tenth century) until the Venetian conquest in AD 1000 (Kazhdan (1991: 578–9, 715–17)).

Alternatively, the original report may have been that Marcellinus was in control of Dalmatia as far as Epidaurus, a city down the coast from Salona, and either this, by scribal error, became Epirus or there was confusion between Epidaurus and Epidamnus (the Greek name for Dyrrhachium).[55] It is just possible, however, that there was some real connection between Marcellinus (or Dalmatia) and Epirus at the time which influenced Damascius' account. Epirus was, like Dalmatia, a prosperous coastal area, important to East–West communications, and was raided by the Vandals in the AD 450/60s.[56] Had Marcellinus perhaps extended his authority down the coast from Dalmatia with, possibly, the agreement of Constantinople, perhaps connected with the need to secure the Strait of Otranto (see p. 50)?

For Marcellinus' subsequent career, we have two fragments from Priscus' history preserved in the *Excerpta de Legationibus*. The first reads:

Since Gaiseric no longer kept the treaty which he had made with Majorian, he sent a force of Vandals and Moors to ravage Italy and Sicily. Marcellinus had already left the island because Ricimer, wishing to drain off his strength, had won over with money his Scythian followers, who were in the majority [or, 'who came to a very large number of men'].[57] As a result they left Marcellinus and went over < to Ricimer [,] and Marcellinus > as a precaution against the plot (since he could not compete with Ricimer's wealth) withdrew from Sicily. Embassies were therefore, sent to Gaiseric, both from Ricimer, warning him not to ignore the treaty, and from the ruler of the eastern Romans telling him to keep away from Sicily and Italy and return the royal women.[58]

Gaiseric's treaty with Majorian was made in AD 460 (or early 461), following the destruction of Majorian's fleet (see Pt. III p. 208).[59] The resumption of Vandal raiding may have

---

[55] Since making this last suggestion I have found exactly this confusion in the Ravenna *Cosmographia* (113, 4). Although this is a late seventh-century AD work, it used a written fifth-century source, together with a fourth-century map (Jordanes, ed. Mierow (1915: 37)). Incidentally, its entry on Dalmatia (16, 8) reads: 'iuxta ipsum Illyricum circa maris litora patria quae dicitur Dalmatia, iam ex colpo [*sic*] pertinens occidentali'.

[56] Kazhdan (1991: 715–17).

[57] Alternative translation by Whitby.

[58] Priscus, frag. 38 (1) (Blockley's translation).

[59] Hydatius, 204 (209) *s.a.* 460 and 205 (210) *s.a.* 461.

occurred after August AD 461 when Majorian was killed, and the treaty hence considered void. But, if Gaiseric decided to break the treaty when news of Majorian's death reached Carthage, it would have been very late in the season for a fleet to set sail in safety, and the spring of AD 462 seems more likely.[60] The other evidence for the date is that Eudoxia and her daughter Placidia were finally returned to Constantinople in the summer of AD 462,[61] which dates Marcellinus' presence in Sicily to early AD 462 at the latest. He probably left the island in AD 461.

The common assumption that Marcellinus was serving at this time under Majorian is based on flimsy evidence. It is not, on the evidence of this fragment, an indisputable fact that Marcellinus was in Sicily on the orders, or at the request, of Majorian; nor that Marcellinus must have reverted to allegiance to the western emperor (given up, according to Procopius, after the death of Aetius), still less that he had been appointed western *magister militum*.[62] The reference to Marcellinus follows mention of Gaiseric breaking the treaty made with Majorian, but no direct association is made between the two and no reason is given for Marcellinus' presence in Sicily prior to the Vandal raid. The reason that Priscus gives for Marcellinus' withdrawal is the loss of his troops, not Majorian's death. The only reasons for believing that Marcellinus was acting for Majorian are the congruence of the dates in which Marcellinus was in Sicily and those of Majorian's reign and abortive attack on North Africa, and the involvement of Ricimer in both Majorian's death and the bribing of Marcellinus' mercenaries.

Working against the idea of Marcellinus being in Sicily under Majorian's orders is the improbability that someone who had exercised independent power for several years would have voluntarily put himself back under the control of a weak western emperor. Personal friendship with Majorian, as hypothesized by some writers, does not seem an adequate motive. It is more likely that Marcellinus' presence in Sicily resulted from some

---

[60] Sea travel was not normally undertaken between November and March, and was inadvisable between late September and May (Jones (1964: i, 403; ii, 843). Gaiseric normally set out in the spring (Procopius, *Wars* III, v, 22).

[61] Hydatius, 211 (217) *s.a.* 462.

[62] For instance, *PLRE* ii, 709, Marcellinus 6; Bury (1923: 333).

kind of alliance with the Italian government. Such an alliance could have been made by Marcellinus for his own reasons, either connected with the escalating Vandal raids in the eastern Mediterranean and the security of coastal Dalmatia (see pp. 49–50), or even with the fact that Constantinople was putting pressure on Gaiseric to return Eudoxia and her daughters. Whatever the exact circumstances, Marcellinus' presence in Sicily is not conclusive evidence of military service under Majorian.

The second fragment reads:

> The Western Romans came to fear that Marcellinus, whose strength was [or, 'military forces were' (Whitby)] increasing, would make war on them while their affairs were troubled in a variety of ways both by the Vandals and by Aegidius... the Western Romans sent envoys to the East to reconcile Marcellinus and the Vandals to them. Phylarchus was sent to Marcellinus and persuaded him not to attack the Romans.[63]

The two fragments refer to events close together in time, but we do not know how they related to each other within the original history. It makes sense to place events in fragment 38 slightly earlier than those in fragment 39; the first relating to events just before AD 462, and the second to a little while afterwards. This is the order in which they appear in the *Excerpta*. The events must date to before AD 465, the date of Aegidius' death. The latter part of fragment 39 (not given above) refers to Eudocia being married to Gaiseric's son Huneric. This was arranged before her mother and sister were returned to Constantinople in AD 462 and presumably was not long delayed. Also, we know that Aegidius was fighting the Goths in Gaul in AD 463.[64]

The reference to the western Romans fearing Marcellinus' strength (or 'forces') increasing might refer to his acquisition of troops to replace those enticed away by Ricimer. That incident would also provide the motive for Marcellinus' threatened attack on Italy, which otherwise needs explanation (and also perhaps explains why he was dissuaded from it by Constantinople, it having been a matter of reaction rather than policy). It is

---

[63] Priscus, frag. 39 (1) (Blockley's translation).
[64] Hydatius, 214 (218) *s.a.* 463.

significant that the Italian government (which at this time means 'Ricimer') did not send ambassadors directly to Marcellinus, but to Constantinople. This would be understandable if, as argued above, Dalmatia had previously been ruled by the eastern empire and still had strong connections with Constantinople under Marcellinus.[65]

Priscus refers to both Marcellinus and Aegidius, but it is not known whether there was any connection between their threats against Italy. Both men may have wanted to remove Ricimer from his position of power in Italy, and it is possible that they had been in contact with each other and had agreed to concert their efforts. Equally possibly, the dual threat may have been coincidental; each had separate reasons to be hostile to Ricimer. There is no other evidence of the two working together. In fact, in AD 464/5 Aegidius was making overtures to the Vandals, perhaps even agreeing a treaty with Gaiseric (see Pt. II p. 94), while Marcellinus, in the same year, was fighting the Vandals in Sicily.[66]

The information in the first fragment that Marcellinus had been in Sicily is confirmed by Hydatius: 'The Vandals, who had been slaughtered by Marcellinus in Sicily, fled from there.'[67] This entry dates to AD 464 or 465. It is conceivable that this refers to the campaign reported by Priscus, and that Hydatius has got the date wrong;[68] but there is no reason why Marcellinus should not have been in action against the Vandals in Sicily twice (or more): once around AD 461 and again, more successfully, in AD 464/5. But why would he have been willing to return to Sicily after the previous débâcle? It surely cannot have been at the request of the Italian government, for this was then dominated by Ricimer. His return to Sicily may have

---

[65] The only thing known of the envoy to Marcellinus, Phylarchus, is that he was a member of another diplomatic mission to Gaiseric (*PLRE* ii, 884, Phylarchus).

[66] Hydatius, 220 (224) *s.a.* 464–5 and 223 (227) *s.a.* 464–5.

[67] Hydatius, 223 (227) *s.a.* 464–5: 'Vandali per Marcellinum in Scilia caesi effugantur ex ea.'

[68] It was suggested by Courtois (1951: 23–54) that the dates in Hydatius' chronicle needed radical overall amendment, but Burgess (1993) has shown this to be mistaken. However, Hydatius did not always get individual dates correct, and it is possible that this item on Marcellinus has been slightly displaced.

been prompted by the eastern emperor Leo[69] (possibly as a result of the embassy of Phylarchus to Marcellinus), and he may have provided ships and manpower. However, it is unlikely that Leo's motive was to assist Italy under Ricimer's puppet emperor Libius Severus, whom Leo did not recognize.

Marcellinus' first campaign in Sicily (probably) and the second (certainly) were not for the benefit of Italy. Marcellinus' motive for intervention in Sicily (and for co-operation with western forces in the first instance) would have been his own fears of Vandal sea power in the Mediterranean and Adriatic. This was, after all, the one barbarian threat that was a real danger to Salona and the Dalmatian coast, especially if the Vandals proved able to establish themselves in Sicily and southern Italy. There is evidence from Procopius, Victor of Vita, and the early sixth-century *Oracle of Baalbek* that the Vandals were raiding Dalmatia at this time,[70] and conceivably Sicily was being used as a base. The key to the security of the Adriatic (and hence Dalmatia) was the Strait of Otranto, for which the key points would be Brundisium, Dyrrhachium, and the island of Corfu. We do not know what, if any, action Italy and Constantinople were taking here, probably very little; the fact that the Vandals raided Dalmatia (and also the island of Zacynthus to the south of Corfu)[71] suggests this. Marcellinus may have taken his own measures to try to secure the strait, to which action on Sicily would be a logical extension.

Max has put forward the theory that at this time Marcellinus played an important part in relations between Leo and Majorian,[72] who may have sought Leo's aid in his abortive attack on Gaiseric. This is associated with a 'recruiting campaign' undertaken by Majorian in the Danube area, close to Dalmatia, which might have alarmed Marcellinus and caused some sort of agreement between Marcellinus and Majorian, perhaps arranged through Leo's diplomacy. This is then connected with Leo's

---

[69] *PLRE* ii, 709, Marcellinus 6.

[70] Procopius, *Wars* III, v, 22–5; Victor Vit. I, 5; and *the Oracle of Baalbek*, 133: 'and from Africa there will arise a rebel named Gaiseric and he will capture Rome ... and Dalmatia will be altogether plunged into the sea, Campania and Calabria will be captured'.

[71] Procopius, *Wars* III, xxii, 16–18.

[72] Max (1979: 232–7).

suspension of payments to the Ostrogoths, who shortly afterwards 'responded by invading those territories independently governed by Marcellinus; they continued down the shores of the Adriatic to the city of Dyrrhachium in New Epirus'. In AD 464/5, when Leo resumed payments and Marcellinus was in Sicily 'fighting the Vandals on Leo's behalf', 'the inference is almost inevitable that Leo's remission and renewal of tribute ... could manoeuvre Marcellinus into any desirable position'. Possibly Leo gave Majorian partial recognition as emperor with some guarantee of aid from Marcellinus, and Marcellinus' second appearance in Sicily is connected with the western delegation to Constantinople.

It is perfectly credible to link Marcellinus' presence in Sicily with either, or both, Majorian and Leo; diplomatic channels existed between the three parties, and Leo certainly had influence over Marcellinus, but there is no need to drag the Ostrogoths in. Also, there is no evidence that Majorian recruited in the Danube area; this is based on Sidonius' anachronistic list of the barbarians in his army, most of whom were, no doubt, already in Italy (see Pt. III, p. 205). The Danube area is, in any case, well away from coastal Dalmatia. The contention that Ostrogoths invaded Marcellinus' lands is surprising. The supposed invasion 'down the shores of the Adriatic to the city of Dyrrhachium' is based on a cryptic notice in an addition to Prosper's chronicle, found in one version only, unsupported by other evidence, that in that year Valamer entered Dyrrhachium.[73] It would also have to be the case that, on the basis of the *Suda* (see pp. 44–6), Marcellinus was the independent ruler of the province of Old Epirus as well as Dalmatia, which, as seen above, is most uncertain. While not impossible, this version of events remains purely speculative.

Marcellinus probably returned to Dalmatia after his Sicilian campaign in AD 464/5 (and between *c.* AD 461 and 464 if there were two campaigns). In the following years he may have visited Constantinople, perhaps seeking eastern assistance. He and Leo

---

[73] *Auct. Prosper ad ed. a 455* (Vatican epitome) 11, following notice of Ricimer's consulship. This is a rather mysterious entry. It is surprising, if this really occurred, that it is not noted by Jordanes. Other Goths took the fortified city in AD 479 (Malchus, frag. 18).

were certainly in contact, as we next hear of Marcellinus in
AD 467 participating in the eastern expedition taking Anthemius to Italy to become western emperor. An entry in Hydatius
reads: 'Directed by the emperor Leo, through the will of God,
Anthemius the brother of Procopius, with Marcellinus and
other picked men as *comites*, and a large and powerful army,
reached Italy from Constantinople.'[74] Anthemius clearly set off
from Constantinople and Marcellinus may have done so too. At
this point in his career Marcellinus was acting very closely with
Leo, perhaps having accepted an eastern military position, although it is unclear from Hydatius' wording whether Marcellinus was one of Anthemius' *comites* or not. It is difficult to be
sure how to reconcile this with his position as independent ruler
of Dalmatia. Perhaps he had discovered that he could not survive without eastern support, rather in the same way that Ricimer was forced into accommodation (see Pt. III, pp. 233–4),
and was forced to relinquish some of his autonomy.

Marcellinus and Anthemius may have already known each
other. Anthemius had campaigned in Illyricum, against the
Ostrogoths, and around Serdica in the 460s.[75] He was believed
by Damascius to have had pagan sympathies and interests,
similar to those of the circle with which Marcellinus was associated. Messius Phoebus Severus, a pagan Roman who had been
studying philosophy in Alexandria, returned to Rome in
AD 467/9 and was made consul (for AD 470), patrician, and
city prefect by Anthemius.[76] According to Damascius, 'Anthemius, who was emperor of Rome, held pagan views and shared
the ideas of Severus, who was devoted to the idols, and whom he
appointed consul; the two had a secret plan to restore the pollu-
tion of idols'.[77] A second reference says that Severus 'was a
Roman and after Anthemius had prompted the hope that
Rome, which was fallen, would be restored again by him, he

---

[74] Hydatius, 230 (234) *s.a.* 465–6: 'De Constantinopoli a Leone Augusto
Antimus frater Procopi cum Marcellino aliisque comitibus uiris electis et cum
ingenti multitudine exercitus copiosi ad Italiam deo ordinante directus ascen-
dit.'

[75] Sidonius, *Pan.* I, 224–6, 232–5, 236–42, 269–80.

[76] *PLRE* ii, 1005, Severus 19.

[77] Damascius, *Vita Isidori*, Photius epitome, *Bibliotheca* (Cod. 242) 108
(Whitby's translation). The anti-pagan attitude is of course Photius'.

returned to Rome, which he had previously left and obtained the post of consul'.[78]

Damascius is, however, the only witness to Anthemius' pagan sympathies, unless the description of 'Graeculus' by Ennodius carries pagan implications (see Pt. III, p. 245).[79] Anthemius came from a Christian family, and according to one source he founded the church of St. Thomas in Constantinople.[80] Sidonius' panegyric to Anthemius when he was western emperor says nothing of his religious beliefs, but does stress his learning in ancient and modern philosophy.[81] It seems likely that Anthemius had intellectual leanings towards classical learning and Neoplatonism, which could easily have been perceived as paganism,[82] especially in the West. When in Rome he also seems to have tolerated Christian heretical sects (see Pt. III, p. 245) and pagan festivals,[83] which would have made him open to suspicion. However, it is most unlikely that he would have been chosen by Leo as co-emperor unless he was at least formally Christian,[84] so if he held pagan beliefs, it was surely 'within the secrecy of his own conscience'.[85]

Sidonius' panegyric pictured Anthemius on a ship, one of a fleet in the Hellespont, probably that which conveyed him to Italy.[86] There is no reason to think that this was one of Marcellinus' ships, as sometimes suggested. Scholars have stated with

[78] Damascius, *Vita Isidori*, Photius epitome, *Bibliotheca* (Cod. 242) 64 (Whitby's translations).

[79] Ennodius, *Vita Epiph.* 54. There is also a coin of Anthemius with the figure of Hercules, which could indicate pagan or classical leanings (Carson and Kent (1994: 198)).

[80] *Chronicon Paschale* (an eastern chronicle written in the AD 630s), *s.a.* 454 and 468.

[81] Sidonius, *Pan.* II, 156 ff.

[82] Something similar happened to Fl. Taurus Seleucus in Constantinople. He was praetorian prefect AD 439–40 and was responsible for numerous public works, but his interests in philosophy and poetry left him open to accusations of Hellenism by his political enemies (John Malalas, 362).

[83] Pope Gelasius I (*Adversus Andromachum Senatorem Caeterosque Romanos Qui Lupercalia Secundem Morem Pristinum Colenda Constituebant*, col. 113) accuses him of tolerating the celebration of the Lupercalia.

[84] He is described as a pious Christian by Theophanes (AM 5957) and by Nicephorus Callistus (*HE* 604); both, however, were writing centuries later.

[85] Chuvin (1990: 121).

[86] Sidonius, *Pan.* II, 505–7.

remarkable unanimity that the main reason for Marcellinus' autonomy was his possession of a navy, sometimes referred to as 'the Salona fleet'.[87] Possession of a fleet of warships would go far towards explaining Marcellinus' influential position; but such historians may be giving a misleading impression of his naval resources.

There is no direct, and little indirect, evidence for the existence of an imperial fleet based in Dalmatia in the late empire. There is no naval force listed in Dalmatia in the *Notitia Dignitatum*, and it is unlikely that a fleet would have been created there after the AD 420s, when it was compiled. The Adriatic would have been covered in the early fifth century by what remained of the *classis* at Ravenna (with secondary base at Aquileia).[88] It is therefore unlikely that Marcellinus inherited a fully-fledged fleet of Roman warships.

The fleet which took Anthemius and Marcellinus to Italy was probably wholly or mainly eastern, as was that which attacked the Vandals in AD 468, and that which took Julius Nepos to Italy. Neither the West nor Dalmatia had comparable resources. (See App. for a fuller discussion of Roman and Vandal sea power.) The best evidence for Marcellinus' possession of a naval force is his campaigning in Sicily, but this only tells us that he was able to transport an unknown number of troops from Dalmatia to Sicily. Vessels would probably have had to be built, or acquired from the commercial shipping still operating from Salona and other coastal cities.[89] Salona probably still had dock facilities which, even if run-down, would have allowed ships to be built and maintenance to be carried out. Marcellinus' ability to requisition or hire ships and men may well have given him a military advantage. However, he would not have been able to use levied or hired ships indefinitely, and though he may have retained a small number in permanent commission, to

[87] For example, Wozniak (1981: 357) referred to a 'substantial fleet based at Salona' giving him 'control of the Adriatic'; and Wilkes (1969: 420) to 'a powerful fleet based at Salona'.

[88] *Notitia Dignitatum*, Oc. XLII, 7 and 4; Vegetius, IV, 31; Zosimus, VI, viii, 2.

[89] However, in AD 488 when Theoderic and the Ostrogoths set out for Italy, they were unable to cross the Adriatic because there were no ships available on the coast, and had to go overland (Procopius, *Wars* I, i, 13).

refer to such access to naval resources as possession of a fleet seems an unwarranted and misleading exaggeration.

When in AD 467 Marcellinus accompanied Anthemius to Italy, he was, presumably, present at his elevation. Given the previous events on Sicily, the meeting between Marcellinus and Ricimer must have been an interesting one,[90] especially as Marcellinus may have been given the title of patrician, attributed by Jordanes and Marcellinus *comes* (who specifies that Marcellinus was patrician of the western empire).[91] The most likely date for him to acquire this title is in the reign of Anthemius. One view is that the title was bestowed by Anthemius, probably immediately on his accession, with the idea of setting up Marcellinus as a counterbalance to Ricimer, who had been *patricius* since AD 457, and who was (rightly) perceived by Anthemius and his supporters as a major stumbling-block to the new emperor exercising full imperial power (see Pt. III, Ch. 14).

This has, however, been questioned, on the grounds that it was impossible for two western generals to hold the patriciate simultaneously. Demandt suggested that Marcellinus *comes* was mistaken in attributing the title to Marcellinus, perhaps giving him Ricimer's title erroneously.[92] Alternatively, if Marcellinus really did hold the title of western patrician, it has been suggested that Ricimer was forced to relinquish the title of patrician while it was held by his rival.[93] From what we know of Ricimer, the chance of him having meekly given up the patriciate to a rival seems extremely remote! It is in fact doubtful whether the initial conception, that only one general might hold the title of *patricius*, is valid.[94] In the time of Aetius there seems to have been more than one military patrician;[95] and there was no

---

[90] However, personal contact between rivals and even bitter enemies was a normal feature of ancient political life, and it is perhaps anachronistic to see a problem here. The formality of the court setting would facilitate matters.

[91] Marcellinus *comes*, *s.a.* 468: 'Marcellinus Occidentis patricius idemque paganus'; and Jordanes, *Getica* 239. As discussed in connection with the sources in general, these sources may not be independent of each other.

[92] Demandt (1970: 685–7). He points out that Marcellinus *comes* (*s.a.* 464) refers to Ricimer only as *rex*.

[93] Piccotti (1928: 3–80), cited by O'Flynn (1983: 189 n. 59).

[94] O'Flynn (1983: 117).

[95] Sigisvult and, possibly, Merobaudes had held the title at the same time as Aetius (Constantius, *Vita Germani* 38). See also Clover (1971: 35–6). In

constitutional reason against it, even had such a convention developed.[96]

Marcellinus *comes'* chronicle is the only reliable source on this; strangely, the western sources for Marcellinus do not note it, as might have been expected were the title conferred in Italy by a Roman emperor. As Marcellinus *comes* was an Illyrian writing in Constantinople, it is possible that the tradition that Marcellinus held the western patriciate stems from an eastern or Illyrian source and may conceivably have related to a title held in Dalmatia. Although it is likely, it remains uncertain whether Marcellinus held the patriciate in the West.

In AD 466, immediately after Anthemius' elevation near Rome, Hydatius recorded that: 'The expedition to Africa organized against the Vandals was recalled due to [the phrase is unclear] and unfavourable sailing conditions'.[97]

Hydatius does not say who organized this expedition; it could have been Ricimer or Anthemius. In the latter case, Marcellinus would be an obvious choice as commander. If it was led by Marcellinus, it is possible that the entry in the *Consularia Constantinopolitana* (see p. 40) refers to this, rather than the later AD 468 expedition.

In AD 468 a major campaign was organized:

The envoys who had been sent to the emperor[98] returned with the news that, in their presence, a very large army with three picked leaders [*duces*] had set off against the Vandals at the command of the Emperor Leo, and that Marcellinus had also been sent off [or, 'was also under orders'?] with a large allied force by the Emperor Anthemius;

the eastern empire it was quite usual for several generals to hold the title at once.

[96] Whether it was or was not theoretically possible for Anthemius to make such an appointment, the viability in reality of setting up a rival patrician to Ricimer may be gauged by the subsequent fates of (certainly) Anthemius and (possibly) Marcellinus.

[97] Hydatius, 232 (236) *s.a.* 466–7: 'Expeditio ad Affricam aduersum Vandalos <ordinata metabularum> commutatione et nauigationis inopurtunitate reuocatur.' On the meaning of the unclear words see Burgess (1993: 132 n. 232). He suggests that this should be translated as 'change of weather'. Rumour of the expedition caused Gothic envoys to return from Carthage and Sueve raiders to be recalled (Hydatius, 236 (240) *s.a.* 466–7).

[98] From entry 234 (238) *s.a.* 466–7 these would seem to be Suevian envoys sent out by Remismund.

[and that] Ricimer had been made son-in-law and *patricius* of the Emperor Anthemius[99]

This eyewitness report should be reliable, but because of Hydatius' style and brevity it is not possible to determine the exact circumstances. The implication is that Marcellinus commanded forces belonging to Anthemius, either from the western army, or eastern units which had accompanied Anthemius to Italy. As the loyalty of the Italian army would have been primarily to Ricimer, the latter is more likely. Hydatius' wording and that in Marcellinus *comes*' report (see p. 59)[100] suggest that Marcellinus was not a regular western military commander, but that some less straightforward arrangement existed.

Procopius gives a detailed description of the expedition, taken from Priscus:

> They say that this army numbered one hundred thousand men. He [Leo] collected a fleet of ships from the whole eastern sea and he showed great generosity to the soldiers and sailors... certainly, they say that he spent one hundred and thirty thousand pounds to no avail... he appointed as supreme commander Basiliscus, the brother of his wife Verina.[101]

There is then an interpolation of non-Priscan material on Aspar.[102] Procopius also records that the second commander was Heraclius, who had been sent from Byzantium to Tripolis, and that the third was Marcellinus. Following this passage comes his description of Marcellinus' background (given in full and discussed on p. 65), and the account then continues:

---

[99] Hydatius, 241 (247) *s.a.* 468: 'Legati qui ad imperatorem missi nuntiantes sub praesentia sui magnum ualde exercitum cum tribus ducibus lectis aduersum Vandalos a Leone imperatore descendisse, directo Marcellino pariter cum manu magna eidem per imperatorem Antimium sociata; Rechimerium generum Antimi imperatoris et patricium factum'.

[100] Marcellinus *comes*, *s.a.* 468.

[101] Procopius, *Wars* III, vi, 1–2 (Blockley's translation). Some of the figures for the number of vessels given are clearly wildly exaggerated, but those of 1,113 vessels (George Cedrenus, *Hist. Compend.* p. 613, probably based on an earlier lost source) and 7,000 marines (Theodore Lect. *HE* i, 25) seem feasible. Basiliscus was the uncle of the wife of Julius Nepos, Marcellinus' nephew.

[102] Blockley (1981–3: ii, 363 and 399 n. 186). The interpolation (vi, 3–4) suggests that Aspar, because of his Arian faith and because Leo had offended him, plotted to ensure that the expedition would fail.

At this time the Emperor Leo courted Marcellianus [*sic*] assiduously, won him over [or, 'won him over by very effective flattery'] and told [or, 'ordered'] him to go to the island of Sardinia, which was in the possession of the Vandals. He drove out the Vandals and held it without difficulty.[103]

The wording of this is rather odd in the circumstances. Marcellinus had just accompanied Anthemius to Italy, at Leo's order or request, so the reference to Leo having to court or flatter Marcellinus at this point seems somewhat incongruous. A context which would fit better might be the slightly earlier time at which Leo was negotiating with Marcellinus for his general support of Anthemius.

Marcellinus was successful in Sardinia and Heraclius also met his objectives. Basiliscus proved to be incompetent, and by delaying on the brink of victory (which Procopius puts down to treachery, but was probably in reality mere bad generalship) gave Gaiseric the time to reorganize his defences, prepare fireships and destroy Basiliscus' fleet.[104] As a result the remaining Roman forces had to withdraw.

Procopius then notes that Marcellinus was assassinated at about the same time as the withdrawal, or shortly before: 'This then was the end of the war, and Heraclius returned home. For Marcellinus had perished by the treachery of one of his fellow generals [or, 'commanders', or 'officers']'.[105] This is one of six notices of Marcellinus' death, the others being brief notices in Cassiodorus' chronicle; the *Fasti Vindobonensis* (which gives the date as August AD 468); the *Paschale Campanum*; Marcellinus *comes*' chronicle; and Damascius. Marcellinus' death is the most widely reported fact about him, and the only fact noted in western chronicles other than

---

[103] Procopius, *Wars* III, vi, 8 (Blockley's translation, Priscus, frag. 53 (3), the two alternative translations by Whitby). Military efforts on Sardinia may conceivably have been prompted by Pope Hilarius (Courtois (1955: 187 n. 3)), who was Sardinian (*Liber Pontif.* XLVIII).

[104] Procopius, *Wars* III, vi, 10–24.

[105] Procopius, *Wars* III, vi, 25 (Blockley's translation, Priscus, frag. 53 (3)). 'Generals' (as this is sometimes translated) is too specific: either 'fellow officers' or 'fellow commanders' is a better translation. The Greek verb has a general meaning of 'to destroy' rather than the more specific 'to murder' or 'to assassinate', though it might also be translated as either of these.

Hydatius.[106] The three western chronicles all state that he was killed in Sicily.[107] As it was previously recorded that Marcellinus had been sent by Leo to Sardinia, either Marcellinus had moved from there to Sicily or one of the locations is an error.

Marcellinus *comes*' entry reads: 'Marcellinus, western patrician and a pagan, while bringing money and assistance to the Romans fighting the Vandals near Carthage, was treacherously stabbed by those very people for whom he had openly come to fight.'[108] Like Damascius, and unlike the western chronicles, Marcellinus makes a point of his namesake's paganism.

Damascius also reports that Marcellinus' death was a result of a ruse or act of treachery by the Romans, and involved the breaking of oaths.[109] The epitome in the *Bibliotheca* refers to Marcellinus' death in the précis of an anecdote about Gaiseric's reaction (see pp. 43–4), which is strikingly similar to the comment made to Valentinian III, that in killing Aetius he had cut off his own right hand with the other.[110]

If his death was a politically motivated, arranged, assassination rather than a murder for personal reasons, Ricimer may have been the instigator;[111] and it is perhaps surprising that

[106] Hydatius reports neither Marcellinus' death nor the failure of the expedition, because his chronicle ends in that same year, probably because the author had died.

[107] *Fasti Vind. Prior. s.a.* 468; *Pasch. Camp. s.a.* 468; Cassiodorus, *Chronica* 1285 *s.a.* 468.

[108] Marcellinus *comes, s.a.* 468: 'Marcellinus Occidentis patricius idemque paganus dum Romanis contra Vandalus apud Carthaginem pugnantis opem auxiliumque fert, ab iisdem dolo confoditur, pro quibus palam venerat pugnaturus'.

[109] Could this refer to some sort of mutual oath of friendship, or at least non-aggression, which Ricimer and Marcellinus had taken (or been forced to take) in Italy? It would have been a logical precaution. It is just possible that an unplaced fragment of Priscus in the *Suda* (A 1660 = Priscus, 67)—'Oaths were given as mutual sureties not only for themselves but also for those who had come from the Roman court to reconcile the men. Priscus says this'—refers to Ricimer and Marcellinus, as we know that Priscus wrote about the Vandal campaign.

[110] Procopius, *Wars* III, iv, 28. Possibly Gaiseric was reusing a well-known quotation, or this was an adage current in the literature of the time, used by both authors.

[111] This is suggested by most modern historians, with the exception of Demandt (1970: 685).

none of the ancient sources insinuates this. The death of Marcellinus removed a serious professional and political rival. Whether Marcellinus and Ricimer were long-standing personal enemies as well,[112] it is now impossible to say. On the other hand, long-distance assassinations are never easy to arrange, and had Ricimer killed him himself we would surely know of it. As far as we know, Marcellinus was in Sicily and Ricimer in Italy. The vagueness of the Greek leaves things ambiguous; while 'fellow generals' could include Ricimer, if Procopius is saying that the person responsible was one of Marcellinus' fellow commanders or officers (see n. 105) this would suggest that it was somebody also involved in the Vandal campaign, who may or may not have been working for Ricimer.

Marcellinus' nephew Julius Nepos became the ruler of Dalmatia. We do not know how this was accomplished, whether solely by inheritance, or also through official or semi-official recognition by Roman authorities. Nepos had a personal connection with the eastern imperial family, as at some point he married a relation of the Empress Verina, wife of the Emperor Leo and mother-in-law of his successor Zeno.[113] In AD 474 Leo made Nepos general and eastern patrician and sent him to Italy as emperor, where he forced his predecessor Glycerius to be ordained bishop (see Pt. III, p. 273); but when, some months later, the patrician Orestes turned against him, he fled to Ravenna and took ship to Salona.[114]

---

[112] As suggested by O'Flynn (1983: 117). One basis for this theory is the proposition that both men had served as subordinate officers of Aetius, and were thus well known to each other, but this is uncertain. The other evidence, the bribing of Marcellinus' Scythians, was not necessarily the result of personal enmity, but of political scheming or even military necessity.

[113] Malchus, frag. 10. Jordanes (*Romana* 338) seems to say that Nepos' wife was a niece of Leo and that the marriage, which took place at Ravenna, was part of the arrangements to install Nepos as emperor in the West. This, if correct, would mean, therefore, that Nepos was not chosen because of a pre-existing marital connection.

[114] *Anon. Val.* 7: 'superveniens Nepos patricius ad Portum urbis Romae, deposuit de imperio Glycerium et factus est episcopus et Nepos factus imperator Romae. Mox veniens Ravennam; quem persequens Orestis patricius cum exercitu, metuens Nepos adventum Orestis, ascendens navem fugam petit ad Salonam et ibi mansit per annos quinque; postea vero a suis occiditur'; John Ant. frag. 209 (2).

John of Antioch and Jordanes testify that Glycerius was made Bishop of Salona,[115] and Glycerius' name appears in the list of bishops of the city.[116] We know little of the Church in Dalmatia at this time, but in the 490s it was in some disarray. There is a break in the recorded series of bishops of Salona immediately after Glycerius,[117] and heresy was rife according to correspondence from Pope Gelasius to Bishop Honorius of Salona.[118] Honorius' recorded surprise at receiving instructions from Rome may indicate poor relations between Salona and Rome, or that he was normally answerable to eastern authority. Salona in the fifth century would have looked towards the East in ecclesiastical matters.[119]

Of Julius Nepos in Dalmatia, before and after he was emperor, we know almost nothing. He held the unique title of *magister militum Dalmatiae* (the implications of which are discussed on pp. 40–1). He ruled in Dalmatia for five years after fleeing Italy and was still formally recognized as western emperor by Constantinople. During this time, Nepos appealed to the Emperor Zeno, to whom he was distantly connected by marriage, for assistance in regaining his position in Italy (by now occupied by Odovacar):

On the same day messengers from Nepos also came . . . to ask him zealously to help Nepos . . . in the recovery of his empire. They asked that he grant money and an army for this purpose . . . At the same time Verina too joined in urging on Zeno, since she was supporting Nepos' wife who was her relative.[120]

---

[115] Jordanes, *Getica* 241. Several other sources (for instance *Fasti Vind. Prior. s.a.* 474, and *Pasch. Camp. s.a.* 474) record that he was consecrated bishop, but do not mention the see. Marcellinus *comes* (*s.a.* 474) implies that he died shortly afterwards.

[116] Wilkes (1969: 431).

[117] Wilkes (1969: 431); Dyggve (1951: 26).

[118] Gelasius, *Epp.* v, *Ad Honorium Dalmatiae Episcopum*, and v i, *Ad eodum Honorium Dalmatae Episcopum*.

[119] Wilkes (1969: 433).

[120] Malchus, frag. 14 (Blockley's translation). For Zeno's reply see Pt. III, pp. 291–2. Contrary to some modern interpretations, although not willing to provide an army, Zeno was sympathetic and seems to have tried to give Nepos some limited support by insisting on his legal title as emperor, and that the title of patrician desired by Odovacar came officially from Nepos.

While still trying to regain the purple, Nepos was assassinated in May AD 480; 'stabbed full of holes', in his villa near Salona.[121] This villa, as previously discussed, was probably Diocletian's residence at Split. It is a haunting picture: the ineffectual figure of the deposed emperor living out his last futile years in the shabby remains of the great buildings, visited perhaps by yet another deposed Roman emperor, now a Christian bishop. One wonders what the shade of Diocletian made of it. Marcellinus *comes* adds further detail: 'Nepos, whom Orestes had a short time before removed from imperial power, was killed at his villa not far from Salona, through the treachery of his *comes* Viator and Ovida.'[122] Malchus associated the ex-emperor Glycerius, then Bishop of Salona, with the conspiracy.[123]

Ovida, perhaps a Goth,[124] was ruler of Dalmatia for a few months (under what title is not known) until he was defeated and killed in AD 481 or 482 by Odovacer, who used Julius Nepos' death as an excuse for invasion.[125] Dalmatia on the death of Nepos should, in theory, have returned to eastern possession, but was invaded and held by Odovacer, who ruled it until AD 489 with the tacit approval of the East, while probably accepting formal eastern overlordship. Possibly significantly, Dalmatia was not then made part of, or returned to, the *praefectus praetorio* of Italy.[126] From AD 493, when Odovacer was killed, Dalmatia would again have theoretically reverted to Constantinople, but was in reality in Ostrogothic control. Dalmatia was probably formally transferred by Zeno to Theoderic in AD 504,[127] reverting again to the East in the Justinian reconquest. It appears that the Ostrogothic rulers

---

[121] *Auct. Prosp. Haun. ordo prior. s.a.* 480: 'Nepos imperator cum Dalmatis imperaret et sumpti honoris sceptra firmare conaretur, a suis inprovisis ictibus confossus interiit X k. lul' (this is reproduced in *Auct. Prosp. Haun. ordo post.* and *marg.*). For the date see also *Fasti Vind. Prior. s.a.* 480.

[122] Marcellinus *comes*, *s.a.* 480: 'Nepos, quem dudum Orestes imperio abdicaverat, Viatoris et Ovidae comitum suorum insidiis haut longe a Salonis sua in villa occisus est'.

[123] Malchus, *Byzantine History*, Photius epitome, *Bibliotheca* (Cod. 78).

[124] An ancestor of Hilderith, King of the Goths, was also called Ovida (Jordanes, *Getica* 113).

[125] *Auct. Prosp. Haun. ordo prior. s.a.* 482.

[126] Mommsen (1906: vi, 444).

[127] Wilkes (1969: 424); Wozniak (1981: 365–6).

were able to run a semi-Roman system in Dalmatia, especially on the coast,[128] and were also able to operate part of the old Roman tax system; also possibly to restore mining in the interior.[129] Some, at least, of the Roman infrastructure had clearly been maintained by Marcellinus and Nepos.

[128] Wilkes (1969: 423–7); Wozniak (1981: 365–6).
[129] Cassiodorus, *Variae* III, 25.

4

The Identity of Marcellinus: Can Procopius and the Other Sources be Reconciled?

The cumulative impression of the above reconstruction is that Marcellinus and Dalmatia had more connections with the eastern empire than with the western empire. To recapitulate: first, there is evidence that much of the diocese of Illyricum belonged to the eastern empire from at least AD 437, and Dalmatia possibly earlier. Second, Marcellinus' nephew and successor Julius Nepos was related by marriage to the eastern imperial royal family. Third, when the Italian government wished to prevent Marcellinus from making an attack on Italy they sent envoys to Constantinople. Fourth, Leo gave the two rulers of Dalmatia direct orders, he sent Marcellinus as one of the *comites* of Anthemius to Italy, he gave Nepos appointments as general and eastern *patricius*, and sent him to the West as prospective emperor, and was possibly also behind one of Marcellinus' campaigns in Sicily. Fifth, Nepos, five years after Marcellinus' death, used a normal bureaucratic procedure to request the eastern emperor for a legal judgment for a domestic case in Dalmatia. Sixth, although this is very tenuous, the *Suda* links Dalmatia under Marcellinus' rule with Epirus, which was definitely an eastern possession.

The evidence in support of a 'western' Marcellinus consists of his activity in Sicily (although, as discussed, he was not necessarily there under the orders of the western emperor). There is his (probably subsequent) threat to attack Italy, though the dealings between Marcellinus and Ricimer may have simply been the consequences of their respective positions in Italy and Dalmatia. The Gallic connection sometimes predicated is non-existent, as the *coniuratio Marcelliniana* has been shown not to be connected to Marcellinus (see pp. 28–9). The other supposed western connection, the identification of Julius Nepos' father with the western *magister militum* Nepotianus, is very doubtful. Julius Nepos is called son of Nepotianus by Jordanes.[1] This is often assumed to be the Nepotianus who jointly led a Gothic army in Spain in A D 460, and is thought to have been Majorian's *magister militum*, which would link Nepos, and hence Marcellinus, to the West. This is proposed, however, purely on the basis of the coincidence of name, which is not an uncommon one. Furthermore, Burgess has very convincingly shown that this Nepotianus was probably not even an imperial general, but a mercenary working for the Visigoths.[2] The main reason that Marcellinus is considered to have been from Italy or Gaul, and an officer of the western army, is a short passage in Procopius' history within his description of the A D 468 campaign. It is therefore important to look closely at this:

There was in Dalmatia a certain Marcellinus, one of Aetius' acquaintances and a man of high reputation. When Aetius died in the manner described, he refused to obey [or, 'be subservient to'] the emperor any longer and, having revolted and having persuaded all the others to secede [or, 'detaching all the others'], he himself held power [or, 'control'] in Dalmatia, since no one dared to confront him. At this time the emperor Leo courted Marcellinus assiduously[3]

It is not absolutely certain that this is, like most of the account of the campaign (see pp. 57–8), taken from Priscus.[4] Elsewhere Procopius has inserted material into the Priscan narrative from other sources, for instance derogatory material on Aspar.[5] The

[1] Jordanes, *Romana* 338.

[2] Burgess (1992: 24–5); see also Pt. II, p. 84.

[3] Procopius, *Wars* I I I, vi, 7–8 (Blockley's translation, Priscus, frag. 53 (3)); the variant translations are Whitby's. The other fairly full account using Priscus, Theophanes' *Chronographia*, has nothing on Marcellinus.

[4] Blockley (1981–3: i, 115–16) writes that most of the material in this chapter could ultimately be from Priscus, and that the relationship between Priscus and Procopius is 'complex and not completely clear', possibly involving an intermediary (1983: 49). Cameron (1985: 208) says that: 'It is far from clear what literary sources Procopius has used . . . he has covered his tracks, and [the] assumption of Priscus is not proved'.

[5] Procopius, *Wars* I I I, vi, 3–4, 25–6. This is indicated by comparing this material with that of the second part of Theophanes' account, where the change of source is stated (Blockley (1983: i, 115–16, and 399 n. 186)).

sentence, immediately after the supposed biographical facts on Marcellinus, beginning 'at this time', does not in fact refer to this time (when he seized power in Dalmatia) but to fourteen years later; and the subsequent reference to Leo 'courting' him also, as previously remarked, seems misplaced. There is an impression here of a break in continuity. It is not impossible that the section beginning 'now there was in Dalmatia' has been inserted by Procopius to give biographical information on Marcellinus when he enters the Priscan action. The possibility that this is non-Priscan material does not, of course, immediately invalidate the material, although Procopius in his non-Priscan material does often make mistakes on western affairs.[6]

Procopius says that Marcellinus was 'in Dalmatia', though he does not give his position or title there, and that he had some connection with Aetius. What exactly this relationship was depends on the translation of the Greek *ton Aetioi gnorimon*. In the translations and secondary sources this is rendered in a wide variety of ways: pupil, friend, *kriegskamerad, waffenge-fährten*, colleague, and acquaintance, but the last, least definite word would seem to be the best translation.[7] Marcellinus is, on this basis, merely acquainted with Aetius, which does not make him Aetius' military subordinate, as so often postulated. There are other possible contexts for a connection.[8]

The vital information is that which follows, which states that Marcellinus, after Aetius' death, refused to obey the emperor, who is unnamed, but from the context must be a western emperor. The obvious candidate is Valentinian III, but it might, if

---

[6] See, for instance, Goffart's opinion of Procopius' introductory section to the *Vandal Wars* in which this material occurs: 'although wholly admirable from a literary standpoint, Procopius' sketch is misleading history...[and includes]...outright legends' (1980: 66).

[7] Blockley's translation of the Greek as 'acquaintance' is to be preferred to any more specific relationship.

[8] For instance, the connection could have been an official one between Italy and Dalmatia and/or linked to the Huns, with whom Aetius, certainly, and Marcellinus, possibly, had dealings over a long period, or even a social one. We have evidence that Aetius was in Dalmatia early in his career. In AD 432, when he fled from Italy, he went first to Dalmatia, before travelling, via Pannonia, to the Huns (*Gallic Chronicle of 452 s.a.* 432). Moreover, Aetius was born in the Balkans, in Durostorum in Moesia on the Danube border (Jordanes, *Getica* 176).

Procopius is condensing his source material, be Petronius Maximus or Avitus. If Valentinian, the date of Marcellinus' coup in Dalmatia would be AD 454 or 455. If, as many writers suggest, Marcellinus reverted to his western allegiance when Majorian came to the throne, he would have had only, at the outside, between October AD 454 and April 457 to rebel, take over Dalmatia, and establish himself as an independent ruler before the return to western overlordship. It is presumed that he then removed his allegiance again when Majorian was disposed of by Ricimer in AD 461, and resumed it in AD 467, when Anthemius became western emperor.[9]

The next phrase in the Procopius passage is interesting: Marcellinus not only revolted and took control in Dalmatia, but persuaded others to secede. Who are these others? This cannot mean Aegidius, mentioned along with Marcellinus by Priscus, as Aegidius did not break with the Italian government until after Majorian's death. There are no reports of other provinces rebelling against Valentinian in AD 454; so others inside, or close to, Dalmatia seem to be indicated. This suggests something more than a coup purely on the basis of military strength.

The conventional portrayal of Marcellinus, based on Procopius, as a western army officer in command of troops in Dalmatia, seems at odds with the evidence of the other sources. This will be discussed further in the concluding chapter. There is, moreover, rather more information available about Marcellinus than has always been realized, and it paints an interesting and complex picture. He proves to be, as Hodgkin once wrote, 'a unique figure of the age and we would gladly know more of his history'.[10]

[9] Removal of Procopius' date for Marcellinus taking control in Dalmatia and of the assumption that he returned to allegiance to Majorian would leave him a much longer possible span of independence.

[10] Hodgkin (1880b: 446).

PART II

Aegidius, Syagrius, and the Kingdom of Soissons

5

The Background and the Sources

NORTHERN GAUL

Less is known of northern Gaul in the fifth century than of the central and southern regions of the country. By the AD 460s, if not considerably earlier, it was no longer under imperial control, although some of the old administrative structure survived, especially in the cities,[1] and the basic *civitas* organization endured into the Merovingian period in ecclesiastical and, to a lesser extent, secular organization. Gallic landowners in general were increasingly concerned with local politics and interests, and taking on new economic, political, and defensive roles. Van Dam's proposal that the first half of the century saw the rise of local leaders from among a newly competitive Gallo-Roman provincial élite particularly applies to northern Gaul.[2] There, as elsewhere, the Church, and in particular the influential bishops of aristocratic birth, grew in authority, and this new power structure strengthened as imperial authority withered away.

On the scanty evidence, central, if not northern, Gaul was still subject to imperial tax in the mid fifth century,[3] but this appears subsequently to have lapsed, and it is unclear what taxation system operated after Aetius' death. Barbarian kings took over some of the imperial tax system, and *civitates* may have done the same, thus converting it into a local resource.

---

[1] There is some evidence for this: for example, in AD 453 the Angers Church council ruled against clerics returning to secular service, and the council of Tours in AD 461 referred to clerics returning to state service; Sidonius Apollinaris mentions criminal proceedings at Troyes (Mathisen (1993: 82)). There are other examples in hagiographic sources.

[2] Van Dam (1985: 181). His more controversial proposal, that these men were the leaders of the Armorican and Bacaudic revolts, has not been accepted by most scholars.

[3] Matthews (1975: 338).

Merovingian taxation was certainly influenced by the late
Roman structure.[4] The long-standing decline in state revenue,
and state intervention in food supply and industrial production,
affected the economy and trade, and the effect of this can be seen
clearly in the archaeological and numismatic record.

It has been argued that northern Gaul in the late antique
period turned away from an enforced focus on the Mediterranean world, back to a more natural place within that of north-
west Europe.[5] This trend can be discerned in the movement of
people and goods between western Britain and Ireland and
Armorica; the Frankish and Saxon settlements in Gaul and,
slightly later, the political and trade connections between Frankish north-eastern Gaul and the kingdom of Kent; and the finds
of north-Gallic coins in Germany and Scandinavia (see Ch. 8
n. 33). It can also be seen in the increasing contrast between the
material culture of northern and southern Gaul found in the
archaeological records in this period.

Connections between Britain and northern Gaul were not
completely severed in the fifth century, as sometimes depicted
in the past; common sense alone suggests that the Channel
would not suddenly become a barrier. The decline in evidence
for contact results from the disappearance of literary sources
and drastic change in the economy and hence in the archaeological evidence. Intercourse must have continued, though
altered in quantity and kind.[6]

In the A D 460s and 470s the establishment of barbarian rule
over Gaul was not yet complete. The most dynamic barbarian
kingdom was that of the Visigothics, which by the 460s
stretched from the Pyrennes to the River Loire, including the
cities of Toulouse, Bordeaux, and Poitiers, but not quite reach-

[4] Wood (1994*b*: 62); Périn and Feffer (1987: ii, 25).

[5] Van Dam (1985: 422).

[6] There is evidence for movement and contact between the Churches in
Britain and northern Gaul, for instance in the *Life of Germanus* and Sidonius
Apollinaris' letters (*Ep.* IX, ix, 6). Jordanes (*Getica* 237–8) describes Riotha-
mus bringing an army to north-west Gaul from Britain. Gildas (*De Excidio et
Conquestu Britanniae*, XX, 1) reports a Romano-British appeal to Aetius.
(Pewter ingots have been found twice in the Thames, stamped with the chi-
rho symbol and the name Syagrius (*British Museum Guide* (1922) 32).
Tempting though it is to link these with our fifth-century Syagrius, the name
must, almost certainly, be that of the late fourth-century consul.)

ing to the Mediterranean coast. In these years the Visigoths concentrated their military and political efforts on expansion in the south. Attacks on Narbonne and Arles were a recurrent feature until they reached the Mediterranean in A D 461/2. By the 460s the Burgundians in south-eastern Gaul had recovered from earlier defeats and were also expanding their borders. Small Alan settlements had been established across Gaul (many of which probably still existed), along the Rhône, and at Valence, also perhaps between Toulouse and the coast and along the Cologne–Amiens–Soissons road.[7]

In *c.* A D 442 Aetius had moved some Alans, under their king, Goar, to the Orleans area, whence they could counter Visigothic intrusions across the Loire, or deal with any trouble from the Saxon colonists (see below) and uprisings among the Armoricans (as in A D 442).[8] At the time of Attila's invasion in A D 451, Orleans was held by Alans under Sangiban.[9] It is not known whether they held the city in the 460s, when Aegidius fought a battle there (see p. 98),[10] although the historical evidence seems to be supported by place-name evidence, which suggests settlement lasted for some time.[11]

North Gaul also contained small groups of Saxon settlers, on the coastal plain between Boulogne and Calais, and in Normandy (the Calvados area around Bayeux was known later as the *Otlinga Saxonia*).[12] There is also evidence for Saxon settlement on unidentified islands, probably in the Loire area

---

[7] Bachrach (1973: 30) on place-name evidence.
[8] *Chronica Gallica a* 452, 127 *s.a.* 442; Constantius, *Vita Germani*, 28.
[9] Jordanes, *Getica* 194–5.
[10] Greg. Tur. *Historiae* II, 7 records Thorismund defeating Alans sometime between A D 451 and 453; and *Addit. Prosp. Haun. s.a.* 453 records that Thorismund defeated Alans in battle; but these were not necessarily the Alans at Orleans.
[11] Bachrach (1973: 62–3). Scattered across northern Gaul are grave-goods of eastern European origin (Marin (1990: 45–99)), and there are even examples in northern and central Gaul of burials showing the practice of artificial cranial deformation (Marin (1990: 112–13)). These could be evidence of Hunnish or Alan presence. Marin associated them with Syagrius' army.
[12] Greg. Tur. *Historiae* x, 9 (for Bayeux). For other historical, archaeological, and place-name evidence see Lot (1915: 17–24); James (1982: 33); Todd (1992: 219).

(see p.104). Other Saxons raided the north and west coasts.[13]
The eastern Saxon settlements may have affected links between
Britain and Gaul. Boulogne was the Roman port for Britain, and
the Germanic presence there, and in Kent, may have prevented
the Roman populations from using the established sea route,
pushing their sea crossings westwards.

In western Armorica migrants from Britain had been arriving in small numbers since the fourth century AD, and in
the middle of the fifth century this escalated.[14] It is unlikely
that this was purely a flight of refugees, and it may best be seen
as a folk movement, like others of this period. The historical,
linguistic, and ecclesiastical evidence for immigrants from
south-western Britain to the area to the north and west of
the Rennes–Nantes–Tours–Vannes line is supported by archaeology and place-name study.[15] A comparatively prosperous
Gallo-Roman culture continued to exist in the east of the peninsula throughout the fifth century, especially in Vannes and
Nantes.[16]

In the fifth century, Britons/Bretons begin to appear in Gallic sources and in AD 469/70 there are references to a British
king, Riothamus, one of the Gallic leaders who opposed the
expansionist Visigoth king, Euric.[17] If, as is usually supposed,
he was from Brittany, it is unclear what relationship he
and his army had to the general population of migrant Britons
and native Armoricans.[18] He may have been a ruler in Brittany,
or merely the leader of a large war band. It is not impossible that Riothamus was at some time allied to Aegidius or
Syagrius.

[13] Sidonius, *Ep.* VIII, 152–3; Greg. Tur. *In Glor. Martyr.* LIX; *Vita
Bibiani (Viviani)*, V; Lot (1915: 15–17).
[14] Galliou and Jones (1991: 129).
[15] Galliou and Jones (1991: 132, 135).
[16] Galliou and Jones (1991: 141).
[17] Jordanes (*Getica* 237) describes him as bringing his army by sea from
Britain. Historians deride this (probably because it has been picked up by some
'Arthurian' writers). Riothamus' existence, which would otherwise be in
doubt, is confirmed by Sidonius Apollinaris' letter to him in AD 469/70
complaining about the rowdy behaviour of his British followers (*Ep.* III, 9).
[18] James (1982: 33).

We also know, from a verse letter from Auspicius, Bishop of Toul, of the Gallo-Roman *comes* of Trier,[19] Arbogast, who was descended from the fourth-century Frankish *magister militum* of the same name (see Introd.).[20] He seems to have been a regional ruler with both military and civil responsibilities. The letter, dating to *c*. AD 470, congratulates Trier on its governor and praises Arbogast's noble character and ancestry.[21] In a letter of AD 477, Sidonius Apollinaris lauds Arbogast as an educated man upholding Roman culture even though Roman rule was absent from the region.[22] Arbogast may originally have been an official imperial appointee, or the title of *comes* may be being used loosely.[23] If this Count Arbogast is the same as the Arbogast who was Bishop of Chartres in the 480s,[24] it would seem that he had retired from, or been driven out of, Trier, probably as a result of Frankish aggression. Chartres was probably in the area controlled by Syagrius.[25] Like Riothamus, Arbogast could have been an ally of Aegidius, who fought Franks in the Rhineland (see p. 107), or of Syagrius.

The sources for this period are so inadequate that it is quite feasible that there were other similar warlords and regional leaders of whom we are not aware. Hagiographical works

---

[19] Trier had, of course, been an imperial sub-capital, and an area of substantial early Germanic settlement (almost certainly initially connected to imperial service).

[20] The name Arbogastus also appears on the list of bishops of Strasbourg, and on bricks there dating to the fourth or fifth century AD (Duchesne (1915: 166, 171)), so there may have been another descendant who entered the Church.

[21] Auspicius, *Epistola ad Arbogastem Comitem Trevirorum*. Toul, further up the Moselle, may well have been under Arbogast's control or influence.

[22] Sidonius, *Ep*. IV, xvii, 1–2.

[23] As elsewhere, for instance when Sidonius is referred to as *comes*, almost certainly a courtesy title (Sidonius, *Ep*. I, xi, 13). See also Barnwell (1992: 37).

[24] Wightman (1970: 251); Duchesne (1899: 421).

[25] Demougeot (1969–79: 677 n. 429) actually describes Arbogast as taking refuge with Syagrius in AD 479/80, following expulsion by Rhineland Franks. He may not have been the only ecclesiastic to take refuge there. A letter (preserved in a sixth-century work) addressed to Bishop Polychronius, probably the Bishop of Verdun and disciple of Lupus, shows that he was in exile from his see (due to barbarian attack) with a Bishop Castor, probably the Bishop of Chartres (Griffe (1964–6: ii, 102 n. 23)).

furnish a few possibilities, such as Hubaldus, a 'pagan tyrant' at Rouen;[26] Ioannes, described as *comes Castrodunensis*, married to the daughter of the *comes Blaesensis*,[27] and Titus, leader of a war band, who moved from Gaul to Constantinople in the reign of Leo.[28]

Crucial to any study of Aegidius and Syagrius are the Frankish settlers in north-eastern Gaul. During the late empire the Franks had played an increasingly important role in Gaul, as allies and *foederati* of Rome and, sometimes, mainly in periods of Roman disunity, as enemies.[29] Aetius had campaigned against Franks, led by the Frankish king, Chlodio, in Belgica II, and other Franks on the Rhine.[30] Chlodio had also seized Cambrai and invaded or raided as far as the Somme. Merovech, Childeric, and Clovis were, according to Gregory of Tours, descended from Chlodio.

When an (unnamed) Frankish king died, Aetius supported the claims of one of his sons and invited the young Frankish prince to Rome, where he was honoured (perhaps even adopted) by Aetius.[31] Franks fought with Aetius at the Battle of the Catalaunian Plains in AD 451, possibly under the same prince.[32] This could conceivably have been Childeric or his father, perhaps named Merovech.[33] It is just possible that a long-standing

---

[26] Mentioned in a version of the *Life of St. Germanus*, VII, 23, *AASS* May I (2 May). Rouen was in an area of Saxon settlement.

[27] *Vita Avetini*, 1–2 and 5, *AASS* (1 Feb.) 484–5. Their children included the bishops Solemnis and Aventinus.

[28] *Vita Dan Styl.* 60.

[29] Historians have always considered the relationship between the Salian Franks and Romans significant because of the later Frankish conquest of Gaul, and the subsequent interaction of the two peoples and cultures in the creation of France. There is a danger that Frankish–Roman relationships at earlier periods are examined with the benefit of this hindsight rather than in their historical context.

[30] Sidonius (*Pan.* V, 210–11) describes Aetius fighting and defeating Franks under Cloio (*sic*) somewhere around Arras in the AD 440s.

[31] Priscus, frag. 20 (3). The Frankish prince is described as having shoulder-length blond hair. Uncut hair would, of course, become a symbol of the Merovingian dynasty.

[32] Jordanes, *Getica* 191; Greg Tur. *Historiae* II, 7.

[33] There is a tradition that Merovech (a relation, though perhaps not son, of the Frankish King Chlodio (Greg. Tur. *Historiae* II, 9)) was leader of the Franks at the time of the Hun invasion (*Liber Historiae Francorum*, 5; Frede-

link existed between Childeric and Aetius' faction, later represented by Aegidius (see p. 97). By the time of Aegidius, the Salian Franks (then under Childeric) are usually thought to have been settled in the region to the east of the river Somme, based around Tournai.[34]

THE SOURCES FOR AEGIDIUS AND SYAGRIUS

It is notable how diverse the sources for Aegidius and Syagrius are in date, content, and style; and the transitional nature of this period is brought home by the need to use such contrasting sources.[35] An important source for Aegidius alone is Priscus' history (one of the sources for Marcellinus). Priscus was a contemporary of Aegidius, and, although his sources for the West are uncertain,[36] his information is thought to be generally accurate. His material on Aegidius occurs in a fragment of his history, preserved in the *Excerpta de Legationibus*,[37] in a section on relations between Italy, Dalmatia, North Africa, and Constantinople (which also mentions Marcellinus).

The chronicler Hydatius was also a contemporary of Aegidius, and nearer to, and more interested in, events in Gaul than

gar, 9). Merovech is said to be Childeric's father in some sources (Greg. Tur. *Historiae* 11, 9; some Frankish genealogies (*Catalogi Regum Francorum Praetermissi*). I see no reason to consider Merovech as totally mythical (although legends certainly attached to him later). Dynastic names may well originate in the personal name of a founder or his father. That it was that of Childeric's father is plausible. However, one Frankish genealogy gives (C)hildericus' father as Genniodus (a Roman name such as Gennadius?). Heinzelmann (1982: 86 n. 408) has tentatively hypothesized a connection between this Genniodus, the Frankish Gennobaudes of the third and fourth centuries and Gennobaudes, Bishop of Laon (married to a niece of Remigius of Reims), whom Genovefa possibly visited and was perhaps related to (see pp. 117–8) nn. 26 and 27).

[34] This is assumed because Childeric was buried there, but it does not necessarily follow that Tournai was his 'capital'.

[35] As different for instance as Priscus, Sidonius Apollinaris, Procopius, Gregory of Tours, fifth- and sixth-century chronicles, Saints' Lives, and medieval works such as the *Liber Historiae Francorum*.

[36] Blockley (1981–3: i, 67–9).

[37] Constantine Porphyrogenitus, *Excerpta de Legationibus Iussu Imp.* = Priscus frag. 39.

Priscus. His view of Gallic events was coloured by his hatred of
the Arian Visigothic invaders of Spain, to him the greatest
enemy; and those who opposed them get favourable treatment,[38] including Aegidius (also the emperors Majorian and
Anthemius). He mentions Aegidius four times: in AD 462 as
the enemy of Count Agrippinus; in AD 463 defeating the Visigoths under Frederic; his embassy to the Vandals in AD 464–5;
and his death in AD 465.

Sidonius Apollinaris makes no mention of either Aegidius or
Syagrius, unless, as is possible, Aegidius is the unnamed *magister militum* in the panegyric to Majorian (see p. 84–5). The
significance of this is debatable, since his letters and poems are
idiosyncratic literary works, never intended to be historical, and
omit many important political events and people. Sidonius
does, however, provide background material (albeit chiefly for
southern Gaul and a restricted social circle). There is also some
material on Aegidius in hagiographic sources, and in entries in
the *Gallic Chronicle of 511* and the sixth-century chronicle
written by Marius of Avenches.

The most important source for both Aegidius and Syagrius is
Gregory of Tours, primarily his *Historiae* (discussed in depth in
Ch. 7). Although in the past widely known as the *Historia
Francorum*, Gregory himself refers to his history as *Decem
Libros Historiarum*, and *Historiae* is now the more accepted
title. This is not mere pedantry; the older title conveys the
erroneous impression that Gregory's aim was to write a history
specifically of the Franks.

Both men also appear in two sources which use Gregory: the
seventh-century chronicle known as 'Fredegar's',[39] and the
early eighth-century chronicle by an anonymous author entitled
the *Liber Historiae Francorum*,[40] both of which are further

[38] Burgess (1992: 22, 27).

[39] In fact produced by several anonymous early medieval authors. The
original seventh-century compilation uses Jerome, Hydatius, and the first six
books of Gregory of Tours (into which additional details are inserted). It is
possible that it was written in Burgundy, but this is uncertain (Collins (1996)
81–111; for an older view see Wallace-Hadrill (1960: pp. xv–xxv)).

[40] There are two main manuscript traditions, designated 'A' and 'B' by
Krusch, the *MGH* editor. My translations are from the 'A' tradition, but
where the variant or addition in the 'B' tradition is of interest, it is given also.

removed in time and culture than the *Historiae*, and more firmly in medieval historical tradition.[41] The compilers of Fredegar's chronicle covered the fifth and sixth centuries by paraphrasing the *Historiae* and Hydatius, with some additions from unknown sources.[42] The *Liber Historiae Francorum* is also strongly based on Gregory, but with some changes and a substantial number of additions.[43]

Because of its late date, the *Liber Historiae Francorum* has been dismissed as a source for the fifth century, but, while it must obviously be treated with great caution, a study by Gerberding has advanced reasons to think that it might include useful information, especially in connection with Soissons. He has shown that the *Liber* was written north of the Loire, in the Seine/Oise region, more probably in the Soissons than the Paris area, possibly at, or using written records from, the Abbey of St. Medard at Soissons, which was one of the great religious foundations of early Merovingian times.[44] The Soissons area is of particular interest to the compiler of the chronicle;[45] he knew the geography intimately and collected a number of popular stories about, and presumably from, the Soissons region, with which he supplemented Gregory's material.[46] These include the story of Clovis' courtship and marriage.[47]

While Aegidius is referred to in a number of sources, virtually all we know of Syagrius is from Gregory of Tours' *Historiae*

'A' may be a Neustrian (the later name for that region of France including Soissons) version, and 'B' an Austrasian version (Wallace-Hadrill (1960: p. xxv)).

[41] The two works are independent of each other (Wallace-Hadrill (1962: 820)).

[42] Wallace-Hadrill (1960: p. xxiii).

[43] Gerberding (1987: 33–44). He counts over eighty additions, some quite substantial. Because the *Liber*, unlike the *Historiae*, was written as an account of the Frankish kings, it ignores the religious sections of the *Historiae* (or the author may not have had these sections, which were largely omitted from the abbreviated version of the *Historiae* commonly in use) and generally takes a Frankish angle (Gerberding (1987: 1, 35)).

[44] Gerberding (1987: 32, 155, 157).

[45] Gerberding (1987: 40).

[46] There are twenty-two mentions of the area, of which nine are independent of Gregory (Gerberding (1987: 154)).

[47] Gerberding (1987: 155).

(and works using it). Contrary to repeated statement, however, Gregory is not the sole authority for his existence; for of the three references to Syagrius in the *Historiae* two occur in Gregory's own narrative, but the other originates in the chronicle probably written in Angers and copied by Gregory. Syagrius' name also appears in a further, often unregarded, source for both Aegidius and Syagrius (in which it is implied that they were kings).

Amongst Frankish poetic genealogies there are lists of the ethnic groups descended from three brothers,[48] preceded in some cases by the names of Roman rulers in Gaul. These are believed to date back to the early sixth century:[49]

Primus rex Romanorum Allanius dictus est [or, 'Analeu']
Allanius genuit Pabolum [or, 'Papulo']
Pabolus [or, 'Papulus'] Egetium [or, 'Egegium']
Egetius genuit Egegium
Egegius genuit Siagrium [or, 'Fadiru'] per quem Romani regnum perditerunt.[50]

The 'Egegius' on the fourth and fifth lines is presumably Aegidius. The name on the third and fourth lines, 'Egetius' or similar, may be that of Aetius, and 'Pabolus' could possibly be the Count Paulus who commanded Roman and Frankish troops in North Gaul. 'A(l)lanius', or 'Analeu', could conceivably come from 'Alan', or be a miscopied 'Alaricus'. I cannot guess why 'Fadiru' and 'Siagrium' appear as alternatives to each other in different versions. During the first few centuries of many of the successor states, genealogies were developed which, along with genuine ancestors, included various high-status names: mythical and biblical persons and real historical people from the late empire. These genealogies were connected to the legitimization (and glorification) of ruling dynasties.[51] This is pre-

---

[48] 'Gothos, Walagothus, Wandalus, Gepides, et Saxones' from the first; 'Burgundiones, Loringus, Langobardus, Baiarius' from the second; and 'Romanos, Brictones, Francus, Alamannus' from the third. This last association reflects sixth-century geographical rather than genetic relationship (Kurth (1893: 96)).

[49] Kurth (1893: 97); Wallace-Hadrill (1962: 148 n. 1).

[50] Amalgamated from *Item de Regibus Romanorum* and *Incipit Generatio Regum* in the *Catalogi Regum Francorum Praetermissi*, p. 851.

[51] See Heather (1991: 22).

sumably the context of this material, which shows that the names of Aetius, Aegidius, Syagrius (and, possibly, Paulus) were, at the least, well known to the Franks, and considered to be prestigious. (See also pp. 133–6 on the use of the term 'king'.)

6

The Career of Aegidius

The context for Aegidius' career is both the situation in Gaul described in Chapter 5 and the struggle for supremacy in the remains of the western empire that had been taking place since the assassinations of Aetius and Valentinian III in AD 454 and 455.

Priscus describes Aegidius as a native of Gaul.[1] The reports by Hydatius and Paulinus of Périgueux suggest that he was a respected man of orthodox beliefs.[2] Modern historians describe Aegidius as being from the aristocratic family of the Syagrii, which originated in the Lyons area,[3] and thereby a descendant of Afranius Syagrius, consul in AD 382. This identification is based solely on the name of Aegidius' son, which, though not proof positive, does make a connection with the family seem likely, either by birth or, perhaps, by marriage.[4]

It is likely that Aegidius was from an upper-class family; every *magister militum* of this period whose pedigree is known to us comes from a background of either aristocratic landed wealth or high-level imperial service (examples include Aetius,

---

[1] Priscus, frag. 39 (1).

[2] Hydatius, 214 (218) *s.a.* 463; Paulinus, *Vita Martini* VI, 111–12.

[3] The statement in some secondary histories that the Syagrii owned land in both the Lyons and Soissons areas is mere circular argument, on the basis of the supposed identification.

[4] Five bishops of the sixth century were named Syagrius: those of Autun, Bourges, Grenoble (two), and, possibly, Le Puy (Duchesne (1894: 179), (1899: 27), (1894: 232, 237), and (1899: 57)), all in the east-central region of France. They may well have been from the senatorial Syagrii family. A Syagrius was the son of the Bishop of Verdun, another the brother of the Bishop of Cahors and another a *vir inlustris* in Laôn (Stroheker (1948: 221 nos. 373, 378, and 371)). The name Aegidius was fairly common all over the country (and later developed into Giles). An Aegidius was Bishop of Reims in the sixth century (Duchesne (1915: 83)) and it is tempting to think that there might be some family connection with the *magister militum*.

Merobaudes, Avitus, Majorian, and Jovinus), or is of noble
barbarian ancestry (such as Ricimer and Gundobad). Among
those whose ancestry is unknown there are no allusions to any
having risen from the ranks or lower classes. The social and
military conditions of the third and fourth centuries, which had
allowed men of humble birth to rise to the highest ranks, had
apparently disappeared. Close association between high social
status and military command would, of course, be a feature of
the Middle Ages.

Gregory of Tours implies that Aegidius became *magister
militum* in Gaul shortly after Majorian's accession,[5] and the
majority opinion is that he was appointed by Majorian, probably in AD 458 when the emperor arrived in Gaul.[6] Priscus
states that Aegidius had served with Majorian under Aetius.[7]
Even so, there is no reason to think that Aegidius and Majorian were personal friends.[8] We do not know what Aegidius'
political allegiance was during Avitus' brief reign, nor whether
he was in Gaul or Italy at that time. Presumably he was of
Majorian and Ricimer's faction prior to the coup, or quickly
joined it.

Following his installation as emperor in AD 458, Majorian
instigated an attack on the Vandal kingdom in North Africa
(see Pt. III, pp. 204–5), and on the way to Spain spent some
time in southern Gaul, both countering barbarian resurgence
and effecting a political reconciliation with the supporters of the
late Avitus. Around AD 456 the Burgundians were expanding
their territory in Gaul, probably by agreement with either Avitus or some Gallo-Roman senators,[9] and possibly also with the

[5] Greg. Tur. *Historiae* 11, 11: 'cui Martianus [*sic*] successit, in Galliis autem
Egidius ex Romanus magister militum datus est'. Hydatius calls him *comes*
(212 (217) *s.a.* 462) and *comes utriusque militae* (214 (218) *s.a.* 461).

[6] Mathisen (1979: 607–9) suggested that because Aegidius came from
Lyons (the assumed connection with the Syagrii) he was a member of a pro-
Avitus party based there, and that Aegidius' appointment as *magister militum*
may have been connected with bringing him (and hence his family) over to
Majorian's side.

[7] Priscus, frag. 39 (1). Not surprisingly, several other contemporary military and political leaders had also served under Aetius.

[8] As suggested by several historians, e.g. Stroheker (1948: 57).

[9] Marius Avent. *s.a.* 456 (2): 'Eo anno Burgundiones partem Galliae occu-
paverunt terrasque cum Gallis senatoribus diviserunt'.

agreement of the Visigothic king, Theoderic.[10] On the basis of Sidonius' typically inexplicit references to the retaking of Lyons from unnamed barbarians by Majorian,[11] it is thought that the Burgundians may have either taken, or been allowed into, that city. Sidonius' panegyric to Majorian, composed shortly after he retook Lyons, for some reason concentrates on the success of Petrus, Majorian's *quaestor epistolarum*, who finalized the recovery of the city and agreed terms with the barbarians.[12] It is usually assumed that this followed a successful military action (though the ending of the siege may have been achieved peacefully). As it is most unlikely that Petrus held a military command, some scholars have argued that the victorious commander was Aegidius, the *magister militum per Gallias*.[13]

Another possible candidate is the inexplicably unnamed *magister militum* who is extravagantly praised by Sidonius immediately before the references to Lyons and Petrus, and who is described as having accompanied Majorian to Gaul.[14] He has, in the past, been tentatively identified as Nepotianus, thought to have been *comes et magister utriusque militiae* from AD 458/9 to 461.[15] Hydatius calls Nepotianus *magister militiae* in an entry for AD 459, and *comes* in AD 460, when he was in joint command of a Gothic army in Spain. He also records that Nepotianus accepted Arborius as his successor, on the orders of King Theoderic.[16] This would be most odd if Nepotianus was an imperial commander. In fact, Nepotianus was probably a Roman working for the Goths, for whom Hydatius uses a Roman-sounding title.[17] This strengthens the case for the unnamed *magister* being in fact Aegidius, having perhaps

---

[10] *Auct. Prosp. Haun. s.a.* 457.

[11] Sidonius, *Pan.* V, 571–86.

[12] Sidonius, *Pan.* V, 565–75.

[13] Mathisen (1979: 607–10 and n. 52); Stein (1928: 559); Loyen (1942: 82–3).

[14] Sidonius, *Pan.* V, 554–7.

[15] See Mathisen (1979: 609 n. 52); Sidonius, ed. and trans. Anderson (1965: 108 n. 2); Heinzelmann (1982: 656); *PLRE* ii, 778, Nepotianus 2.

[16] Hydatius, 192 (197) *s.a.* 459 and 196 (201) *s.a.* 460.

[17] Burgess (1992: 24–5). As he points out, imperial military ranks, such as *comes* and *dux*, were used by both Roman and barbarian.

accompanied Majorian from Italy to take up his Gallic appointment.[18]

If this unnamed *magister militum* was Aegidius, it is surprising that Sidonius does not identify him, presumably a fellow Gallic aristocrat whom Sidonius (who seems to have been acquainted with most of the Gallic aristocracy) would have known, particularly if from the Syagrii family of Lyons. Harries may be correct in commenting that Aegidius' absence from *all* Sidonius' works 'cannot be fortuitous', and in suggesting that references to Aegidius may have been removed when Sidonius edited the poems for publication[19]—because of his break with the imperial authorities; his Frankish connections; his dealings with Gaiseric; because Sidonius favoured his rival Agrippinus; or because Sidonius' reluctant acceptance of Theoderic put them at odds. An alternative explanation is that, as mentioned above, Sidonius was simply not writing history.

Majorian made peace with Theoderic following a Gothic defeat in battle.[20] The location is not given, but many historians have identified this victory with the lifting of a Visigothic siege of Arles,[21] involving Aegidius.[22] The basis for the idea that there was a siege of Arles at this date and that Aegidius was present is a late fifth-century verse life of St. Martin by Paulinus of Périgueux.[23]

---

[18] Although Gregory (II, 11) says *in Gallis*, he was not necessarily appointed *in* Gaul.

[19] Harries (1994: 247–8).

[20] Hydatius, 192 (197) *s.a.* 459.

[21] A few, such as Schwarcz (1995: 49), think it was the other way round, with Majorian besieging the Visigoths.

[22] Though it is hardly likely that he can have been involved in sieges both at Lyons and Arles.

[23] Paulinus of Périgueux (Petrocordiensis), *De Vita Sancti Martini*, VIII, 111–51. Paulinus was bishop from *c.* AD 458 to 488. The first five books rework in verse Sulpicius Severus' prose *Vita*. The sixth, on Martin's posthumous miracles, was composed by Paulinus and taken from a pamphlet by Perpetuus, Bishop of Tours, who promoted the cult vigorously, and possibly initiated the first five books (McDermott (1949: 34)). The work is dedicated to Perpetuus (Van Dam (1986: 565–73)), and therefore the composition of the poem should date to his episcopate, which ran from AD 458 (McDermott (1949: 37)) or AD 460/1 (Wace and Piercy (1911)) to AD 490/1, although

The enemy siege with many a column had walled off Aegidius, a man illustrious for his valour, but more glorious for his kindly character, and great in the faith in which he excels; [the siege] which had fenced off the city walls by confronting them with weapons, cutting off aid and forcibly pressing the enclosed, so that the division made the besieged strength less, and it was impossible to unite the two armies for war. But with the help of the Lord, the [enemy] thousands were cast down and routed; the double gates were thrown open and out came the column, to restore and consolidate its strength now that its leader was safe. Meanwhile the neighbourhood, sad and trembling with fear, grew pale that the great chief was in danger, and the whole anxiety of the frightened peoples hung in suspense while each man thought that he was suffering a similar storm, and in one man [Aegidius] there trembled in the balance whatever stands firm in one man [everyone else].

Then, by chance, one of those whom gruesome wrath had drawn to the hope of drinking blood in slaughter was swept away by the Lord's will, as it were by a headlong whirlwind, outstripping the flying winds across the blasting clouds, and revealed from the body he possessed the sequence of events, proclaiming in the same moment, the same time, that the city had been freed from the siege by Martin's prayers,[24] and that God had granted him the inhabitants and their general. Soon the facts were obvious and believed, and the day itself confirmed the sequence, the hour was the same, with no change in order, and their punishment forced the enemy unwillingly to corroborate. Just as Balaam, wishing to curse the Lord's people, blessed the cheering crowd under God's compulsion, in no other but in just the same sequence came the message that the city had been freed from a great siege, that the Rhône was fast-flowing, which he had subdued with a flexible bridge, and had joined both banks with a connected crossing, to provide a dry passage, [the Rhône] which he controls with pontoons, and over them a swaying path hangs on the burdened river. This too you rescue, Holy one, the ally of [our] effective patron, and you compel the trembling [demon] to admit [the efficacy] of your prayers, which he

the events alluded to could of course predate this. Modern writers variously suggest the 460s, 470s, and 480s for the date of composition, the 460s being preferred, for instance by Stancliffe (1983: 129, 222), seemingly because of a reference to a new church (VI, 265–90) which was built in the mid 460s (Van Dam (1986: 572)). It is assumed that Aegidius was still alive at the time of composition, on the basis of the use of the phrase *inlustrem virtute*, although this is ambiguous (Van Dam (1986: 572 n. 31)). Paulinus' work is difficult to understand, as the text is corrupt, the Latin obscure, and the style convoluted.

[24] Aegidius was possibly a patron of St. Martin's shrine at Tours.

was unwilling should be granted to you. He stands here guiltily and, swifter than the east wind, he speaks of losing the spectacle of slaughter for which he had hoped and is made the herald of a salvation hated by him.[25]

Gregory of Tours also refers to the siege in his *Miracles of Saint Martin*, but is summarizing Paulinus' account:[26] 'Egidius, when besieged by enemies and cut off from relief, [his] troops embattled, was freed [and] the enemies put to flight through the intervention of the blessed man.'[27]

It is difficult to make out the exact circumstances, or even Aegidius' movements, but it seems most likely that he was trapped inside the city. He is also probably the leader (*dux*) referred to later. He had perhaps made a sortie outside the

---

[25] Paulinus of Perigueux, *De Vita Sancti Martini* VI, 'Illustrem virtute virum sed moribus almis plus clarum magnumque fide qua celsior exstat Egidium, hostilis vallaverat agmine multo Obsidio, objectis quae moenia sepserat armis Auxilia excludens, et clausos viribus urgens Ut minus obsessis faceret divisio robor, Nec jungi ad bellum socialia castra liceret. Verum paesidio Domini dejecta fugantur Millia, et egressum portis bipatentibus agmen Restaurat solidas securo principe vires. Interea trepido vicinia moesta pavore Pallebant tanti proceris discrimine, et omnis Anxia pendebat populurum cura paventum Dum se quisque putat similem perferre procellam, Inque uno nutat quidquid consistit in uno. Ergo aliquis forte ex illis quos tetrior ira Traxerat ad votum sorbendi in caede cruoris, Praecipiti ad nutum Domini quasi turbine raptus, Praecedensque citos trans flabra et nubila ventos Gestorum seriem captivo e corpore prompsit, Obsidione urbem Martino orante solutam, Atque ipsum donasse Deum populumque ducemque Mox patuit manifesta fides, seriemque probavit Ipse dies, eadem hora fuit, nihil ordine verso, Invitumque hostem fallere poena coegit. [*sic*] Ut Balaam cupiens Domini maledicere plebem Extorquente Deo coetum benedixit ovantem. Haud alio penitusque ipso rerum ordine venit Nuntius, illam urbem tanta obsidione solutam, Praecipitem Rhodanum molli quem ponte subegit, Et junxit geminas connexo tramite ripas, Ut siccum praeberet iter, quae puppibus instat, desuper et presso nutans via pendet in amne. Hanc quoque praesenti sociatus sancte patrono Erepis, et cogis trepidum tua vota fateri Quae nollet donata tibi, reus astat, et Euro Ocior admissa optatae specularia caedis haec quoque discussis patefecit calculus horis, Ipso ut res docuit, completa et prodita puncto.' I am grateful for Dr Roger Tomlin's considerable help in completing this translation.

[26] His summaries are generally rather inaccurate (McDermott (1949: 33)).

[27] Greg. Tur. *de Virtutibus et Miraculis de S. Martini* I, 2: 'Egidius quoque cum obsederetur ab hostibus et, exclusa solatia, turbatus inpugnaretur, per invocationem beati viri, fugatis hostibus, liberatus est.'

walls to allow reinforcements to get through.[28] The *urbs* is not
named in the poem, but has always been identified as Arles
because of references to the River Rhône and a bridge of
boats.[29] It is known that there was a bridge of boats over the
River Rhône at Arles in the early fifth century.[30] However, the
implication of the poem that the bridge was built at the time of
the siege (by Aegidius or the enemy?) does not fit with the Arles
location, unless this bridge was a replacement for the earlier
one. All that can safely be said on the basis of Paulinus' poem is
that, at some time in his career, Aegidius was involved in the
siege of a city on the Rhône, but all other aspects remain uncertain. It is not really a satisfactory basis for the statement of fact
that in AD 456/9 Aegidius, as commander of Majorian's army,
raised a Visigothic siege of Arles (although this is not, of course,
impossible).

Another problematic source for Aegidius is the *Life of Saint
Lupicinus*,[31] which includes a lengthy, undated, story of a clash

---

[28] Stevens (1933: 50) suggested that the siege was relieved by Majorian,
while Mathisen (1979: 190 n. 91) considered it possible that the *auxilia* in the
poem were troops under the command of Nepotianus, sent to Arles while the
emperor went to Lyons.

[29] The original identification of the besieged city as Arles (and the date)
appears (as far as I am able to discover) to have been by Dubos (1734: ii,
96–8). Dubos's history is surprisingly modern; he addresses problems in the
sources still discussed today and, interestingly, raises the question of the
language which Aegidius would have used to address his Frankish forces
(1734: 56).

[30] Daniel and Heijmans (1992: 97–9). The evidence includes a mosaic from
the forum at Ostia and references by Ausonius (*Urbes* 77) and Cassiodorus
(*Variae* VIII, 10, 6). Also, a story recorded by Gregory of Tours (in *Glor.
Martyr.* 68) and the *Sermo de Miraculo S. Genesii* (perhaps by Hilarius of
Arles, according to Van Dam (Greg. of Tours, *In Glor. Mart.* 1988: n. 82))
tells of a miracle by St. Genesius of Arles, who rescued a procession that fell
into the river when the pontoon bridge collapsed (between AD 427 and 430
according to Van Dam (Greg. of Tours, *In Glor. Mart.* 1988: n. 68)). Stevens
(1933: 50 n. 3) wrote that there may also have been a bridge of boats at Vienne
(citing Jullian (1922), but I have been unable to find this). If so, Aegidius could
have been fighting the Burgundians. However, there are no references to a
bridge of boats in the modern archaeological literature on Vienne (Pelletier
(1974) and (1982); Jannet-Vallat, Lauxerois, and Reynaud (1986)).

[31] Lupicinus was, from *c.* AD 460, Abbot of the abbey of St. Claude (Con-
datiscone or Condat) near Lyons, then within Burgundian territory, and had
previously been an influential figure in the Jura monasteries. At a later date he

between Aegidius and another Gallic official named Agrippinus, in which Aegidius accuses Agrippinus of treason (see pp. 90–1).[32] The enmity between the two is confirmed by Hydatius.[33] It has been suggested that Agrippinus was either Aegidius' predecessor (perhaps appointed by Avitus), or his successor as *magister militum per Gallias* (see also Pt. III, pp. 225–6). Agrippinus' career in Gaul was a fairly long one (stretching from at the least *c.*450 to the early 460s) but what his position, or positions, were is not totally clear.

Hydatius called him *comes* in AD 451, and again at the later date of AD 462 when Agrippinus handed Narbonne over to the Visigoths (see pp. 91–2).[34] The *Life of Saint Anianus* describes Agrippinus meeting Anianus, the Bishop of Orleans, probably in the early 450s,[35] and describes him as 'the illustrious Agripinus [*sic*], who, at that same time, was discharging the duties of

was close to the Burgundian royal family. Agrippinus was perhaps a patron of one of the Jura monasteries, which would explain why the *Vita* takes his side against Aegidius. Mathisen (1989: 218–19) has suggested that the references of Paulinus and Gregory to Aegidius show that he had support in west-central Gaul and in Belgica II, in contrast to Agrippinus, whose support was concentrated in eastern Lugdunensis. This is on the basis of Agrippinus' contacts with Lupicinus (reported below); Anianus, Bishop of Orleans (*Vita Aniani* 3); and Euphronius, Bishop of Autun, who wrote a letter reporting a comet to him (Hydatius, 143 (151) *s.a.* 451). However, the number of sources is really too small to warrant this conclusion.

[32] The *Vita S. Lupicini* (along with the lives of Romanus and Oyend) appears in the *Vita Patrum Jurensium*, which is now believed to be an authentic work written by an anonymous author in *c.* AD 520–30 (Griffe (1964–6: ii, 68 n. 10; Martine (1968: 50–1)).

[33] Hydatius, 212 (217) *s.a.* 462.

[34] Hydatius, 143 (151) *s.a.* 451, recording the letter from Euphronius sent to the *comes* Agrippinus (the title could stem from Euphronius or Hydatius), and 212 (217) *s.a.* 462.

[35] St. Anianus was Bishop of Orleans in AD 451 when Attila invaded Gaul, and his prayers saved the city from being destroyed by the Huns. Gregory of Tours (*Historiae* II, 7), Jordanes (*Getica* 37), the *Liber Historia Francorum* (5), *Vita Genovefae* 42, and Sidonius (*Ep.* VIII, xv) make reference to the same event. According to the *Vita*, Anianus lived for another three years after the Hun invasion, and this would seem to be confirmed by the fact that Duchesne (1894–1915: ii, 455) lists four bishops between Anianus and the Prosper who was corresponding with Sidonius Apollinaris between AD 477 and 480. The meeting with Agrippinus was therefore prior to 454, sometime before the clash with Aegidius recorded in the *Life of Lupicinus*.

magister militum, sent by the emperors [*sic*] to visit all the cities of Gaul for the well-being and enforcement [?] of the state'.[36]

This seems a somewhat odd description of the duties of *magister militum per Gallias*, although this may not be significant in a later hagiographical source. In this period the term *comes*, used by Hydatius and Lupicinus, could apply to any official of the central government, civil or military,[37] and it is conceivable that Agrippinus was not in fact *magister militum per Gallias*, at that time at least.[38] In the *Vita Lupicini* (probably referring to *c.* AD 460) he is also described as *comes* of Gaul, and he addresses Aegidius as *mi domine ac maior*, which suggests that Aegidius was at that time his superior (see below).

The *Vita Lupicini* describes Agrippinus as endowed with exceptional wisdom, and as having, among other honours, been made Count of Gaul by the emperor.[39] It continues: 'Agrippinus was skilfully and maliciously vilified in the eyes of the emperor by Aegidius, then *magister militum*, with the claim that, being jealous of Roman authority and certainly favouring the barbarians, he was attempting by clandestine means to detach provinces from the state'.[40]

The sequence of events following the accusation is confused and unclear, but what seems to have happened is that Agrippi-

---

[36] *Vita Aniani* 3: 'vir inlustris Agripinus [*sic*] qui tunc tempore magistri militum fungebatur officium, principibus fuerat depotatus, ut per omnes civitates Galliarum pro salute et districtione [*sic*] publica habere deberet excursus'. It goes on to describe how Agrippinus, on meeting Anianus, treated him with great respect, but was unable to comply with his request for the release of prisoners. However, Agrippinus was then struck on the head by a piece of masonry falling from a church roof and was cured by Anianus, and in gratitude freed those held in captivity. (Who were these captives, perhaps tax defaulters or similar?) The *Vita* is thought to date to the eighth century (Krusch 1896: 104, Introd. to *Vita*).

[37] Barnwell (1992: 37).

[38] He might even be the Agripinus [*sic*] who appears in the *Acta Agoardi et Agilberti*, 3–5, *AASS* (June V), called *iudex* and *praeses*.

[39] *Vita Lupicini* 11, 11: 'Vir condam inlustris Agrippinus [*sic*], sagacitate preditus singulari atque ob dignitatem militiae secularis comes Galliae a principe constitutus.'

[40] *Vita Lupicini* 11, 11: 'per Aegidio tum magistrum militum callida malitiosaque apud imperatorem arte fuerat offuscatus, eo quod Romanis fascibus liuens, barbaris procul dubio fauens, subreptione clandestina provincias a publica niteretur ditione deiscere'.

nus, while at his post, discovered that accusations were being made, but before he was able to declare his innocence orders arrived for the *magister militum* to send him to Rome. Agrippinus therefore placed himself under guard *ad comitatum* (this was in Gaul), but informers betrayed him to the emperor and he was imprisoned, while protesting and demanding that his accuser come into the open. Aegidius, however, accused Agrippinus of yet more crimes. At this point, Lupicinus was called in by Agrippinus to act as some sort of guarantor. Agrippinus was then sent to Rome.[41] The subsequent events in Italy are covered in Part III. Aegidius is not mentioned again. Agrippinus was eventually returned to Gaul, possibly by Ricimer, perhaps to replace Aegidius in his command there (see the discussion of Ricimer's policies in Gaul, pp. 226–7).

The story continues, for Hydatius reports that in 462: 'The Gaul Agrippinus, a *comes* and citizen, the enemy of the brave and distinguished *comes* Aegidius, to earn the assistance of the Goths, betrayed Narbonne to Theoderic.'[42] This can be seen as supporting Aegidius' previous denunciation of Agrippinus, as

---

[41] *Vita Lupicini* 11, 11–12: 'eumque ut diximus, antequam posset in comminus puritatis adsertione ueris falsa prosernere, nidoris uirosi accusatione turpauerat. Interea memoratus Agrippinus de causa ad praesens in loco mustatione quadam leuiter titillatus, ad comitatum sub quadam custodia cogitur properare. Cumque adhoc in loco positus animos principis aemulo in semet liuore praeuntos quorundam, ut diximus, musitatione sensisset, renti ac reclamare fortiter coepit non se omnino iturum nisi is qui clancule accusauerat rerum conuicturus, palam veniret in comminus. At uero Aegidius non quidem e contra sermone confligere, sed, conscientia conueniente, subtrepidus coepit crebris sacramentorum nexibus innocentiam Agrippini potius inretire quam souere… "Si ergo" inquit Agrippinus "mi domine ac maior Aegidi, nihil est quod illac metuam accusatus, absecro ut mihi sanctus Dei seruus Lupicinus, qui adpreasens est, ex hoc uice Nobilitatis tuae fideiussor accedat". "Fiat" inquit Aegidius. Confestim, adprehensam Dei serui dexteram deosculans, arram foederis tradidit accusato. Cumque, arrepto confectoque itenere, ad Urbem maximam peruenisset'.

[42] Hydatius, 212 (217) *s.a.* 462: 'Agrippinus Gallus et comes et civis Egidio comiti viro insigni inimicus, ut Gothorum meretur auxilia, Narbonam tradidit Theudorico'. It seems strange that, only shortly after this, Sidonius describes Theoderic, in a fit of wishful thinking presumably, as: 'the support and preserver of the Roman people' (Sidonius, *Carm.* XXIII, 71; a poem sent to a Roman friend). Sidonius did not see the loss of Narbonne, apparently, in the same tragic light as he saw the similar, slightly later, surrender of Auvergne. Sidonius, of course, lived in Auvergne not Narbonne.

reported by the hagiographer of Lupicinus.[43] Agrippinus may
have been, as often proposed, acting on Ricimer's orders, to gain
either, specifically, assistance against Aegidius, or the Goths'
general tolerance of Ricimer as *de facto* ruler in Italy. Alternatively, Agrippinus could have been the initiator, to gain Visigothic support for himself, perhaps (seeing that Hydatius
mentions their enmity) against Aegidius. Wolfram has suggested that Aegidius was besieging his rival in Narbonne, causing him to seek Gothic aid, and to give them the city as a reward
(which is not inconsistent with Hydatius' wording).[44]

It is possible that the antagonism between the two men initially arose because Agrippinus was an adherent of Ricimer (see
Pt. III, pp. 225–6), or because he was a supporter of Avitus, and
Aegidius of Majorian.[45] Alternatively, it may have been professional or purely personal. If the treachery of which Aegidius
accused Agrippinus was connected to his betrayal of Narbonne
to the Visigoths in AD 462,[46] then the episode in the *Vita*
occurred after Majorian's death. On the other hand, the *Vita*
calls Aegidius *magister militum*, which suggests (though does
not prove) that it dates to Majorian's reign. The earlier date
seems preferable, because after Majorian's death Aegidius had
broken with Ricimer and was not in a position to have Agrippinus sent to Rome to face charges (see below). Or, alternatively,
as Harries suggested, the story in the *Vita* is 'a garbled version
of two separate events, the first being the rivalry between Aegidius and Agrippinus at the outset of Majorian's reign . . . and the
second being the accusation relating to the surrender of Narbonne'.[47]

A massive shift in Aegidius' career occurred in AD 461, on
Majorian's deposition and death (see Pt. III, pp. 209–214).
Aegidius did not accept Ricimer's creature Libius Severus as

[43] On the psychological readiness of some Romans to come to an accommodation with the barbarians see Schwarcz (1995: 52).

[44] Wolfram (1988: 181).

[45] Mathisen (1989: 200).

[46] Although Mathisen ((1979: 615–18) and (1993: 83–4)) has related it to
the Burgundian aggression of AD 456–8 and Gallic feeling against Majorian
and Ricimer. He connects Agrippinus with the Burgundians via his close
relationship with Lupicinus recounted in the *Vita*.

[47] Harries (1994: 99).

legitimate emperor. Priscus writes that: 'The Western Romans
... were troubled in a variety of ways, both by the Vandals and
by Aegidius, a man sprung from the western Gauls.[48] He had a
large force and, having been a fellow soldier of Majorian's, was
angry at the murder of the Emperor.'[49]

The threatened invasion of Italy was all the more dangerous
because of a similar threat from Marcellinus in Dalmatia but (as
discussed in Pt. I, pp. 48–9) we cannot tell whether the two were
co-ordinated. There is no need to assume that friendship with
Majorian was Aegidius' motive; ambition and rivalry with Ricimer would be reason enough; and recognition of Libius Severus
would have constituted acceptance of Ricimer as the effective
leader of what was left of the western empire.[50] Libius Severus
was not recognized as a legitimate emperor by the senior emperor, Leo (see Pt. III, pp. 216–7), and Aegidius had little
reason to accept him. During the reign of Libius Severus,
Aegidius may have legitimized his retention of his command
of the Gallic army and his independence from the Italian government by asserting his allegiance directly to Leo.

In the event, Aegidius did not launch the threatened invasion
of Italy. Priscus gives the reason: 'in the meantime his disagreement with the Goths in Gaul deterred him from war against the
Italians, for being in dispute with them over some border land,
he fought against them and in the war performed deeds of great
bravery'.[51]

It is possible that the Visigoths had been bribed to attack
Aegidius with the surrender of Narbonne (see p. 92); or that
Priscus is referring to the battle fought between Aegidius and
Visigoths at Orleans (see p. 98), which may have been part of a
larger conflict on the Loire, or to a general continuation of

[48] Priscus almost certainly means the western Gauls as opposed to those of
Galatia in the east.

[49] Priscus, frag. 39 (1) (Blockley's translation).

[50] James (1988: 67–8) has described Aegidius as being at this point 'in
revolt' against the legitimate emperor, but this is unjustified.

[51] Priscus, frag. 39 (1) (Blockley's translation). Priscus' tone (and use of the
term 'Italians') does not fit with the idea of Aegidius being in revolt against a
'legitimate emperor', as suggested by James (see above). It would be interesting to know how Priscus heard about Aegidius' courageous deeds, since his
western information is usually confined to Italy.

hostilities. Possibly Aegidius consciously chose the (unusual) course of keeping his forces for the defence of Roman Gaul rather than attacking a rival, or it may have been strategically impossible for him to march into Italy (with or without the additional pressure from the Visigoths). The failures of both Aegidius and Marcellinus in their intention to attack Italy, and also perhaps Ricimer's inability to control Aegidius, illustrate how the warlords of the late fifth century increasingly lacked the resources to operate directly outside their own spheres of power.

The Italian government dominated by Ricimer would probably have appointed a replacement for Aegidius as *magister militum per Gallias*. As discussed above, this may have been Agrippinus;[52] another possibility is the Burgundian king, Gundioc, Ricimer's brother-in-law, who is known to have held the title of *magister militum*.[53] That whoever officially replaced Aegidius was not, in the event, more effective in bringing Aegidius to heel must have been because Aegidius retained control of a considerable proportion if not all of the military forces in Gaul (see the fuller discussion of this in Ch. 10), a greater problem for Agrippinus than for Gundioc, who could call on Burgundian manpower.

We know something about Aegidius' activities in Gaul between AD 461 and his death in 465 from Hydatius and Gregory of Tours. Hydatius says that: 'In the month of May, the brave Aegidius (mentioned above) sent an embassy to the Vandals by way of the ocean, which returned home by the same route in the month of September'.[54] Hydatius does not clarify the purpose of the embassy, but it is most likely that it was an attempt to organize an alliance against Ricimer.[55] Gaining Gaiseric's assistance would probably have been at Italy's expense (another example of Roman willingness to treat with the empire's enemies to destroy a rival).

---

[52] As suggested by Demandt (1970: 690); O'Flynn (1983: 124).

[53] As suggested by Jones (1964: 241).

[54] Hydatius, 220 (224) *s.a.* 464–5: 'Mense Maio superdicti uiri Egidi ligati per Oceanum ad Vandolos transeunt, qui eodem cursu Septembri mensi reuertuntur ad suos'. The mention of the months hints that the ship carrying the embassy may have called into a Spanish port.

[55] See Stroheker (1948: 141–2).

The strangest piece of information we possess about Aegidius is in the *Historiae*. Gregory says that the Frankish king, Childeric, was deposed by his people because of the debauchery of his private life,[56] and exiled to Thuringia, where he became the lover of the queen, Basina, who followed him back to his kingdom and later bore his son Clovis.[57] Then, Gregory relates: 'After the Franks expelled him they unanimously adopted as their king Aegidius who, as we have said above, had been sent by the government as *magister militum*.'[58] Gregory says that Aegidius then reigned for eight years before the Franks restored Childeric to his throne.[59]

The story is extraordinary, and complicates our understanding of the relationship between Roman and Frank. It was accepted by historians in the past,[60] but has been dismissed out of hand by most modern ones (even though this story gets

[56] Explaining political events on the basis of personal virtues and vices is common in ancient historical writing, and Christian writers were always inclined to stress sexual morality. The exile of Childeric for debauchery probably reflects the moral viewpoint of Gregory, or his source. A reading of the *Historiae* suggests that male misbehaviour would have had to be very extreme to upset the early Franks; the real reasons were probably political.

[57] On the basis of some of Gregory's early Frankish history, it is possible that the Merovingian dynasty (rather than the Salian Franks in general) had connections with Thuringia (Wood (1994*b*: 35, 37–8)). According to the highly embroidered version of Gregory's story in Fredegar's chronicle (II, 11), Childeric went from Thuringia to Constantinople. This Wallace-Hadrill (1962: 162) accepted, thinking that Childeric might have been subsidized to act against Aegidius. However, it would have been Ricimer, not Constantinople, who considered Aegidius dangerous, and it would not fit with what we know of eastern policy. In Fredegar's account Aegidius and Childeric have 'many combats', and Childeric finally cuts Aegidius to pieces during the Frankish invasion of the Rhineland; which illustrates how legends developed over time.

[58] Greg. Tur. *Historiae* 11, 12: 'Denique Franci, hunc eiectum, Egidium sibi, quem superius magistrum militum a re publica missum diximus, unanamiter regem adsciscunt.'

[59] 'Qui cum octavo anno super eos regnaret.' Frye (1992: 7) believed that the period of eight years corresponded to the period between Aegidius being appointed *magister militum per Gallias* and his death, and thus supports the story (this could, however, be just where Gregory got his figure of eight years from in the first place). A problem with this is that there would have been three or four years in which Aegidius was not only the King of the Franks but also *magister militum* of Majorian.

[60] For instance, Dill (1926: 11) considered that there was 'nothing incredible' in Gregory's story.

equal treatment in Gregory with others that are accepted un-
critically). James has argued that Gregory had heard 'some
misunderstood memory of the Franks fighting under Roman
leadership' and wrongly assumed that the Franks had elected
Aegidius as their king.[61] It seems, however, implausible that
Gregory would have concocted a story of a Roman becoming
King of the Franks and connected it to sexual scandal about the
great conqueror's parents merely to explain a folk memory of
Franks fighting under Aegidius (especially if, as James believes,
Gregory was set on glorifying Clovis).

Another recent historian, Frye, returned to the older view
and accepted not only that Aegidius became King of the Franks
but the details of Gregory's story (see below for his interpretation of the reports of a battle at Orleans). In his model, Childeric and Aegidius were rivals for the Frankish throne,[62] with
Franks fighting for both sides.[63] Childeric's activities in North
Gaul are placed in the context of this rivalry,[64] including the
story in later sources of a Frankish victory over Aegidius on the
Rhine, which he attributes to Childeric[65] (although Childeric's
name does not appear in this context). Frye has also suggested
that Childeric may have been acting against Aegidius with the
backing of Constantinople, but the evidence for this is exceed-
ingly weak, and is unnecessary if his other idea of rivalry for the
Frankish throne is correct.[66] Frye's model of rivalry between

[61] James (1988: 68).

[62] That a Gallo-Roman could become the king of a barbarian people he finds
quite credible, believing that in this period ethnicity 'had become fluid'.

[63] Frye (1992: 12) suggested that some Franks 'provided the muscle' for a
powerful anti-imperial separatist movement centred around Aegidius and
involving most of the *civitates* in North Gaul. To imagine an organized anti-
imperial separatist movement is stretching the evidence. Aegidius' refusal to
accept Libius Severus can be explained simply by his opposition to Ricimer.

[64] Périn offered a different interpretation of events, with Childeric on his
return from exile offering his services to Aegidius, thus explaining why he was
fighting with him at Orleans (Périn and Feffer (1987: i, 106)), for which see
below.

[65] Frye (1992: 6–7).

[66] Frye (1992: 8). See n. 57 on this theory as advanced by Wallace-Hadrill
on the basis of a story in Fredegar. As Frye says himself, there may be
confusion here with the similar story of the later Gundovald. The Alamannic
campaign which he cited as proof of imperial support for Childeric, if it
occurred, took place after Aegidius' death, so is irrelevant.

Aegidius and Childeric is not inherently impossible. The problem is that, like the theory of a Frankish–Roman alliance between the two, which he rightly questions, it is a detailed and sophisticated reconstruction of the political and military situation based on evidence that just cannot support it.

A major reason against accepting Gregory's story as it stands is that not one of the Roman sources for Aegidius mentions, or even hints at, such an unusual situation. Indeed, Hydatius says that at the time of his death he guarded lands in North Gaul 'in the name of Rome'.[67] That Childeric was forced into temporary exile in a neighbouring kingdom is not problematic. This was a fairly common occurrence, caused by feuds or rivalry for the throne (similar situations may lie behind the careers of other barbarians serving the empire). The difficulty is the elevation of Aegidius in his place. Other elements of the exile story have the feel of folk tradition, and that might be where Gregory acquired it. The inclusion of Aegidius would then predate Gregory. This story would then be an early example of the sort of legend which could quickly develop around real people and events in this period, comparable to those in Burgundian, English, and British legend. Its basis could be a real memory of Childeric's exile, elaborated to provide a 'birth story' for Clovis, which somehow became combined with traditions about the Frankish relationship with Aegidius. It does, however, suggest that if the basis was an alliance between the Salians and Aegidius, then he was remembered as the dominant partner.

I have a persistent feeling, however, that the story has some greater significance, and that the relationship between Aegidius and Childeric's Franks was an unusual one (reflecting perhaps the complex nature of Roman/barbarian relations in this period). Roman command of Frankish fighting men was, after all, an occurrence too common in the late empire to need any special explanation or the development of this strange tradition. I have even wondered whether there was a connection by marriage between the families of Aegidius and Childeric, since intermarriage may have been more common than we are aware of (see pp. 76–7 for a possible connection via Aetius). Given the

---

[67] Hydatius, 224 (228) *s.a.* 464–5.

inadequacy of the sources, the question of Aegidius' Frankish kingship should perhaps remain open.

In AD 463 Aegidius won what was probably a major battle at Orleans, defeating Frederic, brother of the Visigothic king. Frederic had earlier been campaigning against the *bacaudae* in Spain, on Rome's behalf.[68] This battle is recorded in a number of sources, each with a slightly different angle. According to a chronicle written by Marius of Avenches, the battle, between Aegidius and the Goths, took place between the rivers of the Loire and the Loir, near Orleans.[69] Hydatius reports that, in AD 463,[70] 'in the province of Armorica, Frederic, the brother of King Theoderic, rose up against the *comes utriusque militiae* Aegidius, a man of courage and commendable reputation and pleasing to God for his good works, and, with those with him, was defeated and killed'.[71] The *Gallic Chronicle of 511* entry for AD 463 does not mention Aegidius, but records the death of Frederic near the Loire, when fighting Franks;[72] while Gregory of Tours writes that 'Childeric fought battles at Orleans' (no date given).[73]

The usual reconstruction amalgamates all these notices to create the 'Battle of Orleans', won by Aegidius and Frankish allies, or federates, under Childeric,[74] with the *Gallic Chronicle*

---

[68] Hydatius, 150 (158) s.a. 453–4.

[69] Marius Avent. s.a. 463: 'pugna facta est inter Aegidium et Gothos inter Ligerem et Ligerecinum iuxta Aurelianis ibique interfectus est Fredericus rex Gothorum'.

[70] There is some confusion on Hydatius' dating here. *PLRE* ii (for Aegidius and Fredericus 2) gives Hydatius' date for the battle as 461 (presumably on Mommsen's dating of Hydatius in *MGH*), but Burgess dates some of Hydatius' entries differently from Mommsen. Both Muhlberger (1990) and Burgess (1993) date this entry to AD 463, and this is clearly the correct date, confirmed by the other sources.

[71] Hydatius, 214 (218) s.a. 461. This notice suggests that Frederic was the aggressor, and this is the usual line taken by modern commentators; however, Wolfram (1988: 181) described Aegidius as attacking the Goths in a move against Toulouse, co-ordinated with his encouragement of the Vandals to attack Italy. There is no evidence for this.

[72] *Chronica Gallica a 511*, 638.

[73] Greg. Tur. *Historiae* ii, 18: 'Igitur Childericus Aurilianis pugnas egit.'

[74] It is possible that Gregory, reading or hearing of Frankish involvement, assumed Childeric's leadership and inserted his name, as suggested by James

of 511 entry acting as a link between the Roman sources mentioning Aegidius, and Gregory's reference to Childeric. This is then adduced as proof of an alliance between Aegidius and Childeric (often extended to Syagrius).[75] However, it has been argued that there are problems with this amalgamation, and that the battle that Childeric fought at Orleans recorded by Gregory was not the same as that won by Aegidius in AD 463.[76]

The best reasons advanced are, first, that the *Historiae* describes Childeric fighting more than one battle (*pugnas*),[77] and, second, that it makes no mention of the death of Frederic.[78] Frye described it as unwarranted to manufacture an alliance between Aegidius and Childeric on such slender and insecure evidence. One must say that it is equally unwise to use the same evidence to prove there was a conflict between Aegidius and Childeric, as Frye then does. Gregory is here using a chronicle source, cryptic in style (see pp. 101–2); the omission of Frederic proves little. If one wants to take Gregory literally, then it is perfectly feasible that there was more than one battle at or around Orleans in the AD 460s, one between Aegidius and Frederic and one between Franks, under Childeric, and Goths,[79] but Frye's own point that Childeric is reported as fighting more than one battle at Orleans shows that he must

(1988: 65). This still leaves Aegidius' association with Franks in the battle very likely.

[75] See Périn and Feffer (1987: i, 108); Daly (1994: 624, 627).

[76] Frye (1992: 1–4).

[77] It is *pugnas* in all manuscript traditions, i.e. in the plural, although translated by Thorpe (1974) in the Penguin edition as 'a battle'. It could be a grammatical error or a piece of Gregory's idiosyncratic style.

[78] The version in the *Liber Historiae Francorum* (8), in which Childeric fought at Orleans after Aegidius' death, could also be seen as supporting this view, although this is not mentioned by Frye.

[79] If so, and remembering that there had been an earlier battle between the Huns and the allied Romans and Goths at Orleans, it seems possible that the city (or the area around it) was one that had some strategic significance at this time. Elton (1992: 174) has suggested a trend, in the fifth century, towards battles being fought for or at cities, as with Orleans, Arles, Narbonne, Angers, and Soissons. One cannot be certain that all the battles involved the actual city, as the name of a *civitas* in the sources would cover both the city itself and its surrounding territory; nevertheless there are enough instances in which it is clear that the city itself was the location of the battle to support the idea of a

also have fought *another* battle there, and this presumably was
that involving Aegidius and Frederic.

As well as a battle at Orleans, Gregory's *Glory of the Confessors* records that Aegidius, at an unknown date, fought a minor
engagement at Chinon (in the territory of Gregory's own see of
Tours).[80] In an account of a holy man named Maximus he
writes: 'Then Maximus came to Castrum Cainonense [Chinon],
a town of Tours, and set up a monastery. When the stronghold
was being besieged by Aegidius, and the people of the countryside were confined there, the hostile enemy blocked up [or,
'off'] a well dug in the side of a mountain'.[81] Maximus then
miraculously brought on a storm to provide rain water, and the
enemy fled. It has been suggested that Aegidius attacked Chinon because its people were supporting the Visigoths;[82] that is,
was making war against his own people. It seems more likely
that this episode occurred during fighting between Aegidius and
the Visigoths, perhaps at the same time as the battle at Orleans,
and the people of Chinon got caught in the middle.

It may be that in the early A D 460s, having been successful in
the South, the Visigoths had turned their attention northwards
across the Loire, and it is probable that Aegidius spent a substantial part of the last four years of his life in this area resisting
their attacks, apparently with some success. However, Aegidius
does not seem to have exploited his victory at Orleans by taking
offensive action against the kingdom of Aquitaine. He may have
been in a precarious position because of lack of resources. An-

---

trend that way. This may have been because the cities were centres of whatever
wealth and political functions still existed; it may also reflect a more defensive
military strategy.

[80] The cathedral possibly owned property there (Greg. of Tours, *In Glor.
Conf.*, trans. Van Dam (1988: 38 n. 28)). Gregory probably acquired the story
from local folk memory or ecclesiastical sources at Chinon itself.

[81] Greg. Tur. *Glor. Confess.* 22: 'Deinde ad castrum Cainonensim urbis
Turonicae veniens, monasterium collocavit. Quod castrum cum ab Egidio
obsederetur, et populus pagi illius ibidem esset inclusus, hostis adversus effos-
sum a latere montis puteum . . . obturant.'

[82] Rouche (1979: 36).

other possible reason is the presence of rivals in Gaul such as Count Paulus, Gundioc, Arbogast, and Agrippinus.[83] But Aegidius' lack of follow-up is not unusual; the ability of Roman commanders to beat the Goths in battle, but inability to inflict strategic defeat, was of long standing (and a crucial factor in the West's failure).

Chapters 18 and 19 of the *Historiae* provide further historical information about events in North Gaul.[84] Chapter 18 begins with the report of Childeric fighting battles:

Then Childeric fought battles at Orleans. Adovacrius came with Saxons to Angers. At that time a great plague devastated the population.[85] Aegidius died and left a son called Syagrius.[86] After he was dead, Adovacrius took hostages from Angers and other places. The Bretons [or, 'Britons'] were driven out of Bourges by the Goths, [and] many were killed at the town of Bourg-de-Déols.[87] Paulus *comes*, with Romans and Franks, made war on the Goths and took booty. Then Adovacrius himself came to Angers, and King Childeric arrived the next day; the *comes* Paulus being killed, he occupied the city. On that day a great fire burnt down the church house.

[19] These things having happened, a war started between the Saxons and the Romans, but the Saxons retreated and many of them, pursued by the Romans, were put to the sword. Their islands, after many had been killed, were overthrown and captured by the Franks. In the ninth month of that year the earth trembled. Odovacrius entered

---

[83] As suggested by Elton (1990: 216).

[84] The story of Aegidius as King of the Franks appears in ch. 12. The intervening chapters are religious in character. Contrary to earlier thought, these chapters (and the other religious chapters in the work as a whole) are not now thought to have been interpolated by Gregory into an earlier draft (Goffart (1987: 58–62)).

[85] According to Gildas, there was also plague in Britain at about this time (*De Excidio et Conquestu Britanniae* XX, 2).

[86] It is conceivable that this mention of Syagrius was an interpolation by Gregory into his source material because of his later appearance in his main narrative, but there is no particular reason to think so.

[87] *Dolensis vicus* has been identified as modern Bourg-de-Déols, on the river Indre, close to Châteauroux, approximately thirty-five miles from Bourges (Longnon (1878: 466)).

into a treaty with Childeric [and] they subdued the Alamanni,[88] who
had invaded part of Italy.[89]

The bald factual record in these two chapters is completely
different in style to the surrounding text. In book II Gregory
appears to have made a collection of all, or most, of the information on the fifth century available to him, and these two
chapters have, almost certainly, been copied, with little or no
expansion, from a chronicle, possibly annalistic in form. It is
thought to have been written in Angers, because in chapter 18
Angers figures prominently; the reference to the church house
(the bishop's residence) burning down is particularly telling.
Also, the use of the verb *venire* in relation to Angers suggests
that the author was within that city.[90] As Bishop of Tours,
which is close to Angers, Gregory could well have had access
to written records preserved there.

Unfortunately, it is impossible to set exact dates, or to know
whether days, months, or years separated the recorded events.

---

[88] A minor difficulty here is the lack of corroborative evidence for Odovacer
campaigning against the Alamanni. However, the sources for his reign are very
poor. The Alamanni raided northern Italy in the time of Majorian (Sidonius,
Pan. v, 373–80), and Pope Gelasius writes of unspecified barbarian incursions
into Italy during the reign of Odovacer (Gelasius, *Ep.* VII, *Ad Episcopus
Picenum*). It is also possible that the campaign took place outside Italy. Odovacer was particularly concerned with the security of his northern possessions,
and the Alamanni settled on the Upper Rhine were a threat to Noricum and
Raetia (Hodgkin (1885: 139); Barker (1911: 413)). The Alamanni were later
allies of Theoderic against Odovacer (Barker (1911: 441, 451)).

[89] Greg. Tur. *Historiae* II, 18–19: '[18] Igitur Childericus Aurilianis pugnas egit [*sic*], Adovacrius vero cum Saxonibus Andecavo venit. Magna tunc
lues populum devastavit. Mortuus est autem Egidius et reliquit filium Sya-
grium nomine. Quo defuncto, Adovacrius de Andecavo vel aliis locis obsedes
accepit. Brittani de Bituricas a Gothis expulsi sunt, multis apud Dolensim
vicum peremptis. Paulus vero comes cum Romanis ac Francis Gothis bella
intulit et praedas egit. Veniente vero Adovacrio Andecavus, Childericus rex
suquenti die advenit, interemptoque Paulo comite, civitatem obtinuit.
Magnum ea die incendio domus aeclesiae concremata est. [19] His ita gestis,
inter Saxones atque Romanos bellum gestum est; sed Saxones terga vertentes,
multos de suis, Romanis insequentibus, gladio reliquerunt; insolae eorum cum
multo populo interempto a Francis captae atque subversi sunt. Eo anno mense
nono terra tremuit. Odovacrius cum Childerico foedus iniit, Alamannusque,
qui partem Italiae pervaserant, subiugarunt.'

[90] Wood (1994*a*: 38).

If this was originally an annal, Gregory has restructured it in narrative form and removed the year dates. In some annals of this period some years might not have any entries, others more than one, so we cannot even assign one entry to each year. As Gregory says in his preface to book II that he tried, to the best of his ability, to work in chronological order,[91] what we know of the dating of those events placed by Gregory before and after these two chapters sets the time period as the AD 460s and 470s.[92]

This is substantiated by the internal dating. Although, as covered above, there is a case for caution, it remains a strong probability that the battle of Orleans recorded at the beginning of chapter 18 is the same as that dated by Hydatius and Marius to AD 463. The last item in chapter 19 must, if referring to Odovacer King of Italy, date to between AD 476 (when he took power) and AD 482 (when Childeric died). If the defeat of the Bretons at Bourg-de-Déols is the same battle as that recorded by Jordanes in the region of Bourges (or was part of the same campaign), then a date of *c.* AD 470 would seem appropriate.[93] The most secure date is that of the death of Aegidius, which Hydatius gives as late AD 464 or early 465.[94]

An Adovacrius (amended to 'Odovacer' in the Thorpe and Dalton translations of the *Historiae*) appears in chapter 18 leading Saxon attacks on Angers (perhaps by ship up the river, which is navigable as far as Angers?).[95] These Saxons are presumably the same Saxons who in chapter 19 are described as fighting the Romans, and whose unidentified islands were attacked by the Franks (but this need not necessarily be so).

[91] Greg. Tur. *Historiae*, preface to Book II: 'I recount for you at one and the same time and in the muddled and confused order in which these events occurred . . . so that the onward march of the centuries and the succession of the years down to our own times may be studied in their entirety' (Thorpe's translation).

[92] It seems that Gregory's ordering of events is usually correct (Wallace-Hadrill (1983: 23)).

[93] Jordanes, *Getica* 237–8. The date is based on that of the events immediately following in the *Getica*.

[94] Hydatius, 224 (228) *s.a.* 464–5.

[95] Gerberding (1987: 44).

These islands are consistently described in secondary sources as being in the Loire.[96]

The *comes* Paulus who appears in chapter 18 is not known from any other sources (with the possible exception of the genealogies previously discussed). Like Aegidius he was the leader of both Romans and Franks. He could have been Aegidius' subordinate or successor,[97] a rival of his, or a purely local leader (perhaps based in Angers?). It was once suggested that Paulus was an official appointee of the Emperor Anthemius (who was attempting at this time to organize an alliance in North Gaul against Euric, also including Riothamus), but this seems unlikely at this date.[98]

Childeric's role in these events is unclear. The conventional view was that Childeric was allied to Paulus, as Aegidius' successor. (Later accounts in Fredegar's chronicle and the *Liber* have Childeric fighting and killing Paulus,[99] but this is usually attributed to misunderstanding of Gregory.) It is, however, equally possible from the cryptic and ambiguous text that Childeric was allied to the Saxons, or indeed the leader of a third force.

The identity of the Adovacrius/Odovacrius is problematic. The coincidence of the name has often led to the assumption that this is the same man as the Odovacer, King of Italy,[100] but this causes major difficulties. In the ancient sources Odovacer is variously described as Scirian, Rugian, or Gothic, but never Saxon.[101] From the *Vita Severini*, we know that he travelled

---

[96] See e.g. Greg. of Tours, trans. Dalton (1927: 496 n. 13): 'Piratical Saxons had occupied the wooded islands in the Loire between Saumur and Angers'. After protracted research, I have been unable to find the origin of this 'fact', and can only presume that it is a logical assumption from the internal evidence in the two passages. An alternative location for the Saxon settlements would be islands somewhere off the north or west coast of Brittany. If these Saxons remained settled in the Loire region, they may be those later converted by Bishop Felix of Nantes in the sixth century (Venantius Fortunatus, *Carm.* III, ix, 99–104).

[97] As proposed by Périn and Feffer (1987: i, 1010).

[98] Bury (1923: 346).

[99] Fredegar, 11, 12; *Liber Historiae Francorum*, 8.

[100] See *PLRE* ii, 791, Odovacer; Heinzelmann (1982: 544).

[101] *Suda*, 693; John Ant. frag. 209 (1); Theophanes, AM 5965; Jordanes, *Romana* 344; etc. See Pt. III, pp. 284–7 for full discussion.

from the Danube area to join the imperial army in Italy.[102] There he served in the imperial bodyguard;[103] and was involved in conflict between Ricimer and Anthemius in AD 470–2. It is hard to see how or why the same man would have been leading Saxons in north-west Gaul.[104]

Study of the Latin text suggests a solution to this long-acknowledged problem. Examination of the variant spellings of Adovacrius/Odovacrius in the original Latin shows that in virtually all the manuscripts the name in chapter 18 is Adovacrius (or Adovagrius) and in chapter 19 Odovacrius.[105] The Adovacrius of the first chapter was, I suggest, a Saxon leader, with a name that when Latinized is somewhat similar to Odovacer, while the Odovacrius of the second was Odovacer of Italy. It is interesting that Gregory divided this material into two chapters.[106] The rather ambiguous linking phrase *his ita gestis* ('These things having happened,') is probably Gregory's own. Gregory may have used *two* sources, one for chapter 18 and one for 19, the first being all or part of a chronicle, probably annalistic, from Angers, the second a similar written source from elsewhere.[107] He linked them together because they referred to conflicts in the same region, and because both mentioned Childeric: in one source involved in fighting in northern Gaul which also included a Saxon leader Adovacrius; and in a second source, at a slightly later date, allied to or employed by

---

[102] Eugippius, *Vita Severini* VI, 6.

[103] John Ant. frag. 209 (1); Procopius, *Wars* V, i, 6.

[104] These Saxons are clearly not a federate unit of the imperial army. Frye (1992: 10) suggests that the chronicler may have identified as Saxons what were really Thuringians, which enables their leader to be identified as Odovacer of Italy, but this argument is tenuous in the extreme.

[105] This is true of both the major Corbie and the Bruxelles MSS. Among the very large number of manuscripts of the *Historia* (Greg of Tours, ed. Omont and Collon/Pourpardin (1913: pp. xiv–xix); and ed. Krusch and Levison (1937–51: pp. xxii–xxxi)) there are only one or two exceptions. In ch. 18 only the text in the Leiden MS (for the third reference only) reads Odovacrio. In Ch. 19 again there is only one exception, the Namur MS having Adovachrius.

[106] The chapter divisions in the *Historiae* are those made by Gregory himself (Goffart (1987: 62 ff.)).

[107] It may be relevant here that the *Liber Historiae Francorum* includes the material in ch. 18 (the proposed first source) but not ch. 19.

King Odovacer.[108] The pattern of the variant spellings supports the theory that there are two separate sources, and, if so, the existence of two sources makes it more likely that two different men appear in them.

The material in the *Liber Historiae Francorum* on Aegidius, although thought to be copied wholesale from Gregory, is somewhat different in sequence and details. There is a much more elaborate version of Gregory's story of Childeric's exile and Aegidius' election in his place, which gives an important role to Childeric's loyal Hun advisor Wiomed (who also appears in Fredegar's account).[109] The elaboration presumably developed in Frankish oral tradition or epic. In the *Liber*'s version Aegidius, who is described as a Roman prince and 'that proud and haughty soldier of the emperor',[110] was elected because the Franks followed 'bad counsel'. When Aegidius begins to oppress the Franks, Wiomed asks them: 'Do you not remember in what manner the despotic Romans threw you out and drove your people from their land?'[111] So Frankish tradition seemingly remembered the Romans, perhaps especially those associated with Aegidius, as oppressors. That the Franks were being driven off 'their' lands is totally at odds with the conventional picture of continuous Frankish expansion, and it is interesting that it surfaces from folk tradition. (Fredegar, incidentally, gives details of Aegidius' unbearable oppression: he imposed a poll tax on them.[112])

[108] Some of the gold coins found in his grave could have been payment from Odovacer. The coins, in the names of eastern emperors, date to sometime between AD 475 and 491 (Todd (1992: 195); Périn and Feffer (1987: i, 109)), and, given the context, presumably to the 470s. The theory that they were paid to Childeric directly by the eastern government (see n. 57) seems inherently unlikely. It has been suggested that an alliance between Odovacer and Childeric would have been particularly detrimental to Syagrius (Périn and Feffer (1987: i, 138)).

[109] It is perhaps odd that Frankish legend gives such an important part to a Hun.

[110] *Liber Historiae Francorum*, 7: 'militem istum imperatoris superbum atque elatum'.

[111] *Liber Historiae Francorum*, 7: 'Quare non recordaris quomodo eiecerunt Romani opprementes gentum vestram et de eorum terra eiecerunt eos?'

[112] Fredegar, III, 11. No doubt this reflects the concerns of his own age, though it is not unlikely that Aegidius would have demanded tax or tribute from peoples under his 'protection'.

In the *Liber Historiae Francorum* this story is succeeded by the following passage, which is not taken from Gregory:

In those days the Franks took the city of Agrippina on the Rhine, known as Colonia, as if *coloni* inhabited it. There they massacred many of the Roman people belonging to Aegidius' faction. Aegidius himself escaped [by] flight. They then moved on to the city of Trier on the River Moselle, devastating its lands, and took and burnt it.[113] After this Aegidius, King of the Romans, died, so Syagrius his son succeeded to his *regnum* and established his seat of power in the city of Soissons.[114]

This attack could date to the years in which Aegidius was officially *magister militum*, although, given the mention of his death, it could well be later, when he was acting independently of the Italian government (and in a weaker position).

Then follows an account of the events reported in chapter 18 of the *Historiae*, but not identical to it:

Then King Childeric mustered a great army of the Frankish host and came all the way to the city of Orleans and also devastated its lands. Adovacrius *dux* of the Saxons came with a naval force by sea all the way to Angers and burnt its lands, and he made a great slaughter there. As Adovacrius withdrew from Angers, Childeric the King of the Franks gathered an army and came there; Count Paulus who was then there he killed. He took the city itself, and the residence that was in that city he burnt with fire. He then left.[115]

---

[113] The 'B' tradition adds that not since the Huns had such destruction been inflicted. This attack on Trier could be the context of Arbogast's possible change of career, see p. 75.

[114] *Liber Historiae Francorum*, 8: 'In illis diebus coeperunt [*sic*] Franci Agripinam civitatem super Renum vocaveruntque eam Coloniam, quasi coloni inhabitarent in eam. Multo populo Romanorum a parte Egidii illic interfecerunt, ipse Egidius fugiens evasit. Venerunt itaque Treviris civitatem super Mosellam fluvium, vastantes terras illas, et ipsam succendentes coeperunt. Post haec igitur mortuus est Egidius Romanorum rex. Siagrius enim. filius eius, in regnum resedit, constituit sedem regni sui in Suessionis civitate.' The 'B' tradition calls Aegidius *Romanorum tyrannus*. The chapter continues with a version of events in the *Historiae*, 11, 18.

[115] *Liber Historiae Francorum*, VIII: 'Tunc Childericus rex commovit maximo exercitu hostium Francorum, usque Aurelianis civitate pervenit terras quoque illas vastavit. Adovacrius Saxonorum dux cum navale hoste per mare usque Andegavis civitate venit illaque terra succendit; magna tunc cede in illa fecit [in MS 'B', 'cede populo vastavit']. Redeunte igitur Adovacrio de

Perhaps significantly, the *Liber* does *not* continue with the information in chapter 19 (from the proposed second chronicle) on the Bretons and Childeric and Odovacer. It is probable that the differences between this account and that of Gregory are the result of careless and imaginative rewriting, but it is conceivable that it results from independent contact with the Angers tradition.

The material in the *Historiae* and *Liber Historiae Francorum* is extremely important in reconstructing the history of northern Gaul, but it does not allow us to establish a precise chronology, nor the exact status of the protagonists and the relationships between them (it must always be kept in mind that there may have been more than two sides in this fighting, and that political alliances would have been fragile).

As noted above, Aegidius' death is reported and dated by Hydatius: 'Aegidius died, betrayed, some say in a trap, others by poison. On his passing, the Goths soon [invaded] the regions that he had protected in the name of Rome.'[116] Infuriatingly, Hydatius omits to say who killed Aegidius, or was believed to have done so. It is possible that his death was in fact from natural causes, and then that rumours to the contrary developed and reached Spain. The Visigothic expansion referred to would not seem to have been into the lands north of the Loire, in which Aegidius is thought to have operated, since there is no evidence at all that the Visigoths moved into this area.[117] Perhaps it refers to expansion into Auvergne or the Narbonne area (which would confirm that Aegidius' activities were not confined to north-eastern Gaul).

Andegavis, Childericus rex Francorum exercitu commoto, illac advenit, Paulo comite, qui tunc ibi erat [the 'B' tradition adds, 'qui in ipsa civitate preerat'] occidit ipsamque urbem coepit, domum, qui in ea urbe erat igne succendit, indeque reversus est.'

[116] Hydatius, 224 (228) *s.a.* 465: 'Egidius moritur, alii dicunt insidiis, alii ueneno deceptus. Quo desistente mox Gothi regiones quas Romano nomini tuebatur [inuadunt].'

[117] *Contra* Wolfram (1988: 180–1), who describes the Visigoths pushing north of the Loire on Aegidius' death. In support of this statement he cites Hydatius, 212 (217), 214 (218), and 220 (224), which are ambiguous, and also *Epistolae Arelatenses*, 15; and *Chronica Gallica a 511*, 638. The last citations are strange, since neither seems to refer to Visigothic expansion north of the Loire.

In all the material discussed above, nothing has linked Aegidius to the city of Soissons, still less to a kingdom of Soissons. If one takes all the sources for Aegidius at face value, the sum is a leader of imperial forces in Gaul, who fought possibly at Lyons, almost certainly at Arles, definitely at Orleans and near Tours against the Visigoths, probably in the Rhineland against Franks and possibly against the Saxons in Normandy, led Franks in northern Gaul, threatened to invade Italy, and sent envoys to the Vandal kingdom in North Africa, and a man of sufficient importance to come to the notice of Priscus in the East.[118] All in all, the picture is that of an important Gallic political and military leader rather than that of a local warlord based in a rather obscure *civitas* in the north-east of the country.

The single thing linking Aegidius with Soissons is a throwaway line within Gregory's account of the life of Clovis: 'Childeric died and his son Clovis reigned in his place. In the fifth year of his reign, Syagrius, the King of the Romans, son of Aegidius, had his seat at the city of Soissons, which the previously mentioned Aegidius had formerly possessed.'[119] (The rest of the story is given on pp. 122–3.) All this passage tells us is that Aegidius held Soissons for an indeterminate length of time; and Aegidius' only other link with the city is the very vague one of his association with the Franks, and Soissons' general proximity to their territories. Aegidius would not have had much time after Majorian's death to build up a personal power base at Soissons, even if it were his campaigning headquarters (and a campaigning base further west would have been more effective against the Visigoths).[120] The kingdom of Soissons, if it existed,

---

[118] Johnson (1980: 112) suggests that the famous 'Groans of the Britons', a letter to 'Agitius' reproduced in Gildas's *De Excidio et Conquestu Britanniae* XX, 1, was an appeal to Aegidius. However, as he is called *ter consuli* it was almost certainly Aetius, consul for the third time in AD 446. The two names may, however, have been confused to create the form Agitius (Myers (1986: 8 n. 3)), which would suggest that Aegidius was known to the Romano-Britons.

[119] Greg. Tur. *Historiae* II, 27: 'Mortuo Childerico, regnavit Chlodovechus filius eius, pro eo. Anno autem quinto regni eius Siacrius Romanorum rex, Egidi filius apud civitatem Sexonas/Suessones [some MSS have 'Sexonas', others 'Suessones' or similar variations] quam quondam supra memoratus Egidius tenuerat, sedem habebat.'

[120] Musset (1993: 75) suggests that there was a Roman command on the Loire, organized by Aetius, based at Orleans.

really belongs to his son Syagrius, and should hence be seen as a rather later political development, a step further down the road of fragmentation, localization, hereditary succession, and the translation of military to general power; in other words, towards early medieval characteristics.

7

Syagrius and the Kingdom of Soissons

THE KINGDOM OF SOISSONS IN CONVENTIONAL SCHOLARSHIP AND AS REDEFINED BY EDWARD JAMES

In the conventional version of the history of fifth-century Gaul, Aegidius and Syagrius held most of North and north-central Gaul for about twenty-five years, from c. AD 461 to 485/6 (possibly with Count Paulus ruling between the two). The area of this 'Roman kingdom' is not, of course, given in any primary source, and estimates of its extent are based on the absence of evidence for this region being under the control of any other rulers. The lands they are believed to have controlled encompassed the valley of the Seine and the plain of central Gaul, from the Somme and Meuse west to Brittany, and contained the cities of Amiens, Beauvais, Reims, Troyes, Soissons, and Orleans (see map 2). Some have stretched the kingdom out to Verdun (on Verdun see also pp. 129–30).[1] In this model, this region, 'evolved into a kingdom centred on Soissons, ruled by Aegidius' son Syagrius, known later to the Franks as *Rex Romanorum* and called so because he and his kingdom were recognisably Roman'.[2] Syagrius either inherited this kingdom from his father or, although this seems unlikely, was appointed as a legitimate authority, by Julius Nepos or Anthemius.[3]

In his 1988 book *The Franks* James rejected this traditional model outright.[4] According to James, Gregory never used the

---

[1] For Verdun see Périn and Feffer (1987: i, 135) and Map 2.
[2] Salway (1981: 493).
[3] See Bury (1923: 346).
[4] The following précis of James's argument is taken from *The Franks* (1988: esp. 67–77).

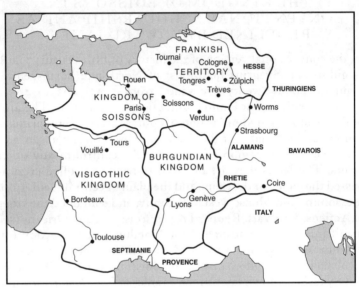

Map 2: Possible extent of the Kingdom of Soissons

phrase 'kingdom of Soissons',[5] which James called a political entity constructed by modern historians, based on 'a desire to fill this political blank with some plausible authority and a feeling that Gregory would not have used the word *rex* if there was not a *regnum* of some reasonable size'. The assumption that Syagrius ruled a large territory from Soissons to the borders of Brittany and Aquitaine has, according to James, resulted in Syagrius being wrongly elevated to being 'a major political force', and portrayed by most historians as a 'bulwark of *Romanitas*'.[6] 'We may', James concluded, 'doubt whether this ghostly "kingdom" ever existed'. James's argument rests partly on the theory that Gregory of Tours deliberately inflated the figure of Syagrius, and hence Clovis' victory over him, both for literary reasons and because of his desire to glorify Clovis (see discussion on pp. 131–2).[7]

James accepted the outline of Aegidius' career as described in the previous section (with the exception of the 'fairy tale' of his reign as King of the Franks), but suggested a new model for late fifth-century Gaul. In this, Frankish military and political domination of northern Gaul dates to the reign of Childeric; for which he finds support in the letter from Bishop Remigius of Reims and in the *Life of Saint Genovefa* (see pp. 118–9). He believed that Childeric held some official or semi-official position in Belgica II;[8] and that the Salians were already playing a major political role in the West in the AD 460s.[9] Syagrius appears 'no more significant than his contemporary Arbogast, count of Trier. Perhaps he was in reality no more than Count of Soissons . . . lying

---

[5] James (1988: 81). However, Gregory (*Historiae* II, 27) *does* refer to a *regnum* slightly later, when referring to the aftermath of Syagrius' defeat: 'Quem Chlodovecho receptum custodiae mancipare praecipit; regnoque eius acceptum, eum gladio clam feriri mandavit'.

[6] As described by Périn (Périn and Feffer (1987: i, 137)): 'et constituait l'ultime bastion de la romanité en Gaule'.

[7] James (1988: 71, 78–80).

[8] The evidence which he gives for this is the letter from Remigius, which is ambiguous, and the presence among his grave-goods of Roman objects including a gold cruciform brooch of the type given to Roman officials on their investiture and worn as a badge of office, and a signet ring (James (1982: 27)). However, the recent discovery of horse sacrifices connected to Childeric's burial (Périn and Feffer (1987: i, 127)) conveys a distinctly unRoman impression.

[9] On the basis of Greg. Tur. *Historiae* II, 18, 19.

within the province which, according to Bishop Remigius, had
"always" been administered by Childeric'.[10]

This minimalist view of Syagrius' status is not impossible
to sustain (especially if James's view on Gregory's aims is
accepted). To assess both James's models and the conventional
ones, the rest of this chapter and Chapters 8 and 9 will examine
in depth the historical sources and other evidence relating to
Syagrius and Soissons.

THE HISTORICAL EVIDENCE FOR SYAGRIUS, SOISSONS, AND NORTHERN GAUL

There is an almost complete gap in our knowledge of events in
North Gaul between the time of Aegidius' death in AD 465 and
that of his son in *c.* AD 486. Our information about Syagrius
comes at the later date, when Gregory says that he was a king of
the Romans who had his seat in Soissons (see pp. 122–3 for
text).[11] As seen, Aegidius' connection with Soissons was slight,
and we do not know for certain how or why Syagrius was there.
Within Belgica II, Reims, the provincial capital, would have
been a more obvious choice (see also pp. 147–8 on Paris). The
fabrica at Soissons, recorded at the beginning of the century,[12]
is unlikely to have prompted the choice, even if it still existed,
and, although Kaiser has made the suggestion that Soissons may
have been easier to defend than Reims because it had a smaller
castrum, this is unlikely to have been of more than secondary
importance.[13] One is thrown back on the old idea that Aegidius
and Syagrius may have had family ties and estates in the Soissons area. Access to the types of resources this would offer may,
by the second half of the century, have been a factor in maintaining independent military forces.

---

[10] James (1988: 71).

[11] Gregory's Syagrius has sometimes been identified with a Syagrius who
appears in the letters of Sidonius (*Epp.* V, v and VIII, viii), but the latter was
involved with the Burgundians, and is now identified as a completely different
person. They may well both have been descendants of Fl. Afranius Syagrius
(Stroheker (1948: 221)).

[12] *Notitia Dignitatum*, Oc. IX, 35.

[13] Kaiser (1973: 140). His other suggestion, that there may have been a
group of aristocrats in the area who favoured resistance, is less plausible.

The names of fifth-century bishops of Soissons in the *Fastes Episcopaux de l'Ancienne Gaule* are taken from a list compiled in the twelfth century,[14] and this gives the bishop at the time of Syagrius as Principius,[15] who other sources say was the elder brother of Remigius of Reims (their father an otherwise unknown Emilius).[16] Principius was the addressee of two letters from Sidonius Apollinaris *c.* AD 475.[17] In one, Sidonius laments that he and Principius live in separate regions and are prevented by *dissociatae situ habitationis* from seeing each other;[18] in the other he refers to the difficulties of the journey between them, which were apparently preventing travel between their homes.[19] Strangely, nowhere else does Sidonius so stress the problems of communication, even when writing to correspondents in Reims or Trier.

The length of time Syagrius is conventionally thought to have ruled for is considerably longer than the four years in which his father was an independent power, and one in which political changes affected Gaul as a whole. Euric came to the Visigothic throne in AD 466, and embarked on a political and religious offensive. The Emperor Anthemius attempted counteraction, but failed (see Pt. III, pp. 242–3). Auvergne was lost to the Visigoths in AD 475 and Provence in AD 476, both ceded as concessions by the Italian government. There is no evidence that the kingdom of Aquitaine succeeded in extending north across the Loire, which suggests that this area was being defended by somebody. The Burgundian kingdom expanded to cover the region from Provence to the Alps and the Massif Central, and the Alamans settled as far west as the Vosges.[20]

From AD 476 Odovacer ruled as king in Italy, so there was no western emperor whom Syagrius could have considered even the most nominal overlord. This, it has been said, finally ex-

---

[14] Duchesne (1915: 83).
[15] Duchesne (1915: 89).
[16] Hincmar, *Vita Sancti Remigii* I, 13–15; Sidonius, *Ep.* VIII, xiv, 2–3. Hincmar, a later Bishop of Reims, wrote his account of Remigius' life in the ninth century AD. It includes Remigius' will.
[17] Sidonius, *Ep.* VIII, xiv; *Ep.* IX, viii.
[18] Sidonius, *Ep.* IX, viii, 2.
[19] Sidonius, *Ep.* VIII, xiv, 8.
[20] Périn and Feffer (1987: i, 135).

posed his legal position for 'the sham it was'.[21] But, should Syagrius have been concerned about having a legal position, which is doubtful, he could easily have considered himself to be formally under the authority of the eastern emperor; this was exactly the line taken by Odovacer while it suited him. In connection with this question there is another ancient source which, just conceivably, relates to Syagrius. The eastern historian Candidus wrote that: 'After the assassination of Nepos and the expulsion of Augustulus, Odovacer in his own person ruled Italy and Rome . . . When the Gauls of the West revolted against Odovacer both they and Odovacer sent an embassy to Zeno. He preferred to support Odovacer.'[22]

These cannot be the same embassies which reached Zeno simultaneously from both Odovacer and Nepos (see Ch. 3),[23] as Candidus would hardly confuse an ex-emperor's ambassadors from Salona in Dalmatia with Gallic ones. Even if there is careless condensation by Photius here, and the embassy from Odovacer in Candidus is the same as the one in Malchus, this still leaves an otherwise unknown Gallic embassy. Some Gallic authority that did not accept the overlordship of Odovacer had a reason (and the resources) to send representations to Constantinople. As far as is known, Odovacer did not make any claims or efforts to rule outside Italy, so an actual rebellion cannot have taken place; but someone in Gaul may, it seems, have wanted to reject any idea of formal allegiance to him in favour of the eastern emperor. Southern Gaul was in the hands of the Visigoths and Burgundians. It is difficult to imagine who in Gaul would have contacted Constantinople in this way if not Syagrius.

For Syagrius, and any other Roman leaders in northern Gaul, relationships with Italy and Constantinople would now be less important than those with the neighbouring barbarian kingdoms, especially the Visigoths and the Franks. We know nothing about relations between the Visigoths and the kingdom of Soissons, except that Syagrius fled there when defeated by Clovis.

---

[21] Wallace-Hadrill (1962: 164).

[22] Candidus, frag. 1 (Blockley's translation); Photius epitome, *Bibliotheca* (Cod. 79).

[23] Malchus, frag. 14.

The often-mentioned alliance between Childeric's Franks and Aegidius rests on slender literary evidence (see Ch. 6); if it existed, it may have continued between Childeric and Syagrius, but if so its nature may well have changed over time. Alliances between Roman and barbarian leaders in this period are still seen in terms of *foedus* by some historians, but this is a misinterpretation; by the middle of the fifth century the balance of military and political power had changed significantly. It has been asserted that an alliance between Soissons and the Franks *must* have existed, to explain the continued existence of a Roman enclave (although this jars with the other view, connected with the archaeological evidence, that the existence of the Soissons enclave blocked Salian expansion for a generation or so). It has also been argued that the alliance was of more benefit to the Franks than to Aegidius and Syagrius and enhanced Childeric's personal prestige.[24]

The *Vita Genovefae*, now believed to have been written *c*. AD 520,[25] includes material important to any assessment of the extent and nature of the Frankish presence in Gaul at this time. There is some reason to believe that Genovefa was of higher social status than she is given in later popular French tradition.[26] It has also been suggested that she was 'de la noblesse franque et une famille de hauts militaires romains'.[27] This might explain her influential position in Gallo-Roman

[24] Périn and Feffer (1987: i, 106, 108); Drinkwater, paper given to the Oxford Conference on Gregory of Tours (1995).

[25] There has been protracted argument on the date (involving, among others, Krusch, Duchesne, and Kurth), which is covered in detail by Heinzelmann and Poulin (1986: 14–19), and Griffe (1964–6: ii, 53–4). Heinzelmann and Poulin (1986: 53) suggest that the author was a clerk or monk from Tours, and that the work may have been commissioned by Clothild, the wife of Clovis.

[26] According to the *Vita* (50) she owned land at Nanterre, acted as a local secular leader (12, 35, etc.), was instrumental in the construction of St. Denis (17–18), and travelled about (to Meaux (28), Tours (45), Troyes (37), Orleans (42), either Lyons or Laon (25), and Arcis (35–6)), as well as having great influence with both Roman and Frankish notables, in this period particularly striking in a woman.

[27] Heinzelmann and Poulin (1986: 81–6, 98). The basis for this is that her name is Germanic, while her parents' names, 'Severus' and 'Gerontia', are Roman, and, while there are many examples of individuals of Germanic descent taking Roman names, there are no examples at this time of those of Roman descent taking, or giving to their children, barbarian names. That her

society *and* with Childeric and Clovis, although is not essential
to do so, as charismatic religious figures could at this time have
huge prestige, as with Severinus in Noricum and Ennodius in
Italy.

The account of Genovefa's life most famously includes her
spiritual and practical leadership of the Parisian citizens during
Attila's invasion, but also touches on the saint's dealings with
Franks, in one case specifically with Childeric:

> I am totally unable to express how much the respected Childeric, when
> he was King of the Frankish peoples, esteemed her. Once, concerned
> that Genovefa would rescue some defeated enemies whom he was
> intending to execute, he left the city and ordered the gates shut.
> [But] when the king's intention reached Genovefa by a faithful mes-
> senger, she speedily hastened to save their lives. Great was the people's
> wonder to see the gate of the city unlock without a key, at the touch of
> her hand. And thus, catching up with the king, she was able to prevail
> on him not to carry out his intention of cutting off the heads of his
> captives.[28]

Although not stated, it seems most likely that this city is Paris,
though, as this episode follows an account of Genovefa travelling to either Lyons or Laon,[29] it might be elsewhere. If Paris,
then the *Vita* tells us that, at an uncertain date, Childeric was in

family were high-ranking military they have deduced from the combination of
the name and her apparent high status in the *Vita*, and it is considered that a
Frankish background is both the most likely in northern Gaul and explains her
influence with Childeric and Clovis. Her father could have been retired and
settled in Nanterre by the time of his daughter's birth (*c.* AD 420), having been
connected either with the defence of the Rhine or the usurpation of Constantine III (one of whose generals, incidentally, was named 'Gerontius'). The
theory is very attractive, but inevitably hypothetical.

[28] *Vita Genovefae* 26: 'Cum esset gentiles Childericus rex Francorum
veneratione qua eum dilexit effari nequeo ut vice quadam ne vinctus
quos interemere cogitabat Genuvefa [*sic*] abreperet egrediens urbem Pari-
siorum portam claudi precepit. Adubi ad Genovefa per fidus internuntius
regis deliberatio pervenit, convestim [*sic*] ad liberandas animas properans
direxit. Non minimum populi mirantes fuit spectaculum quemadmodem se
porta civitatis inter manus eius sine clave reseravit. Sicque regem consecuta ne
vinctorum capita amputarentur obtenuit.'

[29] The text reads *Lugdunensis*. Heinzelmann and Poulin (1986: 22, 101)
make a case for Laon (*Lugdunum Clavatum* in the sixth century), closer to Paris
(and possibly in Frankish territory). They associate this journey with her
suggested Frankish connections (see n. 27).

a position of power there but not how this came about—whether as hostile occupier or as an ally of a Gallo-Roman authority.[30] The chapter that follows tells how Genovefa was known to St. Simeon Stylites, who made enquiries about her with merchants travelling between the East and Gaul, even conveying his greetings to her.[31] If one could be sure that the episodes of Genovefa's life were related in chronological order, this would set the date when Childeric was in Paris at prior to AD 459/60, when Saint Simeon died,[32] and, since Childeric became ruler of the Franks *c.* AD 456, to the second half of that decade. Unfortunately, although the *Vita* is organized overall to move from the saint's birth to her death, some episodes seem to be grouped together schematically, and one gets the impression that, typically, the author was not certain of, or not interested in, a strictly chronological sequence. The most that one can safely say is that the episode is more likely to have been in the late AD 450s or 460s, rather than later in Genovefa's long career, and hence relates to Aegidius' dealings with the Franks rather than Syagrius'.

Further on in the narrative is another reference to Franks:

At that time then, when Paris was enduring a siege, of twice five years as they say, by the Franks, the countryside of that city suffered such a famine that several people are known to have perished of hunger. It happened, however, that Genovefa set out with a naval party[?][33] to the town of Arcis-sur-Aube for the collection of *annona*.[34]

[30] Périn suggested he was a subordinate of Syagrius (Périn and Feffer (1987: i, 108)), and wondered whether he may have been involved in operations against the Saxon pirates. Daly (1994: 627) proposed that Aegidius had granted him administrative authority over Belgica II, and that his various appearances in northern Gaul (and Paris) were due to 'administrative journeys'; which seems a rather unlikely idea.

[31] *Vita Genovefae* 27.

[32] Smith and Wace (1877–87: iv, 679). Simeon was famous and attracted pilgrims from as far as Spain and Britain.

[33] Heinzelmann and Poulin (1986: 44) take *navali effectione* to mean that Genovefa was authorized to utilize the official late-Roman transport system (the *evectio*); however, it seems more likely that the meaning is much less specific.

[34] *Vita Genovefae* 35: 'Tempore igitur, quo opsidionem Parisius bis quinos, ut aint, annos a Francis perpessa est, pagum eiusdem urbis ita inaedia adflixerat, ut nonnulli fame interisse nuscantur. Factum est autem ut Genovefa in Arciacinse opido navali effectione ad comparandam annonam proficisceretur.'

From its position in the narrative of the *Vita*, this siege and famine may be of later date than the episode in which Childeric was involved. It could even date to the early years of Clovis' reign rather than that of his father, perhaps even to the time of the defeat of Syagrius.[35] A continuous investment of the city for ten years is out of the question, and *opsidio* should perhaps be translated as encirclement rather than siege.[36] The period of 'twice five years' may echo the traditional length of the siege of Troy. Probably, the Franks were a sporadic or regular seasonal problem in the whole region for about a decade, possibly besieging or capturing the city on one or more occasions.

Similar situations occurred in Noricum, where populations were normally safe within city walls[37] but the disruption of agriculture caused by the barbarian presence in the surrounding countryside made their position untenable.[38] In the case of Paris, it was apparently the country people rather than the city dwellers who suffered food shortages. In response to the famine Genovefa travelled to Arcis, which is about sixty miles east of Paris, to collect *annona*. It is debatable what this *annona* involved: more probably the collection of local taxation in kind by the *civitas* authorities than an official authorization to collect imperial dues. The fact that we are told that on the way Genovefa miraculously destroyed two 'variously coloured monsters' is a warning that this material must be used with caution.[39] Saint Genovefa lived to a great age, dying in about AD 500,

---

[35] Heinzelmann and Poulin (1986: 101–2, citing K. F. Werner (1984: 298ff.)) date the beginning of the blockade to *c.* AD 476, to an alliance between Childeric and Odovacer, and believe that it occurred in the context of conflict between Childeric and Syagrius, caused because the existence of Syagrius' kingdom hindered Childeric's ambitions for expansion.

[36] Heinzelmann and Poulin (1986: 102 n. 475): 'Pour opsidio dans le sens "d'encerclement" voir *Thesaurus linguae Latinae*, IX 2, col 224–6; en conséquence, la situation décrite en V.G. 35 est à comprendre comme état d'occupation de certaines régions autour de Paris, pendant que le pagus de Paris lui-même était sans doute toujours sous contrôle de Soissons.'

[37] As Wes (1967: 170) has pointed out, the ubiquitous walling of cities left the countryside exposed.

[38] See Eugippius, *Vita Severini*, chs. 4, 26.

[39] While in Arcis, Genovefa cured the wife of a tribune called Passavius (*Vita Genovefae* 36). His title might indicate some existing Roman military organization there, although *tribunus* was used very loosely in the late imperial period.

towards the end of Clovis' reign. Just before the conclusion of the *Vita* she is described as having great influence over Clovis, who is called 'fearful king by right of war'.[40]

Procopius' *History of the Gothic War*, on the origins of the Franks, has sometimes been used as a source for the relationship between Franks and Gallo-Romans in northern Gaul. In book 5 of his history, when the Franks enter the war in Italy, he describes their background. This includes references to the 'Arborychi', generally thought to mean the Armorici (not the inhabitants of the Breton peninsula, but of the old *Tractus Armoricanus* stretching across northern Gaul):

the Arborychi had become soldiers of the Romans. And the Germans wishing to make this people subject to themselves, since their territory adjoined their own and they had changed the government under which they had lived from of old, began to plunder their land, and being eager to make war marched against them with their whole people … since the Germans were not able to overcome them by force they wished to win them over and make the two peoples kin by intermarriage. This suggestion the Arborychi received not at all unwillingly for both, as it happened, were Christians. And in this way they were united into one people …

Now other Roman soldiers, also had been stationed at the frontiers of Gaul to serve as guards … having no means of returning to Rome and … unwilling to yield to their enemy who were Arian, gave themselves together with their military standards and the land which they had long been guarding for the Romans to the Arborychi and Germans[41]

Although the broad elements of Procopius' account do reflect the general course of events in Gaul, to use it as evidence for the details and nature of the Frankish conquest of northern Gaul (still more for its chronology)[42] is investing it with more authority than seems wise. Procopius' knowledge of events in the West (outside Italy in his own time) is notoriously unreliable. It is

---

[40] *Vita Genovefae* 56. This passage also describes her interceding with him to pardon those whom he had imprisoned in an *ergastulum* (i.e. a prison usually associated with slaves).

[41] Procopius, *Wars* V, xii, 12–17 (Dewing's translation). See below (p. 158) for the end of this passage.

[42] See Bachrach (1970: 21–31).

obviously tempting to equate the Roman soldiers of the second paragraph with remnants of the Gallic army, or the forces of Aegidius and Syagrius, but the most that one can safely say is that reports of them may have contributed to the hearsay that reached Procopius. It is, however, of interest to compare Procopius' account with the other sixth-century account of fifth-century northern Gaul, that of Gregory of Tours; illustrating how the past has been dealt with by two authors working in very different genres of historical writing.

In the *Historiae*, following the historical material discussed in the chapter on Aegidius, come seven chapters which cover ecclesiastical matters and Euric's conquests and persecutions in southern Gaul. Gregory then reports that Childeric died and that his son Clovis ruled in his place, or after him.[43] He continues:

Now in the fifth year of his [Childeric's] reign[44] Syagrius the King of the Romans, son of Aegidius, had his seat[45] at the city of Soissons, which the previously mentioned Aegidius had formerly possessed. Clovis, together with his kinsman Ragnachar, who also held a kingdom, came against him [and] challenged him to make ready on the field of battle. In fact he [Syagrius] did not hesitate or fear to resist. And so both sides [fought] against each other and Syagrius, perceiving that his army was shattered, turned in flight and slipped away swiftly to King Alaric in Toulouse.[46] Clovis sent word to Alaric, that he must return him, otherwise he would initiate a war against him if he offered protection to him. He [Alaric] being fearful [and] not wishing to incur the anger of the Franks, for the Goths are naturally cowardly,[47] handed the defeated Syagrius over to the envoys. When Clovis had

---

[43] Greg. Tur. *Historiae* 11, 27: 'His ita gestis, mortuo Childerico, regnavit Chlodevechus, filius eius, pro eo.'

[44] i.e. AD 485/6. For discussion of the dates of Clovis' reign see Périn and Feffer (1987: i, 153).

[45] The word *sedes* can be translated in a number of ways, ranging from 'residence', or 'abode', to 'seat', or even 'throne'. It is used elsewhere in the *Historiae* in connection with kings or emperors, or bishops and other important religious figures.

[46] Why did Syagrius flee to the Visigoths? Presumably a case of 'my enemy's enemy'?

[47] Gregory consistently portrays the Arian Visigoths in an unflattering light.

received him, he threw him into captivity, seized his kingdom [and] ordered him to be put to the sword in secret.[48]

This story is quite detailed and specific. While there is, without doubt, some oversimplification and exaggeration, it is unlikely that Gregory, or oral tradition, could have developed it in the absence of *any* factual basis, especially as this victory was the first of Clovis' conquests. Gregory does not mention a motive for the Frankish attack. In James's model, Clovis, the ruler of northern Gaul, was putting down a rebellion, although the tone and details of the account as it stands hardly suggest the suppression of a rebellious local official. Périn has suggested that Clovis wanted to take Belgica II before the Rhineland Franks did so.[49] In fact, we hardly need to seek a specific reason for the attack; given the vulnerability of any Gallo-Roman enclave in the AD 480s, and the nature of the Franks and their new king, it was probably inevitable.

According to Gregory, Syagrius met Clovis in open battle, although he would surely have been safer remaining within the walls of his city and letting Clovis undertake a siege.[50] Kurth thought this was because Gregory's story was taken from oral tradition, with its convention of single combat between opposing leaders;[51] but the alternative, a successful storming of the city of Soissons, would surely have been remembered, and such

---

[48] Greg. Tur. *Historiae* II, 27: 'Anno autem quinto regni eius Siacrius Romanorum rex, Egidi filius, apud civitatem Suessones, quam quondam supra memoratus Egidius tenuerat, sedem habebat. Super quem Chlodovechus cum Ragnechario, parente suo, quia et ipse regnum tenebat, veniens, campum pugnae praeparare deposcit. Sed nec iste distolit ac resistere metuit. Itaque inter se utrisque pugnantibus, Syagrius elisum cernens exercitum, terga vertit et ad Alaricum regem Tholosa curso veluci perlabitur. Chlodovechus vero ad Alarico mittit, ut eum redderiit, alioquin noverit, sibi bellum ob eius retentationem inferri. Ad ille metuens, ne propter eum iram Francorum incurrerit, ut Gothorum pavere mos est, vinctum legatis tradedit. Quem Chlodovechus receptum custodiae mancipare praecipit; regnoque eius accepto, eum gladio clam feriri.'

[49] Périn and Feffer (1987: i, 138).

[50] It is normally thought that the battle took place at Soissons, but Dill (1926: 79) places the battle (without, infuriatingly, giving his reasons) at Noyon, ten miles north of Soissons, on the edge of its old territory, where the road between Amiens and Soissons crossed the Oise.

[51] Kurth (1893: 216).

an action was, in any case, extremely rare in this period. Syagrius was, it seems, confident that he could defeat Clovis in open
battle, which suggests that their forces were fairly evenly
matched (see Ch. 10 on this), and that Clovis' victory was not
assured. That some Frankish kings remained neutral substanti-
ates this. At least two refused to join Clovis against Syagrius, and
later paid dearly for it.[52] It is very possible that there was an
alliance between Syagrius and Franks unfriendly to Clovis.

Clovis clearly went to some trouble to get Syagrius back into
his own hands, but why did he wait to kill him in secret later?
This aspect of the story would not seem to come from oral
tradition glorifying Clovis, in which one might expect Clovis
to kill Syagrius heroically in battle. Behind this account may be
complex political manoeuvring concerned with the consolidation of the Frankish conquest and Clovis' position. It is possible
that Syagrius was not surrendered by the Goths until some
years after his defeat (Gregory giving no date), perhaps in
AD 493, when a marriage alliance was arranged between Theoderic of Italy and the sister of Clovis, with the Visigoths making
overtures of peace to Clovis and handing Syagrius over.[53] There
seems no overwhelming reason to date the surrender of Syagrius to AD 493; however, it certainly remains true that we do
not know when exactly it took place.

Immediately following the defeat of Syagrius in the *Historiae*
is the famous story of the vase of Soissons,[54] the context of
which is the plundering of a large number of Gallo-Roman
churches by Clovis' troops, and subsequent acrimony during
the sharing out of the loot at Soissons, which was apparently
Clovis' headquarters at that time. Later versions say that the
vessel (and other liturgical items) was stolen from the cathedral
at Reims, and that it was Bishop Remigius of Reims who requested its return.[55]

---

[52] Greg. Tur. *Historiae* II, 41.

[53] Wolfram (1988: 191). He linked this to Clovis' second expansion from
the Seine to the Loire (see below), which he hence dates to AD 493. This
argument is used by Wolfram to disprove the contention of Alaric's timidity.

[54] Greg. Tur. *Historiae* II, 27.

[55] Fredegar, III, 16; Hincmar, *Vita Sancti Remigii* XI; Flodoard, *Historia
Remensis Ecclesiae* XII.

That Clovis used Soissons as his base for some time is suggested by a lengthy account in the *Liber Historiae Francorum*
(not present in the *Historiae*) of the courtship and marriage
of Clovis and Clothild,[56] the niece of Gundobad, which is
set in Soissons.[57] The *Liber* adds a couple of touches to Gregory's account that reflect the milieu in which it was written:
Clovis fighting against Syagrius in the battle;[58] and his
taking possession not only of his kingdom but also his
treasure house (*thesauros*), which may reflect a tradition local
to Soissons.[59]

In the conventional historical version, by defeating Syagrius
Clovis won not only Soissons and its territory but the whole of
northern Gaul as far as the borders of the Visigothic and Breton
lands. His victory over Syagrius is regarded as removing the
main barrier to Frankish expansion. It is also often held that
Clovis took over the functioning Roman administration of Syagrius' kingdom, and this amalgamation of Roman and Frankish
systems has been seen as an important element in the creation of
France. At *civitas* level there was some continuity into the
Merovingian period; but it would be a mistake to see the Frankish kings as inheriting a fully functioning Roman bureaucracy in
northern Gaul, nor is such a view necessary to explain the
existence of elements of continuity.

An important letter written by Remigius, dating to this early
stage in Clovis' rise to power, has survived:

---

[56] An important figure in these negotiations was Aurelianus, Clovis' legate,
who appears in several episodes of Clovis' early career described by the *Liber*;
for example *Liber Historiae Francorum* 11, 12, 14, 15. Although some have
considered him a legendary figure (see Gerberding (1987: 33)), he fits quite
well into the context of the time. His appearance in the *Liber* may be connected
to the fact that he was rewarded with a dukedom in the region in which it was
written. It is conceivable that his descendents had links with monasteries
connected to the author; also that local traditions about the founder of the
family fortunes are the basis of these entries.

[57] *Liber Historiae Francorum* 12: 'accepta Chrotchilde, cum magna gaudio
ad Chlodovechum regem adduxerunt eam Suessionis civitate in Francia'.

[58] *Liber Historiae Francorum* 9: 'Convenientesque ad bellum illis inter se
fortiter conpugnantibus'.

[59] *Liber Historiae Francorum* 9. See also Gerberding (1987: 146–59) on
where the *Liber* was written, and p. 150 on the treasury at Berny-Rivière.

To [our] distinguished lord and most worthy king, Clovis, from Bishop Remigius.[60]

A momentous report reaches us—that you have undertaken the government of Belgica II. It is not new that you should begin to be what your parents[61] ever were. The next pressing matter is that, now that through your humble endeavour you have reached the summit, the judgement of God should not waver from you, because of your merit, for, as is commonly said, the deeds of a man show what he really is. You must summon to you advisors who are able to embellish your fame.[62] Your achievement should be unpolluted and honourable, and you should in future confer with your bishops, and always return to their advice, for if you and they come together in amity, your province will be better able to stand together. Encourage your subjects, relieve the afflicted, assist widows, feed orphans . . . Justice should issue from your mouth, nothing should be exacted from the poor or foreigners [or, 'landless'?] . . . Let your jurisdiction be accessible to all, so that none is turned away in despair. [With] the wealth that you possess from your parents liberate captives and remove the yoke of servitude from them: if anyone comes into your presence, let him not feel a stranger. Jest with the young men [but] consult with the old men, if you wish to rule—govern with honour.[63]

---

[60] Remigius was Bishop of Reims from *c.* AD 460 to *c.* 532/3. As a leading churchman he would have been closely involved in political events in Belgica II, of which Reims had been the provincial capital. On Remigius in general see Schäferdiek (1983: 256–78) and Griffe (1964–6: ii, 308 ff.).

[61] *Parentes* is rather vague and could possibly mean relatives or ancestors.

[62] A (not very subtle) hint that Remigius himself might be summoned?

[63] Remigius, *Ep.* 11: 'Domino insigni et meritis magnifico Hlodoveo regi, Remigius Episcopus: Rumor ad nos magnum pervenit, administrationem vos Secundum Belgice suscepisse. Non est novum, ut coeperis esse, sicut parentes tui semper fuerunt: hoc inprimis agendum, ut Domini iudicium a te non vacillet, ubi tui meriti, qui per industriam humilitatis tuae ad summum culminisque pervenit, quia, quod vulgus dicitur, [ex fine] actus hominis probatur. Consiliarios tibi adhibere debes, qui famam tuam possent ornare. Et beneficium tuum castum et honestum esse debet, et sacerdotibus tuis debebis deferre et ad eorum consilia semper recurre, quodsi tibi bene cum illis convenerit, provincia tua melius potest constare. Civos tuos erige, adflictos releva, viduas fove, orfanos nutre . . . Iustitia ex ore vestro procedat, nihil sit sperandum de pauperes vel peregrinis . . . Praetorium tuum omnibus pateatur, ut nullus exinde tristis abscedat. Paternas quascunque opes possides, captivos exinde liberabis et a iugo servatutis absolvas: si quis in conspectu vestro venerit peregrinum se esse non sentiat. Cum iuvenibus ioca, cum senibus tracta, si vis

When this letter was written is uncertain; it is sometimes thought to have been after the defeat of Syagrius,[64] sometimes round about A D 481, when Clovis came to the throne on Childeric's death.[65] The tone of the letter and absence of condolences suggest that it was not written immediately on Childeric's death; a better context might be a little later, when Clovis had succeeded in establishing his authority over a large part of Belgica II, perhaps following a struggle for power among Childeric's kin.

This letter has been seen as an illustration of continuity in Roman administration; but, apart from the references to the province of Belgica II, there is really nothing that could not as well apply to a medieval king as a Roman governor. The impression of continuity is largely produced by Remigius' hortatorial, anachronistic, and rather patronizing style. Its ambiguity may also be a result of Remigius' need to use tactful and diplomatically vague language in a situation fraught with the difficulties felt by a Gallo-Roman bishop in the face of a powerful pagan barbarian king. The letter as a whole reflects hopes and ideals rather than actuality.

More specifically, James considered this letter to show that 'Childeric had the administration of all Belgica Secunda', and that Remigius implies by his 'always' that Childeric had done so for some years.[66] Thus Clovis inherited Roman authority as well as Germanic kingship. This (as previously mentioned) would mean that Syagrius was some sort of local administrator under Frankish overlordship.[67] There are some problems with this interpretation. First, that Clovis gained kingship of this

regnare nobilis iudicare.' In making this translation I have referred to that by Professor Thomas Charles-Edwards (internal Oxford University special-subject document).

[64] See Bury (1923: 244–5); Tessier (1964: 83–4).

[65] See Daly (1994: 632).

[66] James (1988: 65). He translates the crucial sentence as: 'a strong report has come to us that you have taken over the administration of the Second Belgic Province. There is nothing new in that you now begin to be what your parents always were' (taken from the translation by J. N. Hillgarth (*Christianity and Paganism* (1986: 76))). James does not give a translation of the rest of the letter, nor the Latin original.

[67] James (1988: 65–71).

territory by peaceful inheritance from his father is contradicted
by the contemporary *Vita Genovefae*, which calls Clovis 'king
by right of war'.[68] More importantly, as can be seen above, the
wording of the letter is more ambiguous than James's interpretation of it. It is also possible to interpret the crucial phrase as
meaning that Childeric had held a position in Belgica II, allied
to or subordinate to Aegidius or Syagrius, that gave him local
powers over the population (see above on his activities in
Paris) while retaining tribal kingship (for which there are
fourth-century precedents). Alternatively, it is perfectly possible that the phrase simply means that Clovis had become King
of the Franks, controlling part of the province, just as his
parents or ancestors had been before him.

Also, the recorded plundering of many of the churches of
Belgica II by Clovis' army at the time of his defeat of Syagrius[69]
seems surprising if, as James suggests, Clovis and Childeric had
long been ruling the province in Roman fashion, and indeed co-
operating with the Church there.[70] Moreover, Clovis could not
have inherited the whole of Belgica II as James suggested. Apart
from the possible Roman enclave at Soissons, we know of another Frankish kingdom in Belgica II based on Cambrai, under
Ragnachar, and the lands of another Salian king, Chararic, may
also have been inside the province.[71]

If James was correct in saying that Syagrius was a subordinate
of Childeric and Clovis, then, although he does not pursue the

[68] *Vita Genovefae* 56: 'rex bellorum iure tremendus'.

[69] Greg. Tur. *Historiae* II, 27.

[70] As suggested by James (1988: 65–6).

[71] Greg. Tur. *Historiae* II, 42. Clovis defeated Ragnachar in battle after
suborning his *leudes*, then executed him and his brother Richar, who is also
described as *rex*. A third brother, Rigomer, was executed in Le Mans (*Historiae*
II, 42). If he was in power at Le Mans it would be good evidence of the Franks
being well to the West at an early date, but Gregory simply records it as the
place of his execution. Le Mans may have been one of Clovis' headquarters
during his push westward. For Chararic see Greg. Tur. (*Historiae* II, 41).
Among Clovis' other victims was the Frankish King of Cologne (II, 39).
Longnon (1878: 83 n. 6) cites a 17th-century documentary source for Chararic
being ruler of a kingdom based on Thérouanne (Tarvenna/Tervenna), an
important location in the road network. The *Notitia Dignitatum* (Oc. XLI,
16) records a *Praefectus militum Menapiorum* at Tabernis, which is probably
Tarvenna, so it is conceivable that the origin of a Frankish 'kingdom' there, if it
existed, was a military settlement of *laeti* or federates.

point, the battle between Clovis and Syagrius resulted from an act of rebellion, and his position was wildly exaggerated by Gregory (his use of the title *rex* being in this case preposterous). As seen above, the details of Syagrius' defeat in no way support the idea that Clovis was putting down a rebellious subject. Were James correct, Remigius' letter could not date to Syagrius' defeat, since the subduing of a minor rebel would hardly be described in the terms used in the first line of the letter (nor would Remigius need tidings or rumours when his own cathedral was being looted!). Finally, how the son of Aegidius, *magister militum per Gallias*, could have ended up as a city governor for a barbarian king remains unexplained.

Even if Belgica II *was* Frankish in Childeric's reign, the rest of northern Gaul (the parts of the old province of *Lugdunensis* known in the late empire as the *Tractus Armoricanus*) remains to be accounted for. Although the conventional accounts see these regions as falling into Clovis' hands in one fell swoop through his victory at Soissons, the process may in fact have been more protracted and untidy. The *Liber Historiae Francorum*, in material independent of Gregory, states explicitly that Clovis' conquest of North Gaul had two stages; first to the Seine, and then to the Loire: 'Also at that time, Clovis enlarged his kingdom, extending it as far as the Seine. At a later time he occupied as far as the River Loire. And Aurelianus received *Castrum Melidunensem* and all of that region as a dukedom.'[72]

Northern Gaul did not immediately settle peacefully under Clovis' rule. Several Frankish rulers were later executed by Clovis.[73] About a decade after Syagrius' fall, the city of Verdun was still holding out against Clovis, finally submitting after a

[72] *Liber Historiae Francorum* 14: 'Eo tempore dilatavit Chlodovechus amplificans regnum suum usque Sequanam. Sequenti tempore usque Ligere fluvio occupavit accepitque Aurilianus Castrum Malidunensem [or 'Milidunensem'] omnemque ducatum regionis illius.' (For Aurelianus see above on Clovis' marriage.) *Castrum Malidunensem* is probably Melun, just to the south-east of Paris, described elsewhere as *Mediolanense castrum* (for this identification see Longnon (1878: 468–9)). It is not entirely clear whether Aurelianus gained his dukedom in the first or second stage of conquest. Interestingly, the area south of Paris as far as Melun has a most unusual degree of survival of Roman roads and boundaries, with a high percentage of the Roman villas developing into villages (Percival (1976: 180–1)).
[73] Greg. Tur. *Historiae* II, 40, 41, 42.

siege;[74] and Nantes (occupied by a Gallic rather than Breton population) was also resisting Frankish attack during Clovis' reign.[75] There were probably other unrecorded incidents of resistance and revolt. Nevertheless, by the AD 490s northern Gaul was sufficiently under Clovis' control for him to turn his attention elsewhere; first attacking the Thuringians and the Alamanni to the east, then the Visigothic and Burgundian kingdoms, leading eventually to the extension of his rule over most of Gaul.[76]

THE RELIABILITY OF GREGORY OF TOURS

It is from Gregory's *Historiae* that historians have taken and elaborated the idea of a kingdom of Soissons, ruled over by Syagrius. The controversial assertion that Aegidius was 'King of the Franks' also comes from Gregory. The question of the reliability of Gregory as a historian of the fifth century is therefore an important one. Gregory's detailed and colourful narrative style compares attractively with that of the chronicles (the more usual historical format in this period) and it is easy to be seduced into taking a very positive view of him as a historian. There are obvious problems in using the *Historiae* for the fifth century, though: the distance in time at which he wrote, and the paucity of written records available to him. And, naturally, Gregory wrote with hindsight, from the viewpoint

[74] *Vita Euspicii* 3–4. The same siege is reported in a *Vita* of Maximinus, Abbot of Micy, according to Musset (1993: 75).

[75] Greg. Tur. *Glor. Mart.* 59 describes a miracle at Nantes (performed by Rogatianus and Donatus) when, during the reign of King Clovis, barbarians besieged the city. After about sixty days the enemy army was struck with terror and left the region because a miracle had occurred involving Chillo the commander of the army, who had not then 'been reborn by water and the Holy Spirit'. The last sentence strongly suggests that the tactfully unspecified barbarians were Franks, and that their commander later followed Clovis' lead by being baptized. It is possible that the army was Saxon (Kurth (1923: i, 261–2)), but they were probably not so numerous and organized as this.

[76] Clovis' conquest of Gaul took only about thirty years, in contrast to the Germanic conquest of England, which took 100–150 years. This is not an appropriate place to explore the reasons for this, but it is clear that the difference in time-scale radically affected the subsequent development of the ex-provinces.

of a sixth-century bishop, of Gallo-Roman descent, but living under an established Frankish monarchy. Inevitably he sees historical causation in strongly Christian moralistic terms. Some scholars have suggested that the *Historiae* also suffers from some less obvious and more misleading characteristics.

It has been assumed in the past that in the *Historiae* Gregory wished to set the Franks in the context of universal history and to show them in a positive light[77] (difficult though this was, given their own behavioural and moral norms), whereas the work is now considered to be a general Gallic history with a strong ecclesiastical theme.[78] Some historians (including James) have argued that Gregory's particular brief was the glorification of Clovis, both as the founder of the Merovingian dynasty and as the first Frankish king to accept the Catholic faith; and that to this end he deliberately distorted facts.[79] If correct, this would have implications for Gregory's material on Syagrius and Soissons.

Gregory's account of Clovis, while giving him some credit, is certainly not eulogy. Apart from approving gifts to the Church, there are only two occasions on which he praises Clovis: when he comments, at his birth, that he grew to be a 'great and distinguished warrior';[80] and when he comments that Clovis 'prostrated himself to God every day his enemies [fell] into his hands, and he increased his realm because he walked righteously and wisely in His presence and did what was pleasing in His eyes'.[81] The context of the second comment is Gregory's report of Clovis' bloody conquest of the Frankish kingdom of Cologne, in which he described in detail the king's treachery and mendacity. Gregory either took the simplistic view that Clovis' con-

---

[77] See Wallace-Hadrill (1962: 60–1).

[78] Goffart (1987: 57–76); Wood (1994a: p. i). See also p. 78 on the title of the *Historiae*.

[79] See James (1988: 71). According to James, who wishes to remove the kingdom of Soissons from history altogether, Gregory's account of late fifth-century events is completely distorted by his desire to glorify Clovis. It would be interesting to know whether James's view on the unreliability of Gregory arose from his views on the kingdom of Soissons, or vice versa.

[80] Greg. Tur. *Historiae* II, 12: 'magnus et pugnatur egregius'.

[81] Greg. Tur. *Historiae* II, 40: 'prosternebat enim cotidie Deus hostes eius sub manu ipsius et augebat regnum eius, eo quod ambularet recto corde coram eo et faceret quae placita erant in oculis eius'.

version (and attacks on Arians) excused the most dastardly behaviour, or he was perhaps, as elsewhere, being ironic.

In the rest of his account of Clovis' actions (mainly nasty and violent) and in his report of Clovis' death there is no other favourable comment. He relates many incidents which could hardly have resounded to Clovis' credit, even among the Merovingians; including the murder of blood relations, incitement to patricide, and the bribery and incitement of sworn followers to turn on their lord. Gregory also made no attempt to gloss over the fact that Clovis was born as the result of adultery, which he certainly disapproved of (and the Franks disfavoured in the case of a married woman). The deeds of Clovis must have been well remembered, and it is unlikely that Gregory had scope for drastic emendation; but he could easily have omitted or glossed over some of the more unsavoury episodes, had he so desired. Gregory was perfectly capable of presenting a sophisticated picture of a man who wins earthly success because of his conversion, and yet commits many evil deeds, reported by Gregory in a neutral or ironic manner. In fact, he had no need to distort or invent in connection with Clovis. As Goffart pointed out, saints and martyrs not warrior kings were Gregory's heroes.[82]

Some of Gregory's information on the fifth century seems to have come from oral tradition. This may have been Gallo-Roman as well as Frankish. Wood has pointed to Gregory's use of oral traditions from within his own family (particularly evident in bk. 3).[83] Gregory also used many different secular and ecclesiastical written sources (some named, some not). Book 2, on the fifth century, uses a variety of religious and secular sources: extracts from Roman histories, hagiographic works, consular lists, letters, biblical quotation, oral tradition, and at least one chronicle or annal, all linked by Gregory's own words.

Did Gregory use any written records for his account of Clovis' early career? He quotes from a letter of consolation from Remigius of Reims to Clovis (whom Remigius baptized), and it is known that he had read an early account (now lost) of

---

[82] Goffart (1988: 220).   [83] Wood (1994*a*: 39).

Remigius' life.[84] (From this he may well have taken material, including his story of the 'vase of Soissons', if the bishop involved was indeed Remigius.) It is quite possible that Gregory's account of Clovis' conversion was based on this *Vita* (and also possibly Remigius' own writings), and these may have referred to other events in Clovis' early career, including the part played by Syagrius and Soissons (especially given Remigius' family connection with Soissons through his brother Principius).

THE TITLES ATTRIBUTED TO AEGIDIUS AND SYAGRIUS

Given that Gregory's account is not sheer fabrication, but grounded in some fact, the next question that must be addressed is his use of the term *rex*, and its significance. James argued that Gregory used the term because of his unsophisticated misunderstanding of his sources, perhaps because he lived under a Frankish monarchy.[85] One thing that makes this dubious is that earlier in book 2 Gregory included some competent research in the written records available to him on the origins of kingship among the Franks, and in which he comments on the various terminology used by Roman historians to describe earlier Frankish leaders.[86] He quotes from several authors, clearly discriminating between *reges*, *regales* (subkings or petty kings), and *duces*, trying to reconcile the references, and recording his exasperation at the confusion of terms. He can, therefore, be expected to have been careful in his own use of the term *rex*. Moreover, Gregory was intelligent, well educated, and familiar with much Latin literature; and must have been well aware both that forms of rule other than monarchy existed and that *rex* was not a normal title among Roman leaders.

---

[84] Greg. Tur. *Historiae* II, 31. This *Vita*, probably written by a cleric at Reims, was lost by the time that Hincmar wrote his *Vita c.* AD 880, although he searched for it at the time. Another early work concerning Remigius, erroneously attributed to Venantius Fortunatus, included only theological matters (Demouy (1997: 142–4)).

[85] James (1988: 71 n. 11, citing Bloch (1963: i, 75–6)).

[86] Greg. Tur. *Historiae* II, 9.

Fanning's study of the titles accorded to Aegidius and Syagrius argued that the assertions by Merovingian authors that
both men were *reges Romanorum* have been wrongly rejected by
historians:[87] 'One tradition had [Aegidius] being accepted as
king over the Franks, while another named him "king of the
Romans". Aegidius was succeeded... by his son Syagrius...
who is not known by any traditional Roman title, but is called
"king of the Romans" by... Gregory of Tours.'[88]

The question of the range of titles used by the Merovingian
authors does demand closer examination. In the case of Syagrius, Gregory (as seen above) calls him *Romanorum rex* and
shortly afterwards refers to his *regnum*.[89] Chapter 8 of *Liber
Historiae Francorum* refers to him succeeding to his father's
regnum; in chapter 9 the 'B' tradition MS adds *rex Romanorum*
after his name; and both 'A' and 'B' refer to him having a
regnum.[90] Fredegar, however, calls him *Syagrius Romanorum
patricius*.[91]

In the case of Aegidius Gregory twice calls him *magister
militum*,[92] he describes him as being chosen as *rex* by the
Franks,[93] but in noting his death he gives no title.[94] The *Liber
Historiae Francorum* does refer to Aegidius as *rex* in a rather
confused statement that: 'There was also, at this time, in that
part of Gaul, amongst the Romans, a King Egidius, sent by the
emperor.'[95] Later, Aegidius is twice referred to as *principem
Romanorum*.[96] In the *Liber*'s account of the Frankish attacks
on the Rhine and Aegidius' death (see Ch. 6), the 'A' tradition
refers to him as *Romanorum rex*, while the 'B' calls him *Roman-*

[87] Fanning (1992: 289–90).
[88] Fanning (1992: 289).
[89] Greg. Tur. *Historiae* II, 27.
[90] *Liber Historiae Francorum* 9.
[91] Fredegar, III, 15.
[92] Greg. Tur. *Historiae* II, 11, 12.
[93] Greg. Tur. *Historiae* II, 12.
[94] Greg. Tur. *Historiae* II, ch. 18 v. 9. (In his last reference to Aegidius
(translated above) the term *rex Romanorum* refers to Syagrius rather than to his
father.)
[95] *Liber Historiae Francorum* 6: 'erat quoque tunc in ista parte Galliarum ex
Romanis Egidius rex ab imperatore missus'. Some 'B'-tradition MSS add
miliciae after *rex*.
[96] *Liber Historiae Francorum* 7.

orum tirannus.[97] Fredegar (not mentioned by Fanning) calls Aegidius *comes.*[98] Hence, Fanning's assertion that *both* Syagrius and his father are called 'King of the Romans' relies on the references to Aegidius in the eighth-century *Liber Historiae Francorum.*

Fanning's study showed that the use of *rex* for a Roman is not unique to Aegidius and Syagrius, nor to Gregory of Tours.[99] Gregory uses *rex* once to describe the Emperor Decius,[100] and *regina* once for Helena the mother of Constantine.[101] Other late Roman authors also occasionally use *rex* for Roman emperors (and *regnum* for the empire) including Augustine, Venantius Fortunatus, Ennodius, Prosper, Sulpicius Severus, Hilary of Poitiers, Jordanes, and Orosius, and even writers in the classical tradition, such as Ammianus Marcellinus, who calls Julian *rex*, and Claudian, who occasionally uses the term for the Emperor Honorius. The wide range of Latin authors who sometimes use the terms *rex* and *regnum* suggests that, for literary reasons, it was permissible to make occasional use of these terms with the general sense of 'ruler' and 'dominion'.

Fanning deduced that because the term is sometimes used to describe emperors, this is clearly Gregory's meaning in using it for Aegidius and Syagrius.[102] This is in fact anything but clear. Apart from being false logic, it is not in accord with what we know of late fifth- and sixth-century politics. If Gregory's use of the term *rex* for Syagrius is meaningful at all, then it is more plausible that it equates with the obvious kings known to him, and constantly called so by him, than to emperors only referred to as *reges* extremely rarely.

As to Syagrius' actual title in the late AD 400s, there are three main possibilities. First, he could have taken the title of 'king', and been called so by both his barbarian and Gallo-Roman

[97] *Liber Historiae Francorum* 8. One MS in the 'B' tradition calls him *dux.*
[98] Fredegar, II, 56.
[99] Fanning (1992: 291–6).
[100] Greg. Tur. *Glor. Mart.* 94.
[101] Greg. Tur. *Glor. Mart.* 5.
[102] Fanning (1992: 296–7): 'it would be extremely rash to suggest that Aegidius and Syagrius were in fact Roman emperors but it is clear that Gregory of Tours and the *Liber Historiae Francorum* were using language that meant just that'.

neighbours and followers. Second, he was not called 'king' in his own lifetime, but this tradition developed within the couple of generations after his death (more probably through the medium of folk-tale or epic, rather than as an invention of Gregory of Tours). Third, he may have been known by a Roman title among his own people, but as 'king' by non-Romans, by analogy with their own rulers.[103] Syagrius is indeed called 'Patrician of the Romans' by Fredegar;[104] a surprising term for the compiler to use, and one which may conceivably have reached him from separate Gallo-Roman tradition. If Syagrius did use this title, it may have been because of its high, but general and somewhat ambiguous, status; possibly even to link himself to the powerful Italian patricians such as Ricimer.

Whether he was given the title of 'king' in his lifetime, or in later tradition, if Syagrius was indeed the independent ruler of a distinct geographical area, inherited from his father, then to describe him as a 'king' is not totally inappropriate now, and would not have been in the fifth and sixth centuries.

[103] Kurth (1893: 213–14) suggested *comes* or *dux*; Kaiser (1973: 140 and n. 377) *comes civitatem*.
[104] Fredegar, III, 15.

8

A Survey of the Material Evidence
for Northern Gaul

SETTLEMENT AND BURIAL EVIDENCE

This chapter is a brief, and necessarily superficial, description of
some of the relevant archaeological evidence for northern Gaul
in the period of Aegidius and Syagrius, with particular reference
to the city and region of Soissons. Archaeology shows that the
cities of northern and central Gaul suffered general, gradual, but
very real decline in the late empire and post-Roman periods.[1]
Continued occupation is presumed mainly on the basis of non-
archaeological evidence. Few rural sites show signs of continuity
of occupation and use through the late Roman and post-Roman
periods, although the older scenario of wholesale abandonment
and depopulation is now usually modified.[2]

In the conventional reconstructions, the River Somme and
the hills of the Ardennes have been envisaged as the boundary
between Frank and Gallo-Roman in the time of Aegidius and
Syagrius.[3] Such archaeological evidence as exists points to some
depopulation in the Ardennes in the fifth century AD. Early
'Germanic-type' scattered burials occur from the late fourth
century AD, often associated with late Roman hilltop strongholds.[4] New Frankish or Merovingian cemeteries appear in the
sixth century.

The administrative department of the Ardennes (to the
north-west of Soissons and Reims) has been comprehensively
investigated. Not only is there a dearth of fifth-century material,
but very few Roman cemeteries are found beyond the beginning
of the fifth century.[5] In the same area, but in completely differ-

---

[1] See Wightman (1977: 307).   [2] Whittaker (1994: 232).
[3] Wightman (1985: 304); Périn and Feffer (1987: i, 135; ii, 181).
[4] Todd (1992: 203–4).   [5] James (1979: 70).

ent locations, there are over one hundred Merovingian cemeteries, almost all of which are dated to after *c.* AD 530.[6] The best interpretation is that, even if the area continued to be farmed and inhabited by a reduced population, there was a period of decline and disruption in the fifth century AD.

The Aisne River valley, in which Soissons is situated, was (and is) agriculturally productive and well populated, and had a number of large Roman villa estates.[7] The archaeological record there, and in the valley of the Marne, shows that both remained prosperous in the fourth century. There are significant changes in the following century, both in the pattern of rural occupation and in the disappearance of regular military forts.[8] Of those cemeteries in Belgica II which show continuity of use, most are either in Lorraine or in the region around Soissons.[9]

Soissons itself was a prosperous, though not outstanding, *civitas* throughout the early empire. In common with most Gallic cities, walls were erected in the third century (encircling approximately twelve hectares, a common size) and there is some evidence for the movement of the wealthier citizens from the city to large villa estates in the surrounding countryside.[10] There were an unusually large number of late Gallo-Roman cemeteries close to the city, which show continuity of use through the late Roman and post-Roman periods,[11] suggesting continued occupation of the city, and its territory, by a comparatively large population. This may be connected to the fact that Soissons was the site of an imperial *fabrica*.[12] There is also evidence for continuity of settlement and agriculture in the

[6] Ibid.

[7] Roblin (1978: 274) and a personal visit to Berny-Rivière and to the Musée de Soissons. Roblin writes: 'si les Romains ont possédé Soissons jusqu'à la fin du Ve siècle, c'est bien parce que cette région avait une population nombreuse lui permettant de résister plus longtemps aux assauts des Barbares'.

[8] Wightman (1985: 300, 308).

[9] Wightman (1985: 261).

[10] Ancièn and Truffeau-Libre (1980: 74–6).

[11] Wightman (1977: 253) and (1985: 233–4). There are at least four large cemeteries in the Aisne region which show continuity of use throughout the fifth century AD.

[12] *Notitia Dignitatum*, Oc. IX, 35. It does not say what was manufactured there.

countryside around Soissons.[13] It would seem that the *civitas* of Soissons retained an unusual amount of vitality and prosperity in the fifth century.[14]

Those areas within the empire first settled by the Salian Franks, around the mouth of the Rhine, have been the subject of intense study, charting in some detail the disappearance of the *civitates*, and the drastic reduction of other Roman elements from the third century AD onwards.[15] In the fourth and early fifth centuries AD there is discontinuity in settlement pattern, the disappearance of the remaining Roman strongholds *c.* AD 400,[16] and a large number of coin hoards.[17] New material appears in the archaeological record (including a new type of pottery).[18] The archaeology and history of the entire Rhine frontier region has increasingly been interpreted in the light of the idea of the development of a distinctive frontier culture.[19]

During the early fifth century this new material culture spread gradually out from the north-east into Toxandria (between the Meuse and the Scheldt),[20] and then into areas of Belgica I and II. It is possible that expansion was held back, for a time, by the major Roman road from Arras to Cambrai and Cologne, which may have remained fortified into the fifth century AD; but by the third quarter of the century Franks (probably under Chlodio) had extended their territory to the Somme valley,[21] and had taken Arras and Tournai. There had also been Frankish settlement in the Rhineland; and by the time of Aegi-

---

[13] Wightman (1985: 304).
[14] Wightman (1985: 262).
[15] Willems (1986: 275).
[16] Willems (1986: 27).
[17] Willems (1986: 158).
[18] Willems (1986: 176).
[19] See Whittaker (1994: 222 ff.); Miller (1996: 170). Miller has even proposed that early medieval society was in essence La Tène/Halstaat culture transformed by this frontier culture, only slightly influenced by mainstream late Roman society.
[20] Van Ossel (1992: 125–7, 176–7).
[21] Todd (1992: 195–6). There is historical evidence in Greg. Tur. *Historiae* II, 9; Sidonius, *Pan.* V, 210–13; *Liber Historiae Francorum* 5.

dius there were a number of separate Frankish enclaves from the Channel right down the Rhine valley.[22]

.   Settlement evidence for the subsequent Frankish expansion in northern Gaul in its initial phases is very limited. Research points to continued occupation of many late Roman to post-Roman sites, but combined with drastic change of use and possible change of inhabitants. For instance, at Berry-au-Bac, on a crossing of the River Aisne between Soissons and Reims, the settlement which began no earlier than the late third century AD was in the late fifth century a focus for Germanic-type rectangular wooden halls and *grubenhäuser*, indicating little or no gap in continuity of occupation.[23]

The archaeological data for northern Gaul in the fourth and fifth centuries AD has been dominated by debate about the significance of a group of graves sometimes called *Reihengräber*, which is very briefly explored here.[24] In the late fourth and early fifth centuries a new type of grave occurs, in scattered and diverse contexts. In Gaul they are concentrated between the Rhine and Seine and entirely absent in Brittany. They are also found to the east of the Rhine. These were originally identified as Germanic burials, as they contained grave-goods (including weapons, jewellery, and dress accessories, as well as offerings) of a Germanic style which is now considered largely to be the product of the 'frontier culture' referred to above. This style became popular throughout the western provinces, but is particularly associated with the military and the civil service.

It has been argued that these graves were not, as usually thought, those of ethnic Germans (whether *laeti* or, more likely, *foederati*), but those of the Gallo-Roman provincial élite adopting a new burial rite as part of competition arising from a

---

[22] The Franks of this area were at a later date known as Ripuarians. Expansion along the Rhine was less rapid than that of the Salians, and the city of Cologne was permanently taken only in the AD 460s. By *c.* AD 470 Frankish territory included Trier, Cologne, Aachen, Bonn, and Metz.

[23] Todd (1992: 204–5) and Van Ossel (1992: 82, 87, 98, 127, 341), who also covers two other sites of similar type and date in the Aisne valley. Berry was a large area surrounded by palisades and ditches. It is suggested that this may have been a settlement of *laeti*, but, as no Germanic material has been found, it could have been some other sort of military site.

[24] The seminal work is Böhme (1974).

new power vacuum.[25] This identification is not attractive. It would have involved not only a change in burial rite but a wholesale change in élite attire and status symbols (and hence ideology) dating back to the late AD 300s. While it is possible to see how changes in male dress and status symbols might have taken place via the medium of military attire, it is hard to see by what mechanism such a change could have taken place among women, especially as it would have involved the take-up of a less sophisticated dress style by a supposedly competitive élite.[26]

If the style was primarily associated with the late Roman military, then the normal composition of the armed forces at that time would mean that it was, largely, though not of course exclusively, worn by people of Germanic origins, if quite possibly of Roman culture. The objection has been made that the graves are located in too many diverse contexts to be associated with barbarian military personnel, being found as scattered single graves and in large and small cemeteries, and on military and non-military sites.[27] This is answered if some lived off base, or married or retired into non-military sites.[28] The graves almost certainly are those of the élite of the Germanic military in northern Gaul, some of whom may have become landowners at an early stage.[29] The occurrence of *Reihengräber* peters out in the mid fifth century. The advocates of the 'provincial élite' theory postulate that this was a result of Aetius' activity in North Gaul to re-establish imperial control,[30] but it is doubtful that this was so successful. The cession is better explained by the political and military changes associated with the run-down of imperial forces.

[25] See Halsall (1992: 204–6). This can be linked to Van Dam's model of social change in North Gaul referred to in Ch. 5.

[26] The new types of brooches and pins used as dress fastenings and the layout of fasteners, girdles, and jewellery on the bodies indicate a style of dress different to the Roman norm.

[27] Halsall (1992: 197).

[28] Sivan (1987: 770) has made the very interesting suggestion that terms of barbarian settlement in the fifth century derived from those of military veterans in general. Some of these graves may be those of barbarian officers given veteran rights.

[29] Périn and Feffer (1987: i, 67–8).

[30] Halsall (1992: 206).

Germanic graves later reappear in North Gaul, and include some extremely rich burials. These are normally dated to the very end of the fifth century and the early sixth century, and eventually appear in numbers in areas known to have been under Frankish control. It is generally accepted that these are burials of the new Merovingian élite (and of Gallo-Romans who became absorbed into the new culture). The two groups of graves discussed above have relevance to the kingdom of Soissons. The first group relates to the extent of existing Germanic settlement in northern Gaul prior to the time of Aegidius and Syagrius (and to the prevalent social conditions), the second to the expansion of Frankish power from the time of Clovis. (For further discussion of the archaeological evidence see Ch. 11.)

NUMISMATIC EVIDENCE

In general, the numismatic data for late fifth-century Gaul is ephemeral and inconclusive, and problematic due to the practice of imitation and inadequate distribution patterns. Identification of coins also remains somewhat subjective; influenced in particular by opinions on the extent to which Gaul was still 'Roman'.

Official silver coins were no longer minted in Gaul after Jovinus (AD 411–13).[31] The imperial mint at Arles continued to produce gold coins into the third quarter of the fifth century AD (the Trier mint ceased regular official production earlier). There are also a small number of groups of unofficial coins, varying widely in quality, and minted sporadically at different dates and places in Gaul throughout the fifth century AD.[32] These coins were copies of official issues, using the same types, legends, and in some cases also mint-marks. All these unofficial groups consist of small numbers of finds, many of which have no recorded find-spot, making identification of the mint by analysis of the distribution pattern difficult.[33] One group of these unofficial coins is believed to have been produced by the Visigothic

[31] King (1992: 185).
[32] Kent (1994: 27, 187); King (1992: 184–95).
[33] However, where available, the distribution patterns of some of these groups of coins are striking. Coins of some groups have been found in eastern

kingdom of Aquitaine in *c.* AD 418–23;[34] and other coins of a later date are probably also Visigothic. Some later unofficial coins, however, may have been minted elsewhere, by other authorities.

These include a group of gold coins (minted in the names of Valentinian III, Avitus, Majorian, Libius Severus, Anthemius, Julius Nepos, Leo, Zeno, and Anastasius) and another group of *solidii* and *tremisses* with the same reverse type. Of the second group, the *solidii* were minted in the names of Valentinian III, Majorian, and Libius Severus, and the *tremisses* in the names of Valentinian, Libius Severus, Zeno, and Basiliscus.[35] Although the distribution patterns have been seen by some numismatists as evidence of Visigothic origin,[36] it has also been argued that some, if not all, of these coins were minted by Roman authorities.[37] These, it has been proposed, included Aetius, perhaps using the Trier mint, and even Aegidius and Syagrius.[38]

Another group of unofficial coins, but of silver (of substandard workmanship and rather botched lettering), has a distribution pattern pointing to a mint in north-eastern Gaul, possibly at Soissons.[39] It has been suggested that these coins might be connected to the Roman army in North Gaul. More

and northern France, Belgium, Scandinavia, Czechoslovakia, Poland, Germany, and Britain (one example in Bury St. Edmunds (King (1992: 187–8)). This may support the idea of a new linkage between northern Gaul and the North Sea littoral regions, mentioned in Ch. 5. The occasional far-flung findspots may result from historical accident, or indicate that long-distance contacts and, possibly, trade continued.

[34] Kent (1994: 220–1); King (1992: 185–92). The basic reason for this attribution is the absence of any other likely, non-imperial, minting authority in Gaul at this date.

[35] Kent (1994: 187); King (1992: 186–92); Grierson and Blackburn (1986: 44).

[36] King (1992: 186–92, citing Depeyrot (1986); Callu and Barrondon (1987)).

[37] Essentially, the interpretations differ because of a disagreement in dating the coins. These coins may have been contemporary with the official issues from the mint at Arles, hence dating to 454–65 (King (1992: 189–91)). However, the *solidi* of Severus could have become 'immobilized' in form, with the official series lasting into the mid 470s and therefore distributed in what had, by then, become pro-Visigothic territory (King (1992: 240)).

[38] Kent (1994: 223); Grierson and Blackburn (1986: 45).

specifically they have been associated with Aegidius and Syagrius (possibly following Aetius' practice). Another view is that
they may have been produced by 'local remnants of the Roman
establishment'.[40] These coins are minted in the names of
Majorian, Anthemius, Julius Nepos, and the eastern emperor
Anastasius. (The omission of coins in the name of Libius Severus would fit with Aegidius' political stance, but this may be
merely an accident of recovery.)

This group are ancestral to later, very lightweight and fragile
silver coins, minted in the names of emperors down to Anastasius, on which the legends are progressively more and more
blundered.[41] These coins date to the late fifth century AD.
Their distribution is similar to that of the previous group of
silver coins, with several find-spots along the Rhine, and the
most probable origin of these coins is Frankish kingdoms in
north-east Gaul.[42] If the previous group, which these coins
copy, was indeed produced by Aegidius and Syagrius, then it
is possible that the mint was taken over by Clovis.

If Aegidius and/or Syagrius did mint coins in northern Gaul,
this would be evidence that they were breaking new ground,
becoming more like independent rulers.[43] That they did so is
still uncertain, but *somebody* seems to have been minting unofficial coins in northern Gaul; and the existence of these coinages

[39] King (1988: 201); Grierson and Blackburn (1986: 27, 187, 206); Kent
(1994: 27). There are no mint-marks other than an occasional COMOB (sometimes appearing as CONOB) used to designate a palatine mint, and used by
those at Trier, Arles, and Milan, among others (Kent (1994: 25)).

[40] King (1988: 204 ff.) and (1992: 237, 243). In this category we could
surely include Syagrius.

[41] Kent (1994: 27); King (1992: 193).

[42] Kent (1994: 187, 206, 225); King (1992: 193–4). They may have been
produced as small change or to use as 'largesse' (Grierson and Blackburn
(1986: 112)).

[43] It seems unlikely that Aegidius and Syagrius (especially) would have been
using the Trier mint by this date.

testifies, at the very least, to increasing fragmentation and local autonomy.[44] The coins may have been produced to facilitate the raising of local taxes, payment of military forces,[45] or of tribute and protection money.[46] They may also be connected to the need to legitimize the power of new authorities.

[44] The continued imitation of imperial issues perhaps shows a conservative adherence to the old imperial forms, among both Roman and barbarian (unless this was merely the result of inertia and practical constraints).

[45] King (1988: 203) and (1992: 193).

[46] Although it is difficult to see why payments of this nature would need to be in coin.

9
Traces of the Kingdom of Soissons in the Merovingian Period

The question addressed in this chapter is whether there is any retrospective evidence in the early Merovingian period for the previous existence of a Gallo-Roman kingdom, or enclave, based on Soissons; either of the conventional maximal delineation, stretching westwards right across northern France, or of a smaller unit. The conventional kingdom of Soissons coincides with the older *Tractus Armoricanus* (without the eastern areas settled by the Franks), including much of the central plain of northern France. This region, bounded by the Somme and the Loire, is characterized by excellent farmlands,[1] and from the earliest times to the present day it has had its own agricultural and, to some extent, cultural identity.[2]

In some areas of life there was continuity from the late Roman into the medieval period, but there is no evidence that this was more marked here than elsewhere in France. There are two very small hints of early medieval administrative practices dating back to the imperial period in the region. One relates to the sixth-century practice of recruiting levies on a *civitas* basis; this was confined to Neustria (approximately the old Syagrian kingdom) and Aquitaine (the old Visigothic kingdom) and does not seem to have operated in Austrasia or Burgundy.[3] This was not the normal Frankish system and was presumably based on late Roman practice. Second, the area between the Seine and the Loire (roughly Maine, Anjou, and parts of Poitou), unlike other parts of Gaul, paid a tribute in kind, the *inferenda*, dating back to the Frankish conquest, similar to that later imposed on

---

[1] One reason, according to Braudel (1988: 303), why Roman civilization 'lasted longest' there.

[2] Braudel (1988: 106–8).

[3] Bachrach (1972: 66–7).

peoples who submitted to the Franks but retained some autonomy. Unfortunately, the evidence for this is slight, consisting of seventh- and eighth-century records of exemptions allowed to the church of Le Mans, the monastery of St. Serge in Angers, the abbey of St. Denis, and possibly also in Poitou.[4] Lot also argued that certain unique privileges retained by early medieval Maine (then covering most of the area between the Seine and the Loire) may have originated in the fifth century A D.[5] These minor administrative differences could relate back to a sub-Roman kingdom, but are not strong enough to prove its existence.

Turning to early Merovingian territorial divisions and land-holdings proves interesting. The eastern part of the supposed Syagrian kingdom—the valleys of the Seine, Oise, and Aisne, centred on Paris, and particularly the Île-de-France—rather than the older Frankish possessions to the north-east, was later the heartland of Merovingian and Carolingian royal power and wealth. This area contained the royal domains where the king held the land directly. Paris, Soissons, and Orleans, all within this area, and close to each other, were used as sub-capitals when France was divided between Clovis' sons and grandsons.[6]

From the reign of Clovis Paris seems to have been the chief city of the Merovingians,[7] and Clovis himself was buried there.[8] The old provincial capital of Belgica II, Reims, does not seem to have been used as an administrative centre by Clovis or Childeric. Paris had been a city of secondary status in the early empire, but it had gained importance in the late empire because of its good defensive position. It was the residence of the Prefect of the Fleet on the Seine and was used as a temporary headquar-

---

[4] Lot (1930: 246–53). He suggested that this may have been imposed by either Clovis or Childeric; in fact, he long predates James in speculating that the conquest of northern Gaul was completed by Childeric (Lot (1930: 251–2)).

[5] Lot (1930: 252–3).

[6] The information in the above paragraph is based on Jacobs's *Géographie de Gregoire de Tours* (1858), Longnon's *Géographie de la Gaul au VIe Siècle* (1878), the *Atlas Historique de France* (1885–89), and the *Géographie Historique de la Gaule et de la France* (1983).

[7] Although at first the Frankish occupation may have been almost totally military (Périn and Feffer (1987: ii, 16)).

[8] Greg. Tur. *Historiae* II, 38.

ters by campaigning emperors such as Julian and Valentinian.
Walls were built around the Ile de la Cité which survived into
the fifth century.[9] It would be surprising if Aegidius and Syagrius did not make use of Paris.[10] A sub-Roman enclave may
well, in fact, have been based at both Paris and Soissons. That
we have only a reference associating them with Soissons may be
a historical and literary accident of the paucity of the source
material.

The maximal kingdom of Soissons, if it existed, did not
survive as a single unit after Clovis' death. In the division of
AD 511 each of his four sons took a portion of the oldest
Merovingian possessions (that is, the Salian possessions in Belgica II and the lands thought to have constituted the Syagrian
kingdom), plus a share of the newer conquests (including Aquitaine and Burgundy). The Aisne Valley containing the city of
Soissons and 'Salian' country from the Scheldt to the Somme
went to one son (Clothar); the region from the Seine to Brittany
to another. Soissons became the capital of the one temporary
kingdom and Paris of the other.[11] In the division of AD 561 the
Paris area went to one ruler, the Orleans area to a second, Reims
and the lands of the Meuse to a third, and Soissons and the old
Salian lands to a fourth (combined with a general redivision of
the later Frankish acquisitions), with Paris, Orleans, Soissons,
and Reims again the sub-capitals.[12] In both partitions, the lands
of the sub-Roman kingdom treated with the old Frankish
lands for separate division from the newer conquests; and in
both the partitions, when these older northern possessions
were divided the eastern half, including Soissons, was separated
from the western, and attached to the old Salian lands (see
p. 139).

In the *Historiae*, and associated works, there is considerable
evidence for the importance of the city of Soissons to the early
Merovingian dynasty, out of proportion to its size or location.
Clovis used it as his headquarters before Paris (see pp.
124–5). Soissons was the capital of King Chilperic, Clovis'

[9] Périn and Feffer (1987: i, 165–7).
[10] Périn and Feffer (1987: i, 165).
[11] See Longnon (1878: 100–15) for the divisions, using information from
the *Historiae*.
[12] Longnon (1878: 112–21), based on Greg. Tur. *Historiae* IV, 22.

grandson;[13] King Theudebert was exiled there;[14] King Clothar I founded a church in the city, in which St. Medard was buried,[15] possibly in an attempt to create a religious and burial centre for his dynasty;[16] Clothar, taken ill while hunting in the forest of Cuise, was carried to Soissons to die and was buried at the church of St. Medard;[17] King Sigibert attacked and occupied the city and was later buried there;[18] and the royal treasury was kept at a villa just outside Soissons.[19] Soissons remained an important location for accession ceremonies for some time.[20] As late as AD 721 Pippin, the successor to the Merovingians, was consecrated there.[21] Over the early Middle Ages, however, Soissons totally lost its prominence to Paris and to the old provincial capital of Reims. This was perhaps because Soissons' status had been the result not of long-term factors, but of the historical accident of its temporary importance at the point when it was taken by Clovis.

The early Merovingian rulers did not, for the most part, live in the cities, but in royal villas in the countryside in their vicinity. There was a concentration of these royal villas (and royal landholding in general) around Paris,[22] and to a secondary extent around Soissons.[23] There were also one or two royal villas

---

[13] Greg. Tur. *Historiae* IV, 22.
[14] Greg. Tur. *Historiae* IX, 36.
[15] Greg. Tur. *Historiae* IV, 21.
[16] Gerberding (1987: 150).
[17] Greg. Tur. *Historiae* VI, 21.
[18] Greg. Tur. *Historiae* IV, 51.
[19] Greg. Tur. *Historiae* IV, 22.
[20] See Greg. Tur. *Historiae* IV, 22; IX, 36–7; Fredegar, III, 56; *Annales Regni Francorum, s.a.* 750 and 768.
[21] Gerberding commented that: 'the choice of venue by the usurper indicates how closely the venerable and ancient *sedes regalis* of Soissons was bound to the Merovingians and to the Frankish ideas of kingship' (Gerberding (1987: 155)).
[22] Perhaps as much as 75 per cent of the land (Roblin (1971: 342)).
[23] See Longnon (1878) for the modern locations of these villas. There may be further relevant documentation (perhaps the *Chartae Latinae Antiquiores* series and the *MGH Diplomata Regum e Stirpe Karolinorum*). There is unfortunately nothing in the texts relating to private and public institutions in the Merovingian period in Thevenin (1887).

outside the region.[24] Among the villas ringing Paris were those at Chelles, Noisy, Nogent sur Marne, Nanterre, and Reuil.[25] In the region of Soissons there were royal villas at Compiègne (*Compendium*) in the forest east of Soissons,[26] at Choisy-au-Bac (on the Aisne towards Compiègne),[27] at Montmacq,[28] possibly at Verberie,[29] at an unknown *Casnum* in the forest of Cuise, and a very important one at Berny-Rivière (*Brennacus*), close to the city.[30]

As well as being used as a royal residence and for government purposes,[31] Berny housed the royal treasury.[32] Chilperic's two sons were staying at Berny when they died in an epidemic (and Chilperic exiled one of his relatives there, in the hope that he would die of the same disease).[33] Berny was clearly a very large property capable of accommodating royal retinues, as the kings Chlothar, Chilperic, Sigibert, and Dagobert all spent time there, and the treasury was presumably well guarded. Gregory of Tours knew the place personally, as he was tried there for treason and calumny.[34]

There is, of course, no trace today of the Merovingian villa at Berny-Rivière. There was, however, an early medieval cross, at the site of an ancient crossing of the River Aisne at Berny-Rivière, which may just possibly have been associated with the

---

[24] One at Ponthion, south of Châlons, and an important one at Vitry, probably near Tournai (perhaps the property of Childeric and his predecessors), or possibly at the Vitry south of Châlons on the Marne (Longnon (1878: 409, 414)).

[25] Greg. Tur. *Historiae* V, 39; VI, 46; VII, 4; VII, 19; IX, 13; X, 19; X, 28; etc.

[26] Greg. Tur. *Historiae* IV, 21.

[27] Roblin (1978: 271).

[28] Roblin (1978: 185, 271).

[29] Roblin (1978: 34, 36, 185, 271). There was a palace there in AD 918.

[30] The location of Brennacus at modern Berny-Rivière is based on the philological argument of Longnon (1878: 395–401), which is wholly convincing, and is followed by most translators and writers, including Omont (1886), Omont and Collon/Pourpardin (1913), and Thorpe (1974). An earlier suggested location at Braine (Thierry (1840: 7)) would not invalidate the argument, as this small town is also close to Soissons.

[31] Greg. Tur. *Historiae* IV, 22; IV, 46; V, 23; etc.

[32] Greg. Tur. *Historiae* IV, 22.

[33] Greg. Tur. *Historiae* V, 39.

[34] Greg. Tur. *Historiae* V, 49–50.

villa site.[35] Berny lay at the meeting of two important Roman roads: Soissons–Noyon–Amiens–Boulogne and Soissons–Senlis. There was a large Merovingian cemetery, just to the south of Berny-Rivière, at Chelles,[36] and close by, at Mont-Berny, are the remains of a large, late Roman, defended site.[37]

In addition to the villas mentioned above, the Merovingian royal family is known to have owned other estates in the Soissons area: at Courcy-le-Château and Leuilly close to the city (later given to the Church);[38] at Ressons-sur-Long;[39] and probably at Germigny to the east of Soissons,[40] as well as other unnamed estates;[41] and Chilperic is recorded as giving estates from the 'crown lands' at Soissons to one Godin.[42] It is hard to discern to what extent the two cities of Paris and Soissons became prominent because the Merovingians owned extensive lands in their vicinity, or whether the estates were acquired as a result of the cities' importance, but in either case the overall pattern is interesting.

These Merovingian possessions must originally have been Gallo-Roman estates, acquired mainly in the reign of Clovis.[43] The royal villa estates would have been extensive properties capable of feeding and supporting the royal families and retinues, perhaps including industrial elements, and probably

[35] Seen on a personal visit to the area.

[36] Roblin (1978: 59).

[37] Roblin (1978: 273 n. 19). Its function is uncertain.

[38] Hincmar, *Vita Sancti Remigii* XXXII. The authenticity of this will has been supported by Jones, Grierson, and Crook (1957: 356–73). (Incidentally, the will mentions a nephew, Aetius, who conceivably was named after the patrician.)

[39] The Treaty of Andelot of AD 588, quoted by Gregory (*Historiae* IX, 20).

[40] Given by a member of the Merovingian royal family to the Church in the AD 600s (Gerberding (1987: 53)).

[41] Hincmar, *Vita Sancti Remigii* XXXII.

[42] Greg. Tur. *Historiae* V, 3.

[43] Although some may have been acquired by Clovis' sons and grandsons, the most important were already in Merovingian hands by their time, and the initial conquest was probably the point at which most estates were acquired and assigned. The Merovingians probably took over estates as they stood, with many estate boundaries continuing unchanged. Applebaum (1964: 78), in his study of late Roman agricultural estates, considers that there is evidence in the Soissons/Paris/Reims area of considerable continuity in agricultural estate boundaries from Roman to medieval times. See also Roblin (1978: 289 ff.).

acted as centres for the collection of revenues in kind. These estates were probably not remnants of the imperial fisc; almost certainly, any such would, by the later fifth century, have been 'privatized'. It is more feasible that they were acquired by confiscation from Gallo-Roman landowners (alive or dead), and among these Syagrius and his supporters must be prime candidates. It seems probable that some, at least, of the early Merovingian lands around Soissons (and perhaps Paris) listed above had belonged to Syagrius, perhaps including a principal estate at Berny-Rivière.[44]

It is interesting to speculate whether in the very early Merovingian period the old Gallo-Roman estate buildings were still in use, or whether these royal villas were new buildings in Germanic style (thatched, rectangular, timber halls). There are hints that the complex at Berny included buildings of a Roman rather than Germanic style; Gregory records a conversation that he had with Bishop Salvius there in A D 580, in which he mentions that the king had recently had the roof-tiles (*super-tegulum*) of the house repaired.[45] Gregory calls the residence at Berny both *villa* and *domus* (the second being his normal term for a house)[46] he also, unusually, refers to an *atrium* there, a term which he normally uses only in relation to stone-built religious buildings.[47]

In conclusion, there is only slight evidence from the Merovingian period for an earlier Roman enclave extending across North Gaul; but the importance of the city of Soissons in the sixth century and the existence of the royal estates in its territory do support the idea that in taking Soissons Clovis took an existing power base, and gained personal possession of considerable estates both there and around Paris. This, together with the particulars of the various partitions, suggests that a significant sub-Roman political base did indeed exist at Soissons, though its geographical area may well have been smaller than envisaged in the conventional models.

---

[44] Could the late Roman defended site at Mont Berny (see p. 151) possibly be connected?

[45] Greg. Tur. *Historiae* V, 51.

[46] St.-Michel (1979) *s.v. domus.*

[47] Greg. Tur. *Historiae* V, 49; St.-Michel (1979) *s.v. atrium.*

10

The Military Forces of Aegidius and Syagrius

Evaluating the nature of the forces which Aegidius and Syagrius commanded is difficult but crucial, for, like other warlords, their positions would have been based mainly on military strength. Whether or not he had a personal power base in Soissons, this must have been the reason why Aegidius was able to act independently after Majorian's death. Priscus says he commanded a 'large force',[1] and this is confirmed by his ability to threaten an invasion of Italy and resist the Visigoths. The possible sources of Aegidius' military strength are: the Gallic field army, any other units of imperial forces left in Gaul, the troops gathered by Majorian to attack Gaiseric, and unofficial recruitment of barbarians or Gallo-Romans.

A Gallic field army presumably still existed when Aegidius was appointed *magister militum per Gallias*, and came under his command until the death of Majorian. It would have been smaller and less well equipped than earlier in the century, when it was under the command of Aetius (and of course Aegidius did not have his predecessor's access to Hun manpower). Indeed, it may have been hardly recognizable as the old *comitatenses*. Its continued existence may be verified by the report that the Gallic army was present at the elevation of Avitus in AD 455.[2] Evidence for the survival of the Gallic field army into the 470s may also exist in Paul the Deacon's *Historia Romana*, but this is ambiguous. Paul records that in AD 472 an army

---

[1] Priscus, frag 39 (1).

[2] Hydatius, 156 (164) *s.a.* 455: *ab exercitu Gallicano*. It is possible that this is incorrect, but even so he clearly expected such a presence, and this is supported by Sidonius' reference to soldiers being there (*Pan.* VII, 577–8), though this could be simply because the army was traditionally one of the elements which elevated an emperor.

came to the aid of the besieged Emperor Anthemius in Italy, under Bilimer *Galliarum rector*,[3] who may have been *magister militum per Gallias*, which, by this date, would effectively mean that he was Anthemius' commander in the remaining imperial possessions in Provence. The troops under his command could have been units either of the Gallic *comitatenses* or of the army in Italy.

Events suggest that the majority of the units in Gaul remained loyal to Aegidius in A D 461/2, for had they passed to the command of a new appointee it is hard to see how Aegidius could have retained the authority and independence of action that he did. Aegidius may have been a senior officer of the Gallic army for a considerable time before being promoted to overall command, and in their loyalty to their commander they may have been affected by increasing contact with barbarian concepts of fealty and honour. Of course, personal loyalty to individual commanders had often existed in the Roman army, and had been an important factor in civil wars, but by this time the ties of loyalty to state and emperor had ceased to exert a counterbalance. Other motives may have been feelings of loyalty to Gaul and unwillingness to take orders from Ricimer in Italy. This decision may be seen as an example of the general shift in attachments away from central institutions towards regional interests, and towards individuals rather than institutions.

Aegidius, both as *magister militum* and as an independent warlord, would have had his own *bucellarii*, probably, as was common, mainly barbarian; and possibly these became numerous enough to constitute a sort of private war band comparable to those of barbarian leaders. It is conceivable that, after Aegidius broke with the government in Italy, the distinctions between the remnants of the Gallic field army and Aegidius' personal following of staff and *bucellari* became blurred and insignificant.

Aegidius may also have had access to other remnants of the military structure in northern Gaul, such as *limitanei* and *coloni*. The provinces of Belgica I and II were areas of barbarian military settlement from the third century A D onwards. For instance, settlements of Sarmatians in North Gaul are recorded

---

[3] Paul Diac. *Hist. Rom.* XV, 4. See Pt. III, pp. 253–5 for text and discussion.

in the *Notitia Dignitatum*,[4] and there is place-name evidence for Sarmatian and Alan presence in Belgica II and to the east of Paris.[5] These military settlements have been proposed as a continuing source of military manpower into the Merovingian period.[6] Of course, entries in the *Notitia* are no proof of existence in the AD 480s, and even if, as the place-names suggest, these ethnic groups continued to live where they had been settled, they would not necessarily have remained military in character. Some small city garrisons probably also still existed and may have come under Aegidius' control.[7]

Some of Aegidius' forces may have previously served in the largely barbarian army led into Spain by Majorian in AD 458 (see Sidonius' description in Pt. III, p. 205). It seems that this army was not taken back to Italy by Majorian for continued use, but disbanded in either Gaul or north-west Italy, and the barbarian contingents dismissed from his service.[8] Some of these men may have sought new employment within the empire and been recruited by Aegidius.

Another option for Aegidius was the unofficial recruitment of new manpower, either Roman or barbarians from inside or outside the empire; and Franks are the obvious candidates here. Franks had fought with Aetius against Attila in AD 451, and prior to that had a long history of imperial military service. We know that Aegidius fought with Franks either under his command or as his allies at Orleans. Slightly later, Count Paulus led both Romans and Franks (see p. 101). Aegidius, Syagrius, and the Salian Franks may have had common interests in resisting Visigothic expansion northwards and in containing the Saxon settlements. It is probable that Frankish forces were an important component of Aegidius' military strength, but we do not know whether they fought for him as allies, *bucellari*, or mercenaries (some may even have previously been *comitatenses*).

---

[4] *Notitia Dignitatum*, Oc. XLII, 66, 67, 69.

[5] Bachrach (1973: 59–60, 62).

[6] Bachrach (1972: 5).

[7] The payment of which would provide a reason for the production of local coinages by urban authorities, some numismatists suggest (see pp. 143).

[8] John Ant. frag. 203. See Pt. III, pp. 210–11

Aegidius may also have recruited directly from the ordinary Gallo-Roman civilian population.[9] We know that Ecdicius (for whom see Pt. III, p. 275) collected a force of rural peasants in Auvergne in AD 471/2, to augment a small group of mounted companions in resisting the Visigoths.[10] Such recruitment may have been even more feasible in the North; Armoricans had provided a unit of men to fight under Aetius against Attila a generation earlier. The Romans fighting alongside Franks under Count Paulus may have been local Gallo-Romans rather than part of Aegidius' army. In the Merovingian period the *civitates* provided militias, which practice could date back to these final years of Roman Gaul. The will of landowners to resist recruitment had probably reduced; and the insecure and dangerous situation in northern Gaul had, no doubt, produced less passive and peaceful people; a change which can happen very quickly (as demonstrated many times in the ancient and modern world). This is supported by the reports of unrest and independent action in Armorica in earlier decades, and a similar social change seems to have occurred at this time in the highland areas of Britain.

Whether Aegidius' forces, all or some of which were presumably inherited by his son Syagrius, consisted of the remnant Gallic field army, *foederati*, Frankish allies, local militias, or (most probably) some combination of these elements, one thing is certain: they had to be provisioned and paid or rewarded. Aegidius may have tried to do this by subverting imperial receipts and resources, through local taxation, imprests and sequestration of supplies, by offering booty or land for settlement, or by using his private resources. It cannot have been an easy task. In common with all fifth-century leaders, Aegidius must have found available finance a very limiting factor. Even if Aegidius' forces were comparatively large when they threatened Italy, they may have been considerably smaller by the time of his death. (It is a strange thought that if the units which stayed loyal to Aegidius were in some form inherited by Syagrius, then in a sense the Gallic field army outlived the

---

[9] On the development of landowners' semi-private armies in general see Whittaker (1993: 282–90).

[10] Sidonius, *Ep.* III, iii, 3–6.

empire.) Any force commanded by Syagrius is likely to have been recruited in Belgica II, perhaps from his own lands in the Soissons area, from surviving groups of military settlers, and among Frankish allies. The most effective component of his forces may have been *bucellarii* inherited from his father.

All the above considerations, as well as the general trend of military developments, suggest that the forces which Syagrius led in AD 487 would have been closer in character to those Clovis led against him than to an imperial army of, say, AD 400. If Gregory is correct, Syagrius had no hesitation in fighting Clovis and his kinsman Ragnachar,[11] coming out of the fortified city of Soissons to do so (see Ch. 7, pp. 122–3). This suggests that the two sides were reasonably well matched in the numbers and quality of their fighting men.[12] Descriptions of Frankish forces in the next century show that they fought in a largely unorganized way, in ethnic or regional units, and consisted of a small cavalry élite, plus infantry of variable quality armed with spears and axes, sometimes including archers. It would be surprising if Syagrius' army differed greatly in size or character.[13]

A view has been proposed that runs contrary to this,[14] arguing that there was a strong Roman influence on the Merovingian army, as a result of Clovis' conquest of Syagrius' kingdom and 'acquisition of his army'. Procopius' story about the Roman soldiers who had once guarded the frontiers of Gaul has been used to support this argument:

[11] Greg. Tur. *Historiae* II, 27.

[12] Some modern historians estimate the number of Frankish fighting men at *c.* 6,000. This is based on accounts of Clovis' baptism. Gregory (*Historiae* II, 31) stated that 3,000 Frankish warriors were baptized, and Hincmar, in the ninth century (*Vita Remigii* 30), reported that about half the Frankish warriors accepted conversion initially, hence the estimate of 6,000. For obvious reasons the numbers are highly suspect, and likely to be an over-rather than under-estimate, but they do perhaps indicate the scale of forces at the time, with armies in the region of three or four thousand at most, and usually smaller.

[13] Bachrach (1972: *passim*) sees the Merovingian army as inheriting much of the Roman military tradition and organization, although the direct evidence for this is not strong. Calling the Merovingian army Roman in character is misleading in terms of similarity with fourth-century field armies, but it may well have resembled the forces employed by the later Roman warlords, from Aetius onwards, which were heavily 'barbarized' in appearance and in fighting techniques.

[14] Bachrach (1972: 5, 33–4, 124–8).

and they handed down to their offspring all the customs of their fathers... [who] guard them even up to my time For even at the present day they are clearly recognised as belonging to the legions to which they were assigned... in ancient times, and they always carry their own standards when they enter battle, and always follow the customs of their fathers. And they preserve the dress of the Romans in every particular even as regards their shoes.[15]

Procopius was a member of Belisarius' staff in Italy when Theudebert's Frankish army arrived in AD 539, so some of this might have some basis in fact. No doubt descendants of imperial military forces served in Frankish armies, and pieces of Roman military equipment could have survived for a couple of generations; they would be durable and prestigious items. It is possible that some elements of the Frankish army possessed such things, and that the tale of the fate of the Roman soldiers was developed to explain, in historical terms, an interesting detail that came to Procopius' attention.

Procopius discusses Frankish armies in detail elsewhere,[16] and it is clear that they were not, as a whole, Roman in character. All written sources and the archaeological evidence show that fifth- and sixth-century Frankish armies were Germanic in character.[17] Some survivors of Syagrius' army may have transferred their allegiance to Clovis, but this does not mean that he inherited a functioning Roman army, nor is there reason to think that the units in the Merovingian armies called *laeti* and *milites* in written sources were directly descended in manpower or organization from those of the fifth century. Frankish use of Roman military terms[18] can be explained by their long association with the imperial army.

---

[15] Procopius, *Wars* V, xii, 18–19 (Dewing's translation). This follows on from the excerpt on p. 121.
[16] Procopius, *Wars* VI, xxv, 1–4.
[17] Périn and Feffer (1987: ii, 84).
[18] Others include *dux, comes, tribunus, centenarius*.

Alternative Models for Northern Gaul in the Late Fifth Century

The preceding chapters have examined the strengths and weaknesses of two models, the conventional view of a kingdom of Soissons and James's alternative, and introduced some further evidence into the debate. To the question of the reality of a kingdom of Soissons there cannot perhaps be a final definitive answer, but some conclusions can be drawn (and there is some further discussion in the concluding chapter). James's view of the kingdom of Soissons as a modern construct is, as a negative argument, difficult to disprove, and the existence of a 'Roman' kingdom in North Gaul in the late fifth century under Aegidius and Syagrius can no longer be taken for granted. Equally, it must not be summarily abandoned without further study and debate. Its removal from our understanding of the period has wide-ranging implications: for our perception of late antique Gaul, of the early history of the Franks, and of the career of Clovis, and, perhaps most importantly, for the interpretation of the archaeological record.

Two questions need to be addressed, one minor, the other major. First, why have historians uncritically accepted the existence of the kingdom of Soissons, based on such slight evidence, for so long? One of the reasons is the tendency, until fairly recently, to accept primary historical texts at face value, more so for a period in which they are rare. Also, in the past a rather romantic view was often taken of the empire and its fall. Aegidius and Syagrius have been portrayed as inheriting from Aetius the mantle of the 'last of the Romans' and the banner of *romanitas*; and the destruction of this 'last outpost of empire' has been imagined as the heroic last stand of a civilized world order in the twilight of an age.[1] It is in fact rather surprising, given the postwar reaction in history and archaeology against this mode of thinking, that the idea of a Syagrian kingdom has survived for so long, merely being moderated to that of an 'enclave'.

The reasons for this are rather more involved. Its existence has been useful in explaining an apparent hiatus in Frankish expansion in that part of the century. It is, however, possible that this 'hiatus' is based on the historians' understanding of the interpretation of the archaeological evidence, which is in its turn based on the archaeologists' understanding of the historical interpretation of the sources. The Syagrian kingdom or enclave has also been envisaged as one of the means by which Roman culture was absorbed by the Franks, an initial stage in the acculturation which produced *La France*;[2] and the issue of the relative importance of Gallic and Frankish influence in this is still alive today.[3] Less articulated reasons (as James pointed out) are that the Soissons enclave neatly filled a gap in the map of fifth-century Gaul between the Visigothic, Frankish, and Burgundian kingdoms, and that the story of its defeat has provided a clear, single event to explain the Frankish acquisition of northern Gaul.[4] Historians, like nature, abhor a vacuum.

The second and major question is more complex. If there was no Gallo-Roman political unit covering North Gaul from the AD 460s to the 480s, what was there instead? If the Soissons kingdom is to be removed, then the problem of substituting an equally good, or preferably better, reconstruction must be addressed.

[1] See Dill (1926: 13): 'it illustrates the immense strength and prestige of the old Roman character and civilisation that the little kingdom of Soissons should have made itself a power to be reckoned with and should by skilful diplomacy or military force have maintained its independence for so long'. For a similar French view see Griffe (1964–6: ii, 104–5).

[2] Probably not unconnected to its location in the area which became the Île de France, and to the later national centrality of Paris.

[3] It was only recently written: 'C'est en fait une question fort délicate qui fait toujours l'objet de controverses puisqu'il s'agit en définitive d'estimer les conséquences ethniques de l'expansion franque dans l'empire romain' (Périn and Feffer (1987: ii, 125–7)). In the 1990s Clovis was even adopted as the symbol of the French extreme right wing (article in *The Times*, April 1996).

[4] James (1988: 70, 79).

The model favoured by James is that by the 460s northern Gaul (apart presumably from Brittany and the Saxon and Alan enclaves) was ruled (if not settled) by Franks, with the surviving Roman authorities existing on their sufferance.[5] James's theory envisages the Frankish exploitation of the area's resources being on Goffart's model of barbarian appropriation of tax revenues rather than direct ownership of the land. Soissons lay inside territory long held by the Franks, and if Syagrius ruled there, it was merely as the local count of the city, or equivalent.[6] In this model the Franks fighting at Orleans and Angers would have been fighting on the borders of their own lands (although this makes the involvement of Aegidius there very problematic).

This model is not totally convincing. There is no definite evidence in the contemporary chronicles for a pre-Clovis conquest of North Gaul, as opposed to Franks participating in military action there, which could have other contexts. The *Vita Genovefae* contains strong evidence for long-term campaigning by Franks in, or around, the Paris region, over perhaps a decade or more, and for Childeric himself being in Paris at an unknown date, but does not say that he made permanent large-scale conquests of territory. Even if Childeric did take Paris and territory around it at an early date this would still not rule out a Roman-controlled Soissons, as there is absolutely no reason to think that frontiers between ethnic groups were neat, continuous, modern-style borders.

The burial evidence certainly suggests Germanic, possibly Frankish, presence connected with imperial military forces scattered across northern Gaul by the early fifth century AD (see Ch. 8), and these people may have established some settlements, but this is not the same as Frankish rule. The first evidence for Frankish settlement in northern Gaul west of the Ardennes comes well into the sixth century AD.[7] This is presumably why James suggests exploitation on the Goffart model, although Goffart's theory has not won acceptance among most scholars. James believed that the dates of some of the earliest

[5] James (1988: 72–7).
[6] James (1988: 73–5).
[7] Among others, Galliou and Jones (1991: 140), James (1988: 76), Todd (1992: 204–5). Recent studies confirm that pottery evidence does not show the Franks further west than the Somme before Clovis' reign (Legaux (1993: 44)).

Frankish graves in North Gaul could be pushed back a little way,[8] but this hardly takes them back to the reign of Childeric. There is in fact not only no evidence of Frankish settlement, but very little evidence for any Frankish presence, or cultural influence, in northern Gaul in the second half of the fifth century.[9] Unless there is a real revolution in dating, the archaeological data remain a difficulty for the James version.

There was little Frankish influence in the west of Gaul until the late sixth century,[10] and in areas on the eastern borders of Brittany, such as those around Nantes and Vannes, the archaeological record continues to be strongly Gallo-Roman in character until the late AD 500s.[11] Gregory does not record any conquest of, or major conflict with, the Bretons during Clovis' reign; which would have been likely had the Franks ruled right across northern Gaul in the reign of his father. Gregory states that after the death of Clovis the Bretons were under Frankish domination (*sub Francorum potestatim*) and that their rulers were thereafter known as 'counts' rather than 'kings',[12] but a few lines later refers to a Breton kingdom, and the Bretons were clearly still an independent people. No warfare is recorded until the reigns of Clovis' grandsons, when the two peoples clashed in the Vannes region.[13] This, with a few scraps of other literary evidence (for instance, the *Life of St. Dalmas* refers to a *legio britannica* in Orleans in AD 530),[14] together with the archaeological evidence, suggests that extension of Frankish control to the West may have taken some decades to complete.

Other problems with James's model are his interpretation of the Remigius letter (as discussed in Ch. 7), and the need to

---

[8] James (1988: 76).

[9] Drinkwater, paper at Classical Association Conference, Nottingham, 1996; Van Ossel (1992: 97–106); Périn and Feffer (1987: i, 111, 199–200).

[10] Galliou and Jones (1991: 140).

[11] Galliou and Jones (1991: 141).

[12] Greg. Tur. *Historiae* IV, 4.

[13] Greg. Tur. *Historiae* V, 26. Bachrach (1970: 25–6) referred to Clovis undertaking a campaign against the Armoricans in the period AD 502–5. No such campaign is recorded by Gregory. The basis for this supposed campaign is Bachrach's interpretation of the Procopius material referring to the amalgamation of Franks and Armoricans (whom Bachrach thought were actually Alans settled in Armorica). There is no justification for any of this.

[14] *Vita Dalmatii Episcopi Ruteni* 6.

assume that Gregory of Tours was either totally confused about Clovis' early reign, or that he was willing and able severely to distort historical events. It would be unwise, especially in the absence of better textual analysis, to accept Gregory's account of fifth-century history uncritically. On the other hand, it has been demonstrated that his account of the fall of Soissons should not be dismissed as total fabrication (especially if he is indeed using sources connected with Remigius). James's version also leaves unexplained the undoubted political importance of Soissons in the century that followed.

Following the debate occasioned by James's model, a more sophisticated version of the conventional model has been suggested by Drinkwater.[15] In a number of works he has raised serious doubts as to Frankish strength in the fourth and fifth centuries, thinking it most unlikely that the Franks constituted a major military threat to the empire until the middle of the fifth century, and that, even then, it was the historical accident of exceptional leadership rather than political and military power that acted as the stimulus to their expansion.[16] He argued that the Romans remained dominant in northern Gaul into the second half of the fifth century, and that 'the Roman enclave founded by [Aegidius] and his son was the crucible in which the future Frankish kingdom was forged; it was not the obstacle to Frankish success, but a necessary condition of it'.[17] In this model both Aegidius and Childeric enhanced their personal power by the association, but Childeric, holding military and civil rank from Aegidius, would have remained subordinate.

Yet another model is possible: that in the third quarter of the fifth century northern Gaul was neither already part of a Frankish kingdom nor one Gallo-Roman kingdom, but a complex and shifting patchwork. James's rejection of one single Gallo-Roman kingdom extending right across northern France is convincing, and there is evidence that the Franks were present further west at an earlier date than used to be supposed (if not as far and early as James proposes). Although this reconstruction

---

[15] Drinkwater, papers at Oxford (1995) and Nottingham (1996).
[16] Paper given at the Classical Association Conference (1996) and personal communications. See also Whittaker (1993: 279–81).
[17] Paper given to the Oxford Conference on Gregory of Tours (1995) and personal communications.

still sees Syagrius as an independent ruler, it suggests that the area he controlled from Soissons was smaller than that envisaged in the past (and probably altered in extent over time). Its western boundary may have been the Seine.

Syagrius, in this model, would have been one (comparatively important) ruler among a number, in an ethnically and politically heterogeneous region. We know that northern Gaul contained Saxon, Alan, and British settlements, a count of barbarian descent controlling a city, a British army led by a king, urban authorities, Frankish sub-kings, and powerful Roman bishops, as well as the crumbling remains of the imperial structure. We can assume that it also contained peasant communities, increasingly powerful and autonomous Gallo-Roman landowners, and bands of ex-mercenaries and brigands.

Ethnically the population consisted of a Gallo-Roman majority, with British, Alan, Saxon, Sarmatian, Gothic, Frankish, and other Germanic elements, and no doubt the odd Hun and easterner.[18] As to religious adherence, there were Catholic and Arian Christians, possibly Pelagian heretics, and Roman and barbarian pagans. A comparably complicated situation is described by the *Vita Severini*, set in the western Danubian provinces, at around the same date. Roman authorities and culture and remnants of the military system survived in some of the walled towns (although the political, as well as the spiritual, lead was taken by St. Severinus), while the countryside was dominated by various groups of barbarians, some from an established kingdom, but others in wandering raiding parties. Population movement, slave raiding, and brigandage were common. Scholars who envisage the process of ethnic and political change in these circumstances as consisting of peaceful interaction and acculturation hold the most optimistic and naive notions of human behaviour.[19]

---

[18] In Fredegar, III, 11, based perhaps on oral tradition, Childeric has a Hun retainer named Wiomed.

[19] For one recent example see Daly (1994: 624).

PART III

Ricimer, Gundobad, Orestes, and Odovacer in Italy

12

The Background and the Sources

ITALY

The years in which Ricimer dominated Italy fall at the beginning of a period, from the AD 460s to 530s, in which Italy was virtually a single state (a situation not to occur again until 1815). Outside Italy, all that remained of the western empire were some of the Western Mediterranean islands, parts of Provence, Raetia, and Noricum.

Italy contained the old political and cultural centres: the cities of Rome and Ravenna, the central government institutions, and the increasingly influential bishopric of Rome. Although regional differences were marked and increasing, the country was still unified by a shared language, culture, and infrastructure. The population remained largely unchanged ethnically, with the exception, mainly in the north, of military settlements and garrisons of barbarians.

Most Italian cities survived through the late Roman and post-Roman periods. Walls were vital to survival; many unwalled towns were abandoned.[1] Although urban populations fell, life continued, albeit altered in form and focus. With the exception of Rome, most of the traditional elements of the classical city, including aristocratic urban patronage, ceased in the fifth century.[2] Nevertheless, towns and cities continued to function as markets and social and religious centres, with Christian festivals and local patron saints replacing the older foci of local identity.

Even Rome was changing. Population decline accelerated in the late 400s,[3] as did the decay of the infrastructure.[4] Only in

---

[1] Christie (1991a: 186).

[2] Ward-Perkins (2000).

[3] Potter (1987: 211); Hodges and Whitehouse (1983: 51), who estimate a population of c. 40,000 in AD 452.

[4] Ward-Perkins (1984: 45).

ecclesiastical building was there much activity. It is clear from the novellas of Majorian and the writings of Cassiodorus that, although the basic structure of the city endured, there was widespread dilapidation, desertion of some buildings, and re-cycling of materials for repairs and church building.[5] Rome remained, however, a cultural, political, and ideological centre. The other major exception to urban decline was Ravenna, the residence of the imperial court. During the reign of Valentinian III the erection of defences and new buildings there continued,[6] and Ravenna still had links with the more prosperous Eastern Mediterranean world.

In the Italian countryside the archaeological data show significant regional variation and differing levels of continuity in settlement and prosperity.[7] The decline in the number of identifiable rural sites which began in the third century acceler-ated in the fifth.[8] From then into the early medieval period the rural population of Italy becomes increasingly invisible. This may be because of a real decline in population, or the disappear-ance of enduring material culture, or both,[9] but the evidence points to real change in the Italian way of life.

If the native population hardly appears in the archaeological record, then one cannot expect much material evidence for the barbarian presence attested in literary sources and some place-names. The very limited, non-Roman, intrusive material (such as transalpine-derived grave-goods)[10] has been found only in northern and central Italy, with almost nothing south of Rome. The main concentrations of material are around Milan and Pavia and, to a lesser extent, other cities of northern Italy.[11] It is difficult to date this material, or assign it to any particular group, and it could relate to barbarians serving the empire or to

[5] Krautheimer (1980: 56–67).

[6] Hodgkin (1880a: 450–4); Bury (1923: 263); Christie and Gibson (1988: 193).

[7] Potter (1987: 213–19); Ward-Perkins (2000).

[8] Potter (1987: 207).

[9] For instance, South Etruria had lost 50–80 per cent of its rural sites by AD 500. The extent and timing of the disappearance varied from region to region. For a detailed comparison see Greene (1986: 105–8).

[10] Christie (1993: 486).

[11] Todd (1992: 181–2); Potter (1987: 174); Barnish (1986: 174).

the Ostrogothic settlement. Among the barbarians in northern Italy from the third century AD onwards were Sarmatians, Alans, Batavians, Alamans, Heruls, and Goths. Many of the areas of these early military settlements were later settled by Odovacer's followers and then by Theoderic's Ostrogoths.[12]

Economic and cultural change was less marked and more gradual in Italy than in other western provinces, but Italy was becoming impoverished and unsophisticated in comparison to the East. Recent increased awareness of and archaeological work on the late Roman period in Italy have greatly modified, but not overturned, the conventional conception of decline and collapse.[13] The emerging picture is one of gradual deterioration, starting from the second century AD, although there are periods in which limited recovery occurred. Loss of provinces, warfare, civil insecurity, and political instability affected the economy of Italy, including food production and supply.[14] The total loss of North Africa and loss of secure hold over Sicily[15] particularly affected Italy, whose senatorial class had owned huge estates in both areas, whence food and revenue had flowed. Internal and external trade continued, but were contracting,[16] and specialized large-scale industrial production was disappearing.

Throughout the fifth century taxes did not meet government expenditure commitments, the largest of which was the army.[17] Monetary exchange, although continuing, was reduced in scope.[18] Italian mints continued to operate. Gold coins were struck for all the fifth-century emperors, mainly by the Rome and Ravenna mints (the latter moving on occasion to Arles),[19]

---

[12] The Ostrogoths settled largely north of the Po, especially around Ravenna, Dertona, Milan, Verona, and Pavia, also in the foothills of the Alps and in Samnium (Wickham (1981: 24); Potter (1987: 211); Christie (1991*b*: 424); Barnish (1986: 185–6)).

[13] Christie (1991*a*: 185).

[14] For example *Nov. Val.* 15 (1) 31 and 33; *Nov. Maj.* 2; Sidonius, *Ep.* I, x, 2.

[15] There were constant raids on Sicily (only about three days' sailing time from Carthage (Procopius, *Wars* III, xiv, 8)). The Vandals, however, did not take possession of the whole island.

[16] Ward-Perkins (2000).

[17] Hendy (1988: 33).

[18] Luzatto (1961: 12).

[19] Kent (1994: 31–3).

but there were only sporadic issues of silver coins. The only bronze coins circulating were tiny *nummi*, inadequate in numbers and range of denomination for commercial needs.[20]

Mainland Italy had not suffered from the direct effects of invasion as badly as some provinces. Nonetheless, Alaric's incursions, in the first two decades of the century, had caused devastation in some areas of Italy.[21] The later Vandal threat consisted of raid and pillage rather than invasion, but even so increased public insecurity and economic decline, especially in coastal areas of southern Italy which, as a whole, was more vulnerable and less defended than the North. Defensive measures were taken against the Vandal attacks (which generally took place in the spring).[22]

Those detailed in the ninth novella of Valentinian III (from AD 440, when a large Vandal fleet was known to have set sail), entitled 'The Restoration of the Right to Carry Arms', were probably typical. Measures included the organization by the *magister militum* Sigisvult of guards of soldiers and federates in the cities and on the coasts, and exhortations to the citizens to defend themselves, authorizing them to use such arms as they had, while awaiting Aetius and a 'large force'.[23] Majorian, too, put through legislation in AD 459 enabling citizens to carry arms to defend themselves.[24] There is evidence for the repair and improvement of city defences in the fifth century, including those of Rome, Ravenna, Terracina, Naples, and Albenga.[25]

In addition to Vandal raids, the Italian government had to guard against invasion by land from the north. Many of the barbarian federates were stationed in northern Italy, although they were no doubt deployed throughout the country as needed. Stilicho had used fortified towns, such as Bologna and Modena, as federate garrison centres,[26] and this practice

---

[20] Jones (1964: 207).

[21] Where tax assessments were reduced (*Cod. Theod.* 11, 27).

[22] Procopius, *Wars* III, v, 22.

[23] *Nov. Val.* 3, title 9.

[24] *Nov. Maj.* 8. The text is unfortunately lost.

[25] Christie (1991a: 194); Christie and Gibson (1988: 193); Christie and Rushworth (1988: 82–3).

[26] Zosimus, V, 26, 30, and esp. 35.

probably continued.[27] Surviving regular army units may have been tied up in permanent garrison duties, with some perhaps in camps in or near Rome and Ravenna (see p. 197), also the location of the élite guards units. The defensive system in the Julian Alps, the *Claustra Alpium Juliarum*, had been abandoned by the early part of the century,[28] and nothing had prevented the Hun invasion of Italy by that route.[29] Given Rome's military past the absence of any effective defensive action by her armies when Italy was attacked by Alaric, Attila, and Gaiseric is quite shocking. In AD 452 Aetius, deprived of Hun manpower, was relying on auxiliaries lent by Marcian.[30] Nobody seems to have tried to defend Rome against the Vandals in AD 455.[31] Whatever the detailed circumstances, this speaks of fundamental military weakness.

In one element of Italian life there was considerable continuity: among the senatorial class. Their wealth may have been somewhat reduced, but they continued to control huge estates in Italy, which brought in large incomes; these they used, as ever, to maintain competitive, high-profile lifestyles, and to pursue office. Virtually all senators resided in Rome.[32] The political strength of the Italian aristocracy increased in the fifth century AD.[33] This was especially true of the small number of ultra-powerful families such as the Decii, Anicii, Rufii, Acilii, and Petronii.[34] Between AD 425 and 490 such families had a near monopoly of all major civil offices.[35] In the fifth

[27] Apart from the threat of overland invasion, they may have been stationed in the northern cities because of barracks and other military facilities already in place there.

[28] Christie and Gibson (1988: 188–90).

[29] For geographical reasons it was almost impossible to organize an effective, preclusive defence system across the eastern approaches to Italy anyway.

[30] Hydatius, 146 (154) *s.a.* 452–3.

[31] See esp. *Addit. Prosp. Haun. s.a.* 455.

[32] Chastagnol (1966: 45).

[33] Barnish (1988: 120); Wormald (1976: 224); Matthews (1975: 387) and (1985: 375). The permanent residence of the emperor in Italy and the personal characters of the fifth-century emperors played a part in this progress, as did the continued political ambition, wealth, and social cohesion of the senatorial class.

[34] Matthews (1985: 360).

[35] Matthews (1985: 359).

century, unlike the fourth, emperors usually came from the senatorial class, which clung to many of its traditional values, especially those of self-regard and self-interest. As landowners they consistently resisted the recruitment of rural manpower into the army (by the end of Valentinian's reign normal conscription procedures were effectively abandoned), and fifth-century emperors were no more successful than their predecessors in increasing their minimal share of the tax burden.

Another élite in Italy, distinguishable from, although inevitably closely connected with, the senatorial class, was that of the high-level imperial-service families, including army officers and court officials. Many of these families had origins outside Italy, including those of Aetius, Merobaudes, and Majorian. Increasingly, senior army officers were of barbarian origin. There was a clash of interests between this élite, which relied on public spending on the army and the court, and the senatorial landowners who, while supporting both institutions in theory, preferred not to have to pay for them. Large amounts of money did pass, however, from the Italian upper classes into the hands of the Church, a third élite. Relations between state and Church were, in general, harmonious and, as is well known, throughout the period the Bishop of Rome gradually extended his ecclesiastical authority.

The overall picture from the literary, legislative, and archaeological material is one of a gradual but inexorable decline in prosperity, increasing insecurity and social flux, widespread evasion of taxes and obligations, military weakness, the growing power of the Church, and isolation. Yet change in Italy was not as drastic as in Gaul, Spain, or Britain; there were many elements of continuity. Rather than the dramatic fall of the empire in fire and sword of popular mythology, the image that comes to mind is of a once-great family, its mansion shabby and leaking, the family silver long gone, the bills unpaid, the few servants incompetent, the bailiffs circling; yet still arrogant and proud, giving formal dinners as the roof falls in.

THE SOURCES FOR RICIMER AND HIS SUCCESSORS

The sources for Ricimer are not particularly good, but are sufficient to make possible some assessment of his role in the sequence of events which led to the end of the western empire; and to allow some limited assessment of his aims and motivations; those for his successors are even fewer and more problematical. Some of the sources are the same as for Aegidius and Marcellinus; notably, Priscus, Marcellinus *comes*, and (until A D 468) Hydatius. To these can be added a few sources mainly, or solely, of relevance to this part of the book. In the second category are, primarily, those chronicles, gathered together by Mommsen under the title *Consularia Italica*, which concentrate on Italian events; Jordanes' *Getica* and the letters and poems of Sidonius Apollinaris.

Among the Italian chronicle material, the additions and continuations to Prosper's chronicle, found in a twelfth- or thirteenth-century Copenhagen manuscript, are of particular interest, although there is, unfortunately, a lacuna for the years A D 458–73, hence for most of Ricimer's career. The complicated textual composition of this work is discussed in depth by both Mommsen and Muhlberger, who show that this material comes from authoritative fifth-century sources.[36] Both consular annals and a late fifth-century historical work seem to have been used by the seventh-century compiler.[37] The material in the

[36] Prosper, ed. Mommsen (1892), and preface, *MGHAA*, ix, 266–7; Muhlberger (1984: 50–95).

[37] Briefly, the extra fifth-century material is found in additions to Prosper's text, called *Additamenta ad Prosperi Hauniensis* (cited as *Addit. Prosp. Haun.*), and four continuations, divided and named by Mommsen. Of these four, the first is *Auctarium ad. Prosperi Hauniensis* (cited as *Auct. Prosp. Haun.*) for A D 455–7, then (following a lacuna until 473) *Auctarium Prosperi Hauniensis Priores* (cited as *Auct Prosp. Haun. ordo prior.*), and *Posterior* (cited as *Auct. Prosp. Haun. ordo post.*), which overlap for A D 475–89, and the marginal comments to *ordo posterior* (cited as *Auct. Prosp. Haun. ordo post. marg.*), which are often the fullest, and overlap with the previous two for A D 475–80.

Copenhagen manuscript is unique, often adding specific names, dates, and locations as well as detail.

Another Italian source is Cassiodorus' chronicle, purporting to cover world history to A D 519. In it Cassiodorus has tried to combine two different dating systems (consular dating and that of Jerome). This chronicle, given the author's learning and access to information, could have been most valuable, but is copied mainly (not always accurately) from Prosper's chronicle, and many years have no entries at all. It seems to have been written mainly to lead up to the accession of his patron Theoderic, the Ostrogothic King of Italy.[38]

A small amount of material in Jordanes' *Getica* is of interest, especially in its attitude to Ricimer, but is difficult to interpret. The sources, aims, and reliability of the *Getica*, written *c.* A D 551, are still being debated, but there seems no reason not to take Jordanes' own statement at face value; that is, that it is based on his reading of Cassiodorus' sixth-century history of the Goths, with additions from other Greek and Latin histories, plus his own contributions.[39] Jordanes' *Romana*, written at the same time as the *Getica*,[40] and eastern in orientation and attitude, is a jumble of abridgements taken from well-known histories and chronicles.[41] It includes occasional brief items of relevance here.

Sidonius' panegyrics are of major importance to discussion of Ricimer, but in using them one is faced with the notorious difficulties and subtleties of understanding and using the genre. This subject cannot be examined in depth here, but at no point is the 'information' in the panegyrics uncritically accepted. The material on Ricimer occurs in two panegyrics: to Majorian, of whom he was a *de facto* colleague, and to Anthemius, Ricimer's father-in-law. Ricimer was not present when Sidonius gave the panegyric to Majorian, but was almost certainly present for the panegyric to Anthemius, having just

---

[38] I am grateful to Dr Benedict Salway for this information on Cassiodorus' chronicle.

[39] Jordanes, *Getica*, preface, 1–3. It is evident that he has included elements of oral tradition throughout.

[40] Jordanes, *Getica*, preface, 2.

[41] Jordanes, trans. Mierow (1915: 10–11); Goffart (1988: 28).

married his daughter (see pp. 235–6). Sidonius' letters also include information on Gaul and Italy during these years.

Events of Anthemius' reign, in particular the expedition against the Vandals, and his conflict with Ricimer, are recorded in some eastern histories (the most important being those of Procopius, John of Antioch, and John Malalas), which, as might be expected, view the West from Constantinople's standpoint.[42] Procopius wrote within the tradition of secular, narrative, political history, but unfortunately much of his material on the West in the fifth century AD (incidental to his account of Justinian's wars) is less reliable than the rest of his history. The exception is where he makes use of Priscus. His other sources for the West are uncertain; sometimes he seems to be using oral tradition, while any written sources were probably eastern rather than western.[43]

The Byzantine historian John of Antioch (of whom nothing is known) wrote a world history in the classical tradition, which survives only in fragments. For the fifth century AD he used existing eastern histories, especially that of Priscus, and possibly that of Candidus.[44] Those sections based on Priscus are particularly important for Italy; his other sources for the West are not known. In contrast, John Malalas's much more unsophisticated chronicle has survived in full. Written in the sixth century, it concentrates on eastern affairs, especially those of Constantinople, but refers to the involvement of Leo and Anthemius in Italy. His sources in general included eastern histories, oral tradition, and, possibly, city chronicles,[45] but how he obtained his material on Italy is not known.[46]

Another, marginal, source is the eighth-century *Historia Romana* by Paul the Deacon, who wrote a better-known history of the Lombards. The *Historia Romana* is a six-book continuation of Eutropius' *Breviary*, focusing on the end of the western

---

[42] For a discussion of eastern and western perceptions of AD 476 see Croke (1983: 81–119).

[43] Cameron (1985: 136, 198–9). Procopius does not use Cassiodorus or Jordanes, nor (probably) Marcellinus' chronicle.

[44] Heather (1991: 238).

[45] Jeffreys *et al.* (1990: p. xxiii).

[46] There is nothing on this question in the in-depth study by Jeffreys *et al.* (1990).

empire, from AD 364 to 552. Virtually all the material has been
unskilfully copied and abridged from surviving sources, including Marcellinus *comes*, Hydatius, Cassiodorus, Ennodius, and
Jordanes' *Romana*.[47] Given the derivation and date, it would
not be considered useful at all, were it not for the dearth of
sources for the late fifth century AD. There is occasional independent information, for instance on Ricimer's siege of Rome,
which might come from oral tradition or lost Italian written
sources and, although hard to assess, there seems no reason not
to make very cautious use of this information.

An important source for both Ricimer and Gundobad is the
Life of Epiphanius, Bishop of Pavia (then Ticinum), written
about AD 500 by Ennodius, his successor and one of the few
literary figures of the early sixth century. Ennodius was born in
AD 473/4, probably in Arles, but his childhood was spent in
Pavia with an aunt, and his family included a bishop of Milan.[48]
He knew Epiphanius well, and accompanied him on his later
diplomatic missions. This background makes him an important
source for northern Italy. Pavia had grown in importance in the
fourth and fifth centuries AD as a garrison town, and there is
archaeological evidence for the presence of barbarians in the city
and its territory in the late fifth century.[49]

For Odovacer's coup the most important sources are Procopius' *History of the Gothic War* and a western work by an
unknown author, known as *Anonymus Valesianus*. The accuracy
of Procopius' information is hard to assess; his is the only extant
history to attempt an explanation of the coup, and was written
three-quarters of a century after the events. He spent time in
Italy with Belisarius in the AD 530s, so his sources could have
been Italian, but we cannot be certain.[50] The work known as
Anonymus (or *Excerpta*) *Valesianus* is in two parts, the first
being a fourth-century biography of Constantine the Great.
The second part (covering AD 474–526) is mainly on the reign
of Theoderic in Italy, but right at the beginning includes some

---

[47] Goffart (1988: 49–50).

[48] *PLRE* ii, 393–4, Magnus Felix Ennodius; Burns (1984: 155–6).

[49] Bullough (1966: 83–94).

[50] It is not known whether he had any contact with Cassiodorus in Italy
(Cameron (1985: 198)).

information on Julius Nepos, Orestes, and Odovacer. This second part was written (in bad Latin) by an anonymous author *c*. AD 550 (possibly based on a chronicle written in Ravenna).[51] Again its value is hard to assess, because of the virtual absence of other relevant sources.

[51] Rolfe (1939: 506–7).

13

Ricimer's Early Career and the Reigns of Avitus and Majorian

Sidonius tells us that, unlike the two previous dominant *magistri* Flavius Constantius and Aetius, Ricimer was a barbarian and of noble ancestry.[1] His mother was a daughter of Vallia,[2] King of the Visigoths (AD 415–18), who was probably the brother of Athaulf, brother-in-law of Alaric himself.[3] A connection, however remote, with the Balthi dynasty, while not necessarily giving political advantage, would have bestowed prestige. Ricimer's father, whose name is not recorded, was a Suevian, also of royal blood.[4] It is possible, on the basis of his name, that Ricimer (occasionally spelt 'Recimer', 'Ricemer', or 'Rechimer') was related through his father to the Suevian king in Spain (AD 448–55), Rechiar(ius) son of the Suevian king, Rechila (AD 438–48), or to another Suevian leader in Spain, Rechimund(us).[5]

Ricimer was also connected to the Burgundians. Gundobad, his subordinate and successor, was the son of the Burgundian king, Gundioc[6] (and later himself King of the Burgundians). Almost certainly Ricimer was Gundobad's uncle and Gundioc's

---

[1] Sidonius, *Pan.* II, 360–2, 485–6, *Pan.* V, 266–8.

[2] Sidonius, *Pan.* II, 363, 368–70.

[3] Olympiodorus, frag. 26(1), suggests this. See also Heather (1991: 31).

[4] Sidonius, *Pan.* II, 360–3. 'Sueve' (or 'Suebi') was perhaps a name for a section of the Alamanni; and the Sueve in Spain may have been made up of both Alamanni and Quadi (Heather (1995: 13 n. 1)).

[5] The first element in the names (originally from an Indo-European stem connected with kingship or ruling) could be the Gothic 'reiks' (Hodgkin (1880b: 404 n. 1)), although the same or a similar stem appears in non-Gothic Germanic names, including Frankish ones.

[6] Gundioc claimed descent from the Gothic King Athanaric (Greg. Tur. *Historiae* II, 28).

brother-in-law.[7] What we know of Ricimer's relationship with Gundobad suggests that this personal tie was strong. In Ricimer's family background there were, therefore, at least two examples of intermarriage: the marriage of his parents, and that of his sister. It would be interesting to know whether such unions were common or exceptional (perhaps confined to the upper echelons of barbarian society for political purposes). In AD 455 Gundioc had joined the Visigoths under Theoderic in attacking the Sueves in Spain. He and his people then settled in Gaul. Gundioc ruled the Burgundians there until 473/4, and also held the title of *magister militum*, presumably *per Gallias*.[8]

Although his father was a Sueve, Ricimer was more often associated with the Goths by ancient writers;[9] perhaps because of more exalted connections on his mother's side or perhaps because he was brought up amongst them. It is nowhere stated that Ricimer's grandfather the Visigothic leader Vallia and his successor Theoderic (AD 418–51) were related, but it is quite

[7] See John Ant. frags. 209 (1) and 209 (2); John Malalas, 374. John of Antioch here uses two different sources (Blockley (1981–3: ii, 400 nn. 201, 203)). In the first, John describes Gundoband (*sic*) as Ricimer's brother, but in the second refers to Ricimer's nephew Gundobaules. As Gundobad must have been considerably younger than Ricimer (dying in AD 516), and Malalas says that he (Gundoubarios) was Ricimer's sister's son, it seems most probable that Ricimer's sister had married Gundobad's father Gundioc (perhaps in the 440s). This supports the other evidence that Ricimer's parents were of high rank.

[8] Hilarius, *Ep.* IX, dating to AD 463 (within the reign of Severus). It is uncertain why Gundioc was given this post or by whom. A feasible theory is that he was appointed by Ricimer, his brother-in-law, when Aegidius, the previous senior commander in Gaul, disassociated himself from the new regime in Italy (see Pt. II, pp. 92–3). The reasons why the title of *magister militum* might be given to a barbarian ruler were complex. It was in no way acknowledgement of kingship within the empire, but nor was it mere flattery. It was a way of giving important allied barbarian leaders authority within the imperial hierarchical system, and, as a military title, gave them the authority to command military forces.

[9] For instance, Ennod. *Vita. Epiph.* 67 and Malalas, 373, call him a 'Goth', but perhaps in the sense of a barbarian generally.

likely,[10] and if so, Ricimer would have had a family connection with the ruling Visigothic family in Gaul.[11]

When Vallia led the Goths in Spain they were allies of the Romans, fighting the Vandals and Alans, but not the Sueves (who were settled in the North-West); this might have been when Vallia married his daughter to a Sueve. If so, this would suggest a birth date for Ricimer in the AD 420s, making him somewhere between his late twenties and late thirties as *magister militum* in AD 456–7. This is supported by a reference to him as *iuvenis* in the early 450s.[12]

Ricimer was almost certainly, like other Goths and Sueves, an Arian Christian.[13] An inscription from the church of St. Agatha, still standing, in the central Suburra area of Rome, recorded a dedication showing that Ricimer had decorated or adorned the church in fulfilment of a vow.[14] St. Agatha's is referred to in sixth-century documents as 'the church of the Goths',[15] which might mean that it was, or had been, a specifically Arian church.[16] The date of the inscription must be between AD 459, when Ricimer became consul, and *c*.470, from which date he was in conflict with the emperor and be-

[10] Theoderic was married to Alaric's daughter (Sidonius, *Carm.* VII, 505). The daughter of Theoderic was married to the Suevian Recharius, another possible connection with Ricimer (Hydatius, 132 (140) *s.a.* 449; Jordanes, *Getica* 229). See p. 178.

[11] Wolfram (1988: 202) supports this connection; he believes that Theoderic's son, Retemeris in our sources, had the same name as Ricimer and was possibly named after the patrician. On the names see Schönfeld (1965: 188, 189–92).

[12] Sidonius, *Pan.* V, 266–8.

[13] The Arianism of Ricimer and of most of the barbarian peoples was not Arianism as understood in intellectual ecclesiastical terms; but this is not an appropriate place for lengthy discussion of this. Here, the term is used simply for the Christianity of the fifth-century Goths and others.

[14] The inscription was recorded, along with sketches of the mosaics, in the sixteenth century (Muntz (1886: 308)). The accepted version is: 'Fl. Ricimer ui [vir illustris?] magister utriusque militiae patricius et ex cons. ord. pro voto suo adornauit' (Diehl, *ILCV* no. 1637; Dessau, *ILS* no. 1294; De Rossi, *ICUR* II, no. 127).

[15] Greg. Gt. *Dialog.* III, 30; *Liber Pontif.*, p. 61.

[16] This is an interesting area for speculation. There seem to have been 'Arian' churches in both Rome and Ravenna, so presumably those of Arian beliefs living in Italy at this time preferred to worship in churches with specific

sieging Rome until his death (see Ch. 14). Saint Agatha was particularly venerated in Catane (Catania) in Sicily, where she had been martyred.[17] It is conceivable that there was some connection between the fulfilment of the vow and Ricimer's activities on the island (see p. 187).[18] The dedication was associated with mosaics which were (with the inscription) destroyed in a later renovation by Pope Clement VIII but were recorded in sketches at the end of the sixteenth century. They were of the highest quality and showed the figures of Christ and twelve apostles. If the sketches are accurate they marked an important stage in the development of mosaic art.[19] The fact that we are told that Ricimer 'adorned' the church probably shows that it was already in existence at that time, rather than being built by him, although it is possible that it was Ricimer who was responsible for it becoming an Arian church, if it was not so already. A suggestion that St. Agatha's was Ricimer's burial place is entirely unfounded.[20]

There is no hint in the sources of how, or why, Ricimer entered imperial service and rose to high rank. He may have

Arian adherence or even ritual (unless the Arian churches actually date to the later Gothic period?). This may well have caused difficulties with the Catholic authorities, as subsequent rededications would suggest.

[17] Smith and Wace (1877–87: i, 58–9).

[18] Archaeological data shows that Catania suffered a barbarian raid sometime between *c*. AD 450 and 490 (Wilson (1988: 133–5)).

[19] Muntz (1886: 311); Armellini (1942: 252).

[20] Amory (1997: 246 n. 4). There is an instructive story attached to this suggestion. Amory's evidence for this is a 'bronze dagger' with Ricimer's name on it, supposedly found in the church of St. Agatha, suggesting Ricimer's (extremely unusual) intramural burial there (and supposedly dating the mosaic inscription to 470–2). His cited source for this dagger is an article by Zeiller in the journal of the French School at Rome of 1904, which indeed says that 'une lame de bronze portant le nom de Ricimer et la date de 470 a été ... trouvée dans l'église de Sainte-Agathe' (Zeiller (1904: 20)). This inscribed dagger is, however, unknown to the standard collections of Latin inscriptions. Armellini, in the new edition of his book on the churches of Rome (1942: i, 253), actually records the inscription on this 'lamina', which he also believed to have been found in the church, and it is immediately apparent that it is identical to that on the well-known rectangular bronze object (provenance unknown) in a Berlin museum, bearing Ricimer's name (but no date) described on p. 217. Amory's dagger is in fact a coin weight. The association with St. Agatha's, which predates Amory, seems likely to be conjecture, based on the Ricimer

entered the Roman army as an individual or as one of (or the leader of) a unit of federates. It is conceivable that the reason was connected to his position among his people, possibly to dynastic rivalry; or his parents may have already been in imperial service. Ricimer was probably, from the beginning, in a fairly high position among the Romans, and it seems that from early on he had some sort of personal link with the upper-class Italian Majorian.[21] They almost certainly served together in the imperial army. Majorian is known to have campaigned in Gaul with Aetius,[22] and Ricimer may have done so too. Demandt suggested that one reason for Ricimer's rise was that he possessed great wealth.[23] While not impossible, the only evidence for this is that in Priscus' account of his bribery of Marcellinus' mercenaries (see Pt. I, p. 46), in which Marcellinus is said to have been unable to compete with Ricimer's wealth; and this could have been the state's money rather than his own.

Some possible specific contexts and dates for Ricimer's entry into imperial service can be tentatively suggested. During Vallia's brief reign Galla Placidia was returned to the Romans and it is known that, as a result of her marriage to Athaulf, she had an entourage of Gothic retainers in Italy,[24] which could have included Ricimer's family. Alternatively, these retainers may have formed a core of Goths in imperial service at court, later joined by others from a similar background. Gothic hostages of high

connection. Zeiller's cited authority of Muratori (1739) gives the same inscription, but neither he nor other authorities (including the numismatist Friedlander (1882: 1)) place its provenance in the church of St. Agatha. The confusion seems to have come about from the ambiguities of translation from one language to another (*lame* and *lamina* can mean either 'strip' or 'blade') and been compounded by the temptation to overstretch evidence.

[21] Sidonius, *Pan.* v, 266–8. Aetius' barbarian wife, when trying to turn her husband against Majorian, says: 'Coniunctus amore praeterea est iuveni, grandis quem spiritus armat regis avi.' However, this might reflect the time of the composition of the panegyric rather than that of Aetius.

[22] Sidonius, *Pan.* v, 207–56.

[23] Demandt (1989: 174).

[24] Olympiodorus, frag. 38 (40). They were presumably inherited by her, on her husband's death. Olympiodorus says that she also inherited barbarian retainers from her second husband Fl. Constantius.

rank were also handed over to the Romans in the agreements of
AD 416 and 418.[25]

A more intriguing possibility is a connection with the Gothic
wife of Aetius.[26] The association is admittedly tenuous, but
both Ricimer and one of Aetius' wives were of Gothic royal
descent. Aetius' wife possibly belonged to a line that had been
ousted from the succession, as Sidonius refers to her being
debarred from a Gothic sceptre (though this may merely refer
to her sex).[27] If Ricimer was a close relative, this would explain
his entry into Aetius' corps of officers, and into imperial high
society. In his panegyric to Majorian, Sidonius makes great
play, to an almost ludicrous extent, with the hostility of Aetius'
Gothic wife towards the future emperor, and her insistence on
his exile.[28] If Aetius' wife was related to Ricimer, this may have
been an indirect way for Sidonius to attack Ricimer, or to give
Majorian a coded warning against his colleague. Hydatius refers
to Ricimer as *comes* (presumably *rei militaris*) in AD 456–7[29] of
the Emperor Avitus (who had also served in a senior position
under Aetius).[30] By the time of the overthrow of Avitus in
October AD 456 Ricimer was *magister militum*[31] (we do not

[25] Orosius, 7, 43, and 12–13.

[26] Merobaudes, *Carm.* IV, 15–18; Sidonius, *Pan.* V, 128, 203–6. The
question of the number and identity of Aetius' wives is complex and is discussed very fully by Clover (1971: 31–2). Aetius' Gothic wife could be the ex-
wife of Boniface, Pelagia (probably his second wife), who was wealthy (John
Ant. frag. 201 (3); Marcellinus *comes*, *s.a.* 432) and must have been of high
status—or conceivably a third wife who, it has been suggested, could have been
the daughter of Visigothic King Theoderic (Demandt (1980: 621 and n. 57)).
Merobaudes' poem on Aetius' son's birthday (*Carm.* IV) mentions that his wife
was 'the descendant of kings' (like Ricimer) and calls her father 'Rome's
associate'. It also implies that her father was present in Rome for his grandson's
christening (Theoderic is not recorded as visiting Rome). A connection between Ricimer and Pelagia, who was originally Arian (Augustus, *Ep.* 220, 4)
and whose family may have been in imperial service in the early fifth century, is
perhaps more likely than one with a daughter of Theoderic married at a later
date (although Theoderic may, as mentioned, have been related to Vallia,
Ricimer's grandfather).

[27] Sidonius, *Pan.* V, 203–4: 'nato quae regna parabo exclusa sceptris
Geticis'.

[28] Sidonius, *Pan.* V, 130–304.

[29] Hydatius, 169 (176) *s.a.* 456.

[30] Sidonius, *Pan.* III, 230–2, 241, 251.

[31] *Fasti. Vind. Prior. s.a.* 456 and 457; *Auct. Prosp. Haun. s.a.* 456.

184 Ricimer and his Successors in Italy

know whether *peditum* or *equitum*).[32] He may have been *comes*
prior to Avitus' elevation (even from before Aetius' assassination) and been promoted to *magister militum* by Avitus, perhaps following his victory over the Vandals (see below).
However, Hydatius and other sources often used the term
comes loosely to refer to a holder of high office or member of
the imperial court, rather than to a holder of the specific rank of
comes rei militaris,[33] and so it is possible that Ricimer was, by AD
456, already *(comes et) magister militum*.

Ricimer's entry upon the stage of history is quite characteristic; Hydatius records under AD 456 that:

'In these days, it was reported to King Theoderic that a large number
of Vandals, moving towards Gaul or Italy with 60 ships, had been
destroyed by Avitus,[34] through an encirclement [or, 'a manœuvre' or
'a trick' or 'an ambush'] by the *comes* Ricimer.'[35]

This action presumably took place during the spring or summer
months of that year. Immediately following (but as a separate
entry) are further reports of the same event:

The tribune Hesychius, an envoy sent to Theoderic with sacred gifts,
came to Gallaecia announcing, what I have mentioned above, the
killing of a large number of Vandals in Corsica; and that Avitus had
set off from Italy for Arles in Gaul; [but] ships from the East, coming
to Hispalis, reported that they were killed by Marcian's forces.[36]

---

[32] A Remistus was patrician under Avitus, and, as his name is Germanic
(Schönfeld (1965: 187)), he may also have been *magister militum*. Which man
held which of the two *magister militum* positions is probably not of great
importance. It is unknown to what extent the more subtle distinctions of
the old, imperial-army rank structure had survived into the third quarter
of the fifth century.   [33] Barnwell (1992: 36–8).

[34] Almost certainly an example of the common Roman practice of attributing all military successes to the emperor, whether he was personally involved or
not. Avitus was no doubt busy establishing his position, and probably spent
most of his time in Rome. He was consul for AD 456, which would have been
celebrated there at the beginning of that year. In Sept./Oct. he was in Italy (or
possibly Arles; see the reports of his deposition below).

[35] Hydatius, 169 (176): 'Hisdem diebus Rechimeris comitis circumuen-
tione magna multitudo Vandalorum, quae se de Carthagine cum LX nauibus
ad Gallias uel ad Italiam mouerat, regi Theudorico nuntiatur occisa per Auitum'.

[36] Hydatius, 170 (177) *s.a.* 456–7: 'Esycius tribunus legatus ad Theodor-
icum cum sacris muneribus missus ad Galleciam uenit nuntians ei id quod

These two entries are best interpreted as describing three separate reports which reached the ears of Hydatius by various routes.[37] The first two reports were messages sent to Theoderic, who was at this time in north-west Spain, campaigning as an ally of Rome against the Sueves. Immediately prior to the above chronicle entries, Theoderic is reported as being at Bracara, not far from Aquae Flaviae, Hydatius' probable bishopric, and may have still been there when these reports reached him (he was certainly still in Gallaecia).[38] Hydatius may even have had occasion to attend the king and thus have heard the news. The first report (mentioning Ricimer) came from an unnamed source (the Visigothic capital Toulouse?); the second (perhaps arriving slightly later) from the envoy Hesychius. The third report, originating with easterners, may have reached Hydatius through several intermediaries, since Hispalis (on the southern coast of Spain near Gades) was a considerable way from Aquae Flaviae.

There may have been weeks or more between these various reports reaching Spain and Hydatius. Avitus was deposed in October AD 456, and his fall from power was already under way when the embassy bearing the second report, confirming the victory, set out. The envoy Hesychius was presumably sent by Avitus. The message was perhaps sent as Avitus set out for Gaul, possibly requesting help, and Hesychius probably expected him to have gained Arles by the time he himself reached Theoderic.[39]

Sixty ships would have presented a major problem. They are described as threatening Gaul and Italy; the Vandals may have intended to attack both, but it is more likely that the imperial

supra in Corsica caesam multitudinem Wandalorum et Auitum de Italia ad Gallias Arelate successisse; orientalium naues Hispalim uenientes per Marciani exercitum caesam nuntiant.'

[37] The first and second reports are divided into two separate entries by Hydatius (169 and 170), the emphasis in the content of the two is different, and Hydatius, who strives after brevity, could, if this had been one embassy, have more concisely combined the information.

[38] Hydatius, 167 (174) *s.a.* 456–7 and 171 (178) *s.a.* 456–7.

[39] Strangely, Courtois (1955: 186) thought that the report of victory over the Vandals in Corsica was a fabrication of Avitus as part of a diplomatic ruse; this seems most unlikely.

command was uncertain of their destination. The general direction, towards southern Gaul or north-west Italy, is confirmed
by the location of the subsequent battle at Corsica. Most of the
Vandal raids in the western Mediterranean were aimed at Sicily
and southern Italy, so this may mark a change in strategy,
possibly connected to Avitus' alliance to the Visigothic kingdom. Or, possibly, having sacked Rome in AD 455, Gaiseric
simply felt that it would be more profitable and interesting to try
somewhere different this year. Gaiseric was, at this time, also
conquering those African territories that had been retained by
the western empire in the treaty of AD 442,[40] provoking ineffectual diplomatic protests from Avitus and Marcian.

It is surprising that this victory is, in nearly all secondary
sources, described as a naval battle (which requires the Latin
in Corsica to be translated as 'off Corsica' rather than 'in or on
Corsica').[41] That this engagement was naval is unlikely. Battles
at sea were rare in late antiquity, and it is clear that Rome's naval
resources were extremely weak (see App.). The passage speaks
of men being slain rather than ships being destroyed, which
suggests that the Vandals were defeated after having landed.
The *circumventione* may have involved the time-honoured tactic
of catching raiders, laden with loot, on their way back to their
boats.

It is intriguing that the victory is attributed to a successful
manœuvre, or trick, on the part of Ricimer; he was, it seems,
capable of more initiative than most commanders of the time.
By inflicting a defeat on the Vandals he had achieved what other
contemporary imperial commanders with larger armies, such as
Aspar and Basiliscus, were incapable of. There is, however, no
hint in the sources that he captured the Vandal ships, which
would have been useful for Rome, nor any evidence that Gaiseric's depredations were subsequently curtailed.

The third report to reach Hydatius, claiming an East Roman
victory over the Vandals, is a mystery. Hydatius believed that
it referred to the same Vandal horde, but he may have been

---

[40] Prosper, *Chron.* 1339 *s.a.* 441; Cassiodorus, *Chronica* 1240 *s.a.* 442.

[41] See e.g. *PLRE* ii, 943, Fl. Ricimer; Sidonius, trans. and ed. Anderson
(1937: 40 n. 1); Bury (1923: ii, 327); Moss (1973: 726); O'Flynn (1983: 105);
Demandt (1989: 171).

mistaken. There are no other reports of Marcian's forces fighting Vandals in AD 456, although we know of undated Vandal raids on eastern provinces around this time.[42] The eastern informants, or Hydatius, or both, may have got East Roman wrong. It is food for thought, though, that about this time Marcellinus of Dalmatia was fighting the Vandals in Sicily, possibly at the behest of Marcian and with his assistance (see Pt. I, pp. 49–51).

Priscus also records that Ricimer was in action in Sicily. Following the failure of western and eastern representations to Gaiseric, he says that Avitus prepared for war and sent Ricimer to Sicily with an army.[43] Priscus later makes a further reference to Ricimer in connection with Sicily, when he describes how Ricimer suborned Marcellinus' Scythian troops on the island (see Pt. I, p. 46 for the text). Sidonius Apollinaris also describes Ricimer fighting in Sicily at an unstated date prior to AD 468, on the plain of Agrigentum, on the south coast.[44] We cannot be certain how all these references relate to each other. There may have been a number of campaigns in Sicily in which Ricimer was involved, as there were almost annual Vandal raids on Sicily and southern Italy at this time.[45]

Priscus also provides a useful description of the strategy and tactics of the Vandal raiders and Roman defenders:

Every year at the beginning of spring he [Gaiseric] descended upon Sicily and Italy with his fleet. He did not readily attack the cities which the Italians had garrisoned, but seized the places in which there was no adequate force, laid them waste and enslaved them. The Italians were unable to bring help to all the points at which the Vandals could land, being hampered by the numbers of their enemies and their lack of a

---

[42] Priscus, trans. and ed. Blockley (1994: 68).

[43] Priscus, frag. 31 (1).

[44] Sidonius, *Pan.* 11, 367–9. The city of Agrigentum, which had an important harbour, had allowed its defences to decay (Wilson (1988: 181)), and would therefore have become vulnerable to attack. In his panegyric to Majorian, Sidonius makes another vague reference to a recent Vandal defeat, which might relate either to this campaign or to the defeat of the fleet off Corsica (Sidonius, *Pan.* v, 88–90).

[45] Priscus, frag. 39 (1).

fleet. The latter they sought from the Romans but did not receive it because of the treaty with the Vandals.[46]

It is difficult and perhaps unnecessary to try to piece these brief reports of Ricimer's early military career into a chronology, but it is possible to say that Ricimer seems to have been a competent soldier, who was elevated to high rank by Aetius. Twice he is attributed with having acted with cunning: first in the way in which he defeated the Vandal raiding party, and later in enticing away Marcellinus' troops.

In AD 456 Ricimer moved into a position of political as well as military importance, when he was involved in the overthrowing of Emperor Avitus. His associate in this was his ex-comrade-in-arms, and perhaps friend, Julius Valerius Majorian. The latter had risen to the rank of *comes domesticorum*,[47] possibly when recalled from retirement by Valentinian in AD 454.[48] This post was an influential one. The *protectores domestici* were élite troops, with young Roman nobles among their number, and they functioned as imperial guards, usually stationed at the imperial court. They had an independent commander, the *comes domesticorum*, who hence enjoyed an influential position close to the emperor. Military experience, good social standing and reputation,[49] and imperial favour were

[46] Priscus, frag. 39 (1) (Blockley's translation). This is confirmation that Ricimer's victory is more likely to have been in a land than a naval battle. The Romans (by which he means the East Romans) were not prepared to jeopardize their treaty with the Vandals to assist the Italians. It is noticeable that although his usual phrase is 'West Romans', occasionally Priscus refers to Italians (see elsewhere in frag. 39 and frags. 31 and 41); he also makes reference to the 'western Gauls' (frag. 39). This may well indicate his awareness of the fragmentation of the empire and the increasing split between East and West (and possibly he did not consider that the Italians involved in these cases warranted the term 'Roman').

[47] *Chronica Gallica a 511*, 628.

[48] Sidonius, *Pan.* v, 306–8.

[49] According to Sidonius, Majorian's unnamed father had served under Aetius in a financial position and his mother was the daughter of a Majorianus (perhaps Pannonian) who had held the post of *magister militum per Illyricum* under Theodosius (Sidonius, *Pan.* v, 107–16, 116–25). Service under Theodosius I commonly featured among the ancestors of men in high positions later in the fifth century. There is some disagreement among modern scholars as to whether Majorian's father can be identified with the Domninus, businessman

behind Majorian's rise, plus, no doubt, personal ambition. Majorian certainly, and Ricimer probably, had served under Aetius, and there may have been other elements to this connection, political, personal, and social, that would have brought them both close to the centres of political power.

Most of the sources for the fall of Avitus are not detailed, and tell only of a defeat at Placentia.[50] As discussed above, Hydatius recorded that Avitus had abandoned Italy. Later it is reported that 'Avitus, three years after he was made emperor by the Gauls and the Goths, lost imperial power [and] lacking the promised Gothic support, lost his life.'[51] In between the two entries come others referring to Spanish events, but the gap is not particularly significant; items of news did not necessarily reach Hydatius in the order in which they occurred, and would have been placed by him in rough order and as clarity demanded.[52]

and attendant to Aetius, who, John of Antioch says, was the father of another (otherwise unknown) Maximian, a candidate for the throne after the death of Valentinian (John Ant. frag. 201). Barnes (1983: 268) and Blockley (1981–3: ii, 393 n. 134) would amend this to *Maiorianus*. This would make the text more logical, and the corruption is an easy one; the only caveat is that Domninus is described as an Egyptian businessman who had been successful in Italy, and this background would be an unusual one for Majorian, both as a senior army officer and as a contender in high-level politics. (The Byzantine writer George Cedrenus (p. 606) does refer to 'Majorian, known as Maximus', but is so late that this cannot be taken as proof.)

[50] See e.g. *Auct. Prosp. Haun. s.a.* 456; Vict. Tonn. *s.a.* 456; *Chronica Gallica a 511*, 628.

[51] Hydatius, 176 (183) *s.a.* 456–7: 'Avitus, tertio anno posteaquam a Gallis et a Gothis factus fuerat imperator, caret imperio, Gothorum promisso destitutus auxilio, caret et vita.'

[52] Mathisen has written an article which attempts to reconcile the various accounts of the fall of Avitus (Mathisen (1985: 326–35)). His reconstruction involves Avitus retreating to Gaul, subsequently to return to Italy to be defeated at Placentia. This is only necessary, however, if the information given in Hydatius' chronicle is considered absolutely accurate in detail and sequence. It is simpler to assume that Avitus was intercepted on his way *out* of Italy (as described by John of Antioch). See also Mathisen's articles on Avitus' reign (Mathisen (1981: 232–47) and (1991: 163–6)), the latter in reply to the criticisms of Burgess (1987: 335–45).

Gregory of Tours provides more information. Avitus, he says, was 'soliciting imperial power, chose to pursue excess, [and was] overthrown by the senators'.[53] This *luxoriosae* has sometimes been interpreted as 'debauchery', or 'extravagance' (the latter at least fits with the evidence for financial problems). It could be invented moral causality, typical of Gregory, in which case the otherwise interesting statement that he was deposed by the senate may merely follow from this.

John of Antioch's account is more circumstantial. Its origin is unknown, possibly originally Arvernian ambassadors to the court at Constantinople:[54]

When Avitus was emperor of Rome and there was famine at that time, the people blamed Avitus and forced him to send away from the city of Rome those whom he had brought with him from Gaul. He also dismissed the Goths whom he had brought as his own guard, and gave them a money payment raised from public works, through the sale of the bronze in them to the merchants, for there was no gold in the imperial treasuries. This roused the Romans to revolt ... Majorian and Ricimer also broke into open revolt now that they were freed from fear of the Goths. As a result Avitus, afraid both of these internal disturbances and of the attacks of the Vandals, withdrew from Rome and began to make his way to Gaul.[55]

The details (and disputed date) of the coup have been discussed in such minute and scholarly detail in the past by Mathisen (see above) that it would be unproductive to do so again here. However, it is useful to re-examine the specific roles of Ricimer and Majorian. Why did the two turn against Avitus in AD 456? Ricimer, and probably Majorian, had been trusted by him to hold senior positions in the army, and all three had served under Aetius. Older historians sought Ricimer's reasons for disaffection in his barbarian blood.[56] More specifically it has been suggested that the recent defeat and massacre in Spain of his father's people the Sueves by Avitus' Visigothic ally

[53] Greg. Tur. *Historiae* II, 11: 'ambisset imperium, luxoriosae agere volens, a senatoribus projectus'.

[54] Mathisen (1985: 329 n. 17); Blockley (1981–3: i, 67, 114).

[55] John Ant. frag. 202 (Blockley's translation, Priscus, frag. 32).

[56] Stevens (1933: 38–40) attributed Avitus' fall to his coming into opposition with the barbarian federates represented by Ricimer.

Theoderic had alienated Ricimer.[57] While not impossible, there is no evidence that Ricimer cared anything for the fate of the Spanish Sueves. Equally, Avitus' alliance with the Visigoths, to whom Ricimer was connected, clearly cut no ice with Ricimer.

Almost certainly Ricimer's motives for turning against the emperor should be sought in an Italian context. Ricimer, and perhaps his parents, may have lived most, or all, of their lives as high-status Roman citizens. Ricimer may have thought of himself primarily as Roman, or even as Italian. During his period of power his concern was always primarily with the defence and integrity of Italy. His objections to Avitus may well have been identical to those of Majorian and the Italian senatorial opposition. Avitus lacked support from, or had antagonized, several, if not all, of the Italian interest groups, including the senators, elements of the Roman populace, and some or all of the military.[58]

It is usually thought that Avitus incurred the enmity of the Italian élite because of general anti-Gallic sentiment, combined with dislike of his Visigothic backing[59] and, in the case of senators, his appointment of Gallo-Romans to important civil posts normally held by Italians.[60] This last objection seems petty given the dire state of public affairs, but is all too typical. On the other hand, the opposition to Avitus may have had less to do with general separatism than with his personal unpopularity, and the ambitions of others. The existence, in the person of Majorian (possibly the original instigator), of a younger Italian alternative, acceptable to both army and senate, may have been a major factor.

It is unclear whether the initiative was taken by a military or civilian faction, or an alliance of the two. The sources imply that Ricimer and Majorian turned against the emperor after he had

[57] Gibbon, ed. Bury (1897–1900: iv, 13); Hodgkin (1880b: 393).

[58] This can be compared to Sidonius' (*Ep.* 11, xiii, 5) description of Avitus' short-lived predecessor Petronius Maximus ruling 'amongst the tumult of the soldiers, populace [and] federates' ('inter tumultus militum popularium foederatorum').

[59] Hence, perhaps, Sidonius' portrayal of Theoderic in his panegyric to Avitus as considerably more subservient to Avitus than he must have been in reality (*Pan.* VII, 221–9, 355–6, 432–4).

[60] Mathisen (1981: 232–47) covers this in detail.

already lost general support in Rome, but may not be accurate in this. According to John of Antioch, Ricimer and Majorian took action when the emperor dismissed, on his own initiative, his Gothic forces.[61] It seems unlikely that they could not have defeated them; so they may have been unwilling to take the risk of antagonizing Theoderic, or their removal may have simply been the spur to action. One question is why Theoderic had left his protégé to fend for himself in Rome while he took himself off on an extended campaign in Spain. Had he wished to inherit Aetius' position, as sometimes suggested,[62] he should surely have accompanied Avitus to Italy, or at least remained accessible in Gaul. Hydatius, indeed, suggests (*promisso destitutus auxilio*) that Theoderic in some way deprived Avitus of promised backing.[63]

Avitus, having lost all control, understandably lost his nerve, and made for home. His patrician (and probably *magister militum*) Remistus[64] was killed at Classis, near Ravenna, on 17 September.[65] It may have been Ricimer who led the forces that defeated Avitus at Placentia a month later; the majority of the sources mention only him. Victor of Tunnunna wrote: 'The patrician Ricimer defeated Avitus, whose innocence was spared, and was made Bishop of the city of Placentia.'[66] Likewise The

---

[61] If John is correct in frag. 202 that it was Avitus who took this initiative rather than Theoderic (who was in Spain then), then this could have been because he found his Gothic 'allies' presence in Rome too expensive and provocative. He may have hoped that their withdrawal would defuse opposition to him.

[62] See e.g. O'Flynn (1983: 105).

[63] Hydatius, 176 (183) *s.a.* 456–7.

[64] Remistus may have been a particular rival to Ricimer.

[65] *Fasti Vind. Prior. s.a.* 456; *Auct. Prosp. Haun. s.a.* 456. Rather oddly, perhaps, this is also recorded much later by Theophanes, AM 5948: 'In this year Ravenna was burnt and a few days later the patrician Ramitos [*sic*] was killed at Classe'. He continues: 'twenty-nine days later Amitos [*sic*] was defeated by Remikos [*sic*] and went to the city of Placentia in Gaul [*sic*]' (Mango and Scott's translation). Mango and Scott (1997: 168) comment that Theophanes, although he makes obvious mistakes, had a reasonably reliable source for western events here (possibly from Alexandria or Jerusalem), which was then contracted and garbled in his entries.

[66] Vict. Tonn. *s.a.* 456: 'Ricimirus patricius Avitum superat, cuius innocentiae parcens Placentiae civitatis episcopum facit.' Victor also refers to Avitus when he became emperor as 'vir totius simplicitatis' (*s.a.* 455). It is a

Fasti Vindobonenses reported that 'the emperor was captured at Placentia by the *magister militum* Ricimer, and his patrician Messianus was killed, on 17 October'.[67] A continuation to Prosper recorded:

The Emperor Avitus entered Placentia with a force of his allies. But the *magister militum* Ricimer intercepted him with a great number of the army. When battle was joined, most of his men were slaughtered, Avitus took flight, and his life was spared by Bishop Eusebius who from an emperor changed him into a bishop. Missianus [*sic*] the patrician of Avitus[68] was killed in the same battle on 18 October.[69]

Cassiodorus and Jordanes record the ending of Avitus' rule at Placentia, without naming the victor.[70] However, the sixth-century chronicler Marius of Avenches named both Ricimer and Majorian: 'the emperor Avitus was overthrown by Majorian and Ricimer at Placentia and made bishop in [or, 'of'] the city'.[71] John of Antioch likewise writes:

Avitus, afraid both of these internal disturbances and of the attacks of the Vandals, withdrew from Rome and began to make his way to Gaul. Majorian and Ricimer attacked him on the road and forced him to renounce his throne, put off his imperial robe and flee to a shrine. Then Majorian's followers kept him under siege until he died of starvation, having reigned for eight months. Some say that he was strangled.[72]

---

mystery why Victor, writing in North Africa in the sixth century, took this view of Avitus.

[67] *Fasti Vind. Prior. s.a.* 456: 'captivus est imp. Placentia a magis. mil. Ricimere et occisus est Messiam patricius eius XVI kl. Nov.'

[68] Messianus had assisted Avitus against the Goths (Sidonius, *Pan.* VII, 425–7). He may have been appointed as *magister militum* to replace Remistus (*PLRE* ii, 761–2, Messianus).

[69] *Auct. Prosp. Haun. s.a.* 456: 'Imperator Avitus Placentiam cum sociorum robore ingressns [*sic*] quem cum magna vi[*uis*] exercitus magister militum Recimer excepit. commisso proelio Avitus cum magna suorum caede terga vertit, quem vitae reservatum Eusebius episcopus ex imperatore episcopum facit. interfectus in eo proelio Missianus patricius Aviti XV k. Novem.'

[70] Cassiodorus, *Chronica* 1266 *s.a.* 456; Jordanes, *Getica* 240.

[71] Marius Avent. *s.a.* 456: 'deiectus est Avitus imperator a Maioriano et Recemere Placentia et factus est episcopus in civitate'.

[72] John Ant. frag. 202 (Blockley's translation, Priscus, frag. 32).

The Gallic Chronicle of 511 mentioned Majorian alone, but in
relation to the killing of Avitus rather than to the battle: 'Avitus
was killed by Majorian the *comes domesticorum* at Placentia'.[73]
John of Antioch's account and the statement in the continuation
to Prosper that Ricimer caught up (*excepit*) with Avitus at
Placentia[74] both indicate, as previously discussed, that Avitus
was intercepted as he was heading out of Italy. He still had
enough barbarian troops to make it a battle; while Ricimer
probably led a large force of the Italian army (perhaps from
North Italian garrison cities). The sources are consistent in
saying that Avitus was defeated in battle, then ordained as a
bishop at Placentia.

The Eusebius mentioned by one source as ordaining Avitus
was probably Eusebius, Bishop (and previously Deacon) of
Milan (a city with which Ricimer is later connected) from
AD 449 to 465/6, and famous as a restorer of churches.[75] The
list of bishops in the *Series Episcoporum Ecclesiae Catholicae* for
Piacenza (Placentia) gives Avitus (Aricius) for AD 456, followed
in 457 by a Placidus (no Eusebius).[76] The presence of the
alternative, Aricius, suggests that the compiler has not included
the name of Avitus solely on the basis of the literary sources
above, but presumably from ecclesiastical sources from Piacenza. These may have shown either the name 'Avitus', with
'Aricius' as a variant, or only 'Aricius', which Gams may have
assumed was a corrupt form of Avitus on the basis of the sources
covered above, and amended. In either case, but particularly the
first, it is very likely that Avitus was made Bishop *of* Placentia as
well as *at* Placentia, but, on the basis of this list, was no longer
bishop there the following year.

Avitus died shortly after being made bishop, but there is no
consensus on the circumstances. One Gallic chronicle says that
he was killed by Majorian at Placentia, and John of Antioch

---

[73] *Chronica Gallica a 511*, 628: 'Avitus occisus est a Maioriano comite
domesticorum Placentiae'.

[74] *Auct. Prosp. Haun. s.a.* 456.

[75] Gams (1875: 795); Smith and Wace (1877–87: ii, 360). Another, but
much remoter, possibility is Eusebius of Nantes (fl. *c.* 461), who might conceivably have been in Avitus' company.

[76] Gams (1875: 745). Unfortunately, I have been unable to discover the
source of this information, nor the reason why the two names are given.

blames Majorian's followers for his death by starvation or stran-
gling at a shrine. It has been suggested that these reports are
correct, and that the Italian sources (for instance those above)
that do not name Majorian were reluctant to blame a popular
emperor.[77] The seventh-century A D Church historian Evagrius
has yet another version, suggesting that he died of plague.[78]

Gregory of Tours' account was that:

at the city of Placentia he was ordained bishop. Realizing moreover
that the senate were hostile to him and wished to deprive him of his
life, he set out for the church of St. Julian, the martyr of Auvergne,
with many offerings. But, the course of his life being completed during
the journey, he died, and his remains were carried to the town of
Brioude, and buried at the feet of the above-named martyr.[79]

Gregory had close ties with both Clermont and Brioude, so his
information is likely to be accurate at least in relation to Avitus'
burial place.[80] It seems possible therefore that Avitus did not
die at Placentia, but a short time later, either at the hands of
Majorian's followers or of natural causes. Theophanes (see text
in n. 65) mentions Placentia as being in Gaul, which might well
be a contraction from his original source, which may have
mentioned both Placentia and Gaul. Avitus was probably in
his sixties,[81] and a natural death (albeit unnaturally hastened)
has the virtue of explaining why his devoted son-in-law Sidonius was able to reconcile himself with Majorian later. It is
interesting that during the last decades of the western empire
some deposed emperors or usurpers were allowed to survive; for
example, Attalus, Glycerius, Nepos, Romulus, and, possibly,

---

[77] Mathisen (1985: 327–8).

[78] Evagrius, *HE* i, 2.

[79] Greg. Tur. *Historiae* 11, xi: 'apud Placentiam urbem episcopus ordena-
tur. Conperto autem, quod adhuc indignans senatus vita eum privari vellit,
basilica sancti Iuliani Arverni martyres cum multis muneribus expetivit. Sed
impleto in itenere vitae cursu, obiit, delatusque ad Brivatinsem vicum, ad
pedes antedicti martyres est sepultus.'

[80] Gregory's father Florentius, who was from Auvergne, had a particular
attachment to the cult of Julian at Brioude, and Gregory had visited the shrine
as a boy (Greg. Tur. *De Passione et Virtutibus Sancti Juliani Martyris* 24).

[81] Sidonius, *Pan.* V II, 597–8. When Avitus was an envoy to Fl. Constantius
in *c.* A D 420 he was called 'ephebus' (Sidonius, *Pan.* V I I, 207), which would fit
with this estimate.

Avitus. Enforced or 'voluntary' ordination foreshadows later Byzantine practice.

Ricimer had been able to lead the Italian army against the ruling emperor (not, admittedly, ever a difficult thing to persuade imperial troops to do), but we do not know whether he commanded their loyalty because of his birth or through qualities of military and political leadership in general. He seems to have retained the loyalty of the majority of the mainly barbarian imperial forces in Italy throughout his career, and there may have existed some elements of personal fidelity. This was not, of course, unique to this period, but was a characteristic of times of political instability, such as the late republican period and the third century AD, as well as the fifth.

The period immediately after Placentia, during which Majorian and Ricimer consolidated their positions, is very obscure (and again has been examined in exhaustive detail by Mathisen; for which, see below). There is some controversy as to the exact status of Majorian between the defeat of Avitus, in October AD 456, and December 457, when he was formally installed, and whether he was at this point (or indeed at any time) officially recognized by Constantinople (see pp. 198–200 esp. n. 99). The *Fasti Vindobonenses* alone records the initial move: 'Ricimer the *magister militum* was made *patricius* on 28 February and on the same day Majorian was made *magister militum*'.[82]

Hence, Ricimer's title of patrician, held to the end of his life, was not bestowed by a reigning western emperor, as with his predecessors.[83] The appointments may have been made, or approved, by the emperor in Constantinople, following urgent representations from the two men in the name of the senate,[84] but probably took place in some less regular way. Apart from doubts on the attitude of the eastern emperor, there are considerations of time and distance, especially as Marcian died on

---

[82] *Fasti Vind. Prior. s.a.* 457 (1): 'Ricimer mag. mil. patricius factus est pridie kl. Marcias et factus est Maiorianus mag. mil. ipso die'.

[83] Ricimer is almost always referred to as the 'patrician' in the sources, and this was almost certainly how he was known in his lifetime.

[84] This has been discussed by Baynes (1922: 225–7); Kaegi (1968: 31–3); Meyer (1969: 5–12); Barnes (1983: 268); and Demandt (1989: 172), who described this as the first attempt by the eastern emperor to rule the West through a general rather than an emperor.

27 January AD 457, after a serious illness lasting for five months.[85] Leo was proclaimed emperor on 7 February,[86] only three weeks before these appointments were made in the West.

It was once thought that Ricimer might have given up the rank of *magister militum* when he gained that of *patricius*,[87] but this would clearly have undermined his power, and is most improbable. For the short period from February to April he probably held one *magister militum* post and Majorian, temporarily, the other. The combined possession of the highest military command and the title of 'patrician' was the foundation of Ricimer's position, as it had been for previous occupiers of this role. It has been suggested that, because Ricimer did not owe his position to a particular emperor and retained the rank through more than one reign, the rank of patrician gained an independent status.[88] Although this has some validity, Ricimer was almost certainly regarded initially as the patrician of Majorian and later of Anthemius (see p. 241). It was, in truth, not the rank of patrician which took on an independent status but Ricimer himself. The special role of the *magister militum* and patrician did not long outlive Ricimer; although held briefly by his two successors it was not assumed by Odovacer, nor did it reappear under subsequent rulers.

The *Fasti Vindobonenses* records the next move: 'the emperor Majorian d.n. was elevated on 1 April, at the sixth milestone, in the camp at Columella'.[89] This was presumably the acclamation of Majorian as emperor by the army.[90] The previous weeks were probably spent in completing the disposal of Avitus and his faction and marshalling the necessary political support. There may have been opposition to deal with, and possibly other

[85] Theodorus Lector, *Epitome Historiae Ecclesiasticae* 367; John Malalas, 34.
[86] *Chronicon Paschale s.a.* 457; Theophanes, AM 5950.
[87] See e.g. Hodgkin (1880b: 401); Martroye (1907: 178).
[88] O'Flynn (1983: 107).
[89] *Fasti Vind. Prior. s.a.* 457 (2): 'et levatus est imp. d. n. Maioranus kald. April in miliario VI in campo ad columellas'. The 'd.n.' indicates that Majorian was accepted as a legitimate colleague by the eastern emperor. The location was presumably a major military base, six miles outside Ravenna, or possibly Rome.
[90] Referred to at the beginning of *Nov. Maj.* 1: 'et fortissimi exercitus ordinatione cognoscite'.

imperial candidates.[91] Ricimer and Majorian may also have needed to clarify their relationship.

During the five and a half months from the deposition of Avitus to the acclamation of Majorian on 1 April AD 457 there was no emperor in the West.[92] Strangely, some writers have interpreted this as an attempt by the eastern emperor to administer the West through a 'viceroy', dispensing with a western Augustus.[93] This is surely a misreading of the situation. Majorian and Ricimer would hardly have gone to all that trouble merely to become joint *magistri militae* under the control of Constantinople. Also, Leo was just establishing himself in the East, and would, almost certainly, not have wished to take on board the military and financial problems of the West. His consistent policy later on was that the West should be ruled by its own emperor, acceptable to himself as senior Augustus.[94]

Majorian was formally installed as emperor by the senate eight months later, on 28 December AD 457, at Ravenna.[95] It is likely that Leo's approval had been obtained by this date, if not previously.[96] Marcellinus *comes* says clearly that the appointment was by Leo: 'by the will of Leo, Majorian was proclaimed Caesar at Ravenna'.[97] Sidonius, in his later panegyric,

---

[91] This is probably the time of the 'Marcellan conspiracy' to place another (almost certainly Gallic) candidate on the throne (Sidonius, *Ep.* I, xi, 6).

[92] Technically, of course, first Marcian and then Leo would have been sole emperor.

[93] Kaegi (1968: 31); O'Flynn (1983: 107).

[94] The positions of Leo and Majorian were, at this point, not dissimilar, as Leo had come to power with the backing of the Alan *magister militum* Aspar (see p. 266–7).

[95] Sidonius, *Pan.* V, 387–8; *Auct. Prosper ad ed. a 455* (Vatican epitome), giving the date; Marcellinus *comes*, s.a. 457; Jordanes, *Getica* 236.

[96] Recognition from Constantinople would undoubtedly have been *sought* at some point, either in the weeks prior to April or the subsequent months, between April and December.

[97] Marcellinus *comes*, s.a. 457: 'Leo eidem defuncto successit. Cuius voluntate Maiorianus apud Ravennam Caesar est ordinatus'. Also, Marcellinus calls him 'Caesar', and he gave imperial titles only to those officially recognized in the East. He also distinguished meticulously between junior and senior emperors (Croke (1983: 89)). The *Fasti Vindobonensis Prior. s.a.* 458 records 'et levatus est imp. d.n. Marjorianus', which again indicates legitimacy. Also, Leo, Bishop of Rome, wrote several letters to Leo Augustus in which he called Majorian Augustus, tactless if he had not been recognized by Leo (*Epp.* CLIX,

emphasized the correctness of Majorian's appointment 'by plebs, senate, army, and colleagues together'.[98] Yet this has been doubted.[99] It is difficult to see why recognition should have been withheld. The deposed Avitus had, almost certainly, not had eastern recognition; Majorian had a suitable background, had been favoured by the western imperial family, and had secured the backing of the senate. It is true that there was at least one other potential successor, Olybrius, who was related by marriage to the Theodosian house.[100] Olybrius possibly had the disadvantage of being connected with Gaiseric; rather more pertinently, he was not on the spot with military backing and Majorian was.

The delay until December was attributed by Sidonius to Majorian's modest reluctance to become emperor;[101] this can be safely ignored. Modern scholars have sometimes invested the gap between acclamation by the army and formal installation by the senate with unnecessary significance. Barnes supposes that Majorian continued to regard himself as *magister militum*

CLIXII, CLXIV). Jordanes (*Getica* 236) also reported that Majorian was appointed by Marcian (though is not a sufficiently reliable authority for this to be decisive).

[98] Sidonius, *Pan.* v, 386–8: 'plebs, curia, miles, et collega simul'. This may, however, be a typical Sidonius anachronism (particularly evident in the inclusion of *plebs*).

[99] The question of whether the eastern emperor recognized Majorian (and/or Avitus) has been addressed by many historians, including Seeck (1920: 478–9); Stein (1928: 540–51); Ensslin (1925: 1951–2) and (1930: 585–6); Vassili (1936c: 163–9); Palanque (1944: 294–6); Baynes (1922: 222–4); Kaegi (1968: 31–4); Meyer (1969: 8–10); Nagy (1967); Max (1979: 232–5) and see pp. 50–1 for his theory on the involvement of Marcellinus; Barnes (1983: 268–9); O'Flynn (1983: 185 n. 18); Demandt (1989: 172). The majority view is that neither was recognized, in the case of Majorian mainly because of the absence of his name on Leo's legislation (*Codex Just.* 4, 65, 31; 12, 35, 15; 8, 53, 30, etc.) and the absence of Leo's name on his early legislation. However, Baynes has argued persuasively for the recognition of Majorian (supported by Martindale (*PLRE* ii, 702–3, Maiorianus) and Meyer (1969)). Seeck believed that Majorian was made Caesar as an interim step, based on Marcellinus *comes'* use of the term, but this is used by Marcellinus to indicate the junior emperor, rather than in the tetrarchical sense.

[100] On the dates of Olybrius' betrothal and marriage to Placidia, and his whereabouts at this time, see Clover (1978: 174–82, 192–5).

[101] Sidonius, *Pan.* v, 9–12.

until December AD 457;[102] however, whatever aristocrats like Sidonius thought, it was the acclamation by the army which created an emperor, not the senate. Formal installation could, depending on the circumstances, easily be delayed.

The impression from the sources is that Majorian and Ricimer operated in concert to take power and subsequently intended to share it between them, Majorian as emperor and Ricimer as supreme military commander and patrician. Part of the first novella of Majorian, given to the senate at Ravenna on 11 January AD 458, which constituted both a justification for taking office and a manifesto of the policies of the new regime, supports this idea of shared power:

> Military matters will be the watchful concern of both ourself and our parent and patrician Ricimer.[103] We shall, by the grace of God, protect the position of the Roman world, which we liberated, by our joint vigilance, from the foreign enemy and from internal disaster.[104]

There is no reason not to accept the novella at face value; Majorian could genuinely have wished, or felt it was necessary, to share responsibilities.[105]

---

[102] Barnes (1983: 268).

[103] The title of *parens* goes back to Stilicho (*CIL* ix, 4051; and see Mazzarino (1942: 106–11)). It was also used by Fl. Constantius after his marriage and the birth of his son Valentinian (*CIL* vi, 1719, 1720). Here it is combined with *patricius*, as used at least once for Aetius (*Nov. Val.* 36). In the cases of Stilicho and Constantius, this title was not, given their relationships to Honorius and Valentinian, inappropriate, even in a literal sense, but here seems to have become a formal title denoting unique status, and almost certainly does not imply any more than that.

[104] *Nov. Maj.* 1, given to the senate on 1 Nov. AD 458: 'Erit apud nos cum parente patricioque nostro Ricimere rei militaris pervigil cura. Romani orbis statum, quem communibus excubiis et ab externo hoste et a domestica clade liberavimus, propitia divinitate servamus.'

[105] O'Flynn (1983: 110) saw the official relationship proclaimed in the novella as a humiliation for Ricimer, but this is most unlikely. Majorian was, after all, emperor, which still bestowed considerable status; see e.g. Sidonius' description of a banquet with Majorian present (*Ep.* 1, xi, 10–15). O'Flynn's reason for taking this attitude is the belief that Ricimer wanted to rule as 'viceroy' of the eastern emperor without a western emperor (1983: 108–9), for which there is no evidence. Like most other historians, he sees Ricimer as the 'real ruler' from the end of Avitus' reign onwards.

It is often asserted that Majorian was placed on the throne by Ricimer as a puppet emperor, who later proved too independent.[106] However, Ricimer must have been aware that Majorian, with military experience, command of the *domestici*, status as the preferred heir of the last Theodosian emperor, and personal ambition, was not likely to be a mere puppet. Even if Ricimer was in the stronger position, he still needed an emperor; he presumably considered that, as a barbarian and an Arian, he was not an imperial contender in the eyes of either the Italian élite or Leo. It may, indeed, never have crossed his mind. In this he was following the example and ethos of Stilicho and Aetius.

It is possible that the two men came to an agreement. They had been colleagues, perhaps friends; conceivably they were aware that the position of the West was so bad that more than one active leader was necessary. A more cynical view is that, although shared interests had brought the two men together, the alliance was superficial, and each had every intention to get rid of, or at least gain ascendancy over, the other, as soon as might be convenient.[107]

Two minor questions arise: first, why Majorian (with or without Ricimer) had not made a bid for power previously, on the assassination of Valentinian or of Petronius Maximus, and, second, why Majorian and Ricimer and the Italian senators (supposedly anti-Gallic) had initially accepted Avitus as emperor, only to reject him later? The explanation of the first may lie in the general chaos following the assassinations of Aetius and Valentinian and the second sack of Rome.[108] For the change

---

[106] See e.g. O'Flynn (1983: 109).

[107] O'Flynn (1983: 69) has suggested that by becoming emperor Majorian put himself in a disadvantageous position, being unable thereby to wield effective military power, and that this is the reason that the 'generalissimos' did not usually try to take the title of emperor. But Roman emperors were certainly not formally excluded from military action (Honorius and Valentinian III were recent exceptions to the norm), and as an experienced soldier Majorian was to show that his duties as reigning emperor definitely did not preclude campaigning.

[108] Papini (1959: 133–5) had a theory that Ricimer and Majorian instigated the revolt among a pro-Vandal faction that overthrew Petronius Maximus, and that the absence of any defence of Rome against Gaiseric was a brilliant strategy devised by Ricimer which somehow upset Gaiseric's long-term plans. This is just speculation.

of mind on Avitus, factors may have been: his poor performance in office, the weakening of Theoderic's backing, and, perhaps, the increasing influence of Ricimer.

The political situation and military problems facing Majorian and Ricimer were different from those of Valentinian and Aetius. One of Majorian's tasks was reconciling Gaul, as well as Italy, to his rule (the reverse of that of Avitus). The military imperative was the defence of Italy and the other remnants of the empire, most especially and immediately, against the Vandals. Until late AD 458, when he left for Gaul, Majorian was based in Ravenna, as is seen from the titles of his legislation. Majorian's novellas concerned the remission of tax arrears;[109] the reopening of the post of *defensor civitatis*;[110] the protection of public buildings;[111] prevention of corruption among officials;[112] opposition to some aspects of female celibacy;[113] the problems of decurions;[114] the restoration of the right to bear weapons;[115] inheritance;[116] adultery;[117] and the forbidding of enforced clerical ordination.[118] Interestingly, this last states that if a person is consecrated bishop against his will his ordination stands; and this could just be connected to the enforced consecration of Avitus four years previously, although it is most unlikely that he was still alive. This legislation has been called an energetic programme of reform,[119] but there is nothing really novel in these novellas.

In March AD 458 Leo, Bishop of Rome, wrote to the Bishop of Aquileia answering a number of religious queries caused by the return of Italians from barbarian captivity (they had been gone long enough for some of their spouses to

---

[109] *Nov. Maj.* 2.
[110] *Nov. Maj.* 3.
[111] *Nov. Maj.* 4.
[112] *Nov. Maj.* 5.
[113] *Nov. Maj.* 6.
[114] *Nov. Maj.* 7.
[115] *Nov. Maj.* 8 (text unfortunately missing).
[116] *Nov. Maj.* 9 (text missing).
[117] *Nov. Maj.* 10.
[118] *Nov. Maj.* 11.
[119] Demandt (1989: 172). This was also advanced by Bury (1923: 332 n. 3) and Hodgkin (1880*b*: 427–32).

remarry).[120] He refers to the recent disasters of war and inroads of the enemy, but also to the situation having recently improved. It is not clear where the captives were returning from; it might have been Africa, though, as they were from the Aquileia region, perhaps they had been carried off by the Huns in AD 452.

While Majorian still (i.e. probably before April AD 457) held the title of *magister militum* a group of about 900 Alamanni had crossed the Alps from Raetia to plunder northern Italy.[121] Majorian ordered one Burco,[122] with a small force,[123] to deal with them, which he did. Sidonius refers to Majorian as having then only just laid down his arms,[124] which suggests, but hardly proves, that he had been in some military action against barbarians in AD 456/7. Around the same time Italian forces had been successful in action against Vandals and Moors raiding Campania, under the leadership of Gaiseric's son-in-law.[125] In describing the battle in Campania, Sidonius makes no mention of Majorian personally, so he was probably not present. As the military action in the north was led by Burco, Ricimer, as declared in the novella, may have taken responsibility for the defence of Campania.

Sidonius describes the fighting in detail. Initially the Italian civilians were taken by surprise, but then imperial forces arrived and cut off the marauding bands, mainly Moors, from their

[120] Leo the Great, *Ep.* CLIX, ii, vi, vii, viii. Some references suggest that the captors were pagan, others that they were heretic, which would fit Attila's forces. *Epistole* CLXVI (of the same year) to the Bishop of Ravenna also refers to returning prisoners of war. *Epistole* CLXVII, to the Bishop of Gallia Narbonensis (date uncertain), speaks of people coming over from North Africa, but whether as returning captives or refugees is unclear.

[121] Sidonius, *Pan.* V, 373–87. The number, of 900 raiders, is one of the few definite figures for barbarian forces in ancient texts.

[122] The name Burco is non-Roman, either Germanic or possibly Celtic (Schönfeld (1965: 55, 283)). A 'Burco' appears in Ennodius' *Vita Epiphani.* (21–5), involved in a land dispute with the Church at Ticinum, *c.* AD 460, but the context is such that it is unlikely that the two references are to the same man.

[123] Sidonius, *Pan.* V, 378–9. The phrase 'Burconem dirigis illo exigua comitante manu' suggests that this was some sort of non-regular force.

[124] Sidonius, *Pan.* V, 489.

[125] Sidonius, *Pan.* V, 385–440. Courtois (1955: 196 n. 5) suggested that this was in the region of Volturne.

ships, scattering them into the hills, to be dealt with by local defenders. The raiders left behind with the ships (mainly Vandals) prepared to meet the Romans. They are depicted by Sidonius landing war horses from the ships in small boats, donning mail-shirts, and arming themselves with bows and arrows. Sidonius provides a colourful account of the ensuing encounter, which he portrays as mainly a cavalry battle (although pikemen were also involved).[126] He mentions the dragon standards flying in both armies; the sound of trumpets; showers of arrows; and the use of javelins, pikes, harpoons, lances, and two-edged swords. Some of the Vandals escaped to their ships, but their leader, the son-in-law of Gaiseric, was among the dead, killed by a javelin.[127] This was yet another victory over the Vandals, and these successes must have boosted the imperial partnership and encouraged Majorian's next venture.

The decision seems to have been made, probably very early on, that attack was the best form of defence, and Majorian launched a major campaign against the Vandal kingdom in Africa. Preparations were under way shortly after his installation, including the organization of the necessary fleet and recruitment of barbarian manpower.[128] This offensive may have been a long-term strategic move as well as a response to the raids on Sicily and Italy. The containment of Gaiseric (and hopes perhaps of recovering the vital African provinces) must have been central to western long-term policy at this time. A major victory over the Vandals would not only have reduced the threat to Italy and the islands, but avenged the recent sack of Rome. The decision to take the offensive against Gaiseric was courageous and strategically sound, *provided* that adequate resources were available. Victory could possibly have made a real difference to the viability of the western Roman empire; it would also have greatly enhanced Majorian's personal

---

[126] Sidonius, *Pan.* V, 405–40. It is apparent from this, and other sources, that the later Vandal armies had become cavalry-orientated, probably as a result of Alan and Moorish influence (see also App. pp. 309–10). The Alans were notoriously ineffective without their horses (Isidore, *Etym.* XIX, 23, 7).

[127] Sidonius, *Pan.* V, 438–9.

[128] Sidonius, *Pan.* V, 441–69, 470–83. Max (1979: 232–3) suggested that Majorian may also have sought and received assistance from Leo, but there is no evidence for this.

prestige, perhaps enabling him, had he wished, to rid himself of Ricimer.

It is difficult to decide whether this offensive policy was totally unrealistic or not. The Vandals had been in Africa for nearly thirty years and had a useful naval force (see pp. 308–12). Procopius assessed the Vandal and Alan forces, in the sixth century AD, at 50–80,000 men, plus Moorish support.[129] The later, better-equipped and funded joint East and West expedition of AD 468 was to fail miserably, but it seems to have been fatally handicapped by incompetent leadership; the invasion under Belisarius in the 530s, however, defeated the Vandal kingdom swiftly and decisively.

It is hard to assess Roman strength by the late AD 450s. Procopius refers to Majorian as having a considerable army,[130] and Sidonius refers to thousands being assembled in Liguria under diverse (or separate) banners.[131] The nature of this army is made clear by Sidonius: 'Bastarnian, Suevian, Pannonian, Neuran, Hun, Getan, Dacian, Alan, Bellonotan, Rugi, Burgundian, Visigoth, Alites, Bisalta, Ostrogoth, Procrustian, Sarmatian, Moschan ... all of the Caucasus and the Scythian drinker of the Don.'[132] However anachronistic the ethnic names are,[133] the panegyric in which this list appears was composed while Majorian's army was present in Gaul, and the overall impression—that this was an army of barbarian contingents mainly from beyond the Danube—must be correct.[134]

---

[129] Procopius, *Wars* III, v, 18–22.

[130] Procopius, *Wars* III, vii, 4. The context of this, however, is a legendary tale about Majorian (see n. 174), which makes it suspect.

[131] Sidonius, *Pan.* V, 484.

[132] Sidonius, *Pan.* V, 474–9: 'Bastarna, Suebus, Pannonius, Neurus, Chunus, Geta, Dacus, Halanus, Bellonotus, Rugus, Burgundio, Vesus, Alites, Bisalta, Ostrogothus, Procrustes, Sarmata, Moschus ... omnis Caucasus et Scythicae potor Tanaiticus undae.'

[133] Sidonius is clearly trying to give the impression of a multi-ethnic, fierce, and outlandish crew for stylistic effect. Loyen (1942: 78 n. 3) provided a detailed analysis of the backgrounds of those peoples who are known to have really existed at that time, and of the literary and legendary sources from which Sidonius collected the odd, anachronistic names: such as Dacus, Bisalta, Procrustes, etc. For speculation on the Alites see Bachrach (1968: 35).

[134] Most of the ethnic contingents listed were probably not recruited directly from the Danube area, but were already stationed in Italy as *laeti*,

Majorian led his army across the Alps in person, and Sidonius describes an incident that took place as the emperor was moving from his assembly camp in Liguria. This involved Scythians (probably Huns),[135] under an otherwise unknown Tuldila, who seemingly disobeyed orders and took part in unauthorized pillaging. Other troops then took independent action against the Huns, and slaughtered them.[136] It is (as so often) hard to excavate the facts from Sidonius' elaborate and allusive writing, but references to Caesar quelling a famous mutiny, and to *seditio*, and the threat that barbarians who disobeyed orders in future would be slain,[137] show that Majorian had lost control over some elements of his army;[138] first those led by Tuldila, then other troops who ignored his pardon of Tuldila's offence. Their disobedience was rewarded by 'the booty' (the Huns' gear or their unauthorized plunder?). The episode speaks very poorly of the discipline of his army, and makes one wonder whether this was a factor in the failure of the campaign.

Majorian had built and gathered 300 ships to carry his army from Spain to North Africa.[139] This was paid for partly by a special levy on Gaul,[140] and, presumably, from normal taxation revenue.[141] The decision to attack not directly from Italy but from southern Spain seems odd; it was a long way to march the army and Spain was awash with warring barbarian armies, including the Visigoths, ex-allies of Avitus. The reasons were probably primarily naval: the need to keep the actual crossing

federates, etc. (see pp. 168–9). Any extra recruitment undertaken would have involved additional financial outlay and/or promises of rewards and booty.

[135] Sidonius, *Pan.* V, 483–510.

[136] Schönfeld (1965: 280). Maenchen-Helfen (1973: 162) describes the name as 'Hunnic of the Germanized variety', similar to Attila and Rugila.

[137] Sidonius, *Pan.* V, 508–10: 'vestris haec proficit armis seditio: quadcumque iubes, nisi barbarus audit, hic cadit, ut miles timeat'.

[138] Sidonius, *Pan.* V, 510 and 505–8. Martindale (*PLRE* ii, 1131, Tuldila) repeats an old and strange interpretation, in which Tuldila was the leader of a band of barbarians near the Danube, attacked and killed by Majorian, after refusing to accept his authority.

[139] Priscus, frag. 36 (2).

[140] Sidonius, *Pan.* V, 446–8.

[141] Majorian's legislation made the usual attempts to improve the taxation system (*Nov. Maj.* 2, of March AD 458), but, *contra* Max (1979: 235), says nothing specific about revenue for campaign purposes.

short; the possible acquisition of more transports; and ease of reinforcement.[142] There was also a political objective: for Majorian to visit southern Gaul, *en route* to Spain, to reassert Roman authority over the barbarian kingdoms and to consolidate his personal position with the Gallo-Romans. In leading the expedition personally, rather than sending Ricimer or other commanders, Majorian was raising the stakes of the game. It left Ricimer in Italy in a position of great power, with the joint tasks of defence and, doubtless, the prevention of any emperor-making in Majorian's absence.

Majorian was successful in Gaul, coming to terms with Theoderic[143] and scoring a political and personal success with the Gallic notables. In May AD 460 he led his forces into Spain, from where the vital attack on the Vandals would be launched. If Procopius' version is correct, Gaiseric's responses to the invasion threat show that he took it seriously:

Gaiseric . . . first sent envoys to him in an attempt to settle their differences by negotiation. But when Majorian would not agree, he laid waste all the land of the Moors, to which Majorian's forces would have to cross from Spain and also poisoned the wells.[144]

But, in a massive anticlimax, the attack never took place, and Majorian withdrew to Gaul. The fleet had been awaiting the arrival of Majorian and the army at Elice, on the bay of Alicante. Before Majorian even reached it,[145] Gaiseric captured most of the ships.

According to Hydatius, who was close to events:

In the month of May Spain was entered by the Emperor Majorian. As he continued to the province of Carthaginensis, some of the ships, which were being prepared by him for the crossing against the Vandals, were captured from the Carthaginian shore by the Vandals,

---

[142] Gordon (1960: 117 and n. 3) and Hodgkin (1880*b*: 433) speculate that this route was chosen because Majorian had heard of disaffection among the Vandals' Mauritanian and Numidian allies, but supply no supporting evidence.

[143] Hydatius, 192 (197) *s.a.* 459; Sidonius, *Pan.* v, 562–3.

[144] Priscus, frag. 36 (1) (Blockley's translation).

[145] He had passed through, or possibly got as far as, Caesaraugusta, in northern Spain. The *Chronica Caesaraugustanorum* (*s.a.* 460) records: 'His conss. Maioranus imp. Caesaraugustam venit'.

informed by traitors. So Majorian, frustrated in his plan, returned to Italy.[146]

One wonders why some Gallo-Hispanics (if they had been barbarian Hydatius would not have described them as traitors) found it in their interest to assist the Vandals? They may have been merchants who had business dealings with Carthage (we know from archaeological data that trade with North Africa continued), or simply men out to profit from selling intelligence. Gaiseric must have organized a surprise raid, and boarded the ships, perhaps adding them to his own fleet.

Majorian seems to have made no attempt to salvage the campaign. John of Antioch records that he broke off the war 'on shameful terms' and retreated.[147] As the treaty was described as 'shameful', the terms may have involved the cession of the remaining North African provinces to the Vandals, possibly payments of money, or even the cession of islands, perhaps in return for (worthless) promises to desist from raiding Italy.[148] As well as failing to prevent Vandal raids on Italy, or recover Roman territory, Majorian's abortive campaign must have significantly depleted the limited imperial resources.

Although this fiasco was only one of several Roman failures against the Vandals (other examples being in AD 422, 431, 441, possibly 466, and 468), there have been modern suspicions that it was in some way engineered. It has been argued that Majorian was such an able emperor that only treachery can explain his

[146] Hydatius, 195 (200) *s.a.* 460: 'Mense Maio Maiorianus Hispanias ingreditur imperator; quo Carthaginiensem provinciam pertendente aliquantas naves, quas sibi transitum adversum Vandolos praeparabat, de litore Carthaginiensi commoniti Vandali per proditores abripiunt. Maiorianus ita a sua ordinatione frustratus ad Italiam reveritur.' *Chronica Gallica a 511*, 634, records: 'qui volens Africam profisci naves eius in Hispaniis a Wandalis captae sunt iuxta Carthaginem Spartarium'.

[147] John Ant. frag. 203. Hydatius (204 (210) *s.a.* 461) also mentions envoys from Gaiseric to Majorian: 'Gaisericus rex a Maioriano imperatore per legatos postulat pacem.' This is given several items (including an account of Hydatius' own three-month captivity) later than the one reporting the loss of the ships and Majorian's return to Italy, but this may be another example of Hydatius' inability to date all items that reached him in exact chronological order.

[148] This treaty is also mentioned in Priscus (frag. 38 (1)): 'since Gaiseric no longer kept the treaty which he had made with Majorian' (Blockley's translation).

failure, and dark hints are made about Ricimer's involvement.[149] Connections have been made with the presence in
Spain of Nepotianus (thought by many writers to have been
an imperial *magister militum*),[150] or of the Visigoths.[151] It has
been proposed that Nepotianus was an adherent of Ricimer,
part of a whole ring of Ricimerian 'collaborators' attached by
him to Majorian's army to undermine the emperor.[152] All this is
both unsupported by any evidence and superfluous. Moreover,
as previously mentioned (see Pt. I, p. 65), Burgess has made a
very convincing case for Nepotianus having been a Gothic,
rather than Roman, commander.[153]

We know nothing of Ricimer's whereabouts, or activities,
while the emperor was absent from Italy, except that he was
consul for the year AD 459 (Majorian having been consul for
AD 458).[154] This was the last time that the western *magister
militum* held the consulship (and neither Odovacer nor Theoderic was to become consul). Ricimer did not, like his predecessors, hold the consulship more than once, although Sidonius
expected him to hold it for a second, and even third, time, under
Anthemius.[155] If the Italian aristocracy resented a barbarian
consul, Ricimer was perhaps exercising tact after making the
initial point, and the consulship may have been more useful to
him as a reward for his aristocratic supporters. It is likely that he
spent some of this time in Rome, participating in the traditional
duties and status displays of consulship, and building up his
own power base. Indeed, he so consolidated and strengthened

[149] Vassili (1936*d*: 299). Scott (1984: 29) has commented that 'this only
underscores the strange unwillingness now and perhaps then to recognize the
simple fact that, plan or not, treachery or not, Majorian had to bear responsibility for the debacle'.

[150] See e.g. *PLRE* II, 778, Nepotianus 2; Heinzelman (1982: 656).

[151] Whose presence in Gallaecia is remarked by Hydatius (196 (201) *s.a.*
460).

[152] Vassili (1936*d*: 299) and (1936*b*: 55–66). On a Ricimeran party see
Vassili (1936*a*: 175–80), (1936*b*: 55–66), and (1936*d*: 296–9). He is followed
by Wes (1967: 136 n. 6).

[153] Burgess (1992: 24–5).

[154] *CIL* III, 9522, 13127 and IX, 1372; Leo, *Ep.* 168; etc. The joint eastern
consul, Julius Patricius, was a son of Aspar; there were therefore in that year
two consuls of barbarian origin.

[155] Sidonius, *Pan.* II, 542–4.

his position that he was able to depose and murder Majorian almost as soon as he set foot back in Italy.[156]

The reports of Majorian's assassination in the chronicles are, as usual, very brief, recording his death at Dertona (in the strongly militarized area of north-eastern Italy, close to Placentia, where Avitus had been similarly dealt with), and, generally, naming Ricimer as responsible. The *Fasti Vindobonenses* reported: 'the emperor Majorian was deposed by the patrician Ricimer at Dertona on 2 August and killed at the river Ira on 7 August'.[157] *The Gallic Chronicle of 511* recorded: 'setting out, however, from Arles to Italy, he was killed by the patrician Ricimer at Dertona'.[158] Jordanes named the same place, but seems to get the context wrong: 'then, moving in readiness for battle against the Alans who were disturbing Gaul, he was killed at Dertona, close to the river named Hyra'.[159] There is no other evidence for Alans disturbing Gaul at this time, and the fact that Majorian had dismissed most of his troops (see John of Antioch below) argues strongly against it.

Two writers supply more details. First, John of Antioch:

When he had already crossed to Italy, Ricimer plotted his death. Majorian had already dismissed his allies after his return and was on his way to Rome with his own followers,[160] when Ricimer's men seized

---

[156] He allowed him proper burial; there is a poem by Ennodius (*Carm.* CXXXV) on the tomb of Majorian. His memorial was apparently modest, and Ennodius comments that only bad emperors have grandiose monuments.

[157] *Fasti Vind. Prior. s.a.* 461: 'depositus est Maiorianus imp. a patricio Ricimere Dertona IIII non. Aug. et occisus est ad fluvium Ira VII idus Aug.'.

[158] *Chronica Gallica a 511*, 635: 'Profectus autem ex Arelate ad Italiam a patricio Recimere occiditur Dertona.' Other, almost identical, reports appear in Cassiodorus, *Chronica* 1274 *s.a.* 461; Marcellinus *comes, s.a.* 461; the later eastern writers Evagrius, *HE* ii, 7, Michael the Syrian, IX, 1, and Theophanes (AM 5955), in which the date is incorrect, and AM 5964, a second notice of his death by dysentery, also incorrectly placed (which is no doubt the result of uncritical use of Procopius, whose story about Majorian is out of chronological sequence in exactly the same way).

[159] Jordanes, *Getica* 236: 'dum contra Alanos, qui Gallias infestabant, movisset procinctum. Dertona iuxta fluvium Hyra cognomento occiditur.' Jordanes is clearly using Marcellinus *comes* for the location.

[160] Professor Michael Whitby suggests that 'follower', in the sense of 'members of his retinue', is the best translation of 'tois oikeiois'.

him, stripped him of his purple and diadem, beat him, and cut off his head.[161]

Second, Hydatius:

Majorian was returning to Rome from Gaul and arranging most important matters for the Roman empire and the Roman name,[162] [when] Ricimer, moved by envy [or, 'spite'] and supported by the advice of the envious, deceitfully captured and killed him.[163]

Sidonius, while not mentioning Majorian's assassination in any of his extant works, does in one letter[164] describe Majorian in Arles on his way back from Spain, during which time he was entertained with games at the amphitheatre and held a dinner party for Gallic notables, which Sidonius attended. Sidonius' letter gives a wealth of detail; most of it concerns his own petty affairs, and all we learn of the emperor is that at the dinner party Majorian was cultured, relaxed, and affable.[165]

When he reached Dertona, John of Antioch tells us that Majorian had already dismissed all his military 'allies' (presumably his barbarian troops who had constituted the majority of his army) and was accompanied only by his own retinue. The barbarian troops must have been dismissed either in Gaul or on reaching north-eastern Italy. This left Majorian vulnerable. Both this and his behaviour in Arles suggest that he had no major concerns for his safety; it would seem that he still trusted Ricimer. He was to be rapidly disillusioned. That he apparently had no apprehensions about his return, nor had received any warning or worrying information from Italy about Ricimer's intentions, is perhaps odd. It is, however, possible to interpret John of Antioch's information differently: to suggest that Majorian was almost alone because of a pressing need to travel

---

[161] John Ant. frag. 203 (Blockley's translation, Priscus, frag. 36 (2)).

[162] This may refer to negotiations with Theoderic or Gaiseric.

[163] Hydatius, 205 (212) *s.a.* 461: 'Maiorianum de Galliis Roman redeuntem et Romano imperio vel nomine res necessarias ordinantem Rechimer livore percitus et invidorum consilio fultus fraude interfecit circumventum.'

[164] Sidonius, *Ep.* I, xi. (Sidonius also describes an earlier banquet, attended by Majorian and himself, in Arles or Lyons, in AD 458/9 (*Ep.* IX, xiii).)

[165] Shortly after Sidonius dined with Majorian in AD 461 he was unwilling host (at Arles or Lyons) to ten large and hungry Burgundians (*Carm.* I, xii). It is possible that they were part of Majorian's forces, as suggested tentatively by Anderson (1936: 212–13 n. 1).

immediately and swiftly, alerted to danger and attempting to reach Rome or Ravenna.

A popular, but ultimately unconvincing, theory is that Ricimer turned on Majorian because he had proved himself a capable and successful leader who would hence be difficult to control.[166] Although Majorian had had some success in Gaul, the main (and very important) object of his campaign had not been achieved, indeed not even attempted, and valuable resources wasted. Majorian's personal status must have been affected and he was without any substantial armed forces at his command, while Ricimer had the entire Italian army behind him (and, perhaps, an unblemished military record). If Ricimer wanted an emperor whom he could dominate, then Majorian was in fact a better bet now than he had been before.

Hydatius ascribes Ricimer's treachery to ill will or envy. If Ricimer hated and envied Majorian, then he had hidden it uncommonly well:[167] Sidonius describes them earlier as united in 'bonds of affection', and Majorian had evidently trusted Ricimer. Although the idea of envy has been taken at face value by many modern historians,[168] Hydatius could not, of course, have known what Ricimer's feelings or motivations were. This is simply his own interpretation, probably stemming from the conventional Roman view of barbarian psychology.

It is possible that Ricimer had always wished to exercise supreme power, that his previous acceptance of Majorian had been provisional, and that his action in AD 461 was inevitable. Alternatively, his desire to oust Majorian may have developed during his absence, and have been influenced by his failure to deal with the Vandals, the 'shameful' treaty (conceivably Sidonius' assertion of personal enmity between Ricimer and

---

[166] See e.g. Moss (1935: 60); Stevens (1933: 58); Oost (1970: 231); O'Flynn (1983: 109); Harries (1994: 96).

[167] The idea of Ricimer concealing for years his envy and hatred towards Majorian conforms with some characterizations of Ricimer as a secretive and twisted Machiavellian, almost a Shakespearean Richard III figure; see e.g. Oost (1970: 228).

[168] For suggestions that Ricimer was envious of Majorian's 'energy' see Seeck (1920: 341–2), Stevens (1933: 58), and Jones (1964: 241). For a slight variation see Dill (1926: 19), who wrote that Ricimer 'hated Majorian as a Roman of the old breed'.

Gaiseric was based on some fact), the waste of the new fleet and, perhaps most importantly, his experience of ruling Italy.[169] The decision to act was probably triggered by the simple fact of Majorian's return to Italy.

Ricimer was not alone in plotting against the returning emperor; there were others, described by Hydatius as *invidiorum*, which can be translated as 'envious' or 'holding a grudge'. It is a pity that Hydatius does not say who these were: other barbarian leaders in Italy, or members of a senatorial faction for some reason opposed to Majorian.[170] There is no record of any Italian opposition to Ricimer following the assassination; indeed, we do not hear of any resistance to Ricimer until the time of the fighting with Anthemius. Perhaps his rule was just efficient and fair enough to be acceptable, given that Italy needed an effective defender; or perhaps everyone was sufficiently intimidated by him. In Majorian's absence, the Italians had had some time to become used to Ricimer as their master.

Procopius erroneously asserts that Majorian died of dysentery.[171] This report, like other occasional reports of natural deaths (such as Evagrius' statement that Avitus died of plague),[172] has been seen as the product of Ricimer's 'efficient propaganda machine'.[173] This is totally anachronistic;

[169] Griffe (1964–6: ii, 97) has suggested that the motive was Majorian's action against the Burgundians in Gaul, with whom Ricimer had ties. This appears just possible as a secondary reason.

[170] Oost (1970: 231–3) sees this opposition to Majorian as being from those sections of the Italian élite who were antagonized by his so-called 'reforming' legislation (and the increase in taxes which resulted from the expense of his Vandal campaign), i.e. the great nobles, the Church, and the civil service. Although Majorian's legislation is sometimes described as radical (e.g. Bury 1897–1900: iv, 18–19), on examination much is repetition of previous laws, or deals with a particular case. Nor is there any reason to think that his legislation was any more effectively enforced than usual.

[171] Procopius, *Wars* III, vii, 14.

[172] Evagrius, *HE* I, 2.

[173] See e.g. Oost (1970: 229–30); Sundwall (1915: no. 60, 55); Stevens (1933: 38, 58).

disparities in the sources are easily explained by unreliable transmission and recording of information. Procopius' statement occurs in a romantic story about Majorian in disguise in Africa, and is at variance with more reliable sources.[174]

[174] Procopius, *Wars* III, vii, 4–14. The legend, which he recounts at length, involves Majorian dying his fair hair (for which Procopius says he was famous) black and undertaking a personal espionage mission in Vandal Africa. It is interesting that such a story should have been created about, or become attached to, Majorian. Hodgkin (1880a: 434–5) believed it could have come from a Vandal source, possibly part of a song or saga about Gaiseric. But, as Majorian is the hero, perhaps folklore from Italy is more likely. Majorian may have been particularly remembered as the last heroic or attractive emperor. This idea has recurred in modern writing.

14
Ricimer and the Reigns of Libius Severus, Anthemius, and Olybrius

It was after Majorian's death that Ricimer truly took on a new and unprecedented role, becoming a 'kingmaker' and setting up a figurehead emperor, Libius Severus, while retaining real power for himself. Severus was acclaimed at Ravenna on 19 November AD 461.[1] As following the death of Avitus, there had been a short interregnum of three months.[2] It has been proposed that Ricimer now wanted to dispense with an emperor altogether, hence the August–November gap, Severus being an afterthought when Ricimer encountered opposition.[3] On the basis of his subsequent consistent policy it is clear that, on the contrary, he considered an emperor either desirable or necessary, although preferring one whom he could control or influence. The gap may have occurred because a suitable new emperor had not been chosen in advance, which suggests that Ricimer had not been planning his coup against Majorian for very long.

The appointment was not an attempt to please the senior emperor in the East. Severus may well have been chosen because he was acceptable to the senate; Ricimer needed some senatorial support, even if superficial. Stein argued that there was an alliance between Ricimer and the Italian aristocracy in

---

[1] *Fasti Vind. Prior. s.a.* 461; Cassiodorus, *Chronica* 1274 *s.a.* 461; Marcellinus *comes, s.a.* 461; *Chronica Gallica a 511*, 636; Vict. Tonn. *s.a.* 461 and *s.a.* 461; Theophanes, AM 5955 give a date of 7 July, which would suggest that Ricimer set Libius Severus up before killing Majorian, as suggested by Stevens (1933: 58 n. 5); but Majorian would, surely, have got wind of such action. In any case the date of 19 Nov. has better authority.

[2] In this and subsequent interregnums, it seems that western coins were struck in the name of eastern emperors (Kent (1994: 193)).

[3] Oost (1968: 236); O'Flynn (1983: 115). Seeck (1920: vi, 339) implied that Ricimer wanted to become emperor himself.

general,[4] but there is no real evidence of this, and complex factionalism seems a more plausible model.

Little is known of the new emperor, other than that he was from Lucania[5] (a region of south-west Italy vulnerable to Vandal raids, which might be relevant), and was pious.[6] He may have had the nickname *Serpentios*, but the sources for this are late, and the meaning of the word unclear.[7] It can be assumed that he was of high social rank, almost certainly a senator.[8] The characteristics which recommended him to Ricimer were probably pliability and lack of military expertise; but there cannot have been a shortage of senators with these qualifications. What did Libius Severus gain, or think he was going to gain, by becoming emperor under Ricimer's domination? It is not known how old he was or whether he had heirs he hoped would succeed. The acquisition of the title of emperor, even if empty, would still bring status to self and family, and apart from that he may have had ambitions that never, in the event, materialized.

Severus was recognized by the senate,[9] and assumed the western consulship for AD 462, as was normal for a new emperor.[10] However, it seems that he was not recognized as consul, or as a colleague, by Leo. No source suggests such recognition

---

[4] Stein (1959: i, 380–1). His evidence is that the Roman senate recognized Severus once he had been put forward by Ricimer, but this is hardly proof. Stein also suggested that Ricimer gradually moved away from reliance on senatorial support, which seems plausible. Nagy (1967: 176–7), cited by Scott (1984: 32 n. 55), also saw an alliance of interest, and suggested the Italian aristocracy as the origin of Jordanes' favourable view of Ricimer (see p. 228–9).

[5] *Chronica Gallica a 511*, 636; Cassiodorus, *Chronica* 1274 *s.a.* 461.

[6] *Laterculus Imperatorum ad Justinum I*, written in the time of Justinian: 'ibique religiose vivens decessit'.

[7] Theophanes, AM 5955; see also *PLRE* ii, 1004–5, Severus 18. That some such name was associated with Severus is substantiated by the *Paschale Chronicle*, which gives the consuls for AD 462 (Leo and Severus) as 'Leo and Serpentios'. Oost (1970: 238) suggests that this may have been a *signum* or *supernomen*. Perhaps the term comes from a hostile eastern tradition.

[8] In contrast to the fourth century, in the fifth a number of senators gained the purple (if not for very long); for example Jovinus, Attalus, Petronius Maximus, Avitus, and Olybrius.

[9] Hydatius, 206 (211) *s.a.* 461: 'Romanorum XLV Severus a Senatu Romae Augustus Appellatur anno imperii Leonis Quinto.'

[10] Bagnall *et al.* (1987: 461).

and the wording of Jordanes' *Romana* and the chronicle of Marcellinus *comes* shows that they considered Severus' rule to be invalid, presumably reflecting the official eastern line (Marcellinus also omits his consulship).[11]

History does not record any independent actions by the emperor, but some limited information can be gleaned about his reign in general. During these years Ricimer probably had more power and freedom of action than at any other time, with the possible exception of the last few months of his life. It is at this time that Priscus records envoys being sent to Gaiseric from Ricimer (rather than in the name of the emperor).[12] Probably also dating to this time is a rectangular bronze plaque, or tablet, with inscribed silver lettering, now in a Berlin museum. Its exact provenance is not known, but it was almost certainly found in Rome.[13] This, most unusually, associates the patrician's name with the two emperors, again testimony to his unprecedented prominence. On the reverse it carries the name of an urban prefect, Plotinus Eustathius. The bronze, and hence his term of office, must date to some time between A D 457 (when Ricimer became patrician) and 472 (when he died).[14] The obverse reads:

> salvis dd nn
> et patrici
> o Ricimere

and the reverse:

> Plotinus Eus
> tathius v.c.
> urb. pr. fecit[15]

[11] Jordanes, *Romana* 335–6: 'eius sine principis iussu Leonis Severianus [*sic*] invasit, sed et ipse tyrannidis sui tertio anno expleto Romae occubuit'; Marcellinus *comes*, *s.a.* 461: 'locum eius Severus invasit' and *s.a.* 465: 'Severus qui Occidentis arripuit principatum, Romae interiit.' See Seeck (1920: vi, 483) on this generally, and Bagnall *et al.* (1987: 456–7) on the consulships in his reign.

[12] Priscus, frag. 38. Other embassies described as being from the western Romans or Italians could have been either directly from Ricimer or through the emperor (frags. 39, 41, 50).

[13] Muratori (1739: Thes. CCLXVI no. 3); Friedlander (1882: 1); *PLRE* ii, 436 (Plotinus Eustathius 13). See also Ch. 13 n. 20.

[14] Cantarelli (1888–9: 194–5) has argued for a date between A D 461 and 465 (the reign of Libius Severus).

[15] *CIL* x, 8072.4; *ILS* 813; Cantarelli (1888: 194–5); Muratori (1739: 266).

This bronze is thought to be an *exagium*, an official standard weight for coins.[16]

In a similar, unprecedented, move, the monogram of Ricimer appears on the reverse of certain bronze *nummi*[17] issued in the name of Libius Severus,[18] either during his reign or during the interregnum following his death. The monogram appears on coins bearing the inscription *Victoria Augg*, which also occurs on gold issues, and may be associated with a military victory.[19] The monogram includes the letters R, C, M, and E, and is most naturally read as the monogram of the patrician; although occasional examples look as if an A is included, which would be problematic.

1. RⅭE. RⅭE 2. RⅭE

Fig. 1: Monograms attributed to Ricimer (from J. P. C. Kent (1994) *The Roman Imperial Coinage*, x (Spink))

No other convincing interpretation of the monogram has yet been put forward, and Kent (with reservation if the A is really present) and others were willing to consider this to be Ricimer's monogram, notwithstanding the 'enormity of the constitutional implications'.[20] Gundobad (when King of the Burgundians) and Odovacer both later struck coins carrying their monograms, perhaps copying Ricimer's example.[21]

---

[16] Kent (1994: 9); *CIL* xv, 886–9.

[17] The use of an *imperial* monogram was an eastern custom.

[18] These coins were of too low a value to have been produced for military or diplomatic purposes, but in too small a number for effective commercial use.

[19] Kent (1994: 408–9).

[20] Kent (1994: 190–1). See also Grierson and Blackburn (1986: 24). The coins were originally identified by Friedlander (1849: 5–6). Carson and Kent (1960: 63, 110) suggested this might be the monogram of Severus, but it looks much more like Ricimer's. Ulrich-Bansa (1949: 275) argued that these coins do not date from Severus' reign, but to the following interregnum, and that the presence of the monogram indicates that Leo had delegated to the patrician the power of signing public acts until a new emperor was chosen; but this seems to be stretching the evidence too far.

[21] Hendy (1988: 46); Grierson and Blackburn (1986: 75–7); Kent (1994: 213, 464).

There have been suggestions that this innovation went even further. There was a report in 1864 of a bronze coin carrying the name of Ricimer (Fl. Ricirus), but this coin cannot now be found, and it is likely to have been misread.[22] Another unique coin (minted in Ravenna) carrying two figures in military dress wearing diadems, and with the inscription *PAX*, has been associated with Ricimer, the figures being Anthemius and himself, with the coin dating to their brief reconciliation in AD 471.[23] However, the figures may be those of two emperors.[24]

More recently two works have appeared by Lacam[25] which place a new interpretation on the RCME monogram *nummi* of Severus. Lacam's theory is that these coins were struck not only in the reign of Severus, but in the interregnum that followed and during the civil war between Ricimer and Anthemius; the earliest being produced by the mint at Rome and the later (on stylistic and weight grounds) at Milan (where Ricimer is known to have resided) and then at other Italian mints. Ricimer also, it is proposed, issued gold coins from Milan (without his monogram). In addition, Lacam has suggested that an unusual coin, normally tentatively assigned to Majorian's reign, with a scene symbolizing Roman glory, was struck by Ricimer, at the time that he came to an agreement with Leo.[26]

Most exciting is Lacam's interpretation of two *nummi* (in extremely poor condition)[27] which have Ricimer's monogram on the reverse, and on the obverse a rough portrait of a man, not wearing a diadem (ubiquitous in imperial portraits), but with long hair tied back at the nape of the neck (and possibly also a helmet and beard).[28] One of the two coins has a wreath of laurels around the monogram (see pl. 3). Lacam's interpretation is that this is a portrait of Ricimer, dating to the period of civil war with Anthemius.

---

[22] O'Flynn (1983: 287 n. 34); Kent (1994: 190).

[23] Friedlander (1849: 56–7).

[24] Ulrich-Bansa (1949: 284–5).

[25] Lacam (1986) and (1988: 219–46).

[26] Lacam (1988: 236–8).

[27] One coin is in the Bibliothèque Nationale, the other (more important because clearer) came to light when sold in the 1980s to the Garrat Collection.

[28] Beards are unusual on imperial portraits in the fifth century, which had become more and more stylized and anonymous; however, some are known, for instance on coins of Avitus (Kent (1994: 44)).

Plates 3 and 4: Obverse and reverse of *nummi* of Severus, showing the monogram attributed to Ricimer and the (possible) head of Ricimer (from G. Lacam (1986) *Ricimer, Leon I et Anthemius: Le monnayage de Ricimer*, courtesy of Madame Lacam)

Unfortunately the authoritative *Roman Imperial Coinage, x,* covering the late Roman period, has rejected the idea that coins of this monogrammed series were produced at mints other than Rome, or at dates after Severus' death, as suggested by Lacam. (Although it does not seem inconceivable that monogrammed *nummi* might have been produced during Severus' reign at the Milan mint.) Lacam's views are described as 'entirely conjectural and supported by no valid argument'.[29] *Roman Imperial Coinage, x,* makes no mention of the coins with a supposed

[29] Kent (1994: 191).

portrait of Ricimer, and we must, presumably, sadly conclude
that this portrait of Ricimer is merely a badly produced and
preserved imperial head.

It does, however, seem probable, for historical reasons, that
the mint at Milan was under Ricimer's control. Milan had, from
the reign of Valentinian III, a permanent detachment of the
palatine mint, perhaps established by Aetius, which remained
under the control of the *magister utriusque militum* as a source of
coinage (for primarily military purposes), independent of the
emperors' control. Coins were struck at Milan in the names of
all the late fifth-century emperors (with the exception of Petronius Maximus) and later for the Ostrogothic King Theoderic.[30]
It is interesting that, apparently, in late AD 467 the Milan
producers, for a short period, had considerable influence on
the mint of Rome, even supplying it with an obverse die.[31]
This is probably connected to Ricimer's taking of the city.
The numismatic evidence is difficult to interpret, but, even if
Lacam's theories are untenable, control of the Milan mint
would have enhanced Ricimer's status and autonomy.

It has been thought that at some point before the reign of
Anthemius a formal change was initiated, either by Aetius or
Ricimer, by which high-ranking military officials gained prece-
dence over civil ones. This is based on a remark in a letter of
Sidonius Apollinaris, from early in Anthemius' reign, that certain senators were 'of the most elevated order, excepting the
privileged military class'.[32] The reign of Severus is thought to
be the most likely context,[33] and it has been seen as part of a
general aggrandizement of the status of the military under Ricimer, but the circumstances and date are very uncertain. There is
one recorded novella issued by Severus, dating to AD 463, and
addressed to Basilius, the praetorian prefect. The first title (of
two) refers to 'The Abrogation of the Unjust Chapters of the
Law of the Sainted Majorian Augustus'. However, disappoint-
ingly, this refers to the sixth novella of Majorian, which is

[30] Kent (1994: 30).
[31] Ibid.
[32] Sidonius, *Ep.* I, ix, 2: 'in amplissimo ordine seposita praerogativa partis
armatae'. This is discussed by Stein (1959: 380, and 599 n. 87).
[33] Demandt (1970: 674); Stein (1959: 599 n. 87).

concerned with inheritance rights from mothers to children, and the amendments are almost certainly the result of specific cases among the Italian élite.[34] The second title concerns the status of the children of *laeti* who had consorted with *coloni* and slaves, following complaints brought to his notice by Ausonius, praetorian prefect and patrician. The ruling, that children of members of any of the public guilds and *coloni* or slaves have servile status, could be seen as pro-senatorial (and as possibly reducing available military manpower, in the case of *laeti*). If, as seems likely, the *laeti* referred to were of barbarian origins, this is also evidence of intermarriage among the lower as well as upper classes.

These novellas were issued at Rome. Libius Severus seems to have resided principally there (as did his successor Anthemius, and perhaps Nepos), rather than at Ravenna,[35] in contrast to previous emperors such as Valentinian, Honorius, and Majorian. In the case of Anthemius this may reflect his classical and cultural interests, but it may have been more than an accident of personal preferences. As the power of the western imperial throne diminished, it may have seemed useful to associate it with the ancient centre of power; perhaps it was also felt useful to be close to the great aristocratic clans. Ricimer would have spent much of his time close to the army in North Italy, and thus the emperor was free to reside at Rome, perhaps more comfortable at a distance from the patrician. Those men who gained high office under Severus must, it can be presumed, have met with Ricimer's approval, perhaps even being part of a faction centred upon him. Unfortunately, information on this is limited. The western consul for AD 462 was Libius Severus himself, and for AD 463 Flavius Caecina Decius Basilius. In the other two years of Severus' reign both consuls were eastern, and apparently recognized in the West.[36] Plotinus Eustathius may have been *praefectus urbis Romae* during Severus' reign, and certainly was during Ricimer's supremacy (see

[34] *Contra* Oost (1968: 38), who wrote of Severus revoking 'the more offensive of Majorian's anti-clerical legislation' (The English version of the title is from Pharr's translation.)

[35] This is the impression from historical records, the titles of their novellas, and the minting of their coins; for the last see Kent (1994: 189, 195).

[36] Bagnall *et al.* (1987: 462–5).

p. 219),[37] as, possibly, was Flavius Synesius Gennadius Paulus (some time shortly before A D 467).[38] In 461/3 Caelius Aconius Probianus held the post of *praefectus praetorio Italiae*,[39] as did Basilius (ex-consul and patrician) A D 463–5; he had held this post under Majorian in A D 458.[40]

These men were members of powerful and wealthy Italian noble families. Clearly, there was no break from normal fifth-century practice under Ricimer. Basilius, a member of the Decii family, is described by Sidonius, who sought his patronage early in the reign of Anthemius, as one of the most influential men in the senate.[41] His family was still influential under King Odovacer. Plotinus Eustathius was perhaps related to the literary figures Macrobius Plotinus Eudoxius and Macrobius Ambrosius Theodosius. Synesius Gennadius Paulus (a friend of Sidonius Apollinaris)[42] may have been connected to Rufius Synesius Hadrianus (urban prefect prior to A D 483[43]), to Gennadius Avienus (an ex-consul influential in the senate in Anthemius' reign),[44] and to the powerful Rufii family.[45]

Romanus, *magister officiorum* (and *patricius*), whose affiliations are unknown, is recorded at a slightly later date, but may have been appointed at this time, and was a friend of Ricimer.[46] In contrast to the civil officials, the majority of the known military commanders under Ricimer were barbarian: Gundobad, Burco, Bilimer[47] (all three of which are discussed

---

[37] *PLRE* ii, 436, Eustathius 13.
[38] *PLRE* ii, 854–5, Paulus 36.
[39] He was consul in A D 471 (*PLRE* ii, 909, Probianus 4).
[40] *PLRE* ii, 216–17, Basilius 11.
[41] Sidonius, *Ep.* I, ix, 5–6.
[42] Sidonius, *Ep.* I, ix, 1.
[43] *PLRE* ii, 527, Rufius Synesius Hadrianus.
[44] Sidonius, *Ep.* I, ix, 3.
[45] *PLRE* ii, 855, Paulus 36.
[46] John Ant. frag. 207; Cassiodorus, *Chronica* 1289 *s.a.* 470. It is just possible that this man might be connected to the Romanus who was an imperial officer and Aetius' envoy to Attila in A D 449 (Priscus, frag. 11 (2)).
[47] Bilimer is described by Paul the Deacon (*Hist. Rom.* XV) as *Galliarum Rector*; as he was clearly of barbarian origin it is assumed that he held a military position.

more fully later), Everdingus,[48] Thorisarius,[49] Alla,[50] Sindila,[51] and Flavius Valila.[52]

In Gaul, we know something of two Roman officials of this time, Agrippinus and Arvandus. It is known that Agrippinus held office as *comes*, and possibly *magister militum*, in Gaul in the AD 450s and in 461/2 (see Pt. II, pp. 88–92). His position at the later date may have been given to him by Ricimer. Arvandus was *praefectus praetorio Galliarum* from AD 464 to 468 and was of comparatively humble origin.[53] His trial, famous from Sidonius' account, took place in the reign of Anthemius, but his initial appointment was made during that of Severus. Both these men were the target of allegations, which appear to have been well founded, of acting against the interests of Rome and of favouring the Visigoths. Agrippinus had, almost certainly during the reign of Majorian, been accused by Aegidius of favouring the barbarians (see Pt. II, p. 90–1) and in AD 462 he surrendered Narbonne to the Visigoths.[54] Arvandus, at a slightly later date, admitted having corresponded with Euric, advising him to turn on Anthemius and to extend his realm north of the Loire, dividing Gaul between himself and the Burgundians.[55] It is possible that Agrippinus was an adherent of Ricimer, or became one because of his enmity with Aegidius.

Agrippinus, following Aegidius' accusations, and Arvandus, after being arraigned by Gallic notables, were both eventually

---

[48] *PLRE* ii, 414, Everdingus. See also n. 138.

[49] *PLRE* ii, 1115, Thorisarius. See also n. 138.

[50] *PLRE* ii, 60–1, Alla.

[51] *PLRE* ii, 1016, Sindila.

[52] Fl. Theodobius Valila is recorded as *magister militum* in AD 471 and again in 476/83 (*PLRE* ii, 1147, Fl. Valila). He was probably appointed by Ricimer and was perhaps his second in command. Ensslin (1931: 492) suggested that he was *magister equitum praesentalis*, and a strong supporter of Ricimer. (He appears to have been very fully assimilated into Roman life and may have founded an aristocratic line.) He was presumably also an adherent of Odovacer, as his name appeared on the seats in the Colosseum in his reign (Chastagnol (1966: 74)).

[53] Sidonius, *Ep.* I, vii, 3.

[54] Hydatius, 212 (217) *s.a.* 461; *Vita Lupicini* XI. It is not clear how the two relate to each other (see Pt. II, p. 91–2).

[55] Sidonius, *Ep.* I, vii, 5.

brought to trial in Italy.[56] The *Life of Lupicinus* records that Agrippinus appeared 'without delay before the patrician in the presence of the senate'.[57] The emperor, who is unnamed, was consulted on the appropriate penalty for a traitor, and he, without allowing Agrippinus a hearing, imposed the death penalty. This is a striking illustration of Ricimer's power.

Arvandus, before his trial, and at the trial itself, behaved in such a reckless and strange way as to engender the suspicion that he either had good reason to believe that the charges would not stick or was mentally deranged.[58] Both men escaped serious consequences. Arvandus was, to his surprise, sentenced to death, but later this was commuted to exile.[59] Agrippinus, according to Lupicinus' biographer, avoided execution by escaping from prison and going into hiding, but was then mysteriously found to have been innocent and, having given himself up, was acquitted and returned to Gaul. This may have been because Aegidius, his accuser, had become an enemy of Ricimer.

When Agrippinus handed Narbonne over to the Visigoths[60] it is often thought to have been on Ricimer's instruction, to gain the Visigoths' assistance in order to tie Aegidius down in Gaul,[61] or to gain general support for the patrician. The surrender of Narbonne was a major step, giving the Visigoths the vital access to the Mediterranean which had been denied them since the settlement by Flavius Constantius in AD 418.

---

[56] *Vita Lupicini* 11, 96–110. This definitely says the trial was in Rome, though Mathisen thinks it more likely to have been at Ravenna (1979: 616 n. 79). The emperor was either Majorian or Severus.

[57] *Vita Lupicini* 11, 12: 'confestim patricio iuxta insinuationem pristinam praesentatus, adscito quoque senatu'.

[58] The latter is plausible (Sidonius, *Ep.* 1, vii, 1–3, 6–10). Harries (1994: 163–4) suggested that Arvandus genuinely did not think his letter could be construed as treasonable; but this seems doubtful.

[59] Sidonius, *Ep.* 1, vii, 12 (recording the death sentence); Cassiodorus, *Chronica* 1287 *s.a.* 469; Paul Diac. *Hist. Rom.* XV, 2 (his exile).

[60] Hydatius, 212 (217) *s.a.* 462 (see Pt. II, p. 91 for text).

[61] Priscus (frag. 39 (1)) says that Aegidius was deterred from attacking Italy by fighting over disputed borderlands with the Goths; Hydatius (212 (217) *s.a.* 462) that Agrippinus handed over Narbonne to obtain Gothic aid. By putting the two together, it is thought that Ricimer exchanged Narbonne for Gothic assistance against Aegidius; but, while plausible, this is not certain.

There are, of course, other examples of Romans co-operating with barbarian kings on their own initiative; but it is possible that both Agrippinus and Arvandus were following a lead from above, and, if so, logically this was from Ricimer. Ricimer's policy towards Gaul was one of neglect, which allowed the Visigothic kingdom to strengthen and expand. His motivation is open to question. His policy could have been actively pro-Gothic, because he was half-Gothic himself, his loyalty being ultimately to his mother's people, but could equally result from a policy of 'Italy first'. He may have acted for purely pragmatic reasons, such as, amongst others, the need to contain any threat to Italy from Aegidius, military weakness and commitment to other more pressing causes, the growing strength of the Visigoths, and lack of support in Gaul.

Severus' reign was marked by difficult relations between Italy and Marcellinus in Dalmatia, Aegidius in Gaul, the emperor in Constantinople, and the Vandals in Carthage. As seen, already, Ricimer successfully neutralized Aegidius and Marcellinus: by bribing Marcellinus' mercenaries and applying diplomatic pressure via the eastern empire; possibly by using the Goths against Aegidius; and conceivably by assassination. With the other two Ricimer was less successful. Most seriously, Constantinople not only did not recognize Severus, but refused the Italian request for ships to use against the Vandals (to replace those lost by Majorian?) on the grounds that it had a treaty with Gaiseric.[62] Ricimer was also unable to eliminate the constant menace of the Vandals. He and Gaiseric remained at odds, the raids continued, and diplomatic efforts got nowhere.[63] Presumably, Ricimer annually organized expensive defensive measures against the Vandal attacks on Italy and the islands, but it would have been impossible to prevent all the raiding parties from causing destruction and damage.

[62] Priscus, frag. 39 (1).

[63] Priscus, frag. 38 (1). Gaiseric either had or pretended to have three reasons for his continuing aggression: that the treaty with Majorian had lapsed with his death, that he wished Olybrius placed on the western throne, and a claim to the property of Valentinian and Aetius in the names of Eudocia (now his daughter-in-law) and Aetius' son Gaudentius, who was 'living with him' (John Ant. frag. 204). The last, at least, sounds like a pretext, rather similar to Attila's claims prior to his attack on Gaul.

During Severus' reign Ricimer was involved in military action against Alans in North Italy. As this attack is reported in a number of western and eastern sources and was led by an Alan king, this was not merely a minor engagement with a small raiding party. Ricimer led the Roman defensive force in person, and there is no question of the victory being attributed to Severus. The sources (which are consistent with each other) include the *Fasti Vindobonenses*: 'Beorgor, King of the Alans, was killed at Bergamo at the foot of the mountains'.[64]

Marcellinus *comes* briefly reported that 'Beorgor, King of the Alans, was killed by King Ricimer'.[65] Jordanes, wrongly placing the episode in the reign of Anthemius, wrote that the emperor 'sent his son-in-law Ricimer against the Alans, an outstanding man, who at that time was almost unique in Italy in his military ability. In the very first engagement he defeated, overthrew, and massacred the host of Alans and their king, Beorg.'[66]

There are several interesting features in the reports. First, Jordanes' description of Ricimer is quite complimentary (later he takes a similar pro-Ricimer view of the conflict with Anthemius).[67] As Jordanes' views were generally eastern in orientation this is surprising; eastern tradition should be pro-Anthemius and hence anti-Ricimer.[68] Jordanes is not quoting Marcellinus. Cassiodorus' lost history of the Goths is a possibility, but Cassiodorus is normally perceived as following a senatorial, anti-Ricimer tradition (and the same would apply

---

[64] *Fasti Vind. Prior. s.a.* 464: 'occisus est Beorgor rex Alanorum Bergamo ad pede montis VIII idus Februarias'.

[65] Marcellinus *comes*, *s.a.* 464: 'Beorgor rex Halanorum a Ricimere rege occiditur.'

[66] Jordanes, *Getica* 236: 'Recimerem generum suum contra Alanos direxit, virum egregium et pene tunc in Italia ad exercitum singularem. Qui et multitudine Alanorum et regem eorum Beorgum in primo statim certamine superatos internicioni prostravit'. The first sentence is not straightforward to translate (and may be corrupt) and I am grateful for Dr Roger Tomlin's advice, which I have followed here. Other translators read this passage as meaning that Ricimer *alone* was in charge of the army in Italy. (Paul the Deacon (*Hist. Rom.* XV, 1) gives a similar account of the incursion (probably from Jordanes).)

[67] Jordanes, *Getica* 239.

[68] It is unlikely to result from an anti-Alan bias as suggested by Bachrach (1973: 28).

to the lost history of Symmachus).[69] A remote possibility for the origin of this view of Ricimer is one of Jordanes' named sources, the lost work of Ablabius or Ablavius,[70] who may have collected Gothic oral traditions.[71] He seems to be Jordanes' source for early Gothic history, but may have also contributed to later sections. Another possibility is some late fifth-century Visigothic history, that may have been used by Jordanes.[72]

As has often been remarked, Marcellinus' chronicle calls the patrician *Ricimere rege*.[73] Why did Marcellinus give Ricimer this title? We do not know Marcellinus' source(s) for this entry. Official eastern records and city chronicles (if the latter existed; it is debatable) may have been his sources for western items;[74] but these are unlikely to have considered Ricimer in any sense King of Italy.[75] Although Marcellinus was writing when kings ruled Italy, it is unlikely that this is an anachronistic slip; from what he wrote elsewhere, especially on A D 476, it is clear that he was well aware that emperors had ruled Italy at this time. A mistake connected to the fact that he alone calls Marcellinus of Dalmatia 'patrician', Ricimer's title, has been proposed,[76] but this is unconvincing. It has been speculated that the title simply reflected Ricimer's great power in Italy, but again this does not really account for the use of *rex*. The title might reflect Ricimer's royal Gothic origins;[77] *rex* is sometimes used of barbarian leaders of royal birth, even if not what we would consider kings.[78] Perhaps Marcellinus, or his source,

---

[69] It is Cassiodorus who reported the accusation that Ricimer poisoned Severus and who strongly criticized him in connection with Anthemius.

[70] Jordanes, *Getica* 28, 82, 117.

[71] Mommsen (1882), preface to Jordanes' *Getica*, p. xxxvii.

[72] Heather (1991: 64–5) suggested that such a work might have been produced at the court at Toulouse.

[73] The chronicle also notes Ricimer's consulship in A D 459 and his killing of Anthemius, but uses his name only.

[74] Croke (1983: 87–8).

[75] Croke (1983: 87–90, 102–4). Incidentally, Croke asserts that the chronicle contains nothing about the West that was not also of significance to the East, which this entry contradicts.

[76] Demandt (1970: 685–7).

[77] Demandt (1989: 171).

[78] For instance, Sarus, when a military leader in imperial service in A D 406–12, is called 'king' by Marcellinus *comes* (*s.a.* 406) and Jordanes (*Romana* 321), but *dux* by Orosius (V I I, 37, 12).

considered Ricimer a king of the barbarians. It is possible that the origin of this entry could have been a western tradition, perhaps folk tradition rather than a historical work. (See also p. 247–8 and n. 153 on Ennodius calling Ricimer by the title of *princeps*.)

Ricimer apparently met the Alan threat promptly;[79] perhaps he was already in northern Italy. It has been proposed that these Alans were a disbanded unit of Majorian's army;[80] such groups *could* have been a nuisance since AD 457, but this seems a remote possibility.[81] Another possibility is that they were Alans from outside the empire, released by the recent break-up of the Hun empire. The location of the battle at Bergamo suggests that these Alans may have come over either the Brenner or the Septimier Pass from the north, through Raetia or Noricum, which supports the latter origin.

The attack could also have been made from the Alan settlements in Gaul (although there is nothing in the Gallic sources). Alan kings are known in Gaul, such as Goar, Sambida, and Sangiban; Beorgor could have been another. As to the reason why Alans settled in Gaul would attack Italy—Aegidius is a possible instigator. He made contact with the Vandals, presumably to organize an alliance against Ricimer, so may have done the same with the Alans in Gaul. Around AD 463 he had defeated Visigoths at Orleans, which in the 450s had been an Alan stronghold (see Pt. II, p. 73) and probably still was; and Aegidius may have had an alliance with them. Alans had also been settled around Valence by Aetius,[82] and there is place-name evidence for Alan settlements in that area and

---

[79] Suggested by the fact that Jordanes describes the battle as 'the first engagement', and given that no prior destruction or pillaging is recorded.

[80] Bachrach (1973: 33), on the grounds that Alans are listed by Sidonius as among the contingents (*Pan.* v, 474–8). Bachrach thinks these Alans were recruited in Gaul, but Majorian brought the contingents listed by Sidonius over the Alps from Italy *into* Gaul.

[81] Bachrach (1973: 33) surmised that they had spent the intervening years raiding southern Gaul and North Italy; while not impossible, there is no evidence to support this. True, it might explain Jordanes' reference to Majorian returning to Italy to deal with an Alan threat, but this, as discussed on p. 210, is almost certainly a mistake by Jordanes.

[82] *Chronica Gallica a 452, s.a.* 440.

further north,[83] possibly intended to protect the passes to Italy.[84]

There were also probably Alan settlements in northern Italy.[85] Alans had been in imperial military service in Italy since the fourth century A D, among Stilicho's forces for instance.[86] Bergamo was in the militarized region of barbarian settlements and garrisons. A further possible context, therefore, is a rebellion of a powerful Alan group in Italy (settled originally as *laeti*, or *foederati*), caused by disagreement among the barbarians controlled by Ricimer, and quickly stamped on by him. In addition to fighting Alans, Ricimer was possibly also in action against Goths in Noricum towards the end of Severus' reign, or in the subsequent interregnum (see p. 238).[87]

Libius Severus died in the palace at Rome in A D 465, having reigned for four years.[88] The date given by the *Fasti Vindobo-*

---

[83] Bachrach (1973: 32–3, 68–71). As well as place-names there are also a number of fifth-century 'deformed skull burials' found to the west and north of Lake Geneva. (These burials, also found in northern France, are not specifically Alan, but associated with steppe nomad cultures in general.)

[84] Bachrach (1973: 70–1).

[85] Bachrach (1973: 39). Examples of place-names are Allain near Aosta, Alagna (2), Alan d'Riano, Alegno, etc.

[86] Zosimus, v, 26; I v, 35; Orosius, *Hist. ad. Paganos* v I I, 37. For Alans in Stilicho's forces see Claudian, *De Bell. Goth.* II, 580–97, *De Cons. Hon.* v I, 223–6. *Comites Alani* are listed among palatine troops in Italy by the *Notitia Dignitatum* (Oc. v I, 8; v I, 50; v I I, 163). The Alan leader Saul, who fought under Stilicho, is described as a prefect, the normal title for the commander of a *laeti* colony, by Claudian (*De Bell. Goth.* 583). The *Origio Gentis Langobardum* I I I includes possible evidence for Alan soldiers in Ravenna *c.* A D 487: 'exivit rex Audoachari de Ravenna cum exercitu Alanorum'. Also, Bachrach (1973: 36–8) has suggested that some of the military colonies described in the *Notitia* as Sarmatian were, in fact, Alan, or that Alans were later settled in the same locations. Among these Sarmatian colonies in North Italy (dating from before the fifth century) were Pollentia and Cremona (*Notitia Dignitatum*, Oc. X L I I, 63 and 55).

[87] Sidonius, *Pan.* I I, 377 (dating to Jan. A D 468) suggests this, and it appears to have been fairly recent. Although this comes from panegyric, military action in that region is not implausible.

[88] *Fasti Vind. Prior. s.a.* 465 (which gives the erroneously early date of 15 Aug.); *Pasch. Camp. s.a.* 465; Jordanes, *Getica* 236, *Romana* 336; *Chronica Gallica a 511*, 644; Cassiodorus, *Chronica* 1280 *s.a.* 465 which locates the death 'in the palace'; and Marcellinus *comes*, *s.a.* 465. For the Nov. date see Seeck (1919: 412).

nenses, of 14 August, cannot be correct, as Severus issued a law on 25 September. The date of 14 November given by the *Paschale Campanum* is more likely. Only Cassiodorus reported rumours of foul play: 'it is said that Severus was killed by the deceitful Ricimer by poison, in the palace at Rome'.[89] Sidonius stated explicitly in his panegyric to Anthemius that Severus' death was natural,[90] yet several scholars have suspected Ricimer's hand in the emperor's demise.[91] If Sidonius was, as has been suggested, being ironic, he was taking a risk, as Ricimer was almost certainly present when the panegyric was read out (see p. 236).

The traditional forensic questions concern 'means' and 'motive' Cassiodorus mentions poison, which makes Ricimer's involvement less likely. Poison was commonly blamed in the past in cases of illnesses not then understood, such as food poisoning, and its efficient use is more difficult than fiction and rumour have it. Ricimer was perfectly capable of killing Severus, but poison seems unlikely and out of character. On the other hand, it is easy to see how and why such suspicions could have arisen and rumours circulated. Ricimer's motive for murder is hard to perceive. If he wanted a docile puppet emperor, then, according to all we know, that is what he had in Libius Severus.

It is true that our picture of Severus as a docile puppet is an argument from silence. Oost speculated that he was showing signs of independence because he felt that his position was threatened.[92] However, the basis of Oost's case is the circular argument that Severus must have been becoming more assertive, otherwise why did Ricimer murder him? For Oost, reports to the contrary are either the result of 'Ricimeran propaganda' (see pp. 213–4) or, in the case of Sidonius, a coded message actually

---

[89] Cassiodorus, *Chronica* 1280 *s.a.* 465: 'ut dicitur Ricimeris fraude, Severus Romae in Palatio veneno peremptus est'.

[90] Sidonius, *Pan.* II, 317–18. Paul the Deacon (*Hist. Rom.* XV, 1) also describes the death as natural (though his usual source is Jordanes, who simply says that Severus died).

[91] Esp. Oost (1970: 228–40).

[92] Oost (1970: 228–40) followed by O'Flynn (1983: 113). The supposed threat to Severus is the elevation of Olybrius, a potential emperor supported by Gaiseric and Leo, to the eastern consulate for AD 464, and (or alternatively) the fact that Ricimer now regarded him as an obstacle to western reconciliation

supporting the idea of murder. It is an ingenious argument, but unconvincing. It is a great deal simpler to accept the records that say Severus died a natural death at face value. This is not to say that friction between emperor and patrician, nor intrigue on the part of either, did not occur. Even a nonentity would gain prestige from the purple, and Ricimer would always have had to rule through the emperor. A puppet emperor could still act as a focus for opposition.

Following Severus' death there was another interregnum, this time lasting for over seventeen months, from November AD 465 to April 467.[93] During this, not inconsiderable, time Ricimer must have been the major decision maker in legislative, military, and judicial matters.[94] These interregnums may have acclimatized Romans to the lack of an emperor, making it easier to accept after AD 476. Rather than setting up an Italian emperor by himself, as previously, Ricimer made contact with Leo, sending an embassy which was probably in the name of the senate.[95] Possible reasons are not hard to see: pressure from the senate; a wish for reconciliation with Constantinople; the status that a fully recognized emperor would possess; and, especially, the need for Leo's assistance against Gaiseric. Had he been able, on his own, to stop Gaiseric by diplomatic or military means, he might well not have approached the East.[96]

---

with Leo and/or Gaiseric. Seeck (1920: vi, 352) also saw the removal of Severus as the price of eastern aid. However, if Severus really feared that he might be disposed of as inconvenient, it would have been courageous of him to attempt to topple Ricimer; a better option might have been abdication and ordination.

[93] The fact that Ricimer had not got a replacement lined up for Severus sustains the view that he did not kill him.

[94] As he knew of the later emperor Anthemius, it is probably to this interregnum that Theophanes (using his source for western affairs) referred when he recorded that 'Severus [ruled] three years. After these men there was no emperor, but Rekimer [*sic*] controlled affairs, commanding the army and invested with great power' (AM 5947: Mango and Scott's translation).

[95] For the embassy in the name of the senate see Evagrius, *HE* ii, 16; Theophanes, AM 5957.

[96] The Italian government had been refused eastern naval assistance in Severus' reign (Priscus, frag. 39 (1)). The situation in Gaul had also deteriorated; the new Gothic king, Euric, was less pro-Roman than Theoderic, and on the offensive.

To gain these advantages Ricimer took the serious risk that an eastern appointee would become a political and personal threat to him (as indeed proved to be the case). He was, perhaps surprisingly, willing to accept this risk and to act against his personal best interests. The urgent military and political necessity to find some way of dealing with the Vandal threat must have overridden other considerations; it is even conceivable, if unlikely, that the decision was made for the sake of what remained of the western empire. Ricimer may have thought, moreover, that, if the need arose, he could deal with an uppity emperor.

Leo was willing to co-operate, one reason being, no doubt, the Vandal nuisance in the Mediterranean and their raids in the eastern Mediterranean (including Illyricum, and the mainland and islands of Greece).[97] The *Life of St. Daniel Stylite* recorded a rumour current in Constantinople around this time that Gaiseric even intended to attack Alexandria.[98] The explicit task of Leo's chosen candidate was to make war on the Vandals,[99] for the benefit of both Italy and the East.

Leo selected Anthemius, a distinguished man, the son-in-law of Marcian (thus with a remote connection to the house of Theodosius), and an experienced military leader,[100] acceptable to the conservative faction in Italy and, on the face of it, an excellent choice. In spring A D 467 (as described in Pt. I) Anthemius was accompanied to Italy by an eastern army, his *comites*, and Marcellinus of Dalmatia. His proclamation as emperor near Rome on 12 April is recorded by a large number of sources. It took place at somewhere called Brontotas at the third milestone from the city, according to one source; at an unnamed location eight miles from the city, according to another.[101] A number of important events of the time are recorded as taking place outside

[97] Procopius, *Wars* III, v, 22–5 and xxii, 16–18; Victor of Vita, I, 5.

[98] *Vita Dan. Styl.* 56.

[99] Procopius, *Wars* III, vi, 5.

[100] Sidonius, *Pan.* II, 199–201. He had held the titles of *magister militum* and patrician and had been consul in A D 455 (Sidonius, *Pan.* II, 205–6; Marcellinus *comes*, *s.a.* 467; Jordanes, *Getica* 236, *Romana* 336).

[101] Cassiodorus, *Chronica* 1283 *s.a.* 467: 'qui tertio ab urbe miliario in loco Brontotas suscepit imperium'; Hydatius, 231 (235) *s.a.* 467 (giving the location of eight miles outside Rome); *Fasti Vind. Prior. s.a.* 467 (giving the date);

Rome or Ravenna, and this may well have been because they occurred at major military bases (this is specified in the case of the proclamation of Majorian at the camp of Columellas). Brontotas may have been another such. This gives some indication of the location of some, at least, of the fifth-century army. These military bases outside Rome and Ravenna were probably those of the élite 'guards' units.

Later that year Ricimer married Anthemius' daughter Alypia in Rome.[102] Presumably, this had been agreed as part of the deal between Ricimer, Leo, and Anthemius.[103] Anthemius may have considered this a great concession.[104] Ricimer perhaps regarded the marriage as one of temporary political convenience, but it is more likely that he valued it. It publicly recognized his status and he gained a kin relationship with the ruling emperor, similar to that of Stilicho with Theodosius and Honorius, and Flavius Constantius with Honorius, and such as Aetius (and perhaps Gaiseric) had desired with Valentinian. Both Stilicho and Aetius (and perhaps Gaiseric) hoped to see their sons or grandsons wearing the purple, and hence to become themselves part of an imperial lineage; Flavius

Sidonius, *Pan.* 11, 212–15; *Pasch. Camp. s.a.* 467; Marcellinus *comes, s.a.* 467; *Chronica Gallica a 511*, 645; and many later writers. Brontotas does not appear in either *RE* or the *Lexicon Topographicum urbis Romae*. Perhaps the name dates to the sixth century.

[102] Since she is spoken of as being of royal blood (see p. 239), Alypia's mother was probably Aelia Marcia Euphemia, daughter of the emperor Marcian. This would mean that Alypia was about fourteen years old, at most, on marriage (Anthemius and Euphemia married *c.* AD 453). However, as she had a brother, Anthemiolus, who was killed fighting the Goths as joint commander of the army in AD 471, for which *c.* 18 years seems rather young, both may have been the children of an unknown earlier wife, and hence older. The marriage gave Ricimer a remote but real connection with the prestigious Theodosian dynasty.

[103] Sidonius, *Pan.* 11, 484–6, *Ep.* 1, v, 10 and ix, 1; John Ant. frag. 209 (1); Ennodius, *Vita Epiph.* 67; Hydatius, 241 (247) *s.a.* 468; *Chronica Gallica a 511*, 650; Jordanes, *Getica* 236; Marcellinus *comes, s.a.* 472; Procopius, *Wars* 111, vii, 1; John Malalas, 378; and others. Most only record the marriage indirectly, by calling Ricimer Anthemius' son-in-law. Typically, only one source, John of Antioch (probably using Priscus) bothers to record the name of Alypia.

[104] Ennodius, *Vita Epiph.* 67 (see p. 250), but see the comments on p. 252 for caution here.

Constantius alone had achieved this. Ricimer may well have had similar ambitions.[105] Ricimer, who must surely have been in his thirties at the very least, was perhaps a widower. Unlike Stilicho, Flavius Constantius, Aetius, Orestes, and Odovacer, Ricimer does not appear to have had a son to sharpen his ambition (indeed, no children are recorded). This is substantiated by his later appointment of his nephew Gundobad as his successor. Ricimer was Arian and Alypia Catholic, but political pragmatism clearly triumphed over religious scruple.

The marriage was celebrated in extravagant style and amid general festivity, and had, apparently, the general approval of all sections and factions of the population of Rome.[106] Sidonius saw the marriage as providing grounds for hope for the future security of the state.[107] He had happened to arrive in Rome when the wedding was taking place; bringing a petition to the new emperor from Auvergne. Its subject is not known, but from other evidence the deputation was probably seeking both defensive measures and action against abuses of power by officials. To help his cause, Sidonius composed a panegyric to Anthemius, delivered on 1 January.[108] Its content indicates what the senatorial class hoped for from the new emperor: an active and successful leader against the Vandals.[109] Its other major theme was unity between East and West.

The panegyric includes a section in praise of Ricimer. Although lengthy, it is worth close study, as one of the few sources to indicate how Ricimer was seen by his contemporaries, and, perhaps, indirectly, by himself. Ricimer was almost certainly present at the occasion of its reading (being Anthemius' first western consulship, celebrated shortly after the wedding). Sidonius was not unintelligent and very anxious for his mission to

---

[105] O'Flynn (1983: 115–16) considered that marriage to Alypia would not have been as attractive to Ricimer as to his predecessors, but this is doubtful. There have been many instances of important men, powerful enough to make and unmake monarchs, still finding it useful and pleasing to have a personal relationship with a royal family.

[106] Sidonius, *Ep.* I, ix, 1.

[107] Sidonius, *Ep.* I, v, 10: 'in spem publicae securitatis'.

[108] Sidonius, *Ep.* I, ix, 5–6.

[109] Sidonius, *Pan.* II, 382–6.

succeed,[110] so the content of the panegyric would surely have been made acceptable to both emperor and patrician. Sidonius was perfectly capable of sycophancy, mendacity, gross exaggeration, and the omission of inconvenient fact,[111] but his (occasional) factual statements are presumably correct.

A goddess representing Italy speaks to the river god of the Tiber thus:

> Furthermore, unconquerable Ricimer, to whom the destiny of the state looks anxiously, his own efforts alone hardly repulse the pirate who roves across the countryside, who avoids battle, who becomes the victor by flight. Who could endure such an enemy who refuses both peace and war? For he will never make a treaty with Ricimer. Harken to why he hates him so much. He is born of an uncertain father, while a slave-woman was certainly his mother. Now, [to show] that he is the son of a king, he proclaims his mother's adultery. Especially he envies Ricimer because two kingdoms call him to kingship; for he is Suevian through his father and Gothic through his mother. And at the same time he [Gaiseric] remembers that in the Tartesian lands [i.e. Spain] his grandfather Vallia, cast down the Vandal armies and their allies in war the Alans … But why relate ancient flights and former defeats? He [Gaiseric] recalls his losses on the plain of Agrigentum. Ever since then he rages, because he knows that he [Ricimer] is the true grandson of the hero at whose sight the Vandals always turned in flight [Vallia]. Certainly you Marcellus were no more glorious when you returned from the lands of Sicily …
> … Noricum holds back the Ostrogoth because he [Ricimer] is feared; Gaul ties down the might of the Rhine because he inspires terror; because the Vandal hosts and their relatives the Alans plundered me [Italy] bare, he himself then took vengeance by his own arms. But, for all that, he is only one man; who can only accept so many risks alone.[112]

---

[110] It proved successful for Sidonius himself because, as a result of the panegyric, he became urban prefect (Sidonius, *Ep.* 1, ix, 6).

[111] Given that Ricimer was jointly responsible for the overthrow and death of Sidonius' father-in-law Avitus, and for that of Majorian, Sidonius' reference to previous western emperors (346–8) is masterly in its tact and evasiveness; their fate is blamed on the caprice of Fortune: 'quemcumque creavit axe meo natum, confestim fregit in illo imperii Fortuna rotas'.

[112] Sidonius, *Pan.* 11, 352–82: 'Praeterea invictus Ricimer, quem publica fata respiciunt, proprio solus vix Marte repellit piritam per rura vagum, qui proelia vitans victorem fugitivus agit. Quis sufferat hostem qui pacem

The panegyric goes on to state that Ricimer's efforts alone, however, cannot save Rome, and this leads into Italy's need for Anthemius, Sidonius' main theme. Within a panegyric to the emperor, over thirty lines is a considerable amount to devote to another man. Compare this with the victorious *magister militum* of Majorian, who got five lines, and is never named (Pt. II, p. 84). This reflects both Ricimer's personal power and, even more, his new relationship with Anthemius. For an account by Sidonius it is comparatively informative. The main themes are Ricimer's military prowess (to which there are further references elsewhere in the panegyric), and his noble birth contrasted with Gaiseric's bastardy.[113] To praise Ricimer's military skills was not only safe but accurate; he is not known to have suffered a defeat. Apart from the Vandals, the Ostrogoths in Noricum are mentioned, and the 'armed might of the Rhine'; the wording is ambiguous, but Ricimer may himself have campaigned in Noricum (possibly against Goths from Pannonia),[114] and possibly in Gaul (perhaps under Aetius at an earlier date). It is very striking that Sidonius describes him as *invictus Ricimer*, as this title was once reserved for members of the imperial family alone. He compares the patrician favourably with Marcellus, the captor of Syracuse, and also likens him to Metellus, who defeated the Carthaginians (presumably because

---

pugnamque negat? Nam foedera nulla cum Ricimere iacit. Quem cur nimis oderit audi. Incertum crepat ille patrem, cum serva sit illi certa parens; nunc, ut regis sit filius, effert matris adulterium. Tum livet quod Ricimerem in regnum duo regna vocant; nam patre Suebus, a genetrice Getes. Simul et reminiscitur illud, quod Tartesiacis avus huius Vallia terris Vandalicas turmas et iuncti Martis Halanos . . . Quid veteres narrare fugas, quid damna priorum? Agrigentini recolit dispendia campi. Inde furit, quod se docuit satis iste nepotem illius esse viri quo viso, Vandale, semper terga dabas. Nam non Siculis inlustrior arvis tu, Marcelle, redis . . . Noricus Ostrogothum quod continet, iste timetur; Gallia quod Rheni Martem ligat, iste pavori est; quod consanguineo me Vandalus hostis Halano diripuit radente, suis hic ultus ab armis. Sed tamen unus homo est nec tanta pericula solus tollere'.

[113] See e.g. ll. 502–3: 'hos thalamos, Ricimer, Virtus tibi pronuba poscit atque Dionaeam dat Martia laura myrtum'.

[114] John of Antioch records the Goths in Pannonia beginning hostilities around the time of the reign of Anthemius (John Ant. frag. 206 (2)). See also Wolfram (1988: 263) and Bury (1923: 332). It is possible that Ricimer had some connection with the Sueve settlements in Noricum and Pannonia.

of the analogy of their victories, but also, one suspects, so he can introduce a parade of elephants).[115]

Ricimer's barbarian ancestry is not glossed over but stressed. There is no attempt to make him an honorary Roman, to describe his good Latin, classical learning, or civilized virtues, as Sidonius does elsewhere.[116] His birth cannot have been something that Ricimer tried to disguise (indeed he may have played on it).[117] This can be seen as a reflection of the attitude of Ricimer himself, or that of Sidonius and contemporary society, or both. It shows the change that had taken place in the West: that barbarian ancestry could be considered an asset rather than a handicap. Indeed, it is probably safe to say that Ricimer's barbarian royal ancestry actually gave him status, among both the barbarians and Romans of Italy. This is clear in a later passage in the panegyric: 'Hereafter, accompany your public alliance with a private one. May the parent Augustus become the fortunate father-in-law of Ricimer. [Both] shine with nobility—she is your royal maiden, he is my [Italy's] royalty.'[118] The idea of Ricimer as Italy's royalty is striking and rather surprising.

Whatever was proclaimed in the panegyric, the relationship between emperor and patrician must, from the first, have been complicated and, perhaps, fraught. However, it took three years for open conflict to break out between them. These were dominated by military reversals, which may have affected the political and personal status quo. Very little is known about affairs in Italy during these three years. Ennodius describes Ricimer at this time as 'directing the government of the state, second only to the Emperor Anthemius'.[119] From what other sources indicate, and what Ennodius says elsewhere, this seems a fair enough assessment.[120]

[115] ll. 373–6, omitted above.
[116] See e.g. Sidonius, *Ep.* I, ii, 6 and IV, xvii, 1–2.
[117] This might connect with Marcellinus *comes*' description of him as 'king' (see pp. 229–30).
[118] Sidonius, *Pan.* 11, 484–6: 'Adice praeterea privatum ad publica foedus: sit socer Augustus genero Ricimere beatus; nobilitate micant: est vobis regia virgo regius ille mihi'.
[119] Ennodius, *Vita Epiph.* 51: 'secundis ab Anthemio principe habenis rempublicam gubernabat'.
[120] See e.g. Theophanes, AM 5947; Marcellinus *comes*, *s.a.* 464.

There is one novella of Anthemius on record, given at Rome in spring AD 468,[121] but it is uninformative for our purposes, being on family law. Marcellinus *comes* noted an earthquake in the Ravenna region and an eruption of Vesuvius;[122] and the *Fasti Vindobonenses* an outbreak of cattle disease in AD 467.[123] There was pestilence in Italy, particularly in Campania.[124] In both East and West this was a time of disasters and unusual events including: the fire in Constantinople in AD 465;[125] earthquakes and floods in the eastern Mediterranean;[126] falls of ash;[127] celestial phenomena in AD 467;[128] and famines.[129] All this may have contributed to a general feeling of insecurity, even of doom.

Ricimer was not given command of either the major campaign led by Basiliscus and Marcellinus against the Vandals (see Pt. I, pp. 56–60),[130] or that led by Anthemius' son against Euric in Gaul (see pp. 242–4), and this may have been resented.[131] From subsequent events, we know that he must have remained in command of substantial forces in Italy. Towards the end of Anthemius' reign, Sidonius wrote: 'If the state has no soldiers, no defences, if [as is reported] the Emperor Anthemius has no resources'.[132] There were still large barbarian contin-

---

[121] *Nov. Anth.* 1 (the last recorded novella of a western emperor in the *Theodosian Code*).

[122] Marcellinus *comes*, *s.a.* 467 and 472.

[123] *Fasti Vind. Prior. s.a.* 467. *The Oracle of Baalbek*, 125, also mentions an epidemic of sheep and cattle disease in the mid fifth century.

[124] Gelasius, col. 113.

[125] Evagrius, *HE* ii, 13; *Chronicon Paschale s.a.* 465; Theophanes, AM 5954; Marcellinus *comes*, *s.a.* 465.

[126] Evagrius, *HE* ii, 14.

[127] John Malalas, 372.

[128] Hydatius, 238 (244) *s.a.* 467.

[129] Theophanes, AM 5964; Sidonius, *Ep.* I, x, 2.

[130] It is conceivable that the aborted expedition against the Vandals in AD 467, which was cancelled or recalled because of adverse conditions (Hydatius, 232 (236) *s.a.* 466–7, see Pt. I, p. 56), had been initiated by Ricimer.

[131] John Ant. frag. 207: '[Ricimer] summoned six thousand men who were under his command for the war against the Vandals.'

[132] Sidonius, *Ep.* II, i, 4: 'Si nullae a republica vires, nulla praesidia, si nullae, quantum rumor est, Anthemii principis opes'. Given that the context is complaint about the lack of imperial assistance for Clermont, this may of course be exaggerated.

gents in Italy, so either Sidonius is exaggerating for effect or these forces were not considered to be under Anthemius' control, and were, presumably, under Ricimer's.

The idea that Ricimer might at this time have relinquished the title of *patricius*, so that it could be assumed by Marcellinus, has already been rejected (see Pt. I, p. 55–6). Indeed, Hydatius records envoys reporting 'that Ricimer had been made son-in-law and *patricius* of the Emperor Anthemius'.[133] Presumably, Ricimer was confirmed in his title by Anthemius; this again may have been an agreed precondition. It is also possible that Ricimer and Marcellinus swore oaths of friendship or at least non-aggression (see Ch. 3 n. 109).

The Vandal raiding continued and became more serious. Priscus records that: 'The Emperor Leo sent Phylarchus to Gaiseric to announce to him the sovereignty of Anthemius and to threaten war if he did not *evacuate Italy and Sicily*. He returned with the report that Gaiseric refused to accept the emperor's commands and *that he was engaged in preparation for war*' (my italics).[134] This embassy may have been a last-ditch attempt for peace, or a piece of misdirection, for Leo had already determined on a campaign against the Vandals, the disastrous course of which is covered in Pt. I. The failure of this campaign (and, to a lesser extent, the death of Marcellinus) must have been very damaging to Anthemius. A victory over the Vandals was desperately needed and had been the reason for his welcome in Italy. Ricimer may have been glad to see the back of Marcellinus, but unhappy that the expedition had failed; he had, after all, put himself out to gain eastern help in this direction, and now Italy was not only no better off, but had suffered a further wasting of limited resources.

In what remained of Roman Gaul the imperial position was desperate. It has been suggested that Anthemius' policy in Gaul was to encourage imperial loyalties in Gaul and Spain and to weaken Ricimer's support there. The first suggestion seems logical enough, although the actual evidence for this as a policy

---

[133] Hydatius, 241 (247) *s.a.* 468: 'Rechimerium generum Antimi imperatoris et patricium factum'.

[134] Priscus, frag. 52 (Blockley's translation).

is not that strong.[135] O'Flynn considered that Ricimer would have regarded Anthemius' attempts to establish good relations with the various barbarian peoples as encroachment on 'his territory'.[136] There is no reason, though, why arranging the alliances could not have involved Ricimer as well as Anthemius. In AD 472 when Ricimer's Burgundian nephew Gundobad came to Italy from Gaul he was (according to Malalas) *magister militum*.[137] As Malalas is the only source for this, and as he is not a reliable source for the West, it seems advisable to treat this information with caution, but it is usually presumed that he was *magister militum per Gallias* (a title previously held by his father). If Gundobad did hold this post, it may have been at his uncle's instigation, possibly as part of a formal alliance between Romans and Burgundians at the time of the campaign against Euric, who was a threat to both. (Riothamus, possibly an ally of Rome at this time, fled to the Burgundians when defeated by Euric: see below.)

Anthemius did not wish to abandon the last Roman possessions in southern Gaul. In AD 471 an army was sent from Italy to attack the Visigoths; one of the four leaders was his son Anthemiolus.[138] Shortly before this Anthemius had made an

---

[135] Stein (1959: 389–90) cited the favouring of Gallic notables such as Sidonius and Ecdicius, the 'removal of Arvandus' (who may or may not have been a creature of Ricimer's), and the 'striving for good relations' with the Visigoths, Bretons, Franks, Burgundians, Sueves, etc. This is shaky: Riothamus was an ally of Anthemius (according to the not very reliable Jordanes (see p. 243)) from either Britain or Brittany; but the reference to the Franks rests on extremely tenuous reasoning connecting Childeric to Anthemius by way of Count Paul; Hydatius (241 (247) s.a. 468) records an embassy from the Sueves to the western emperor, but nothing more; the Burgundian connection seems to rest on the appointment of Gundobad as *magister militum*, which may be nothing to do with the Burgundian kingdom; and, so far from trying to establish good relations with Euric, Anthemius sent an army against him!

[136] O'Flynn (1983: 118).

[137] John Malalas, 375.

[138] *Chronica Gallica a 511*, 649: 'Antimolus a patre Anthemio imperatore cum Thorisario, Everdingo et Hermiano com. Stabuli Arelate directus est: quibus rex Euricus trans Rhodanum occurrit occisisque ducibus omnia vastavit.' ('Anthemiolus was ordered to Arles by his father, the Emperor Anthemius, with Thorisarius, Everdingus, and Hermianus, the Count of the Stables. They were met and destroyed by King Euric, across the Rhône, and all the

alliance with the British, or Breton, leader Riothamus with the intention, presumably, of attacking Euric on two fronts. Riothamus, however, was defeated by Euric north of the Loire, 'before the Romans could join him', and fled to the Burgundians.[139] According to a Gallic chronicle, the army sent by Anthemius was defeated and destroyed somewhere *trans Rodanum*.[140] All the commanders, including Anthemius' son, were killed, making this a personal tragedy, as well as yet another military and political reverse. Euric went on to begin the conquest of Auvergne, and within five years had obtained all the remaining Roman possessions in southern Gaul. By this time the relationship between Ricimer and Anthemius (probably one of distrust from the outset) had developed into a struggle for power, and was ultimately to become, in effect, civil war.[141] This process may have been fuelled by Ricimer being sidelined from major

commanders were killed.') (At least two of the other three *duces* were of barbarian ancestry.) By this time Anthemius and Ricimer were already at odds with each other, so possibly these men represented a barbarian faction in Italy opposed to Ricimer and loyal to the emperor. An alternative would be that the army was dispatched during the temporary truce associated with St. Epiphanius' efforts to make peace around this time (Ennodius, *Vita Epiph.* 51).

[139] Jordanes, *Getica* 237. Assuming that the Romans were Anthemius' forces from Italy, they were possibly delayed in setting out. One would not normally place much value on this bit of Jordanes, but it certainly would have made sense for the two armies to attack Euric simultaneously, and this might have been the plan. If the army's arrival in Gaul was delayed, thus preventing them from co-operating effectively with Riothamus, the cause could well have been Ricimer's rebellion or lack of co-operation. It is obviously speculation, but Anthemius may have blamed Ricimer in part or full for his son's death, accentuating the personal bitterness of the conflict. Alternatively, as suggested by Stevens (1933: 112 n. 2), these Romans were Syagrius and his forces, with whom Riothamus was to rendezvous somewhere in north-west Gaul.

[140] A minor point, but, assuming that 'trans Rodanum' would normally mean east of the river to somebody writing in Gaul (*PLRE* ii, 93, Anthemiolus) and the army was sent to Arles on the Rhône (still presumably in Roman hands), and given that Euric's kingdom was to the west of the river, why was the lost battle to the *east* of the Rhône? Did they in fact never arrive at Arles, but were met by the advancing Goths? Had they failed to retake Arles, already in Gothic hands, and been in retreat?

[141] As indeed it is called by John of Antioch, frag. 209 (1), *Fasti Vind. Prior.* s.a. 472, *Pasch. Camp.* s.a. 472, and Pope Gelasius I, writing in the 490s (*Adversus Andromachum* col. 115): 'Et nuper cum Anthemii et Ricimeris civili furore subversa est'.

campaigns and by the death of Anthemius' son. Ricimer probably found it possible to move against Anthemius in A D 470 not
only because of the emperor's weakened political and military
position, but because in the East Leo had become involved in a
power struggle with Aspar and was therefore unlikely to intervene. Anthemius remained, however, able to command the
adherence of a large part of the Italian élite and the populace
of Rome. The fact that the siege of Rome carried on for months
confirms the existence of support for him.

Did personal and political animosity overlie a more fundamental dichotomy? Ricimer and Anthemius were seen by
nineteenth-century and early twentieth-century writers as representatives respectively of a Germanic or barbarian party and
of a conservative and Roman party. Bury, for instance, wrote:
'the question of Roman or German ascendancy which had
underlain the situation for fifteen years was now clearly
defined'.[142] There was in fact no straight ethnic division. Ricimer commanded barbarian armed forces, but there were also
barbarians on the emperor's side and Romans on the patrician's.[143] Ricimer's ethnicity was a factor in the view of many
ancient sources, for instance Malalas;[144] it is, however, debatable to what extent Ricimer should really be seen as barbarian
(see pp. 252–3 and pp. 263–5).

Was there, however, some sort of split into two factions
among the western Roman élite itself? Although it is possible
to discern among the Roman upper classes both conservative
sentiments and a more pragmatic willingness to come to terms
with the barbarian presence,[145] it would be simplistic to envisage a straight dichotomy. The reality must have been more
complex; factions among the Roman élite were normally mut-

---

[142] See e.g. Bury (1923: 339).

[143] For instance, Romanus, presumably a Roman, was a close friend of
Ricimer, while Bilimer, presumably a barbarian, tried to assist Anthemius
(see below). Also, Ricimer proclaimed Olybrius emperor before Anthemius
was killed, and must have had some Roman allies to be able to do so.

[144] John Malalas, 368: 'he had aroused the enmity of his son-in-law Ricimer
the *magister militum* and was afraid of him as he was a Goth'. (Jeffreys'
translation).

[145] Sometimes, indeed, in the same person; Sidonius Apollinaris is the
obvious example.

able, and account must always be taken of the promptings of self-, kin, and class interests.

A further factor was that Anthemius was from the 'Greek' East, and may have been unpopular for that reason alone, especially among those who disliked the idea of domination, political or religious, by Constantinople. There are hints of such sentiments in the writings of Ennodius, where he is called 'an excitable Galatian' by Ricimer, and *Graeculus* by the Ligurians;[146] and in a letter of Sidonius, who calls him 'the Greek emperor'.[147] There is also the possibility (discussed in Pt. I) that Anthemius had pagan leanings, or what appeared to be so in the unsophisticated West. Anthemius' classical interests may have made him popular among sections of the aristocratic and intellectual élite in the city of Rome, but are unlikely to have won him friends outside such circles. It has also been argued that these Hellenic sympathies made Anthemius particularly anti-barbarian,[148] hence making collaboration with Ricimer and others in Italy more difficult.

Anthemius had also clashed with the Bishop of Rome. One Philotheus, an adherent of the Macedonian heresy, had accompanied him to Rome. He had tolerated celebration of the Lupercalia (see Pt. I, pp. 52–3). Worse, he had attempted to introduce a measure of toleration by allowing all Christian sects to hold conventicles in Rome. Pope Hilarius protested, and Anthemius was forced to promise that such heretical sects would not be allowed to do so again in future.[149] All this may have lost him important Church support.

The conflict between Ricimer and Anthemius escalated over a couple of years; in reconstructing its progress one is forced to reconcile a small number of disparate sources, which

---

[146] Ennodius, *Vita Epiph.* 53 and 55. In the latter case, *Graeculus* is contrasted to *catholicus et romanus* and this may be intended to refer to religious rather than, or as well as, ethnic difference.

[147] Sidonius, *Ep.* I, vii, 5: 'Graeco imperatore'.

[148] Vassili (1938a: 38–45).

[149] Gelasius, *Ep.* XIII, *ad Episcopos Dardaniae*: 'Sanctae memoriae quoque papa Hilarius Anthemium imperatorem cum Philotheus Macedonianus ejus familiaritate suffultus diversarum conciliabuta nova sectarum in urbem vellet inducere, apud beatum Petrum apostolum palam ne id fieret clara voce constrinxit, in tantum ut non ea facienda cum interpositione sacramenti idem promitteret imperator.'

do not provide a coherent chronological narrative. The reconstruction that follows arranges the fragmentary information into what seems the most rational course of events.[150] The incident which triggered open conflict (probably in AD 470) was, according to John of Antioch, the execution of one Romanus:

> Anthemius...became seriously ill as the result of sorcery and punished many who were caught in this crime, especially Romanus, who had held the office of master and was enrolled amongst the patricians. He was a very close friend of Ricimer who, out of anger over Romanus, left Rome and summoned 6,000 men who were under his command for the war against the Vandals.[151]

As *magister officiorum*, Romanus held a post central to the imperial court and close to the emperor, involving administration inside and outside the palace and possibly civil security. Anthemius' attribution of his illness to sorcery may have been a genuinely held belief (followed possibly by a panicky witch-hunt and the use of torture to gain confessions), or a pretext to rid himself of those in his court whose loyalty was primarily to Ricimer rather than to himself.

John of Antioch's figure of 6,000 men is one of the few estimates of military numbers in this period. If originally from Priscus, it might be accurate, but it is unclear whether it relates to the total strength of the army under Ricimer or to forces that had been specifically gathered for use against the Vandals. As it

---

[150] The suggested chronology is as follows. Romanus was executed sometime in AD 470. A short while afterwards Anthemius and Ricimer became openly hostile and Ricimer withdrew to Milan. Sometime between then and early AD 471 Epiphanius effected a temporary reconciliation, but this broke down. About June/July AD 471 Ricimer moved on Rome. Nine months later, in March/April, Bilimer arrived to assist Anthemius and was defeated. Knowing that Anthemius' situation was now hopeless, Ricimer proclaimed Olybrius emperor round about May (and perhaps now summoned Gundobad), but the siege dragged on for another five months, as Anthemius' support drained away. Gundobad arrived, Ricimer made an attack with the extra troops, and Anthemius was killed in July AD 472. Ricimer died in Aug. 472 and Olybrius in Nov. 472 (in the seventh month of his reign).

[151] John Ant. frag. 207 (Blockley's translation, Priscus, frag. 62). It is recorded by Cassiodorus (*Chronica* 1289 s.a. 470) that Romanus was punished for a 'capital crime against the state', and by Paul the Deacon (*Hist. Rom.* XV, 2), perhaps using Cassiodorus, that Romanus was guilty of treachery.

is likely that Gaiseric would have followed up his defeat of the imperial fleets in AD 468 with further attacks, these troops may have been assembled for defensive purposes; but it could be that an offensive campaign against the Vandals (perhaps in Sicily) had been prepared.

The other major source for the conflict is Ennodius' account of the life of St. Epiphanius, Bishop of Pavia. This, as hagiography, is completely different in character to John of Antioch's history, and it is tricky to reconcile the two into one chronological sequence (see n. 150). The easiest way is to place the events described by Ennodius (below) after the initial rift, but before the siege of the city of Rome in AD 471. The relevant section begins with the description of Ricimer governing second only to the emperor (quoted on p. 239). Ennodius begins his account of the conflict in Milan (probably in early AD 471), where Ricimer was living, perhaps in the old imperial palace:

Now, when the emperor was in Rome, that envy which divides rulers sowed the seed of conflict between them, and equality of power became a cause of discord. So much anger and distrust arose, that both prepared for war. And not only were there reasons for their enmity, but the quarrel was encouraged by the counsel of their supporters. The well-being of an endangered Italy was rocked and was gravely afflicted by these troubles, while expecting yet more troubles in the future. Meanwhile, the nobles of Liguria gathered at Milan, where, during this stormy period, the patrician Ricimer was residing, and, with bended knees or prostrate on the ground, begged for peace between the rulers (*principes*), and so that both sides should abandon discord begged to be offered the chance of grace from one of the parties. Ricimer was softened, and, touched by the tears of so many, assured them that he wished to restore concord. 'But', he said, 'who can take on the very great weight of this embassy? Who can endure the care of such a grave business? Who can call back to sense an excitable Galatian and emperor? For, when begged a favour, he, who does not control his temper with natural moderation, always loses control.'[152]

[152] Ennodius, *Vita Epiph.* 51–4: 'Nam imperatore Romae posito seminarium inter eos iecit scandali illa quae dominantes sequestrat inuidia et par dignitas causa discordiae. Surrexerat enim tanta rabies atque dissensio, ut

There are several interesting things in this account. Significantly, to Ennodius both Anthemius and Ricimer are *princeps*, a term at this date for the emperor. It is impossible to say in what sense Ennodius is applying the word to Ricimer, but it certainly implies both rulership and equality of status with Anthemius.[153]

Ennodius does not conventionally blame the envy of the barbarian for the conflict, but 'that envy' (or perhaps 'hostility' would be a better translation) natural between rulers of equal power. Again similar status for Ricimer and Anthemius is implied. Ennodius also states that the quarrel was exacerbated by supporters of each side. This seems a very plausible explanation, although there were, no doubt, also more concrete and immediate causes, including the execution of Romanus. According to Ennodius, the leading Ligurians initiated the attempt at reconciliation. It seems unlikely that the patrician would have heeded such pleas were he not already predisposed to reconciliation, and it is possible that the initiative was his. Ricimer sent envoys to Epiphanius, who accepted the mission and travelled to Rome. At no point does Ennodius suggest that Ricimer's Arian beliefs affected his veneration for, and readiness to make use of, a Catholic bishop, nor Epiphanius' willingness to act on his behalf.[154]

mutuo bella praepararent, et praeterquam origo irarum proprios suggerabat stimulos, lis ipsa circumstantium consilio nutribatur. Nutabat status periclitantis Italiae et adfligebatur ipsis discriminibus grauius, dum expectabat futura discrimina. Interea apud Ricemerem patricium Mediolani ea tempestate residentem fit collectio Ligurum nobilitatis, qui flexis genibus soloque prostrati pacem orabant principum et ut ab scandalo utraeque partes desinerent, occasiones gratiae ab una precabantur offerri. Quid plura contexam? Mulcetur Ricemer et uelle se reparare concordiam permotus multorum fletibus pollicetur. "Sed qui" ait "potissimum huius legationis pondus excipiet? Quem tantae molis cura maneat? Quis est qui Galatam concitatum reuocare possit et principem? Nam semper, cum rogatur, exuperat qui iram naturali moderatione non terminat".'

[153] There is something similar in the *Life of St. Anianus*, which describes Agrippinus being sent 'by the emperors [*principibus*] to visit the cities of Gaul' (*Vita Aniani*, 3; where *principibus* would seem to have to refer to the emperor and Ricimer.

[154] There are parallels in the *Life of St. Severinus*: see e.g. Eugippius, *Vita Severini* VI and VIII.

Ennodius then moves to Rome, where Anthemius, speaking to those who announce the bishop's arrival, is portrayed as saying: 'I sincerely doubt, however, that Ricimer shall obtain what he wants from me, for I know him to be rash in making promises, and not to hold to the boundaries of reason in proposing conditions'.[155] When he formally meets the emperor, Epiphanius makes a lengthy address, in the course of which he says:

the patrician Ricimer has requested my humble oratory, believing, without doubt, that a Roman will confer, as a gift to God, the peace which is requested by a barbarian ... I know of no kind of warfare which requires greater courage than to struggle against rage and to load with benefit the shame of the savage Goth. It will plunge him into disgrace if his requests are granted now, who until now was ashamed to ask ... Consider, moreover, how double-edged are the fortunes of war: in that, if the evils of war prevail, your realm will lose what either side loses. For, whatever is safe with Ricimer as a friend is also shared with you by the patrician. Also consider, that he well orders his cause who first offers peace.[156]

Thus, Ennodius has Epiphanius use three rhetorical arguments: the contrast of Ricimer's barbarian status with that of the emperor; the incentive of the enhancement of Anthemius' reputation if he agrees to peace; and the warning of the damage to be done to Italy, and to the positions of both men, by civil war. It is a clever speech, designed to make it easy for Anthemius to come to terms, while preserving his pride.

[155] Ennodius, *Vita Epiph.* 61: 'Dubito tamen an Ricemer apud me quod poscit optineat, cuius scio uotorum intemperantem esse personam et in condicionibus proponendis rationis terminum non tenere.'

[156] Ennodius, *Vita Epiph.* 64–5: 'Ricemer patricius paruitatem meam oratum direxit, indubitanter coniciens, quod pacem Romanus deo munus tribuat, quam precator et barbarus ... nescio quae species fortior possit esse bellorum quam dimicare contra iracundiam et ferocissimi Getae pudorum onerare beneficiis. Grauius enim percellitur, si postulata inpetret quem puduit hactenus supplicare. Tractandus deinde anceps bellandi euentus: in quo tamen si ita preaualuerint peccata certamine, uestro regno defrudabitur quod partes utraeque perdiderint. Nam quaecumque apud Ricemerem, si amicus est, salua sunt, cum ipso a uobis patricio possidentur. Cogitate pariter, quia bene causae suae ordinem dirigit qui pacem primus obtulerit.' Note that Ennodius has Epiphanius speak of Anthemius' *regnum* (the area over which he rules?) whereas

Anthemius replies:

Holy bishop, we have reasons for resentment against Ricimer. We have
given him the greatest favours, but all for nothing. We have even (not
without dishonour, it must be said, to our throne and to our own
blood-line) allowed him to join our family through marriage, which
we conceded for the love of our country though it would inflict shame
on us.[157] For, who among past emperors has ever done this before:
that, among other gifts that needed to be made to a skin-clad Goth, an
emperor included his daughter to gain peace for his people. We did not
think to spare our own blood for the sake of a foreigner. None, however, should believe that the reason we did this was because of our own
fear: for in such an act of foresight for the safety of all, we did not think
only to fear for ourselves . . .

   But, so that we might make clear to your reverence his continuous
acts; as Ricimer has been showered with the greatest gifts from us, the
greater his hostility has appeared. He has prepared war against the
state. What raging fury among foreign peoples has been stirred up by
him. Finally, indeed, where he was not able to do harm himself he
nevertheless kindled trouble.[158] Shall we now grant this man peace?
Shall we sustain under the cloak of friendship an internal enemy, when
neither the bonds of friendship nor of marriage have been able to hold
him to his agreements? It is a great precaution to have known the mind
of an enemy, for then he at once feels himself to have been beaten . . . If
the astuteness of his cunning has beguiled even you, let him take up the
struggle already wounded.[159]

Anthemius speaks earlier of the *rei publica* (the imperial state); this may not be
coincidental.

   [157] If this was Anthemius' attitude to his 'sacrifice' of his daughter, it would
hardly be surprising that Ricimer was alienated (but see comments on p. 252).
   [158] Perhaps a reference to Romanus?
   [159] Ennodius, *Vita Epiph.* 67–70: 'sancte antistes, aduersus Ricemerem
causa doloris sit et nihil profuerit maximis eum a nobis donatum fuisse beneficiis, quem etiam (quod non sine pudore et regni et sanguinis nostri dicendum
est) in familiae stemma copulauimus, dum indulsimus amori reipublicae quod
uideretur ad nostrorum odium pertinere: quis hoc namque ueterum retro
principum fecit umquam. Ut inter munera, quae pellito Getae dari necesse
erat, pro quiete communi filia poneretur? Nesciuimus parcere sanguini
nostro, dum seruamus alienum. Nemo tamen hoc credat propriae causa factum
esse formidinis: nam in tanta circumspectione salutis omnium solum pro
nobis timere non nouimus . . . Sed ut tuae ueneratione ad liquidum conatus
illius aperiamus: quotiens a nobis maioribus donis cumulatus est Ricemer,
totiens grauior inimicus apparuit. Contra rempublicam bella praeparauit?
Quantas externarum gentium per illum uires furor accepit? Postremo etiam,

According to Ennodius, Anthemius did, in the end, grudg-ingly respond to Epiphanius' plea for reconciliation (ostensibly because of his eloquence). The bishop left Rome on the twenti-eth day after Easter and returned to Ticinum, but for some unstated reason did not go to the patrician in Milan, as must surely have been expected. Ennodius reports, possibly disin-genuously, that the Milanese summoned him to the city, but that he declined the invitation as he did not wish to seem to be seeking expressions of gratitude. This and the fact that hostil-ities continued later lead us to the conclusion that Epiphanius' mission was, in reality, a failure. Perhaps he got some promises of concessions from Rome, but not all that Ricimer demanded. There may have been a temporary truce while Epiphanius' mission took place. Ennodius skips over the rest of the civil war, jumping to the point in 472 at which, he says, Ricimer and Anthemius being dead, Olybrius took the throne.[160]

As this passage appears within the larger context of a laud-atory hagiographic account of Epiphanius' life, there will be some distortion. One can expect and allow for a natural em-phasis on the bishop's holiness and eloquence (for which he was famous) and on the effectiveness of his interventions. The ques-tion is, to what extent, if any, Ennodius is reproducing Rici-mer's and Anthemius' real positions and attitudes (albeit at second or third hand) or putting his own fabricated words into their mouths purely for reasons connected with his eulogy of Epiphanius.

Ennodius was born at about the time of this civil war and wrote the *Vita* about thirty years later, but he knew Epiphanius personally, and probably others who accompanied him to Rome. He may also have had access to written records covering the period. Epiphanius was obviously not present at Milan when the embassy was proposed; but members of the Milanese clergy could have been involved, and Ennodius grew up in

ubi nocere non potuit, nocendi tamen fomenta suggessit. Huic nos pacem dabimus? Hunc intestinum sub indumento amicitiarum inimicum sustinebi-mus, quem ad foedus concordiae nec adfinitatis uincula tenuerunt? Grandis cautio est aduersarii animum cognouisse: etenim hostem protinus sensisse superasse est . . . si solitae calliditatis astutia etiam te fefellerit, certamen iam uulneratus adsumat.'

[160] Ennodius, *Vita Epiph.* 79.

Milan and entered the Church there. As Bishop of Pavia later in his career, he may well have had access to Epiphanius' correspondence, even conceivably a letter requesting him to act as go-between.

Some information on the meeting between Anthemius and Epiphanius in Rome could have come from Epiphanius himself or from other eyewitnesses. It is, of course, most unlikely that the actual wording of the conversations would be remembered, but the general tenor of what was said may have been, and the same applies to the scene with Ricimer in Milan. It seems likely that Ennodius composed the speeches of Epiphanius, Ricimer, and Anthemius using his own words and perceptions of the three men, but on the basis of real memories. The general course of events reported almost certainly took place. Moreover, while it is clearly inappropriate to use specific phrases as direct evidence of the sentiments of Anthemius and Ricimer,[161] and although this is very much Ennodius' version of events, his North Italian background and closeness to Epiphanius make his account valuable. At the very least, it shows how an upper-class Roman in northern Italy, only a generation later, regarded Ricimer and the struggle between him and the emperor (although his views may, of course, have been affected by intervening events and the reigns of Odovacer and Theoderic).

This material is the closest we ever get to Ricimer. It is impossible to say to what extent the portrayal of Ricimer is accurate or the merely conventional topos that as a barbarian he must be warlike, cunning, and untrustworthy. On the oft-quoted reference to Ricimer as a 'skin-clad Goth', Hodgkin once commented that Ricimer's toga was surely as faultless as that of Anthemius.[162] No doubt this was true. Then again, Ricimer probably spent much of his time in military attire, which was, by this date, closer to barbarian than traditional Roman dress, so maybe there is some underlying truth in this rhetorical device.

Significantly, Ricimer is not portrayed in Ennodius' account as a barbarian enemy or a rebellious general, but as the junior of

---

[161] As many modern historians do; e.g. Bury (1923: 339); Jones (1964: i, 243); Oost (1970: 234); O'Flynn (1983: 190 n. 63).

[162] Hodgkin (1880a: 482 n. 1). Oost (1970: 234) calls this a 'canard'.

two rulers who have fallen out. As previously mentioned, the two men are called *principes*, and Ennodius actually specifies equality of power in his reasons for the conflict. It is probable that the division of power was by this date, to an extent, geographical, with Ricimer ruling most of northern Italy from Milan[163] and Anthemius the peninsula from Rome (for further discussion see concluding chapter).

John of Antioch described the conflict thus:

Ricimer became hostile towards Anthemius . . . and, even though he was married to his daughter Alypia, fought a civil war within the city for nine months.[164] The authorities and the populace of Rome fought on Anthemius' side, while Ricimer was supported by a force of his own barbarians. Also on Ricimer's side was Odovacer . . . Anthemius resided in the palace, while Ricimer blocked the area by the Tiber and afflicted those inside with hunger[165]

Another account of this stage of the civil war is given by Paul the Deacon (after a summary of Ennodius' account of Epiphanius' mission). Paul's attitude to Ricimer is more hostile than Ennodius':[166]

---

[163] Paul Diac. *Hist. Rom.* XV, 3: 'Ricimerem patricium qui tunc Mediolani positus praeerat Liguriae'. In this period the more resilient western cities were beginning to become centres of strengthening regional loyalties, and this may have happened quickly in the case of Milan because of its previous status, and as Rome and Ravenna were declining in importance.

[164] John of Antioch's durations—of a nine-month civil war within the city and later of Rome being gripped by a civil war of five months—most probably relate to different stages in a conflict that took place, on and off, from roughly AD 470 to 472.

[165] John Ant. frag. 209 (1) (Blockley's translation, Priscus, frag. 64 (1) (continued below)). There is some overlap between the beginning of this fragment and the previous fragment. As remarked in Ch. 13 n. 7, John of Antioch seems to have utilized two sources in his account of the conflict, Priscus and another unknown source, which were not completely synthesized. Theophanes (AM 5964) records that Ricimer revolted against Anthemius, who was ruling righteously in Rome; and there are brief references in *Chronica Gallica a 511*, 650, Jordanes, *Getica* 236, and *Fasti Vind. Prior. s.a.* 472. Theophanes (AM 5964) also reports famine during the war.

[166] Paul Diac. *Hist. Rom.* XV, 3: 'magnus discordiarum fomes exortus est . . . deinde barbarica perfidia foedus Ricimer inrumpens'. Paul may have taken this hostile view from Byzantine tradition (see *Hist. Rom.*, ed. Crivellucci (1914: 207–8)).

Then with barbarian treachery Ricimer broke the treaty because he was of the Gothic race, and soon afterwards marched on the city with mighty force, and pitched camp by the *pons Anicionis*.[167] Consequently Rome was divided, some supported Anthemius but others followed the treachery of Ricimer. During these events Olybrius, sent to the city by the Emperor Leo, although Anthemius was still living, took possession of the royal power.

Bilimer, Rector of Gaul, learning of Ricimer's conspiracy against Anthemius, hastened to Rome, wishing to give Anthemius assistance. He joined battle with Ricimer at the *pons Adriani*, where he was defeated and killed. On the death of Bilimer, the victorious Ricimer then entered the city, and killed with the sword Anthemius, in the fourth year that he held imperial office. Not only was Rome devastated by the hunger and disease which afflicted it in this time, but it was also gravely ravaged, except the two regions in which Ricimer was with his own men. All the rest of the city was devastated by the greed of the looters.[168]

It is feasible, particularly because locations are given, that Paul's source for this unique information was Roman, and it

[167] The identification of this bridge is problematic. No other mention of a bridge by this name exists (confirmed personally by Professor Steinby). Hodgkin (1880b: 484 n. 2) quotes Tillemont as considering that this should read *pons Anionis*, which Tillemont identified with the *ponte Molle* (in his day a name for the old *ponte Milvio* (Macadam (1979: 257))). But why Tillemont amended 'Anicionis' to 'Anionis' and why he equated Anionis with the Milvian bridge I have not been able to discover, as Hodgkin gives no reference. A *pons Anionis* could be across the river Anio to the north of Rome, but this is probably too far out from the city. The *ponte Milvio* does fit, in that it carried the *via Flaminia* across the Tiber, which was the main road from the north (Richardson (1992: 415–16)). Another possibility is that the bridge derived its name at that time from somebody called Anicius, who had perhaps repaired it (several members of the Anicii clan were urban prefects).

[168] Paul Diac. *Hist. Rom.* xv, 4: 'Deinde barbarica perfidia foedus Ricimer inrumpens, erat enim Gothus prosapia, cum manu mox valida Urbem contendit atque apud Anicionis pontem castra composuit. Divisa itaque Roma est et quidam favebant Anthemio, quidam vero Ricimeris perfidiam sequebantur. Inter haec Olibrius a Leone Augusto missus ad Urbem venit vivoque adhuc Anthemio regiam adeptus est potestatem. Bilimer Galliarum rector cognita adversus Anthemium conspiratione Ricimeris, Anthemio ferre praesidium cupiens, Romam properavit. Is cum Ricimere apud Adriani pontem proelium committens continuo ab eo superatus atque occisus est extincto Bilimere mox victor Ricimer Urbem invadens quarto iam anno agentem iura imperii Anthemium gladio trucidavit. Praeter famis denique morbique penuriam quibus eo tempore Roma affligebatur, insuper etiam gravissime depraedata est et excepto

may be broadly accurate. Bilimer is otherwise unknown;[169] he may have been Anthemius' appointee as *magister militum per Gallias*. John of Antioch may be reporting this same battle in part of his account of the progress of the conflict: 'a pitched battle was fought and many of Anthemius' party were slain'.[170] The battle is described by Paul as taking place at the bridge of Hadrian, which must have been on the site of the modern *Ponte Sant' Angelo*,[171] by Hadrian's mausoleum, now the *Castel San Angelo*. This had, by that date, been converted into a fortress.[172] It is possible that Ricimer either occupied or besieged it (he is described by John of Antioch as having occupied those areas of Rome across the Tiber).

On the evidence of Paul (above) and Malalas (below) Ricimer initially blockaded the city rather than besieged it, preventing food from getting in. After defeating Bilimer, he felt able to enter the city (probably with little opposition) and sacked it (or possibly lost control of his barbarians). This third sacking of Rome is also referred to by Cassiodorus, who notes that at the time of the elevation of Olybrius (see pp. 256–7) the city suffered great destruction.[173] The effects of this civil war in Italy, including the blockade and the third sack of Rome, are often ignored or underestimated in modern histories, yet it must have been a major factor both in the political changes that followed and in the increasing poverty and disruption of Italy.[174]

We now reach the last few months of Ricimer's life. At this stage three new characters appear: Odovacer, Gundobad, and Olybrius. The first two will be discussed in the next chapter; the third, Olybrius, a Roman aristocrat and briefly emperor (the last

---

duabus regionibus, in quibus Ricimer cum suis manebat, coetera omnia praedatorum sunt aviditate vastata.'

[169] His name may be Ostrogothic, on analogy with Valamer, Vidimer, etc.

[170] John Ant. frag. 209 (1) (Blockley's translation) following on from the section on p. 253.

[171] Known as *pons Hadrianus* or *pons Aelius* (Richardson (1992: 296)).

[172] I am grateful to Professor Margareta Steinby for confirming this.

[173] Cassiodorus, *Chronica* 1293 *s.a.* 472: 'cum gravi clade civitatis'.

[174] In a polemic against the celebration of the Lupercalia, Pope Gelasius lists the civil war between Ricimer and Anthemius alongside the Gauls' sack of Rome and that of Alaric (Gelasius, *Adversus Andromachum* col. 115).

connected to the Theodosian dynasty), is a difficult character to evaluate.[175] Following the crushing defeat of Anthemius' supporters, the patrician elevated Olybrius as emperor while still outside Rome. This was, says Cassiodorus, in defiance of all decent feeling,[176] as his father-in-law Anthemius was still alive and trapped in the city. A few eastern sources say that it was Leo's decision to send Olybrius to Italy, whether or not intending him to become emperor,[177] although Olybrius himself may have decided to take the initiative. John of Antioch's account continues: 'Ricimer subdued the rest by treachery and proclaimed Olybrius emperor. Rome was gripped by a civil war of altogether five months'.[178]

John Malalas has a fuller and intriguing account; unfortunately these very characteristics make it somewhat suspect:[179]

He [Leo] sent to Rome the Roman patrician Olybrius ... He was told to reconcile the emperor Anthemius and his son-in-law Ricimer, as they were both Roman senators. Leo's orders were, 'After Anthemius and Ricimer have become friends, leave Rome and go to Gaiseric the Vandal ... since you have free access to him because he has your wife Placidia's sister as his son's bride, and persuade him to become my ally'.

---

[175] His career has been effectively studied by Clover (1978: 169–96) and it would be gratuitous to do so again; so he is discussed here only in terms of his connection with Ricimer. (Bizarrely, Olybrius is the eponymous subject of an Italian opera.)

[176] John Ant. frag. 209 (1); *Fasti Vind. Prior. s.a.* 472; Cassiodorus, *Chronica* 1293 s.a. 472; *Pasch. Camp. s.a.* 472; etc.

[177] The *Chronicon Paschale* (*s.a.* 464 [*sic*]) says that he was sent to Rome by Leo and was then compelled by the western senate to become emperor. Theophanes (AM 5964) recorded that 'Leo, because there was again disorder in Rome, hastily sent Olybrius the husband of Placidia to Rome to become emperor, which he had previously declined' (Blockley's translation). Had Olybrius declined or Leo? According to Malalas (see below) Leo wanted to be rid of Olybrius because he was a threat to his own throne. It is unlikely that Leo intended him to replace Anthemius. Most probably, Leo was so involved with eastern affairs at the time that the situation in the west was of little concern to him. Olybrius' wife and daughter probably remained in Constantinople (John Malalas, 374).

[178] John Ant. frag. 209 (1) (Blockley's translation, Priscus, frag. 64 (1)).

[179] John Malalas' account is sometimes confused; for instance (375): 'Then Ricimer chose another emperor ... Majorian, but they killed him as well, since he supported Gaiseric ... To replace him Ricimer chose yet another emperor ... named Nepos.'

But the emperor Leo suspected that Olybrius supported Gaiseric and was on his side, and so Leo was on his guard against him in case, if Gaiseric were to declare war on Leo, Olybrius should betray Constantinople to Gaiseric (being a relative) and Olybrius should become emperor in Constantinople. After Olybrius had travelled to Rome... Leo wrote through a *magistrianus* to Anthemius as follows 'I put to death Aspar and Ardabour, so that nobody should oppose my orders. You too should execute your son-in-law Ricimer to prevent him giving you orders. See, I have also sent to you the patrician Olybrius. Execute him too and reign as one who gives orders rather than as one who takes them'. Now Ricimer had stationed a guard of Goths at every gate of Rome, and at the harbour, and whoever was entering Rome was asked what he was carrying. When the *magistrianus* Modestus ... arrived and was searched, the imperial rescripts from Leo to Anthemius were removed and taken to Ricimer. He showed them to Olybrius. Then Ricimer sent to Gundoubarios, his sister's son and summoned him from Gaul where he was *magister militum*. He arrived and killed the emperor Anthemius while he was in the holy church of the apostle Peter. Then Goundoubarios immediately returned to Gaul. Ricimer crowned Olybrius emperor with the consent of the Roman senate.[180]

This is truly Byzantine. Perhaps the easiest solution is to treat the story as fantasy. However, there are some elements of the concoction that do approximate to what we know of happenings in Italy.[181] It is quite possible that Olybrius was sent to Italy by Leo, and a letter to Anthemius may well have existed. The implausible part is the secret instruction advising Anthemius to put Olybrius to death (possibly inspired by the story of Bellerophon?).

Olybrius was a member of one of the most important and influential Roman senatorial clans;[182] one that may have been part of a faction supporting Aetius,[183] and possibly Ricimer as his effective successor.[184] As Olybrius was married to

---

[180] John Malalas, 373–5 (Jeffreys' translation).

[181] Plus some factual-sounding detail; or is this merely a case of embellishing with circumstantial detail an otherwise bald and unconvincing narrative?

[182] Clover (1978: 173). The Olybrii were a branch of the Anicii.

[183] Clover (1978: 182–92) tentatively suggests that the Anicii had been supporters of Aetius; they certainly became increasingly influential in the reign of Valentinian III.

[184] Perhaps including those senators who appear in prestigious posts in the reign of Libius Severus.

Valentinian's daughter Placidia[185] he will have been a potential
imperial candidate for some years. But how and why did he
come to the throne at this particular time? We are handicapped
by knowing virtually nothing of the man himself; both in ancient and modern historical writings the emphasis has always
been placed overwhelmingly on his familial, and supposed political, connection with Gaiseric.

Olybrius had spent a long time in Constantinople,[186] from
around the time of the Vandal sack of Rome in AD 455.[187]
Placidia and her mother were released by Gaiseric in *c.* AD 461
and joined Olybrius in Constantinople.[188] Gaiseric had married Placidia's sister Eudocia to his son Huneric and, subsequently, Gaiseric took, or pretended to take, the view that this
gave him a legitimate connection with the dynasty of Valentinian, and even property rights.[189] The ancient sources are
divided on Gaiseric's policies here. According to Procopius,
Gaiseric repeatedly demanded publicly that Olybrius be given
the western throne; while according to John of Antioch, although he wished this he did not advertise it, but used property
claims as pretexts for interference.[190] It has been suggested, by
both ancient and modern writers, that the fact that Gaiseric was
the father-in-law of Olybrius' wife's sister created a close personal and political link between the two men (the cause of Leo's
distrust, according to Malalas).

I suspect that Gaiseric made more of the connection than
Olybrius was inclined to do, and that the latter's 'friendship'
with Gaiseric, if it existed at all, was superficial. It may have
suited Olybrius to appear as a possible avenue of negotiation and
reconciliation with Gaiseric, but Olybrius surely had no desire

---

[185] The exact dates and circumstances of their betrothal and marriage are
debatable, and Clover (1978) discussed this at length. It is enough here to say
that Olybrius was married to Placidia at some time in the AD 450s.

[186] Where he was consul in AD 464 (Bagnall *et al.* (1987) 463).

[187] Evagrius, *HE* ii, 7; John Malalas, 361; Nicephorus Callistus, *Historia
Ecclesiastica* XV, 11.

[188] Priscus, frag. 38 (1); John Malalas, 366; Theophanes, AM 5949; etc.

[189] Priscus, frag. 39 (1); John Ant. frag. 204.

[190] Procopius, *Wars* III, vi, 6; John Ant. frag. 204. The other version from
Priscus (frag. 38 (1) in *Exc. de Leg. Gent.*) does not clarify this disparity. John
of Antioch seems marginally more convincing, if only because the alternative
would probably have put Olybrius at risk.

for Gaiseric, or Huneric, to become the power behind the throne in Italy. However, whether Olybrius was really a friend and ally of Gaiseric and hoped for his backing as emperor (for which, no doubt, Gaiseric would have expected a return), or whether this just appeared a possibility at the time because of his family connection, his elevation by Ricimer clearly demands explanation.

Attempts have been made to rationalize this in terms of complex high-level political intrigue. None is particularly convincing. Some scholars have envisaged Ricimer making a deliberate decision to promote Olybrius, and thereby gain an alliance with Gaiseric, at the time when he initially rebelled against Anthemius.[191] It is hard to see how any such alliance between the two could ever have worked. Ricimer and Gaiseric seem to have been old enemies, and the idea of shared barbarian/Arian interests can be discarded (see pp. 263–4). Ricimer would certainly not have been willing to relinquish his position in Italy to Olybrius' brother-in-law Huneric, Gaiseric's son. It is, however, just possible that as he had not been able either to defeat or negotiate with Gaiseric, Olybrius was attractive as a means of coming to terms with the Vandal king. Another resolution is to disregard all deep motivation in favour of short-term opportunism and self-interest. Leo may have seen personal benefit in removing Olybrius by sending him to Italy; Olybrius may have recognized a good moment to try for the dubious glory of imperial power; and Ricimer may have then elevated Olybrius, not because of a major reversal of policy towards Gaiseric, but because he was at hand, and would attract Italian support away from Anthemius.

The whole Ricimer–Gaiseric–Olybrius–Anthemius relationship might subsequently have proved very interesting, but, in the event, Anthemius, Ricimer, and Olybrius all shortly met their deaths. Anthemius' end was, for one who had been a brave and successful general, particularly demeaning:

Anthemius, his supporters having surrendered to the barbarians and left their emperor defenceless, mingled with the beggars and joined the

---

[191] O'Flynn (1983: 120); Collins (1991: 87); implied by Stein (1959: 394).

supplicants at the church of the martyr Chrysogonas.[192] There his
head was cut off by Gundobad, Ricimer's brother [*sic*, see pp. 178–9].
He had reigned for five years, three months and eighteen days.[193]

Ricimer gave him a royal burial (perhaps because of Alypia),
and installed Olybrius in the royal palace.[194] Olybrius died a
few months later, in autumn AD 472, of dropsy.[195]

Ricimer only survived Anthemius by a few weeks: 'When
Olybrius had received the sovereignty . . . Ricimer died within
thirty days after vomiting up a great deal of blood.'[196] According to Cassiodorus, Ricimer 'not for long continued glory-
ing in [his] wicked deed and died after forty days. Olybrius also
[after] seven months as emperor lost his life'.[197] The date was
18 or 19 August.[198] There is no suggestion among ancient

---

[192] This third-century church still exists in the Trastevere area of Rome
(Krautheimer (1937: i, 144–5)). Malalas substitutes the more famous church
of St. Peter in his account. Trastevere is west of the Tiber, just south of the
Vatican and Ricimer's camp at the Bridge of Hadrian. Interestingly, all the
locations given by the sources for the siege are on the west side of Rome.

[193] John Ant. frag. 209 (1) (Blockley's translation, Priscus, frag. 64 (1)).
The Gallic Chronicle of 511 (650) also records the killing of Anthemius by
Gundobad, so this is not an eastern fabrication.

[194] John Ant. frag. 209 (2).

[195] John Ant. frag. 209 (2), giving his reign as about six and a half months;
Pasch. Camp. s.a. 472 (giving the date of 2 Nov.); *Fasti Vind. Prior. s.a.* 472
(giving the date of 23 Oct.). A number of other sources, eastern and western,
briefly note his death. He was interred in the family mausoleum (Wes (1967:
158–9)). Ricimer was already dead, otherwise modern writers would no
doubt suspect him of another murder. Procopius (*Wars* III, vii, 1 (Dewing's
translation)), who was unaware of the correct dates, indeed did so: 'now
Anthemius . . . died at the hand of his son-in-law Ricimer and Olybrius succeeding to the throne, a short time afterward suffered the same fate'.

[196] John Ant. frag. 209 (2) (Blockley's translation, Priscus, frag. 65).

[197] Cassiodorus, *Chronica* 1293 *s.a.* 472: 'non diutius peracto scelere glor-
iatus post XL dies defunctus est. Olybrius autem VII imperii mens vitam
peregit'.

[198] *Fasti Vind. Prior. s.a.* 472: 'et defunctus est Ricimer xv kl. Septemb.';
Pasch. Camp. s.a. 472: 'moritur Recimer xiiii kal. Septembr'. Cassiodorus
(*Chronica* 1293 *s.a.* 472) gives the date as forty days after Anthemius' murder,
i.e. 19 Aug. John Malalas (375) reports simply 'Then Ricimer died'; similarly
Ennodius (*Vita Epiph.* 79). The confusion is understandable given the close-
ness of the three deaths.

writers that Ricimer's death was suspicious.[199] Suddenly, as
had happened so often in the past,[200] the major players had
been swept from the board.

[199] Theophanes (AM 5964) says he, like Olybrius, died of disease. The two
deaths so close together could have seemed suspicious, and (were this fiction)
Alypia (whose fate is unknown) might be a suspect. However, conditions in
Rome following a long summer siege were perhaps responsible.

[200] E.g. with the deaths of Aetius, Valentinian III, and Attila.

15
Assessments of Ricimer

As Stilicho and Aetius had dominated the western empire in the first half of the fifth century AD, so Ricimer was to dominate its last two decades. Historians of the period have often held strong views about him and his role in events, and—not surprisingly, given the nature of much historical study—on the basis of the same (and extremely scanty) evidence, the widest possible range of views has been put forward by them. Most evaluations of Ricimer are negative and, typically, characterize him as treacherous, and as maker and destroyer of emperors.[1] This is especially so among those scholars who have seen the fall of the Roman Empire as unmitigated catastrophe. To some writers Ricimer was totally evil. For example, to Oost writing in the 1970s 'the German patrician was a cold calculating sinister man who hesitated at no crime, no murder, no treason, or perfidy to maintain himself securely in power'.[2] Other versions see Ricimer as an arch-plotter and masterly deceiver. An extreme version of this appeared in articles by Vassili in the 1930s, which proposed an organized ring of 'Ricimerian conspirators'.[3] There has been what Scott described as 'an annoying readiness on the part of modern scholars to credit any treachery of unspecified authorship to Ricimer'.[4] Conversely, Majorian has had an almost consistently good press, and is generally portrayed as a heroic figure.[5]

[1] See e.g. Gibbon, ed. Bury (1897–1900: iv, 14, 16, 24–5, etc.); Seeck (1920: 258); Ensslin (1930: 589); Stevens (1933: 39, 99, 107); Dill (1926: 12, 17); Kent (1966: 146); O'Flynn (1983: 104 ff.).

[2] Oost (1970: 228).

[3] Vassili (1936a: 175–80); (1936b: 56–66); (1936d: 296–9); (1938b: 399–451).

[4] Scott (1984: 29 n. 18).

[5] See Procopius (p. 214); Gibbon, ed. Bury (1897–1900: iv, 15, 24); (1897–1900) Hodgkin (1880b: 434); Barker (1911: 423); Dill (1926: 18); Solari (1938: 400–20); Stein (1959: 341); Max (1979: 281).

Other scholars have qualified their harsh judgements of Ricimer with provisos. For instance, Hodgkin wrote in the nineteenth century that: 'There is only one thing to be said in mitigation of our abhorrence for this man . . . he does seem to have been faithful to Rome . . . Rome seems to have . . . accepted him, with all his odious qualities as the necessary man for the situation'.[6] While Bury, although supporting the critical view, thought it 'repugnant to the ideas and traditions of his training to have cast off all allegiance to the empire . . . his own attachment to the system under which he was the successor of the great masters of the soldiers'.[7]

In contrast, a number of Italian scholars have held unconventional views on Ricimer. For example, Solari, in the 1930s, while accepting Ricimer as the leader of a barbarian faction, also saw him as the great social progressive of the age, working towards a new society (a view, one imagines, that would come as something of a surprise to the real Ricimer). A comprehensive vindication of Ricimer was put forward by Papini in 1959, defending his strategies and sense of duty, and, indeed, totally justifying all his actions.[8]

In the nineteenth and early twentieth centuries Ricimer was usually considered to be primarily barbarian in allegiance and culture. There was, said Barker in 1911, 'nothing Roman in his make-up and little that was Roman in his policy . . . a jealous barbarian, erecting puppet after puppet . . . his power rested nakedly on the sword and the barbarian mercenaries of his race'.[9] Even a 1990s book by Barnwell speaks of Ricimer as 'not wanting an emperor who would oppose his kin group interests'.[10] And Demandt in 1989 described Ricimer as the prototype of the later Germanic emperor makers and mayors of the palaces.[11] Taking the idea of barbarian allegiance to an

[6] Hodgkin (1880*b*: 404).

[7] Bury (1923: 341).

[8] Papini (1959) and see Ch. 13 n. 108. Demandt (1989: 175 n. 30) uses the German term *Ehrenrettung* for this, and how much better 'honour rescue' is than the more usual English 'whitewash'.

[9] Barker (1911: 422). Dill (1926: 19) called him 'a true barbarian to the core'.

[10] Barnwell (1992: 43).

[11] Demandt (1989: 174).

extreme, Ricimer became a member of a sinister international barbarian/Arian commonality of interest, also involving Aspar and Gaiseric.[12]

As previously discussed in connection with the Visigoths in Gaul, examples of Ricimer's supposed pro-barbarian policy are tenuous and better seen as political realism than ethnic solidarity. This conspiracy theory reflects early twentieth-century thinking more than the reality of Ricimer's day. Rather than conspiring with the Goths or Vandals, Ricimer generally seems to have acted within the military and financial constraints that he inherited, making decisions for the sake both of the defence of Italy and of his own position. He appears to have been inherently realistic and pragmatic rather than ideologically or ethnically motivated.

A rather different slant, but connected to the idea of a fundamental gulf existing between Roman and barbarian, is the idea advanced by several early twentieth-century scholars, of a straightforward two-way split among the West Romans, into pro- and anti-barbarian parties.[13] However, the Roman élite was chronically addicted to factionalism, even in the absence of any barbarian question, and the western Roman political scene was complex and shifting, rather than a straightforward dichotomy. The second half of the twentieth century saw a great change in the way that the barbarians of the late empire were perceived and studied. Jones, in 1964, described all the barbarian *magistri* as serving the emperor to the best of their ability and being 'thoroughly assimilated'.[14] The emphasis moved towards the integration and Romanization of barbarian leaders, setting their actions and motives firmly within Roman ideology and politics; and hence in the history books Ricimer has become a much more Romanized figure.[15] In

[12] Barker (1911: 426); Solari (1938: 439–41); Vernadsky (1941: 64), cited by Scott (1984: 26 n. 14). See also pp. 266–7 on Aspar.

[13] See e.g. Solari (1938–43: 399–451); Barker (1911: 394–5, 424); Vassili (1938b: 399–450).

[14] Jones (1964: i, 182).

[15] It is often pointed out that the barbarian leaders did not *want* to destroy the empire, and this is clearly the case. But this does not mean that their actions did not contribute towards this result. The natural desire to close the door through which you have entered to others that follow is not always achievable.

Ricimer's case, however, the reaction against the older thinking and the consequent recent stress on his 'Roman-ness' may have gone too far. Compared to Stilicho, who was thoroughly Romanized and integrated into the Roman élite of Theodosius' regime (and whose half-barbarian birth we learn of almost by accident), Ricimer seems to have been somewhat less culturally assimilated. The ancient sources stress his high-status barbarian ancestry, and this seems to have been important not only in his relations with other barbarian rulers and the army in Italy, but also within Italian society.[16] By the 460s it was an asset rather than a problem. Many barbarian kings now ruled within the old empire, and this, as well as Roman decline, must have altered ingrained Roman attitudes, even if this fact was generally unspoken and unacknowledged. There are hints (for instance in Sidonius' panegyric) that his noble birth may have been of great personal importance to Ricimer.

Returning to the question of Ricimer's motivations: in contrast to the earlier views, more recent writers have taken a more pragmatic line. O'Flynn, writing in 1983 about the late Roman 'generalissimos', ascribed mixed motives to Ricimer, those of self-interest and of attachment to the ideal of empire (as with other warlords),[17] with his policies essentially carrying on the work of his predecessors, especially those of Aetius. Rather paradoxically, however, O'Flynn also asserted that Ricimer's real aim was to rule the West directly, without an emperor, as the patrician of the emperor in Constantinople.

Scott's 1984 article on Ricimer focused on the background of anti-barbarian sentiment and prejudice within the empire, which affected the barbarian *magistri*.[18] The sources show considerable prejudice among the upper classes and intellectuals, but over time an increasing ambiguity of attitude, as the reality of barbarian presence and importance within the empire grew. Indeed, prejudice did not prevent Ricimer from reaching a position akin to that of Aetius.

---

[16] For an example of how a barbarian was more acceptable if a royal barbarian see Sidonius on Theoderic (*Ep.* 1, ii). There were similar imperial British attitudes to Indian rajas.

[17] O'Flynn (1983: 123–8).

[18] Scott (1984: 23–7).

It is interesting to compare Ricimer's career with that of his contemporary, the eastern *magister militum* Aspar, an Arian of Alan descent,[19] who was for many years a dominant figure in eastern military and political affairs. Aspar, who followed his father into the post of *magister militum*, which he held from the 430s to his death in AD 471, was *patricius* and once consul.[20] No contact is recorded between Aspar and Ricimer, but it probably existed in some form. There are some parallels with Ricimer. In both cases their positions were based on control of the army. Both were influential in the succession of emperors; in Aspar's case, Marcian and Leo, who had both served under him. Marcian was not placed on the throne by Aspar alone,[21] but Leo is described as being Aspar's choice by Priscus[22] and Procopius.[23] However, though he undoubtedly had great influence, both Marcian and Leo were active and able rulers, and neither was remotely a puppet of Aspar's. A sixth-century source stated that Aspar himself was once offered the purple by the senate, but refused, not wishing to establish a precedent.[24] If correct, this would show that some at least of the eastern élite would have considered a barbarian emperor, but that, like Stilicho and Ricimer, Aspar was, for practical or psychological reasons, not ready to do so.

Because of his birth and Arianism, Aspar, like Ricimer, has been accused of disloyalty by both Byzantine and modern

[19] He was related by marriage to leading Gothic families (Theophanes, AM 5964; 5970; Dessau, *ILS* 1299).

[20] *PLRE* ii, 164–9, Fl. Ardabur Aspar. He had grown up as part of the eastern élite (if somewhat apart because of his birth and Arianism). Underlying anti-barbarian prejudice was always present in the eastern empire (Bayless (1976: 71–4)), but the Alans may have suffered from this less than the Goths.

[21] John Malalas (367) says he was the choice of the senate; the *Chronicon Paschale* (*s.a.* 450) suggests that he was nominated by Theodosius on his deathbed. Other sources stress Pulcheria's role (Theophanes, AM 5942; Evagrius, *HE* ii, 1).

[22] Priscus, frag. 19.

[23] Procopius, *Wars* III, v, 7.

[24] *Acta Synhod. Habit. Rom.* v, 23–6: 'aliquando Aspari a senatu dicebatur, ut ipse fieret imperator: qui tale refertur dedisse responsum "timeo ne per me consuetudo in regno nascatur" '. This is thought to have occurred on the death of Marcian (Stein (1959: i, 353–4)).

scholars who stress his religious persuasion.[25] Yet his recorded
actions, especially in fifth-century sources, show little evidence
of the disloyalty, and even less of the Arian conspiracy with the
Vandals (and Goths), suggested by a number of historians.[26]
His reluctance to undertake a major attack on the Vandals seems
justified by military prudence. Aspar's son Patricius[27] married
Leo's daughter Leontia, and was declared *caesar*. It is at this
time (AD 470/1), when the question of succession had become
an issue (Leo's only son died in infancy), that the relationship of
Aspar (and his son Ardabur) with Leo broke down. They were
both assassinated by Leo in AD 471. The consequent epithet for
Leo of 'the butcher,'[28] hints that this may have caused shock
and disapproval in Constantinople, where Aspar had built a
water cistern, and taken an active and courageous role in
fighting the great fire.[29] The differences that exist between the
careers of Aspar and Ricimer can, in many cases, be attributed
to the inherent differences between the political situations in
eastern and western empires at this date. In the East the emperor finally destroyed Aspar, while in the West Ricimer destroyed the emperor.

In the West, Ricimer was very much the political and military
successor to the great Aetius, with the significant difference that
Ricimer did not have as his nominal master a member of the
prestigious Theodosian dynasty. Like Aetius, Ricimer's policies
were in the most part defensive, reactive, and cautious. The

[25] Procopius, *Wars* III, vi, 3–4; Theophanes, AM 5961; George Cedrenus,
pp. 607, 613; Theod. Lect. *Epitome* 399; Zonaras, *Epitome* XII–XVIII. See
also Stein (1959: i, 353–61 and *passim*); Demandt (1970: 748–53); Ensslin
(1925: 1955–8); Bachrach (1973: 45–7); Courtois (1955: 202 n. 2), who refers
to a 'parti alain'.

[26] See e.g. Theophanes, AM 5961; Nicephorus Callistus, *Historia Ecclesiastica* XV; XXVII; Procopius, *Wars* I, vi, 3–4. See also Gautier (1932: 239–40);
Ensslin (1925: 1955), who calls him 'offenkundiger Vandalenfreund';
Bachrach (1973: 46–8); Seeck (1920: vi, 358); Stein (1959: i, 387). See Scott
(1976: 59–69) for a convincing argument to the contrary.

[27] On the basis of his name, and this elevation, Patricius may have been half-
Roman. Aspar married three times (Candidas, frag. 1). Two of his wives were
Gothic, but the third may have been Roman.

[28] See e.g. Malchus, frags. 1 and 3; *Suda*, A 783; George Cedrenus, p. 607.

[29] *Chronicon Paschale s.a.* 459 (on the cistern); 465 (on the fire); 467 (on
unrest amongst Goths and others in the city); Candidus, frag. 1; Theophanes,
AM 5954; Marcellinus *comes*, *s.a.* 465; etc.

major difference between their strategies was that Aetius concentrated his efforts on trying to hold Gaul, while Ricimer concentrated on defending Italy, particularly against the Vandals, and made little attempt to reverse the losses in Gaul. It is usually, and probably correctly, presumed that Ricimer participated in Italian civil government; he must have taken charge during the later interregnums. Although he clearly intervened at the highest levels, we have (probably because of the dearth of sources) no record of any involvement in internal administrative or legal matters (with the exception of Agrippinus' trial). Nor is there any record of him becoming involved in Church affairs, unlike Aetius and Aspar. Most of his recorded actions concern military and foreign affairs and the imperial throne. Ricimer was a military man, perhaps essentially so, which had implications in an age of increasing rift between the civilian and military classes. But, as well as being a successful general, Ricimer was able to participate in the complex and dangerous power games of upper-class Roman life, and in international diplomacy and politics.

Like other men who gain similar positions of power, Ricimer was no doubt hard, self-seeking, and ruthless. Although involvement in the deaths of Aegidius, Marcellinus, and Libius Severus is unlikely, he was certainly a prime mover in the deposition and death of Avitus, and the instigator of the deposition and death of his colleague Majorian and his father-in-law Anthemius. However, the common characterization of Ricimer as a particularly treacherous man seems somewhat misplaced.[30] While the assassinations of Majorian and Anthemius were ruthless, in neither case is there evidence of the envy, deceit, and long-term Machiavellian plotting that have been attributed to him by some historians. His behaviour was, in fact, no worse than that of most previous masters of the Roman Empire. A final thought on Ricimer: unlike many of his contemporaries and predecessors, and against all reasonable expectation, he managed to die, at a good age, of natural causes.

---

[30] Some of the accusations of treachery in the sources seem to be no more than the conventional characterization of a barbarian: John Ant. frag. 209 (1); Hydatius, 205 (210) *s.a.* 461; Paul Diac. *Hist. Rom.* XV, 3; Theophanes, AM 5964; Evagrius, *HE* ii, 7; Nicephorus Callistus, *Historia Ecclesiastica*, p. 604.

16
Gundobad, Orestes, and Odovacer

The man who immediately inherited Ricimer's position was his nephew Gundobad. Gundobad was summoned to Italy by Ricimer during the civil war. As discussed above, he was responsible for Anthemius' death after the fall of Rome to Ricimer.[1] Ricimer may have called him to Italy because he needed extra manpower for his attack on Rome, or he may have wanted Gundobad himself for some other reason. When recalled to Italy Gundobad held the title of *magister militum*;[2] this is usually assumed to be *per Gallias*. He was possibly Ricimer's replacement in Gaul for the ill-fated Bilimer, but the time-scale seems very short for this, so he may have been appointed at an earlier date as part of the campaign against Euric (see p. 242–3). The possibility also exists that he was in fact a subordinate *magister militum* in Italy.[3] Gundobad seems to have been in Liguria for a fairly long period at some time before the final stage of the civil war (see pp. 270–1), so if Malalas is correct that he was summoned from Gaul, his presence there may have been temporary, and his arrival in Italy may best be seen as a recall.

---

[1] *Chronica Gallica a 511*, 650: 'Anthemius imperator acto intra urbem civili bello a Ricimere genero suo vel Gundebado extinctus est.': Malalas, 374–5 (text on p. 257 above); John Ant. frag. 209 (1) (text on p. 260). He was not the first Burgundian to be connected to the death of an emperor. Sidonius writes of Petronius Maximus: 'the Burgundian with his traitorous leadership extorted from the [city of Rome] the panic-fury that led to an emperor's death' (*Pan.* VII, 440–3, Anderson's translation). Who this was is not known; he may have been a high-ranking army officer; conceivably there was a family connection with Gundobad.

[2] John Malalas (374–5) says that Ricimer summoned him from Gaul, where he was the *magister militum*. Although Malalas is the only source for this and is not very reliable, it is not unlikely that Gundobad would hold this rank. It is supported by the fact that he used this title later when King of the Burgundians (*Vita Lupicini*, X).

[3] Stein (1959: i, 394).

On Ricimer's death Gundobad effectively succeeded to his position. At some point, perhaps even on his death-bed, Ricimer may have formally designated Gundobad as his legal and political heir,[4] although Gundobad must have been quite a young man (he lived until AD 516). A slightly different view is that on Ricimer's death the barbarian army chose Gundobad as its leader, and that this transference of loyalty carried with it the role of dominant patrician and general.[5] It is possible that the power vacuum and struggle that followed Ricimer's death gave a large amount of initiative to the army overall, and also that Ricimer had died without nominating a successor. The evidence is not adequate to decide the question, but a combination of the two factors seems most likely.

Gundobad was literate and spoke good Latin, and, as Burgundian king, was described by Ennodius as shrewd and eloquent.[6] Like Ricimer he was an Arian,[7] though this was not the case for all the Burgundian royal family, and may not have been for all the Burgundians.[8] He had spent time in Italy, at Liguria, almost certainly as an ally or subordinate of Ricimer, and so was perhaps involved in Italian politics before his uncle's death. The evidence for his presence in Italy comes in Ennodius' account of Epiphanius' mission to Gundobad (then joint king of the Burgundians) during the time that Theoderic ruled Italy. Gundobad had attacked Liguria and carried off captives, whom

----

[4] The outbreak of war with his father-in-law may have caused a breakdown in his marriage, such that he could no longer expect to have children and heirs by Alypia, inducing him to turn to his sister's son.

[5] Hodgkin (1880a: 489).

[6] Ennodius, *Vita Epiph.* 151, for him as *astutiae*, and 164–5: 'ut erat fando locuples et ex eloquantiae dives opibus et facundus ad sertor'. Epiphanius speaks to him without a translator (in contrast to King Euric, whom Ennodius describes as mumbling in an unknown tongue (*Vita Epiph.* 89)).

[7] Greg. Tur. *Historiae* II, 32.

[8] Wood (1994b: 45) considered that Gundobad's beliefs were different from those of his people, and possibly the product of his connection with Ricimer. They may also be associated with his time in Italy. Although there is evidence for the Burgundians' Arian adherence, Orosius implied that they became Catholic early in the fifth century (7, 41). There is no reason why there cannot have been a mixture of Arians and Catholics among the fifth-century Burgundians (or indeed among other peoples). Some Burgundians may have converted when settled by Aetius *c.* AD 436.

Epiphanius had been sent to ransom. The substance of Epiphanius' appeal is almost certainly correct, as Ennodius was himself a participant in this embassy.

The whole tone of the address as well as numerous explicit phrases suggest that Gundobad was well known in Liguria and active in defending its people; and it is implied that Gundobad had previously been acquainted with Epiphanius.[9] Gundobad is asked to listen to the prayers of the Italians who have 'confidence in him'. Epiphanius refers to Italy as 'never divided from Gundobad and trusting in his mercy'. He portrays the Italian captives asking Gundobad whether he remembers the many times that he defended them from their enemies, and whether those whom he once protected against outsiders should now be attacked by their protector. The appeal continues in the same vein:

we know and acknowledge that you are surely our Burgundians. How many times have these hands which you now presume to bind paid tribute to our common master [Gundobad]...Our former master loves the province, as it is cherished by its new master [Theoderic]... free our Liguria, that you know so well[10]

Gundobad was almost certainly present at the imperial court on his uncle's death, and shortly afterwards he was made, or confirmed as, *patricius* by Olybrius;[11] a signal that he was assuming Ricimer's position in Italy. It is possible that had Olybrius lived Gaiseric might have made moves to intervene in

---

[9] Ennodius, *Vita Epiph.* 140, 151.

[10] Ennodius, *Vita Epiph.* 157–62: 'Audi Italiorum supplicum uoces et de te praesumentium preces serenus admitte. Audi Italiam numquam a te diuisam et multum de animi tui clementia confidentem quae si una uoce uteretur, haec diceret: quotiens pro me, si reminisceris, ferratum pectis hostibus obtulisti? Quotiens pugnasti consilio, ne bella subriperent, ne aliquis meorum duceretur in quacumque orbis parte captiuus? Quos nunc detines, tu nutristi: dolose mihi uirtus tua beneficium praestitit, si quos ab extraneis tutatus est custos inuasit...Quis se subduceret, cum armorum tuorum crepitus audiretur, in quo in necessessitatibus tutissimum habuere perfugium...scimus et euidenter agnoscimus nonne uos estis Burgundiones nostri?...Quotiens istae quas ligare praesumitis manus domino communi tributa soluerunt?...Antiquus dominus prouinciam diligit, quam et modernus amplectitur. Uacua sentibus illam quam bene nosti Liguriam'.

[11] *Fasti Vind. Prior. s.a.* 472: 'eo anno Gundobadus patricius factus est ab Olybrio imperatore'.

Italy on the basis of his relationship with the emperor, possibly promoting Huneric as a replacement for Gundobad. However, Olybrius' death, within only a couple of months, changed the situation again and threw the responsibility of establishing a new emperor on Gundobad.

Almost nothing is known of Glycerius, who was proclaimed emperor at Ravenna in March AD 473,[12] following an interregnum of four months. John of Antioch and Cassiodorus both state explicitly that Glycerius was made emperor by Gundobad. Like Majorian he held the post of *comes domesticorum*, presumably he was an upper-class Italian with some military experience, and he had been an adherent of Ricimer.[13] His accession had not been agreed with Leo, who would probably have been unwilling, on principle, to co-operate with the murderer of Anthemius. Ennodius seems quite favourable to Glycerius, but this may be because once Glycerius had pardoned a man, who had done an injury to his mother, at the request of Epiphanius.[14]

According to Ennodius Glycerius took measures to secure the safety of his people; this almost certainly refers to the entry, during his reign, of Vidimer and his Goths into Italy, described by Jordanes. Glycerius gave them gifts and they were persuaded to divert to Gaul, where they joined with the Visigoths.[15]

---

[12] John Ant. frag. 209 (2): 'Ricimer was succeeded in his position by his nephew, Gundobaules. He made Glycerius, who held the rank of count of the domestics, emperor'; Cassiodorus, *Chronica* 1295 *s.a.* 473: 'H. C. Gundibado hortante Glycerius Ravennae sumpsit imperium'; *Fasti Vind. Prior. s.a.* 473: 'levatus est imp. Glycerius Ravenna [*sic*] III non. Martias'; *Pasch. Camp. s.a.* 473: 'Licerius [*sic*] imperator levatus est v non. Mart'; Evagrius, *HE* ii, 16 (referring briefly to Glycerius' appointment); Marcellinus *comes*, *s.a.* 473: 'Glycerius apud Ravenna plus praesumptione quam electione Caesar factus est'. Marcellinus' assessment of the illegality of the elevation is copied by Jordanes (*Getica* 239): 'Glycerius apud Ravennam plus presumptione quam electione Caesar effectus', and (*Romana* 338): 'Glycerium, qui sibi tyrannico more regnum imposuisset'.

[13] Theophanes (AM 5965) calls him a 'not disreputable person', by which he probably means 'well born'.

[14] Ennodius, *Vita Epiph.* 79. Glycerius' mother was at that time in the Pavia region; if she was there as part of Glycerius' court, the emperor may have been keeping prudently close to the army, or to the Burgundians, as Hodgkin (1880*a*: 493) suggested.

[15] Jordanes, *Getica* 284, *Romana* 347.

Leo sent Julius Nepos to depose Glycerius, which he did with ease:

> when Leo, the emperor of the East, learned of the elevation of Glycerius, he sent a force against him, appointing Nepos general. When he took Rome, he overcame Glycerius without a fight, ejected him from the palace, and made him bishop of Salona. He had enjoyed sovereignty for eight months.[16]

Gundobad, having elevated Glycerius, presumably to act as his figurehead, did nothing to support him. There is no record of any military opposition to Nepos, and the fact that Glycerius' life was spared indicates that he did not resist deposition. It may be that both Glycerius and Gundobad bowed to the eastern emperor's moral right to choose a western colleague.[17] Perhaps Gundobad's power base in Italy was inadequate, or he may have thought Italy not worth the trouble.

It is possible that the patrician was out of Italy in Gaul when Nepos landed,[18] either involved in military action[19] or because of the death of his father. The death of Gundioc occurred around this date, and Gundobad, if he wanted to rule in Burgundy, would have needed to be on the spot, especially as he had three brothers. Gundobad's decision to abandon Glycerius may have been a calculated choice of barbarian kingship in preference to being the power behind the imperial throne in the Roman Empire, perhaps indicative of changed political realities. But we have no way of knowing whether Gundobad actu-

---

[16] John of Antioch, frag. 209. Also described by *Anon. Val.* (7): see Pt. I, p. 60. Nepos may have been proclaimed in Constantinople in August AD 473. This would explain why Glycerius' reign is reduced to five months in some chronicles. His arrival in Italy may have been delayed by Leo's illness, or just the necessary preparations.

[17] From the evidence of the letters of Avitus, Bishop of Vienne, during the reigns of Gundobad and his son Sigismund both seem to have been keen for good relations with Constantinople (Avitus, *Epp.* 46, 78, etc.). Gundobad issued coins in the name of the eastern emperors (Hendy (1988: 46)). See also Demougeot (1969–79: 667–9).

[18] John Malalas (375) says that after killing Anthemius 'Gundoubarios immediately returned to Gaul'.

[19] At this time Sidonius mentions the Burgundians fighting the Visigoths in Auvergne, supposedly to protect the Gauls (*Ep.* III, vii, 1). This action could have been led by Gundobad as a continuation of his previous assignment to defend the last imperial lands in Gaul.

ally made a definite decision to this effect or was simply over-
taken by events, especially if he was not in Italy at the time.

In two letters dating to the autumn of AD 474 Sidonius makes
mention of certain Gallo-Romans in Burgundy[20] being suspected by Chilperic[21] of transferring the adherence of the
town of Vaison to the *partibus novi principis.*[22] This 'new prince'
was taken by Anderson to refer to the new emperor (Nepos),[23]
but it seems more likely that this is a reference to the return of
Gundobad, which would have been of much more immediate
concern to Chilperic (and Vaison) than Nepos in Rome. Perhaps
Vaison was on the border between their respective territories.

Gundobad made no moves to re-establish his power in Italy
during Nepos' brief reign, nor during that of Odovacer (although he did, as previously mentioned, attack Italy in the
reign of Theoderic); instead he concentrated on consolidating
his position in Burgundy, becoming by *c.* AD 500 sole ruler
(achieved by murdering his brothers and their families). It
seems very likely that Gundobad held on to the title of *patricius*
when king; it was used by his son and successor Sigismund in
the sixth century.[24] Gundobad and Sigismund also seem to
have valued the title of *magister militum.*[25] This was probably
not so much idealistic attachment to the old empire as personal
attachment to prestigious titles.

[20] Sidonius, *Epp.* v, vi and v, vii. Among those suspected was Apollinaris,
the uncle of Sidonius and brother of Thaumastus, to whom the second letter
was addressed.

[21] This could be Gundobad's uncle Chilperic or his brother Chilperic, but
as Sidonius calls Chilperic *tetrarch* (*Ep.* v, vii, 1), which surely refers to the
division of the kingdom between the four sons of Gundioc, the latter seems
more likely. Sidonius refers to Chilperic as *magister militum* (*Ep.* v, vii, 1–2).
This appointment was perhaps made by Gundobad.

[22] Sidonius, *Epp.* v, vi, 2; v, vii, 1.

[23] Sidonius, ed. and trans. Anderson (1936: 185 n. 5).

[24] Avitus, *Ep.* 9. The title of 'patrician' may also have been assumed by
Clovis (Greg. Tur. *Historiae* 11, 38, title only). In Italy it was held by Orestes,
Odovacer (probably), and Theoderic (bestowed in the East: *Anon. Val.* 11, 49;
and others). The title of *patricius praesentalis* was also used in Ostrogothic Italy
in the early sixth century AD (*PLRE* ii, 6779, Liberius, and 1132, Tuluin).
Thereafter the title of 'patrician' went out of use in the West.

[25] Avitus, *Epp.* 9, 78, 93, 94 (and possibly 46?). Avitus wrote on behalf of
Sigismund to the eastern emperor asking that the title(s) of his father be passed
officially to him, and, although it is not totally clear, this was probably, or

Gundobad was to prove the greatest of the Burgundian kings; a strong and ruthless ruler, and also a progressive one who introduced coinage and written laws.[26] It seems likely that his later policies were influenced by his time in Italy with Ricimer. Gundobad was unique among the series of dominant military patricians in Italy in that his dominance was not terminated by his death there, but rather he moved on to a different sphere of power. If this was his own choice it proved, for him personally, a wise one; he reigned in Burgundy for over forty years and died peacefully in old age.

The reign of Julius Nepos lasted just over a year, from June AD 474 to August 475. What little we know indicates that he was concerned about the remaining Roman possessions in southern Gaul, which were falling to the Visigoths. He sent an embassy to their king, Euric, headed by Bishop Epiphanius, which succeeded in negotiating a peace treaty.[27] Nepos' first choice as *magister militum* to take military action against Euric was the Gallic aristocrat Ecdicius,[28] who was also granted the title of patrician.[29] According to Jordanes:

Euric had occupied the city of Arverna, which at that time was commanded by the *dux* of the Romans, Ecdicius . . . Ecdicius fought for a long time with the Visigoths, [but was] not strong enough to stand against them. So he forsook his homeland, and especially the city of Arverna, to the enemy, and regrouped in a place of safety. The Emperor Nepos hearing of this therefore ordered Ecdicius to leave Gaul

included, that of *magister militum*. The title of *magister militum* had also been held by Gundobad's father Gundioc (Hilarius, *Ep.* 9) and by Gundobad's brother Chilperic (*Vita Lupicinus* 10; Sidonius, *Ep.* v, vi and vii). It has been suggested that the post of *magister militum per Gallias* became virtually hereditary in the Burgundian royal family (Stein (1959: i, 386, 394)). In Italy the role of the senior *magister militum*, that is, of commander-in-chief of the army, was held by the king, thus reverting to normal imperial practice until the fifth century.

[26] The Burgundian legal code very probably dates to his reign. For Gundobad as king see Perrin (1968: 435) and Frye (1990: 205) who described him as being 'of a different mind-set' to previous tribal rulers.

[27] Ennodius, *Vita Epiph.* 85–94.

[28] He was from the Arverne, the son of the Emperor Avitus, and Sidonius' brother-in-law (see *PLRE* ii, 383–4, Ecdicius 3).

[29] The title was conferred in late AD 474 and had been promised to him by Anthemius (Sidonius, *Ep.* v, xvi, 1–2).

and come to him; in his place he appointed Orestes as *magister mili-tum.*[30] This Orestes took over the army, and, setting out towards the enemies from Rome, reached Ravenna and, delaying there, he made his son Augustulus emperor.[31]

It is one of those historical facts so odd that it is completely memorable, that Orestes had previously been the secretary of Attila the Hun.[32] The usual translation of *notarius* as 'secretary' is more in the sense of a senior civil servant than a PA. He would have been an important man at Attila's court.[33] Orestes was of a Roman family from the part of Pannonia close to the River Save, which had 'become subject to the barbarian by the treaty made by Aetius'.[34] This may have been when Orestes entered Hun service (his father Tatulus was also at the Hun court), or he may have provided by Aetius, like others on Attila's staff. The Roman authorities (especially Aetius) needed Romans in Hun service to maintain diplomatic links, and probably also for intelligence. However, because of this previous career Orestes may have been regarded in Italy later with some degree of distrust and distaste.

Anonymus Valesianus cannot be correct in saying that: 'His father Orestes was in fact a Pannonian, who at that time when Attila came to Italy, joined with him, and was made his *notarius*; whence he advanced [and] rose all the way up to the rank of

---

[30]   From this it would seem that Orestes was appointed *magister militum per Gallias*, but, given Jordanes' unreliability, he could have held the rank of *magister militum praesentalis.*

[31]   Jordanes, *Getica* 240–1: 'Arevernam occupans civitatem, ubi tunc Romanorum dux praeerat Ecdicius... Ecdicius, diu certans cum Vesegothis nec valens antestare, relicta patria maximeque urbem Arevernate hosti adtutiora se loca collegit. Quod audiens Nepus imperator praecepit Ecdicium relictis Gallis ad se venire loco eius Orestem mag. mil. ordinatum. Qui Orestes suscepto exercitu et contra hostes egrediens a Roma Ravenna pervenit ibique remoratus Augustulum filium suum imperatorem effecit.'

[32]   Priscus (in frags. 11 (2) and 15 (2)) makes a number of references to an Orestes in Attila's service in A D 449 and 452, his envoy to Constantinople twice in A D 449. The connection with the later patrician and *magister militum* in Italy is made by *Anon. Val.* (8): see discussion pp. 277–8.

[33]   Without, however, going as far as Musset suggests (1993: 176), who considered that 'Attila may have been inspired by a Roman, his secretary Orestes'!

[34]   Priscus, frag. 11 (1) (Blockley's translation).

patrician.'[35] The only time that Attila 'came' to Italy was when he invaded in AD 452, and we have Priscus' eyewitness testimony that Orestes was already working for the Huns before this date.[36] Orestes did have contacts within the western empire at this time, for when Priscus visited the Huns he was married to the daughter of Romulus, a *comes* under Aetius, who was sent as an envoy to Attila.[37] If she was the mother of Orestes' son Romulus, as seems likely from the name, she may have come from Campania.[38]

There is, then, a gap of over twenty years before Orestes appears again in the records, during which time we can only guess at his activities. In fact, the above passage from Anonymus Valesianus is the only evidence that Orestes the *notarius* to Attila, met by Priscus, is the same Orestes who twenty years later made his son emperor in Italy. The possibility exists that the two are not the same man. It is conceivable that Anonymous Valesianus knew Priscus' work, and, coming across the name Orestes in another context, assumed that the two were the same, and added the part about Orestes joining Attila in Italy (which, as seen above, is incorrect) to connect the two.

If we accept the usual view that the Italian Orestes was the same as Priscus' Orestes, he may have quitted Hun service on, or shortly after, the invasion of Italy. Alternatively, he could have made his way back into the empire after AD 453 in the confusion following Attila's death (see pp. 202–3 for evidence of returning captives). When he appears in the sources in AD 475, it is as *magister militum* and patrician under Nepos.[39] Orestes must have been an exceptional man if indeed he first success-

---

[35] *Anon. Val.* 8, 38: 'Enim pater eius Orestes Pannonius, qui eo tempore quando Attila ad Italiam venit se illi iunxit et eius notarius factus fuerat. Unde profecit et usque ad patriciatus dignitatem pervenerat.'

[36] Maenchen-Helfen's theory (1973: 106–7), on the basis of the *Anonymous Valesianus*, that Attila hence visited Italy prior to AD 449 has nothing to support it.

[37] Priscus, frag. 11 (2).

[38] *Anon. Val.* 8, 38 (on Romulus' deposition): 'eum intra Campaniam cum parentibus suis libere vivere'.

[39] Jordanes, *Getica* 240–1 (trans. on pp. 275–6); *Fasti Vind. Prior. s.a.* 475 and 476; *Auct. Prosp. Haun. ordo prior. s.a.* 475 and 476; *Auct. Prosp. Haun. ordo post. s.a.* 475 and 476; *Auct. Prosp. Haun. ordo post. marg. s.a.* 476; *Anon. Val.* 7, 36; 8, 37–8; Ennodius, *Vita Epiph.* 95; Eugippius, *Ep.* 8.

fully held down a (to put it mildly) demanding job as Attila's
notarius, extricated himself, then re-established a career in the
empire, two decades later becoming the most powerful man in
Italy. Also, his duties for Attila would have been civil, diplomatic, and administrative, rather than military, yet he later
became a senior general (which perhaps puts doubt on the
connection). Orestes could have gone directly to Italy. Alternatively, he could have first found his way to the eastern empire, or
Dalmatia, and taken service under Nepos. As the sources say
that he commanded an army for Nepos in Italy, it seems marginally more likely that he accompanied Nepos there, rather
than having risen under Ricimer or Gundobad.

The rebellion of Orestes is so poorly recorded that it is only
possible to guess at the circumstances. According to Jordanes,
the abortive campaign in Gaul under Ecdicius' command (see
pp. 275–6) immediately preceded Orestes' promotion in his
place to *magister militum*, and his subsequent deposition of
Nepos. This may or may not be so; Orestes may already have
been a *magister militum*. Possibly when Nepos realized that he
must give up Auvergne he had to replace Ecdicius, who might
not have accepted this. Orestes, however, led the army against
the emperor, rather than against Euric. One of the additions to
Prosper describes Nepos as over complacent:

> Then, while successes adorned him, and good fortune favoured him,
> the spur of vanity prevented him from prudently anticipating the
> causes of his own deposition. The following year . . . the patrician
> Orestes with the power of the army was sent against Nepos at Rome,
> who in despair at the state of affairs did not dare put up resistance,
> [but] fled by ship to Dalmatia on 28 August.[40]

Although Nepos set sail from Ravenna, it is possible that he
was in Rome when the coup began, and was chased across Italy

---

[40] *Auct. Prosp. Haun. ordo post. marg. s.a.* 475: 'postquam dum sibi victoriae
decore prosperoque eventu pollere nequaquam causam caute usurpationis
dicare sentiret praeveniente vanitatis stimulo. Sequentique anno . . . Orestes
patricius cum robore exercitus contra Nepotem Roma mittitur. Qui cum
desperatae rei negotium resistendo sumere non auderet, ad Dalmatias navigans
fugit V k. Septemb'. (Here *mittitur* appears to be in the passive tense, but there
does not seem to have been anybody who 'sent' Orestes, so perhaps this is just a
grammatical error.) *Auct. Prop. Haun. prior. s.a.* 475 and *post. s.a.* 475 give
similar accounts.

by Orestes.[41] Like Glycerius, Nepos put up no resistance. He was not Italian and had had little time to build up support in Italy. He probably thought his best course was to obtain eastern aid. Unluckily for him, in the same year Zeno, the eastern emperor, was forced to flee Constantinople, and was in no position to intervene.

Orestes made his son emperor, rather than taking the purple himself. An addition to Prosper records: 'After Nepos' flight, Orestes, although supreme, did not dare add to the vows of his damnable temerity [or, perhaps, 'fearing to increase his chances of damnation'?], but made his son Augustulus emperor in the city of Ravenna on 31 October'.[42]

Romulus was apparently young (probably in his early teens) and of attractive appearance.[43] He, of all the late fifth-century emperors, is most clearly a mere figurehead. There is a hint as to the public's attitude to Romulus' elevation in his nickname Augustulus or 'little Augustus', which has affectionate-cum-contemptuous overtones.[44] His father clearly intended to exer-

---

[41] One source says that Orestes attacked Nepos in Rome (*Auct. Prosp. Haun. ordo post. marg. s.a.* 475); another (*ordo prior. s.a.* 475) that Nepos was residing in the 'city' when Orestes came against him; another (*Anon. Val.* 7 (36)) describes Nepos coming to Ravenna after becoming emperor at Rome, followed by Orestes. Jordanes (*Getica* 424) has Orestes setting out from Rome against the enemy, but going instead to Ravenna, where he invested his son, causing Nepos to flee.

[42] *Auct. Prosp. Haun. ordo post. marg. s.a.* 475 (2): 'Post cuius fugam Orestes elatus quamquam sibi vota damnandae temeritatis augere non auderet, Augustulum filium suum penes Ravennam urbem imperatorem fecit pridie k. Novembris'; Jordanes, *Getica* 241, *Romana* 344; *Auct. Prosp. Haun. ordo prior. s.a.* 475: 'Levatur Augustulus in imperio pridie k. Novemb.' ('Augustulus was raised to imperial power on 31 October.'); *ordo post.* 'Augustulum filium suum Ravennae imperatorem facit II k. Novemb.' ('Augustulus, his son, was made emperor at Ravenna on the 31 October.'); *Fasti Vind. Prior. s.a.* 475: 'eo anno Augustulus imp. levatus est Raven [*sic*] a patricio Oreste patre suo prid. kl. Novembres.' ('In that year Augustulus was made emperor at Ravenna by his father, the patrician Orestes on 31 October.'); *Pasch. Camp. s.a.* 475; Marcellinus *comes, s.a.* 475, 2; *Anon. Val.* 7, 36; 8, 37; Cassiodorus, *Chronica* 1301 *s.a.* 475; Theophanes, AM 5965.

[43] *Anon. Val.* 8, 38.

[44] *Anon. Val.* 8, 37: 'Augustulus, qui ante regnum Romulus a parentibus vocabatur' ('Augustulus, who, before he took the throne, was called Romulus by his parents'); Procopius, *Wars* V, i, 2: 'Augustus, whom the Romans used to call by the diminutive name Augustulus because he took over the empire while still a lad'.

cise the real power; as one of the additions to Prosper describes, 'Orestes, asserting primacy and all authority, made his son Augustulus emperor at Ravenna; however, he himself shouldered the burden of external government'.[45]

Orestes was not debarred by birth or religion from becoming emperor, and there was no reason, either constitutional or practical, why he could not have taken the imperial title and continued to command the army. There must either have been some reason why he did not want to become emperor himself, or something that made his young son acceptable while he was not. Whether it was his first choice or not, Orestes had gained with comparative ease what Aetius and Stilicho had lost their lives trying to achieve: the post of patrician and *magister utriusque militum* and a child wearing the purple.[46]

Surprisingly, perhaps, Procopius speaks well of Orestes as 'a man of the greatest discretion'.[47] According to Paul the Deacon, a treaty was concluded with Gaiseric, on Orestes' initiative.[48] This, if true, may have been a popular success. Evidence that Orestes had support among certain sections of the nobility or the Church occurs in one of Eugippius' letters: 'A certain Pirmenius, a presbyter of the Church in Italy, and a man of noble birth and great authority, fled at the time when the patrician Orestes was unjustly killed, because he feared Orestes' murderers, since he was said to be like a father to the murdered man'.[49] As a Roman with Italian connections, Orestes may have hoped

---

[45] *Auct. Prosp. Haun. ordo prior. s.a.* 476: 'Orestes primatum omnemque sibi vindicans dignitatem Augustulum filium suum apud Ravennam positus imperatorem facit, ipse vero omnem curam externorum praesidiorum gerit.' The last phrase could also be translated as 'external defences' or 'foreign policy', but Orestes would not have limited himself to this area (as the previous sentence shows), so I have left this more open. (Possibly 'external' is in the sense of 'external to the imperial palace', which was left to the young emperor?)

[46] O'Flynn (1983: 134).

[47] Procopius, *Wars* v, i, 2 (Dewing's translation).

[48] Paul. Diac. *Hist. Rom.* xv, 7: 'Annali deinceps circulo evoluto cum rege Wandalorum Genserico foedus initum est ab Oreste patricio.' As with his information on Bilimer, his source is unknown.

[49] Eugippius, *Ep. ad Paschasium Diaconum*: 'Pirmenius quidam presbyter Italiae nobilis et totius auctoritatis vir qui confugerat tempore quo patricius Orestes inique peremptus est, interfectores ejus metuens eo quod interfecti velut pater fuisse diceretur'.

for civilian support amongst those who neither wanted an eastern appointee nor a barbarian military man as ruler.[50]

Some writers have made much of the fact that Orestes, although of Roman birth, had the confidence of Rome's barbarian army;[51] it has even been bizarrely suggested that Orestes' post with Attila, a couple of decades before, somehow made him acceptable as paramount military leader.[52] It is clear, however, from what happened next, that Orestes was *not* in control of the vast majority of the barbarian army in Italy. It is possible that his coup had not been supported by the army in general, but only by certain, possibly palatine, units from Rome or Ravenna see nn. 41 and 42. His period in power was so brief (lasting a maximum of twelve months, quite possibly much less) that it may be best to think of it as a failed coup.

The end of the western Roman empire in AD 476 was, in essence, the mutiny of its army against the last warlord, rather than the last emperor (there were, after all, three emperors still alive). The uprising of the barbarian soldiers against Orestes was precipitated, according to Procopius, by Orestes' refusal to cede land in Italy to them.[53] Procopius paints a grim picture of barbarian domination over the Italians at this time (to what extent this is exaggerated is controversial):

the Romans a short time before had induced the Sciri and Alani and certain other Gothic nations to form an alliance with them ... as the barbarian element among them became strong, just so did the prestige of the Roman soldiers forthwith decline...they were more and more tyrannised over by the intruders and oppressed by them; so that the barbarians ruthlessly forced many other measures upon the Romans ...and finally demanded that they should divide with them the entire land of Italy. And indeed, they commanded Orestes to give them the third part of this, and when he would by no means agree to do so, they killed him immediately. Now there was a certain man among the Romans named Odoacer [*sic*],[54] one of the bodyguards of the

---

[50] O'Flynn (1983: 134).

[51] See e.g. Bury (1923: 404).

[52] O'Flynn (1983: 134).

[53] Though Stein (1959: 398) had a theory that the mutiny was caused by Orestes' inability to pay them, and this may well have also been a factor.

[54] Neither here nor elsewhere, when discussing Odovacer (for instance V, i, 26–8), does Procopius remark that he was a barbarian.

emperor, and he at that time agreed to carry out their commands, on condition that they should set him upon the throne[55]

Settlement of groups of barbarians within the imperial frontiers was hardly novel. Why did Orestes, a man in an insecure position, refuse this, and antagonize the army? It is unlikely that he was motivated by Roman tradition and pride.[56] In refusing settlement, Orestes might have been concerned about antagonizing the native Italians, particularly the influential landowners, whose support for his son he needed. However, when settlement took place under Odovacer shortly afterwards, there is little evidence of widespread, or even aristocratic, opposition, either physical or verbal. It is likely that, quite separately from the settlement question, Odovacer was already a rival to Orestes, and Orestes' refusal of the request may have been for immediate political, rather than ideological, reasons.

Procopius certainly need not be taken literally when he says that a third of *all Italy* was demanded. Moreover, it is possible that the word originally meaning 'third' used by Procopius (and other writers) need not be interpreted in its older precise and technical sense (from the old *hospitalitas* system); its meaning may have become nothing more than 'a share'. The move was almost certainly primarily from garrison cities and towns to imperial and other underused lands around them,[57] wholly within those areas of northern Italy in which the barbarian troops and their families already lived (and which Ricimer had previously controlled), thus merely legitimizing a *de facto* situation. Goffart has advanced the theory that tax revenues not estates were granted to the barbarians in Italy, but argues this only for the Ostrogothic settlement, not for that under Odovacer, on which he leaves the question open.[58]

---

[55] Procopius, *Wars* v, i, 3–8 (Dewing's translation).

[56] As suggested by Vassili (1939: 261–6) and Solari (1938: 462), who saw Orestes as having assumed the mantle of Majorian as defender of *romanitas*.

[57] Barnish (1986: 191).

[58] Goffart (1980: 100). This theory in general flies in the face of the fact that throughout the ancient and medieval European world it was always the ownership of actual land that conferred security and status, and that this is, therefore, surely what was demanded. Barnish (1986: 170–95) provides a much more convincing account of the barbarian settlement in Italy.

Cassiodorus, in the sixth century A D, made a number of references to barbarians who held property prior to the Ostrogothic invasion, some of whom had apparently married Roman women, and these are probably from Odovacer's settlement.[59] In the Po-valley region there was a preponderance of large estates, as a result of the establishment there of the court and army in the fourth century A D,[60] which may have been available to Odovacer to award to his chief supporters. Movement of the federates from billets to their own farms and estates may well have been welcomed by the cities, and it may also have decreased the taxation burden.[61] However, it must also have rendered them more static and less valuable militarily. The Ostrogoths who entered Italy in A D 489 settled in northern and central Italy, mainly in and around cities, especially Milan, Pavia, Verona, Ravenna, and Ancona (see pp. 168–9 and n. 12). This may have been partly because these were already areas of Germanic settlement (and where lands would be available from Odovacer's defeated supporters).

In A D 476 events were now moving rapidly. In modern accounts, the history of Italy in the 470s often appears as a linear succession of short-lived rulers and warlords. It is better to think of it as one power struggle, lasting about five years from the death of Ricimer (or even the beginning of the civil war), in which a number of men, including Orestes, Odovacer, Nepos, Gundobad, and perhaps others not known to us, vied for power. In A D 477 Odovacer killed a *comes*, Brachila or Bravila, who was opposing his rule,[62] and the following year an Ardaric who was rebelling against him.[63] Either, or both, may have been further contenders for power.

---

[59] Cassiodorus, *Variae* I, 18; I, 19, 4; I, 14, 5 and 6.
[60] Bullough (1966: 117).
[61] Barnish (1986: 175).
[62] *Fasti Vind. Prior. s.a.* 477; *Auct. Haun. ordo prior.* (describing him as a nobleman), *ordo post.* and *marg. s.a.* 477; Marcellinus *comes, s.a.* 477; Jordanes, *Getica* 243. The name is clearly barbarian, so it is odd that Jordanes says that he was killed by Odovacer to intimidate the Romans; if this is more than confusion on Jordanes' part, it is conceivable that he was closer to the Italian nobility than Odovacer was.
[63] *Auct. Prosp. Haun. ordo prior., ordo post.,* and *marg. s.a.* 478.

The eventual winner, Odovacer, was, like Ricimer, of barbarian ancestry.[64] The sources associate Odovacer with a number of different tribes. Theophanes and Marcellinus *comes* (typically) call him a Goth (although Theophanes adds that he was brought up in Italy).[65] Gregory of Tours is thought to have associated Odovacer with Saxons (but see Pt. II, pp. 104–6). The additions to Prosper stress the role of the Heruli in Odovacer's coup.[66]

In his description of the civil war between Ricimer and Anthemius, John of Antioch wrote that 'on Ricimer's side was Odovacer a man of the tribe called the Sciri, whose father was Edeco and whose brother was Onoulf, the bodyguard and murderer of Harmatius'.[67] Like John of Antioch, Anonymous Valesianus names Odovacer's father as Edico or Aedico.[68] This has given rise to a theory which makes Odovacer a Hun.[69] That a large number of sources would completely fail to notice that the King of Italy was a Hun seems incredible, and this idea has since been discredited.[70] Eugippius also calls Odovacer and Onoulf brothers.[71] Onoulf (elsewhere called 'Onoulph/us', 'Unulf', or 'Hunulf') later joined his brother in Italy and was also killed by Theoderic.[72]

Recently it has been proposed that Odovacer was the nephew of the eastern empress Verina, wife of Leo, and hence of East

[64] His name appears in the ancient sources as 'Odoacer', 'Odovacar', or 'Odovacer'. As the form on his coins is Flavius Odovac., and the variant without the 'v' seems to be the softened eastern form (see Hodgkin (1880a: 528), Odovacer seems the best choice.

[65] Theophanes, AM 5965; Marcellinus *comes*, *s.a.* 476: 'Odoacer rex Gothorum'.

[66] *Auct. Prosp. Haun. ordo post. marg. s.a.* 476, 1–2. See pp. 288–89 for text.

[67] John Ant. frag. 209 (1) (Blockley's translation, Priscus, frag. 64 (1)).

[68] *Anon. Val.* 10, 45.

[69] Reynolds and Lopez (1946–7: 36–53) on the grounds that there was a Hun notable, mentioned by Priscus (frags. 11 (1) and (2) and 15 (1) and (2)), named Edekon, a name similar to that of Odovacer's father. Priscus, who should know, as he met the man, is quite clear that this Edeco was a Hun by birth. Jordanes (*Getica* 277) reports that Edica and Hunulf (Onoulf) were chieftains of the Sciri.

[70] Maenchen-Helfen (1946: 837–9); McBain (1983: 323–7).

[71] Eugippius, *Vita Severini* XLIV, 4.

[72] John Ant. frag. 214; *Chronica Gallica a 511*, 670.

Roman descent himself.[73] The basis for this is the passage of John of Antioch above. The *magister militum* Harmatius (or 'Armatus') referred to was the nephew of Verina, and of her brother the usurper Basiliscus.[74] Harmatius was involved in Basiliscus' rebellion against Zeno and, as confirmed elsewhere, was killed by Onoulf, Odovacer's brother, then in the eastern army. The most obvious translation of the Greek is that Onoulf was the brother of Armatus. However, this phrase has traditionally been amended (as by Blockley above, and *PLRE* ii) to read that Odovacer was the brother of the Onoulf who was the killer of Harmatius. This fits better with both the sense of John of Antioch's account in general and with the other accounts. Neither Malalas,[75] nor Malchus, for instance, suggests that Harmatius was killed by his own brother. Indeed, Malchus says that Onoulf was befriended by Armatus when he arrived in the eastern empire from amongst the barbarians, and that Onoulf paid him back with barbarous treachery.[76] The *Suda* says that Onoulf was the son of a Thuringian father and Scirian mother.[77] That Odovacer was closely related to the eastern imperial family seems unlikely; it does not fit with other sources for his origins, and is not commented on when he is later in power in Italy. It may be possible that there was a remoter connection and that Basiliscus and Verina's family had some barbarian blood.[78]

Jordanes mentions Odovacer four times: as 'king of the Torcilingi, having with him Sciri, Heruli and allies of various races';[79] 'Odoacer king of the peoples';[80] 'Odoacer, by birth a

---

[73] Krautschick (1986: 344–55), followed by Demandt (1989: 178) and Amory (1997: 282–3).

[74] John of Antioch, frag. 209 (1).

[75] John Malalas, 381–2.

[76] Malchus, frag. 1 (Photius *Bibl. Cod.* 78, i) and frag. 4.

[77] *Suda*, κ, 693. All the other sources of information on his father say that he was Scirian, so there seems to be a mistake here. Perhaps it should be the other way round; a Thuringian mother would fit very well. (It is also possible that Odovacer and Onoulf were half- rather than full brothers.)

[78] Krautschick (1986: 350) points out that Basiliscus is called 'barbaros' in an account of the life of Daniel Stylites.

[79] Jordanes, *Getica* 242: 'Odoacer Torcilingorum rex habens secum Sciros, Herulos diversarumque gentium'.

[80] Jordanes, *Getica* 243: 'Odoacer rex gentium'.

Rugian, leader of Torcilingi, Sciri, and Heruli;'[81] and 'underk-
ing of the Torcilingi and Rugi'.[82] Contradiction and confusion
are hardly alien to Jordanes, and he may be using several traditions. The 'Torcilingi' have attracted attention from some
modern writers, as an otherwise unknown people,[83] possibly
speaking a Turkic language.[84] The boring truth is that this is,
almost certainly, Jordanes' misspelling of Thuringi. This apparent confusion is a result of the nature of the sources, and of the
confused times, rather than a real historical problem. Odovacer's
coup is associated with a number of tribes because the Roman
army in Italy consisted of men from a number of different
tribes,[85] many recruited from the Danube region (only a couple
of weeks' travel from northern Italy), as is shown by Sidonius'
description of Majorian's army in AD 458 (p. 205); neither Sciri
nor Heruli are mentioned, unlike the Rugi, but they may be
included under the heading of Pannonians. The Sciri are mentioned by Procopius (along with Alans and Goths) as present in
Italy just before Odovacer's coup (see p. 281). Sciri, Rugi, and
Heruli may have entered Roman service as a result of intertribal
conflict (such as that which decimated the Sciri in *c.* AD 469).[86]

  The confusion as to Odovacer's personal ethnicity is, actually, not as great as sometimes portrayed. The theories that he
was Saxon, East Roman, or Hun can almost certainly be dismissed. Odovacer was surely Germanic, probably half-Scirian,
half-Thuringian, and he may have had connections with other
tribes through intermarriage.[87] The Sciri and the Rugi (the

  [81] Jordanes, *Romana* 344: 'Odoacer genere Rogus, Thorcilingorum Scirorum Herulorum'.

  [82] Jordanes, *Getica* 291: 'sub regis Thorcilingorum Rogorumque'.

  [83] They only appear in Jordanes and later sources using Jordanes, such as
Paul the Deacon's *History of the Lombards* I, i, and I, xix.

  [84] See e.g. Thompson (1982: 64); Reynolds and Lopez (1946: 44), who turn
them into a royal clan of the Huns (as part of their argument that Odovacer was
a Hun: see p. 284).

  [85] Moreover, these tribes were not totally discrete entities outside the
empire.

  [86] *Contra* Reynolds and Lopez (1946: 43), the fact that Odovacer, as King
of Italy, fought the Rugi in the Danube region in AD 488 (Eugippius, *Vita
Severini* 44) in no way makes it impossible for Odovacer to have led the Rugi in
imperial service in Italy at an earlier date.

  [87] Burns (1984: 72) has described the loyalty of the barbarian army to
Odovacer as being based on the oaths of warriors, not on blood ties and

latter connected with Odovacer by Jordanes) are both recorded in the Black Sea region in the second and third centuries A D, and both probably fought alongside the Gepids to free themselves from the Huns (Sidonius lists both in Attila's army in A D 451).[88] The Sciri were allied to the Rugi *c.* A D 469.[89] The *Vita Severini* refers to the Thuringians, as well as the Rugi and Sciri, making attacks on Noricum and on each other.[90] Odovacer was born *c.* A D 433 and was hence about forty-four years old when he became ruler of Italy.[91] For the first twenty years of Odovacer's life his people were probably under the dominion of the Huns. In about A D 469 his father was probably the leader of (all or part of) the Sciri when they were defeated by the Ostrogoths.[92] Unlike his (perhaps elder?) brother Onoulf, who stayed with the Sciri and then entered the service of Constantinople, Odovacer went westwards. This was probably in the 450s, perhaps shortly after the death of Attila, as he is described in Eugippius' *Life of Saint Severinus* at this point in his life as *iuvenis* (see below), and also because he appears very early in the book, which begins with Attila's death.[93] Severinus was both spiritual and temporal leader of the Romans living along the Danube in Noricum. Among his visitors were barbarians on their way to Italy:

Among those who came was Odovacer, who afterwards ruled Italy, at that time a young man of tall stature, very poorly clad. While he bent down so that his head did not touch the roof of the humble cell, he learned from the man of God that he would become famous. For, as

marriage networks, but it is entirely possible that intertribal marriage ties may have been forged, and have affected relationships.

[88] Sidonius, *Pan.* V I I, 321–2.

[89] Jordanes, *Getica* 277–8.

[90] Eugippius, *Vita Severini* X X I V, 3 and X X V I I, 3.

[91] He was sixty years old when he was killed by Theoderic in A D 493 (John Ant. frag. 214).

[92] Jordanes, *Getica* 277: 'ipsas Scirorum reliquias quasi . . . cum Edica et Hunrufo eorum primatibus'. ('summoned the last remnants of the Sciri with Edica and Hunulf, their leaders').

[93] The later dates of O'Flynn (1983: 136) and *PLRE* ii (791–3, Odovacer) are based on the assumption that he spent time leading Saxons in Gaul, and do not fit with Eugippius' testimony. An earlier date also gives Odovacer sufficient time to establish his undoubtedly influential position in Italy and with the army.

Odovacer said farewell, Severinus said to him, 'Go, go to Italy. Now you are clad in poor skins, but soon you will bestow great largesse on many.'[94]

In Italy, Odovacer became a member of the imperial body-guard.[95] This probably means he was a member of one of the units of court guards; possibly he reached the rank of *comes domesticorum*. We do not know Odovacer's rank at the time of his coup. He is never called *magister militum* by the sources, but, given his influence with the army, it is possible that he had risen to that position. He is mentioned by John of Antioch as a supporter of Ricimer during the civil war,[96] and his experience in military and political matters must have been gained under the patrician. In his subsequent reign, Odovacer has been described as continuing many of Ricimer's 'social policies',[97] though this was probably less conscious emulation than similar pragmatism and respect for Roman culture. Odovacer's main adherents may have been his own tribesmen, but he must have also gained support among other barbarians in the army (although clearly not in such a way as to alarm Ricimer).

As well as Procopius, and a number of very brief references, there are four Italian sources for Odovacer's coup, two in additions to Prosper; the first of these reads:

And among the unfortunate and unforeseen disasters of the state at that time, while the strength of Rome was being destroyed by the civil war, the foreign peoples who with pretended friendship were subject to Roman authority rebelled against it. For, the Heruls, living in Italy,

---

[94] Eugippius, *Vita Severini* VII: 'inter quos et Odovacer, qui postea regnavit Italiae vilissimo tunc habitu iuvenis statura procerus advenerat. Qui dum se, humillimae tectum cellulae suo vertice ne contingeret, inclinasset, a viro dei gloriosum se fore cognovit. Cui etiam valedicenti, "Vade" inquit "ad Italiam vade, vilissimus nunc pellibus coopertus, sed multis cito plurima largiturus."' This is paraphrased by *Anon. Val.* 10, 45–6. Severinus' words to Odovacer were not necessarily a prophecy of future kingship, but just reflect knowledge that a warrior might gain riches in Roman service. (When king, Odovacer evacuated the Roman survivors from Noricum, including the disciples of Severinus, carrying the saint's bones with them (*Vita Severini* XLIV, 4–5).)

[95] Procopius, *Wars* V, i, 6.

[96] John Ant. frag. 209 (1). He may be mentioned as an important supporter of Ricimer or because he became king, or because of the eastern connection through his brother.

[97] O'Flynn (1983: 136).

created a king named Odovacer, a man of both ability and intelligence and versed in military matters.[98]

The second, briefer and vaguer, notice reads: 'Everywhere misfortune arose in the state. On every side we were oppressed by foreign tribes, and provinces and sovereignty were lost'.[99]

The third account was written by Ennodius. His version of events is that Satan (purely to incommode Epiphanius in Ticinum):

raised up an army against the patrician Orestes, and as a secret destroyer implanted the crime of dissension: he unsettled the minds of depraved souls with the hopes of new things. He excited in Odovacer ambition for the throne, and, so that this evil would take place in the city of Ticinum, he [Odovacer or Satan?] invited Orestes there with an assurance of protection. Huge numbers were assembled in the city, inflamed with lust for plunder.[100]

Stilicho and the families of his barbarian troops who had been massacred by Romans in this same region two generations before were avenged.[101]

Ennodius says nothing about demands for settlement, but blames Odovacer's desire to rule. As previously suggested, Odovacer was probably *both* (even primarily) a political and military rival to Orestes *and* the (or a) leader of the barbarian demand for settlement. The two men met in Pavia, probably to discuss the settlement demands. The rioting and pillaging which ensued over two days may well have been in response to Orestes' refusal to accede to the demands. Churches and many

---

[98] *Auct. Prosp. Haun. ordo post. marg. s.a.* 476, 1–2: 'Interque mala et inopinata rei publicae naufragia dum sese interius Romanae vires perimunt, externae gentes quae simulata amicitia Romano iuri suberant adversum eum consurgunt. Nam Heruli intra Italiam habitatores regem creant nomine Odoacrem, hominem et arte et sapientia gravem et bellicis rebus instructum.'

[99] *Auct. Prosp. Haun. ordo prior. s.a.* 476: 'Undique rei publicae mala consurgentia, ab omnibus undique gentibus oppressi et provincias et dominationem amiserunt.'

[100] Ennodius, *Vita Epiph.* 96: 'Exercitum aduersus Orestem patricium erigit et discordiae crimina clandestinus supplantator interserit: spe nouarum rerum perditorum animos inquietat. Odouacrem ad regnandi ambitum extollit et, ut haec pernicies in Ticinensi ciuitate contingeret, Orestem ad eam fiducia munitionis inuitat . . . fit maximus in urbe concursus, praedandi rabies inardescit.'

[101] Zosimus, V, 35.

houses were destroyed and citizens taken hostage. Orestes left
Pavia, but was seized and 'butchered' at Placentia, on 28 August
AD 476.[102] Once Orestes was killed at Placentia the worst of the
disorder there ceased.[103] On 23 August AD 476, five days
before the execution of Orestes, Odovacer was proclaimed *rex*
by the army, probably at Ticinum or Placentia.[104] In September he moved to Ravenna (see below).

According to the fourth source, Anonymus Valesianus:
'Then Odoacar came on the scene with the Sciri and killed the
patrician Orestes at Placentia and his brother Paulus at the pine
wood outside Classis at Ravenna. Then he entered Ravenna and
deposed Augustulus'.[105] Classis was the port area of Ravenna.[106] Paulus may have been trying to defend the city,
which was strongly fortified, or, perhaps more likely, trying to
flee by sea. Romulus Augustulus, who was hardly a serious
threat to him, was spared, and retired to Campania (to lands
belonging to his mother's family) with a pension.[107] It is

---

[102] Ennodius, *Vita Epiph.* 95–100; *Anon. Val.* 8, 37; Jordanes, *Getica* 242;
Fasti Vind. Prior. s.a. 476; *Auct. Prosp. Haun. ordo prior., post.*, and *marg. s.a.*
476; Cassiodorus, *Chronica* 1303 *s.a.* 476; Marcellinus *comes, s.a.* 476.

[103] Ennodius, *Vita Epiph.* 100: 'tamen Oreste et propter Placentiam urbem
extincto depraedationis impetus conquerit'.

[104] *Fasti Vind. Prior. s.a.* 476; *Pasch. Camp. s.a.* 476; *Auct. Post. Haun. ordo
prior. s.a.* 476: 'intra Italiam Eruli, qui Romano iuri suberant, regem creant
nomine Odiacrem x k. Sept'; *Auct. Prosp. Haun. ordo post. s.a.* 476: 'Odoachar
ab exercitu suo rex levatur x k. Sept.'.

[105] *Anon. Val.* 8, 37–8: 'Superveniens autem Odoacer cum gente Scirir-
orum occidit Orestem patricium in Placentia et fratem eius Paulum ad Pinetum
foris Classem Ravennae. Ingrediens autem Ravennae deposuit Augustulum de
regno'.

[106] *Anon. Val.* 8, 37; *Fasti Vind. Prior. s.a.* 476; *Auct. Prosp. Haun. ordo
prior., post.*, and *marg. s.a.* 476; Cassiodorus, *Chronica* 1303 *s.a.* 476. The fact
that the death of Paulus is particularly noted in the Italian sources may mean
that he was a prominent person in Italy in his own right. It is conceivable that
Pinetam actually refers to the name of an army camp.

[107] Marcellinus *comes*: 'Augustulum filium Orestis Odoacer in Lucullum
Campaniae castello exilii poena damnavit'; *Anon. Val.* 8, 38: 'Misiteum intra
Campanium cum parentibus suis libere vivere' ('sent him to Campania to live
as a free man with his relatives'); Jordanes, *Getica* 242; Cassiodorus, *Variae*
III, 35. Could this *Lucullum . . . castello* be the luxurious villa built near Naples
by the famous Lucius Lucullus in the first century BC? We do not know his
fate. Although he presented no real personal danger, he could, of course, have
provided a future focus of opposition to Odovacer or to Theoderic.

possible that Odovacer, who proved to be good at mollifying the Italian upper classes, did not wish to antagonize them by killing the young emperor. A precedent existed in the peaceful removal of Glycerius (and possibly Avitus). He may well also have had political reasons, connected with his plan to establish himself in a novel position of authority in Italy and to sell this to the eastern government. Leo, who had been willing to intervene in the West, had died in AD 474, and, as mentioned above, in 476 his successor Zeno was distracted by the revolt of Basiliscus. The death of Orestes and removal of Romulus may not have worried those Romans who still considered Julius Nepos to be the legitimate emperor.

Odovacer's exact legal and constitutional position in Italy, and *vis-à-vis* the eastern emperor, has been much debated. It appears ambiguous now and probably was so then, particularly up to the death of Julius Nepos. This ambiguity was almost inevitable in the political situation. Envoys, ostensibly from Romulus and the senate, but really from Odovacer, travelled to Constantinople, to announce that there was no longer any need for a western emperor, one shared emperor being quite sufficient, and that they had chosen Odovacer to rule them and requested that Zeno appoint him *patricius*.[108] Odovacer perhaps desired this mainly because it had been Ricimer's title. Perhaps 'patrician' was now seen as a viable alternative to the title of 'emperor', made so by the power of the previous holders of the title in the West. It would not, of course, give Odovacer any legal right to rule Italy, but would have denoted some degree of formal acceptance by Constantinople. It may have been a temporary expedient.

It is not certain whether Odovacer subsequently actually assumed the title of patrician or not. Malchus' account of the representations of Odovacer and Nepos to Zeno hardly clarifies matters:

Zeno gave the following reply... since their emperor was still alive, they should entertain no other thought than to welcome him on his return. To the representatives of the barbarian he replied that it was better that Odovacer had received the patriciate from... Nepos, although he would have confirmed it if Nepos had not done so first... he congratulated Odovacer in thus beginning by preserving the order of

---

[108] Malchus, frag. 14.

government appropriate for the Romans ... if Odovacer wished to act
justly he would quickly receive back the emperor who had honoured
him ... he sent to Odovacer a royal letter ... addressed to him as patrician[109]

Thus Zeno gave some moral support to Nepos, but did not
provide him with the requested resources to regain his
throne.[110]

From AD 476 there was no longer an emperor of the western
empire.[111] Thus Odovacer assumed a role different from that of
Ricimer, Aetius, Stilicho, or their predecessors, for, although he
inherited their position as commander of the armed forces
and effective political leader, there was no longer a western
emperor who was his legitimate overlord. Nor did he become
emperor himself, as numerous Roman generals and nobles had
done in the past. All the sources are perfectly clear in calling
Odovacer 'king' (whether this meant King of Italy, or primarily
of the barbarians in Italy).[112] Cassiodorus states clearly that
although he took the title of 'king', he did not assume the purple
nor the imperial regalia.[113] There had been no significant imperial possessions beyond Italy for some years, and this development recognized the reality: Italy was now a unit similar to
the kingdoms of the Visigoths or Burgundians.

[109] Malchus, frag. 14 (Blockley's translation). See Pt. I, p. 61 for the
beginning of this account.

[110] Julius Nepos was, of course, the last legitimate Roman emperor, but
historians, then and now, have been unable to resist the irony of Romulus
Augustulus' names.

[111] Although it may not have been realized at the time that this would prove
to be permanent. There had been short periods without an emperor when
Ricimer was dominant.

[112] There has been debate as to whether he was only king of the barbarian
non-citizens, as suggested originally by Mommsen (cited in Thompson
(1982: 65)). However, as well as being referred to as king of barbarian peoples,
Italian sources (including, as Jones (1962: 126) points out, two documents
dealing with Roman subjects) call him *rex* without qualifier or reservation. It
may have been easier for the senatorial order and the educated to accept a
barbarian king than a barbarian as emperor, with all the emotive baggage of
that title. Whatever he was called, he was *de facto* ruler of the people of Italy,
both barbarian and Roman.

[113] Cassiodorus, *Chronica* 1303 *s.a.* 476: 'ab Odovacre Orestes, et frater
Paulus extincti sunt nomenque regis Odovacar adsumpsit, cum tamen nec
purpura nec regalibus uteretur insignibus'.

Odovacer is a Janus figure, as *patricius* looking back to Aetius and Ricimer, and as *rex* looking forward to the Ostrogothic kings. The proclamation of Odovacer as king marks the end of the situation prevailing during most of the fifth century: a legal and symbolic emperor of Roman birth, dominated in varying degrees by a warlord whose strength rested primarily on barbarian military forces (see Conclusion). However little actual change there may have been in culture and everyday life, the year AD 476 is the marker and symbol of the end of a centuries-old political system and ideology.[114] It is at that point that this account, like the Roman empire in the west, comes to an end.

---

[114] Less than a year later Gaiseric, greatest of the empire's enemies, died of natural causes, after over fifty years of hostility to Rome.

Conclusion

From the studies of the individual warlords in this book some conclusions can be drawn and suggestions for further research made. To move from there to more general conclusions or models of the late fifth century proves, however, more problematic.

In the case of Marcellinus there is better information, both in terms of quantity and interest, than often realized in the past. The conventional picture of Marcellinus (based on Procopius) as a western general in command of troops in Dalmatia seems at odds with the evidence of other sources. Procopius' evidence undoubtedly remains a problem for any reassessment of Marcellinus. However, it should not be taken as the one and only starting-point. The most convincing line of argument is probably that Marcellinus was Dalmatian in origin, and eastern in education and culture. (Although we will never know how exactly Marcellinus gained his classical education, commitment to paganism, and contacts with the Neoplatonists.)

An interesting question remains as to exactly how Marcellinus came to power in Dalmatia if, as proposed, this was not through the agency of a western army command there. His rise may well have been based primarily on a local power base in Dalmatia, possibly built on the prosperity and strategic importance of Salona. This could be another example of the rise in the importance and power of local landowners, as seen elsewhere in the late empire. It is interesting also to speculate on the dynamics of his subsequent relationship with both Constantinople and Italy. Was he, perhaps, subsidized financially by Constantinople? And how did his probable paganism affect these relationships, particularly with Anthemius? One might also ask to what extent Marcellinus' importance in the 460s was based on his own personality and talent, or the result of the Vandal threat, his access to naval resources, or the increasing strategic importance of Dalmatia to an eastern emperor intervening in the West.

It also seems very possible that Salona remained strongly connected in some way to the eastern empire. The reality of the administrative situation in the Balkans in the fifth century may well have been more complicated than has sometimes been thought, *and* the situation on the ground was no doubt at variance with bureaucratic theory. Given the likelihood that the political map altered several times and the paucity of the available sources, it is beyond reconstruction; but there is reason to think that some areas, including coastal Dalmatia, may have been effectively autonomous from an early date.

Like Aegidius, Syagrius, and Majorian, Marcellinus has been seen as carrying the 'banner of Romanitas': 'The region [Dalmatia] became the depository of the highest and most noble values of the Roman world and assumed the mission of ensuring the continuity of the empire. These values were seen in their purest form in . . . Marcellinus'.[1] While this assessment is partisan and extravagant, it does seem that he and Julius Nepos may have kept a Romanized regime going in Dalmatia for longer than many other provinces.

There is no hint in the ancient sources that Marcellinus attempted to take the purple personally. Certainly he would have had little chance of achieving power in the East, but Italy was a different matter.[2] Priscus tells us that he threatened to attack Italy, but was dissuaded by Constantinople.[3] It is conceivable therefore that he, at least temporarily, considered ousting Ricimer and making a bid for the western imperial throne. It is interesting that Aegidius, who at a slightly later date withdrew his allegiance from the Italian government, also made no bid for the imperial title. Marcellinus was a much more powerful and influential figure than Aegidius, but there are other points of resemblance. Both achieved positions independent of central authority in areas once part of the empire. Both were effective military leaders, who actively resisted barbarian

---

[1] Praga (1993: 34).

[2] Especially if the conventional view that he was an associate of Aetius and a high-ranking, possibly aristocratic, western general is accepted.

[3] Priscus, frag. 39 (1).

expansion, and both were opponents of Ricimer. In both cases, they passed their authority on to their kinsmen.

Why did men like Avitus and Petronius Maximus grasp the imperial title (in the long tradition of Roman history), while Aegidius and Marcellinus, who had as much, probably more, status and as many military resources, did not? Marcellinus' much less impressive nephew Julius Nepos did become western emperor, albeit only with eastern support. That Marcellinus was prepared to put his support behind Anthemius, rather than make a bid for supreme power for himself, perhaps suggests that his position was not in fact as strong as it might seem from the sources (perhaps because of where his power base lay), or that his pagan beliefs stood in the way. It is perhaps more surprising that Aegidius neither proclaimed himself, nor any other aristocratic Gallo-Roman, emperor. The former move would certainly have been natural in the past, and the second similar to what Ricimer was doing in Italy. Even if he lacked the strength to move against Italy, he could have set up a separatist emperor in Gaul. Perhaps lack of support from a major barbarian made this impossible. That neither man took this traditional action argues for a radical change in political realities. It is also possible that the title of emperor was by now hardly worth usurping outside Italy and that the position of emperor was, to an intelligent man, no longer worth aiming for.

Although what once appeared in the history books as 'the Kingdom of Soissons' has been downgraded first to a sub-Roman enclave and finally to a 'phantom state',[4] future debate should not be limited to a simple opposition between the older conventional picture and the opposite extreme of total dismissal. We can consider more complex and interesting possibilities. The potential exists for other models that can be used in both historical and archaeological interpretation.

It is important to stress that the complex situation in northern Gaul described at the end of Part II was (as elsewhere) a temporary and transitional stage, before one element was able to impose itself as dominant; in the event, the Salian Franks under Clovis. This effectively began with the capture of Soissons, a city which may have been for some time within a shifting

[4] Martin (1951: 35).

Roman/Frankish zone (Aegidius and Syagrius being a part of Frankish as well as of late Roman history). It took Clovis several more years to bring the whole of North Gaul under his political and economic control (by, perhaps, a combination of peaceful and violent means, and in several stages which are virtually unknown to us, but, probably, first to the Seine and then to the Loire). This fits well with the idea that Clovis' first conquest, the kingdom of Syagrius, had a western border on the Seine. Substantial Frankish settlement of most of northern Gaul began only a generation or so later, and place-name evidence suggests it remained heaviest between the Rhine and the Seine.[5]

There are hints of similar developments in the almost unknown history of fifth-century Britain; miles away, in every sense, from the still prosperous and sophisticated Mediterranean world, but still perhaps sharing characteristics with northern Gaul and northern Spain. In the historical and legendary sources can be glimpsed a fragmented and complex situation, in which Celtic and Germanic warlords and kings existed alongside Roman leaders of imperial descent, Romano-British *curiales*, and influential religious figures.[6] This alternative model of northern Gaul, into which one can place Arbogast, Goar, Germanus, Riothamus, Aegidius, Syagrius, Childeric, and Clovis, looks convincingly like a context into which one could also place Ambrosius, Gildas, Patrick, Hengist, and even such semi-legendary figures as Vortigern and Arthur.

One might take this further. Northern Gaul retained elements of late Roman or 'late antique' culture. Could it be possible that the ex-province of Britannia was not quite the 'special case' sometimes portrayed? Britain (in at least some regions—possibly the South-West) might also have, in some ways, remained within the mainstream late antique world. This could be the case, for instance, in its Christianity, and aspects of urban and intellectual life.

The existence of a Gallo-Roman leader named Syagrius, ruling the city of Soissons and defeated by Clovis in A D 485/6,

[5] Périn and Feffer (1987: ii, 128), and see pp. 146–7 on Maine.

[6] Gildas refers to sixth-century British *reges* with names such as Aurelius and Constantius (*De Excidio et Conquestu Britanniae*, 27–31) and Nennius calls Ambrosius *rex Britonum* (*Historia Brittonum*, 31, 2, and 49, 5), although Gildas refers to him as *dux* (*De Excidio*, 25).

seems more probable than not. The story in the *Historiae* is a detailed and coherent one, and the names of people, places, and battles are highly durable items in oral history and legend. The kingdom based on Soissons was the creation of Syagrius rather than his father, although it may have had its beginnings in his career. Aegidius, *magister militum per Gallias*, is still recognizably a figure of the late empire, Syagrius hardly at all; and the two decades of North Gallic history that wrought this change are almost totally obscure to us. It is likely that Syagrius was one of the last (perhaps *the* last) independent Gallo-Roman rulers, as indeed stated in Frankish genealogies. (If he, somehow, inherited his position at Soissons from Aegidius, then it is arguable that some sort of Roman political and military presence continued there for about a generation longer than elsewhere in Gaul, perhaps constituting an element of continuity in this transitional period.) This may be linked with the durability of the *civitas* system as a whole, especially as it must have gained new roles in local defence and tax collection. The larger and more secure cities would also benefit from the growing political and cultural regionalism (as, similarly, perhaps, with Marcellinus and Salona and Ricimer and Milan).

Syagrius' defeat marked the beginning of Frankish dominion of Gaul. That the victory at Soissons had political as well as military significance is substantiated by the surprising importance of Soissons in the following century; this can best be explained if the city was taken over as the centre of an important Gallo-Roman political unit. Perhaps in the process Clovis came into personal possession of substantial landed estates, previously belonging to Syagrius and his supporters, which became Merovingian royal estates.

Against the developments in the western empire as a whole, and North Gaul in particular, Aegidius and Syagrius as independent regional rulers do not appear out of place. Even the title of 'king' is not as incongruous as it might appear at first sight.[7] Apart from the considerations of inexact terminology and the

---

[7] As James himself admitted (1989: 46). He pointed out that there was another King of the Romans recorded in the same period. In *c.* AD 508 Masuna held the title, in North Africa, of *Rex gentium maurorum et romanorum* (James (1989: 46)).

difficulty of reconciling German and imperial forms, it may also reflect a real confusion at the time. Ambiguous situations did exist, notoriously in the case of Odovacer. There was an increasing crossover between barbarian and imperial status systems. Several barbarian leaders, from Alaric to the kings of the Burgundians, also held imperial ranks and titles. By the middle of the fifth century Roman citizens held offices bestowed by barbarian kings, and may sometimes have been known by Germanic titles; for instance, those Gallo-Romans in Visigothic service. This does not prove that Aegidius or Syagrius had the title of 'king', or even acted as a king-like ruler, but that this was not (especially in the latter case) impossible. Many classically minded historians have recoiled in horror from the idea of a Roman king, but the basis for this, the traditional Roman antipathy to kingship, is by the fifth century an irrelevance.

For Ricimer, a crucial question, relating both to his place in history and to our understanding of him, is his relationship with the institution of empire. How did he want the western empire ruled, and what were his personal ambitions in this direction? Some historians have thought that Ricimer wanted to become the emperor himself; perhaps it would have been better for Rome if he had been able and willing to do so. But, working from Ricimer's recorded actions, rather than from hypotheses about his essential allegiance and motivation, it is clear that at no point, not even after defeating Anthemius, did Ricimer attempt to make himself emperor. Although capable of directing the government of Italy during those periods in which there was no western emperor, he always chose (or accepted the necessity for) an emperor. However, after the reign of Majorian, when he had established his position, he preferred one who would be a figurehead under his control or his influence (the difference is nice but real). He may have been loyal to the concept of Rome, but he was not loyal to the emperors as individuals, or prepared to work with one who challenged or clashed with him. He probably saw this both as in the best interests of Italy and imperial traditions, and as intelligent self-preservation (he no doubt remembered the fate of his old commander, Aetius, and of Stilicho). If this seems ambivalent, so it probably was in reality. It is also possible that his policies, ideas, and ambitions varied over time, being very different in the 470s to in the 450s.

There is evidence that Ricimer had greater power and independence in Italy than his predecessors; evidence including the interregnums of AD 456–7 and 465–7 during which he was _de facto_ ruler; the title of _rex_ given by Marcellinus _comes_; his command of the loyalty of the Italian army; the appearance of his monogram on the _nummi_ of Severus; and Ennodius' implications that he and Anthemius were _principes_ of equal power. One might also include Theophanes' statement that 'there were no more emperors but Ricimer controlled affairs commanding the army and invested with great power'.[8]

Ricimer's position may have been much closer to that of Odovacer than has been portrayed in the past. It seems that in some ways Ricimer was the inheritor of the fighting emperors, who had used Milan as one of their bases.[9] His presence in Milan was a reversal of that removal to Ravenna in AD 401 often described as a great strategic error.[10] Milan was a good location from which to guard Italy from land invasion. Evidence is emerging that, even after the breakdown of the old Alpine fortified defensive systems at the beginning of the fifth century, the northern borders continued to have some sort of defensive system, including small fortified _castra_, which continued through the fifth century.[11] Milan in the late fourth century had massive walls, imperial palaces, many public buildings, and a mint,[12] as well as an important and wealthy church. It was almost certainly still an important centre in the later fifth century, and continued to be important in the Ostrogothic/Byzantine period.[13]

It is likely that for many years Ricimer was a virtually independent ruler at Milan, whence (as described by Paul the

[8] Theophanes, AM 5947 (Mango and Scott translation). This is, admittedly, a late and unreliable work. Theophanes' source for this information does not seem to be known. It is repeated in George Cedrenus, p. 606.

[9] Incidentally, Stilicho may have previously had a residence in Milan: a house south of the cathedral later given to the Church (Cagiano de Azevedo (1977: 479)).

[10] Ferril (1986: 115).

[11] Christie (1991_b_: 420–2).

[12] Ausonius, _Ordo Urbium Nobilium_, vii.

[13] Christie (1993: 487).

Deacon) he governed Liguria,[14] probably also the Alpine areas and Aemilia, and perhaps Venetia. This region was heavily garrisoned, and settled by barbarians.[15] It was perhaps developing into a separate unit (the major regions of Italy have always had a tendency to separate in the absence of strong central control). This makes the subsequent, apparently acceptable, settlement of Odovacer's followers and Theoderic's Goths in the region more understandable.[16] It seems likely that there was a developing split between northern Italy and central and southern Italy, beginning in the middle of the fifth century AD or perhaps even earlier. Milan was probably becoming a focus of regional loyalty.

If, as well as being a late Roman figure in the tradition of Aetius, Ricimer in many ways anticipates Odovacer and Theoderic, the crucial question is not why Ricimer did not make himself emperor, but why he did not make himself King of Italy.[17] What was probably out of the question in AD 458 (only a couple of years after Valentinian) may in AD 472 (four years before Odovacer's coup) have been attainable, had Ricimer so wished. The crucial political and psychological break may have occurred not in AD 476 but at some point when Ricimer became *de facto* an independent ruler (with Orestes as a very temporary and untenable reversion to the previous system).

Perhaps controversially, it might be productive in the cases of Ricimer, Gundobad, and Odovacer to pursue an interpretation subtly different from either the old characterization of them as barbarian agents of disintegration, or the newer one of them as totally assimilated and Romanized.[18] Here, and with other previous barbarians in imperial service, we may be looking at

---

[14] For his high status in Liguria see Paul Diac. *Hist. Rom.* XV, 3: 'qui tunc Mediolani poitus praeerat Liguria'; Ennodius, *Vita Epiph.* 51–8. Liguria was larger then, of course, than the present coastal region so called.

[15] Paul Diac. *Hist. Rom.* XV, 4.

[16] Tellingly, where Ostrogoths were settled outside this region, in Samnium, there were some problems (Cassiodorus, *Variae* II, 13; V, 26; VII, 26).

[17] By the AD 460s there were many other kings within the former Roman empire: Vandal, Gothic, Burgundian, Breton, Frankish, Suevian, etc.

[18] Recent academic notions that individual cultural and ethnic identity is often fragile, easily mutable, and transferable seem to me very dubious. People generally have a clear idea of who they are.

exceptional men who lived comfortably in (or within the élites of) two different worlds, equally well adapted to both; bilingual and bicultural and able to move easily between one and the other. In connection with this line of thought, one might consider Miller's very striking image:

The Germanic masters of soldiers who held consulships and intermarried with imperial dynasties may have been Romanised to the extent that they could be comfortable in an imperial court but they would probably have been even more comfortable in a La Tène princely Hall.[19]

Although the 'La Tène princely Hall' may be considered an extreme suggestion, it is possible to see these men as part of a process of amalgamation of late Roman and barbarian élites and their ideologies, which helped create the early medieval world. This is not totally dissimilar to earlier Italian views of the barbarian *magistri* as a progressive force building a new culture. This, for Italy specifically, is, however, one of history's 'might have beens'; we will never know how the Italy of Odovacer and Theoderic might have developed.

Given the differences between late fifth-century Dalmatia, Italy, and Gaul, and between the personalities and situations of the various warlords, few generalizations are possible that would not be merely superficial. Within the same basic framework, that is, the political decline and break-up of the Roman empire, there is, diversity of regional development and human response. Trying (as O'Flynn did) to treat all the 'generalissimos' in common, and to establish shared characteristics and motivations, seems a rather pointless exercise. Nor has this book attempted to produce anything on the level of general explanation of the final fall of the western empire.[20] To a great extent, in historical study, the questions as to 'how' events occurred

---

[19] Miller (1996: 171).

[20] It is always easy to identify weaknesses in societies; they will inevitably have many, but all do not lead to decline and collapse. The underlying structural reasons for the, apparently virtually inevitable, collapse of complex societies are best covered by Tainter (1988); and Williams and Friell's idea of a 'ratchet effect' operating in the late Roman period seems a useful one (1994: 160).

must push aside those as to 'why' they did so. Indeed, they may, if answered fully, go a long way towards explaining the 'why'.

Alongside long-term forces and structural factors there existed elements in causality that were not predetermined but interactive and contingent, and individuals, as well as being shaped by external forces, could sometimes influence events. One or two features of the final decades of the western empire, however, have appeared repeatedly in the previous pages, or seem to be of special significance, and these are therefore worth repeating.

It has always been clear that a vital element of the course of events in the fifth century was the split, from AD 395, between the eastern and western parts of the empire. This has been reaffirmed many times in this study. As this political, economic, and cultural division widened over the fifth century, eastern political and military involvement in the West was sporadic, seemingly occurring as the result of a sense of duty, often only when the West made a direct appeal. This division in itself weakened the West politically and financially, helping to allow rivals to the emperors to appear and gain more influence than they were to do in the East, yet denying them the resources to decisively defeat the barbarians. However, the presence in Constantinople of a senior emperor who could legitimize and support (or not) an emperor in the West, and who might at any point intervene, politically or militarily, was a constant factor in the political and diplomatic thinking of all western emperors and warlords.

Also of relevance to the careers of the warlords was the split that had developed from the late fourth century AD between formal and military leadership. The relinquishing of military leadership and control by the ruling emperor allowed the emergence of the dominant generals, and political power soon accrued to military power. The widespread acceptance of this development may be connected to the political and emotional desire, recurring throughout history in times of difficulty, not only among the ordinary people but, often, also among the social and intellectual élite, for a military saviour, a strong leader with quick solutions. However, the emperor retained for a long time his legal and ceremonial role, and formal, almost mystical, status. He also united the separate civil and military hierarchies at the top, and access to his person remained important to the powerful and ambitious. It is difficult to say how long this situation could have continued. It was, in any case, undermined by the death of Valentinian III, which radically changed the political parameters.

It has become clear that the power of the late fifth-century warlords was seriously restricted, and constrained by military and financial inadequacies. It was also limited geographically. This becomes apparent when one compares them with Stilicho, dominating the whole western empire and attempting control in the East, or even with Aetius. Another consistent feature is that all the main characters in this book were much more concerned with their own security, their personal status, and competition with rivals, than with the long-term interests of the state; and made political decisions accordingly (in many cases counter-productive for the empire). This, of course, is neither unnatural nor unusual. There are many previous examples of it; for instance, in the careers of Stilicho and Aetius. In the same way, emperors had almost always considered the barbarians at the frontier as less of a threat than usurpers, real or potential, and were always willing to abandon the frontiers for civil strife. The Narbonne handover by Agrippinus is only one example of internal rivals being seen as more of a real threat than the barbarian leaders. The prevalence in the fifth century of what appears to be highly destructive behaviour among the élite invites comparison with the late Roman Republic and the period of the wars of succession following the death of Alexander the Great; all of which are depressing to contemplate. The charitable view is that the long-term effects of this sort of behaviour may only be perceptible with hindsight.

Lastly, there is still no really satisfying explanation for the long-standing problem of the disintegration of the West's military superiority in the fifth century; what Collins has called 'the mysterious disappearance of the Roman army'.[21] Roman forces were still efficient and effective for most of the fourth century.[22] When and why did this change? Scholars have, in the past,

---

[21] Collins (1991: 89).
[22] Tomlin (1981: 256–7) and (1989: 235–7 and 241); Liebeschuetz (1993: 265); etc.

tended to see either the period immediately after Adrianople or the two decades either side of A D 400 as decisive. More recently and controversially, Elton's work has dated western Roman military collapse to post A D 450 (and played down the extent of military barbarization).[23] However, arguments about how long the imperial armies continued to be able to defeat the barbarians in battle are, really, somewhat irrelevant. The point is that Rome's armies lost the strategic ability to enforce its political objectives (one of which must, initially at least, have been to remove independent barbarian groups and kingdoms from within the empire, by expulsion or withdrawal of their autonomy). However sophisticated an army may be compared to its adversaries, if it cannot do this, then it must be considered to be ineffective.

This book has been written very much as traditional history, in that it has tried to offer rational, if, obviously, not definitive, narrative reconstructions of events in chronological order, and in that it has focused on individuals (to the extent that this is possible in the fifth century).[24] The transitional nature of this period has been demonstrated by the need to use such contrasting sources as Priscus' classical history, the poems and letters of Sidonius Apollinaris, Procopius' *Wars*, the work of Gregory of Tours, cryptic chronicles and annals, Christian writings such as saints' lives, Byzantine literature, and medieval works such as the *Liber Historiae Francorum*. The underlying and unifying context is the course, and aftermath, of the collapse of the political structure and the ideology of a great empire, and the varied human survival strategies which developed to meet it; a subject which may well prove not irrelevant to the twenty-first century.

[23] Elton (1990) and (1996).
[24] One of the fascinating aspects of working in periods like this, when it is almost impossible to 'know' anything, let alone deal with well-known characters, is when one just occasionally catches a glimpse of real personality.

APPENDIX
Naval Power in the Fifth Century

All naval historians of the ancient world agree that Roman sea power had been run down to almost nothing by the late fourth century AD,[1] and most pass over the next couple of centuries in a few sentences. The only major sea battles in the late antique period were those between the emperors Constantine and Licinius in AD 324, involving over 500 vessels, mainly levies from the ports of the eastern Mediterranean,[2] and the naval battle off Italy between the Ostrogoths and the Emperor Justinian's forces in AD 551.[3]

This disappearance of sea power applies especially to the western empire, but it is difficult to establish just when permanent fleets would have ceased to be available. In the early fifth century AD the *Notitia* recorded some naval units, both sea and river, in the West,[4] but we do not know how run-down these were, nor how out of date this information was. Some naval writers have considered that the fourth-century imperial fleets in the Mediterranean were adequate for policing purposes, but not strong enough to deal with barbarian attacks by sea.[5] But Vegetius, writing in the late fourth century, actually referred to the

---

[1] See e.g. Starr (1941: 198); Lewis (1951: 18–19); Haywood (1999: 57); Casson (1991: 213). To keep warships and crews in a state of readiness and efficiency is a costly business. Well-made ships of the classical period only had a life of twenty to twenty-five years (Casson (1971: 90, 119)). Ships could be stripped down and kept in storage in dockyards, in which case they might have been reused up to twenty years later. Casson (1971: 120) gives an example of this (though it dates to 48 BC). A recent book on the Roman army supported the continued existence of a standing fleet into the later fifth century, and explained the contradictory evidence by suggesting that it was not in permanent commission (Elton (1996: 98–9)). However, a fleet consisting of hulls in dockyards, without trained crews, would, given western lack of resources, have been much the same as no fleet.

[2] Zosimus, II, 22, 26.

[3] Procopius, *Wars* VIII, xxiii, 9–13, 29–38.

[4] The *Notitia* did not list the main eastern fleets, such as the one known to be based at Constantinople (although it did record some minor eastern units, such as river flotillas in Moesia). This is probably a textual omission.

[5] Lewis and Runyan (1985: 4–8).

Roman navy in the past tense,[6] as did Sidonius in the mid fifth century;[7] and Priscus said explicitly that the western Romans lacked a fleet in the 460s.[8] On the other hand, Claudian wrote of Stilicho in *c.* AD 400 preparing a fleet of corn transports and another of warships[9] (Claudian is, though, notorious for poetic licence).

The paucity of evidence has not prevented scholars arguing for a fully active fifth-century navy. Moss, for instance, argued, ultimately unconvincingly, that the western empire still retained a navy and was able to carry out naval blockades in the early fifth century.[10] The extreme opposite view was taken by Courtois: that in the West from the Severan period onwards naval tactics were unknown and that state ships were not warships but transports only, either for corn or men.[11] Courtois' theory does seem to be supported for the West by some of the scanty information from the late fifth century AD. Marcellinus used ships to transport men to Sicily, but we do not hear of him using them in naval engagement. Ricimer's so-called naval victory over the Vandals was probably nothing of the sort (see Pt. III, pp. 184 and 186). If he did have naval resources in AD 456, when he defeated the Vandals in Sicily and Corsica, they were not capable of defending Italy against Gaiseric's raids. The fleet built and marshalled by Majorian in AD 460 against Gaiseric (see Pt. III, pp. 206–7) seems to have been intended only to transport his army from Spain to Africa.

---

[6] Vegetius, 4, 31. He is referring to the fleets at Misenum and Ravenna. However, he described the river patrol boats on the Danube as being in increased use (4, 46). He stated with approval that the Roman empire (presumably in contrast to present-day practice) did not 'fit out the fleet on the spur of the moment in response to some crisis, but always kept it in readiness'.

[7] Sidonius, *Pan.* 11, 386: 'Romula desuetas moderentur classica classes'.

[8] Priscus, frag. 39 (1).

[9] Claudian, *Cons. Stil.* 1, 308: 'duplices disponere classes, quae fruges aut bella ferant'.

[10] Moss (1973: 725). However, the sources he cited are hardly evidence of the existence of a proper navy. His example of Fl. Constantius hampering the Visigoths at Narbonne by 'forbidding and cutting off all passage of ships and the importation of foreign merchandise' (Orosius, 7, 43) is ambiguous. The cited case of Stilicho actually says that he 'shut off the coasts and ports with many guards to prevent access' (*Codex Theod.* 7, 16, 1); and the cited blockade of the Vandals in Baetica by Castinus (Hydatius, 68 (76) *s.a.* 422) seems actually to have been a siege.

[11] By the fifth century, fleets came under the command of army generals; no naval command structure existed.

Fleets for major campaigns had to be assembled by levying ships and crews from the commercial sector,[12] combined, if it was important enough, with shipbuilding, as for Majorian's campaign:

Meanwhile, you construct, on two shores, fleets for the Upper and Lower Sea. Into the water fall all the forests of the Apennines; for many a long day there is felling on both slopes of those mountains so rich in ships timber ... Gaul ... is now eager to gain approval by a new levy for this purpose[13]

In the sixteenth century AD it took the arsenal at Venice about two years to build a galley of seasoned wood (which in turn takes decades to be ready). In emergencies ships can be made of unseasoned timber in a few months, as above, but they would be of inferior quality and seaworthiness.[14] Perhaps a life of one or two seasons was considered adequate for Majorian's ships, or perhaps they had no option but to use unseasoned timber.

From the descriptions by Procopius and others of the fleet sent against Gaiseric in AD 468 (see Pt. I, pp. 56–7), it is clear that Constantinople was still capable of raising a substantial fleet for an important campaign. However, the fleet sent against Gaiseric in AD 468 was not a standing force; Leo 'collected a fleet of ships from the whole eastern sea and he showed great generosity to the soldiers and sailors ... they say he spent one hundred and thirty thousand pounds'.[15] The important factors were adequate financial resources and a pool of available seagoing expertise, neither of which was readily available in the West.

The question of the West's naval resources has direct bearing on that of Vandal naval strength. It is beyond dispute that the Vandals made use of substantial numbers of ships. In AD 440 a novella of Valentinian records that Gaiseric had brought 'a large fleet out of Carthage'[16] (to be used to raid the coasts of Italy). He went on to capture Corsica and Sardinia, and make repeated raids on Italy, Sicily, and other Mediterranean coasts. In AD 456 we hear of a Vandal fleet of sixty ships (see Pt. III, p. 184). This evidence has caused some historians to write of widespread Vandal piracy and of the Vandals gaining supremacy at

---

[12] Which goes some way towards explaining their ineffectiveness.

[13] Sidonius, *Pan.* v, 441–8: 'Interea duplici texis dum litore classem inferno superoque mari, cadit omnis in aequor silva tibi nimiumque diu per utrumque recisus, Appennine, latus, navali qui arbore dives ... Gallia ... hoc censu placuisse cupit nec pondera sentit quae prodesse probat'.

[14] Casson (1971: 120 and n. 82).

[15] Procopius, *Wars* III, vi, 1–2.

[16] *Nov. Val.* 9.

sea and control of the Mediterranean.[17] An important consideration here is what sort of ships the Vandals had. The only way in which the Vandals could have come into possession of a fleet of warships would have been by capturing them from the western imperial navy in their conquest of Africa. But were such ships stationed there?

The *Notitia* does not list any naval units stationed at Carthage or elsewhere in western North Africa either; most obviously because there were none, or conceivably as a result of an accident of organization, recording, or textual omission. Orosius and Marcellinus *comes* did record Heraclian using a fleet to transport his troops from Africa to Rome in AD 413, but this seems to have been the corn fleet. Heraclian is said to have had 3,700 ships! Even Orosius is doubtful about this figure.[18] The supply of corn from North Africa to Rome still continued in the mid fifth century, but there is no hard evidence that the late empire maintained a naval force to protect it.[19] Common sense suggests that cargoes of grain would not be prime targets for pirates, who would prefer cargoes of valuable luxury goods (and slave-taking). Courtois argued that the vessels that the Vandals came into possession of were the transports of the corn fleet.[20] These were, of course, large, round-bottomed, sailing vessels, broader in the beam and heavier and much less manoeuvrable than war galleys.[21] Courtois concluded that 'no Vandal navy existed except in the minds of some historians'.[22]

Transport vessels would have enabled the Vandals to carry the men and horses of their raiding parties to Sicily and Italy and other coastal areas. It is known from Sidonius[23] that the raiding Vandal ships carried men and horses. Horses would not be easily transported in fighting galleys. Were cargo ships adapted to enable horses to be loaded and offloaded? For raiders to take horses with them is unusual; most, like the Vikings later, would have rounded up horses when they had landed. The immediate possession of mounted men may well have given the Vandals an advantage. There were horse transports in the

---

[17] See e.g. Schmidt (1911: 309); Stein (1959: 324); Barker (1911: 412); Moss (1973: 728). For Moss, this is vital to his central thesis that Aetius was culpable in not using Roman naval resources (which existed according to Moss) to counter the Vandals.

[18] Orosius (7, 42); and Marcellinus *comes* (*s.a.* 413).

[19] See e.g. Schmidt (1924: 306, 309); Moss (1973: 723); Lewis and Runyan (1985: 6).

[20] Courtois (1955: 207). His arguments are very detailed and only reported very briefly here.

[21] Casson (1994: 126).

[22] Courtois (1955: 207).

[23] Sidonius, *Pan.* V, 395–400 (see Pt. III, pp. 203–4).

Hellenistic and Republican periods, which were converted old triremes rowed by only sixty oarsmen and carrying thirty horses in the lower rowing decks.[24] Such vessels would have been unable to defend themselves. The eastern empire transported cavalry in the fifth and sixth centuries AD;[25] we do not know that these ships were 'specially designed horse transports'.[26] However, reliance mainly on this sort of vessel would not have enabled them to engage in large-scale piracy, naval actions at sea, or widespread disruption of Mediterranean communications. That the Vandals did not in fact do this in the fifth century AD has, of course, been argued by a number of scholars from Pirenne onwards,[27] and has some support from the archaeological record.

In AD 468 Gaiseric defeated a (mainly eastern) naval attack. Do the tactics of that victory provide any information on the type of ships under his command? Procopius (using Priscus) describes how the Vandals took advantage of Basiliscus' hesitation[28] to set sail towards the imperial fleet, towing boats which they then used as fire-ships, causing panic and disorder, then moving in to ram and sink ships.[29] Although this is open to different interpretations, on balance it sounds as if Gaiseric did possess some warships.[30] Of course, the Vandals had acquired shipbuilding facilities, and even if they had not captured a fleet of warships it is possible that they had had some constructed.[31] The evidence overall suggests that while the Vandals possessed some warships (perhaps of the newer type described below), they were primarily a threat as raiders rather than as pirates, mainly using

[24] Morrison and Williams (1968: 93).

[25] Menander, frag. 23 (1); John Lydus, *De Mag.* III, 43; Procopius, *Wars* III, xi, 2–16. In the last case, the way in which their capacity is given suggests that they were grain carriers.

[26] As described by Elton (1996: 98).

[27] Pirenne (1922: 223–35); Baynes (1955: 309–16). More recent writers have not taken such a strong line as Pirenne: e.g. Lewis and Runyon (1985: 10); Hodges and Whitehouse (1983: 169). Interestingly, the latter detect a brief revival in Mediterranean economy and communications in the mid to late fifth century; in other words, during the dominance of Aetius, Ricimer, and Odovacer (Hodges and Whitehouse (1983: 52)).

[28] Bass (1972: 134) suggested the Romans were trying to avoid a sea battle.

[29] Procopius, *Wars* III, vi, 12–24.

[30] As Gautier concluded, there is not enough evidence to be certain of the size or nature of Gaiseric's fleet (1932: 217–21), but it is hard to believe he did not have some warships not reliant on wind power (1932: 219).

[31] Construction did not cease at Carthage under the Vandals (Courtois (1955: 208)). Victor Vitensis (III, 20) recorded prisoners being sent to 'cut timber for the king's ships' under Gaiseric, or his son.

their ships to transport forces rather than to attack ships at sea. The Vandals do seem to have developed naval skills (or skilfully used those of the conquered provincials), but their naval superiority may have been more a result of Roman weakness and disorganization than their own expertise.[32] Rougé has argued that the fleet of ships which Gaiseric acquired would have deteriorated in quantity and quality over his reign and that of his successors,[33] and this is quite possible.

The late imperial period was a watershed between two different types of navy, both in strategic and tactical terms and in terms of ship design. Roman naval squadrons had traditionally been made up of a combination of large triremes (often with platforms for artillery) to which the faster and lighter *liburnae* had been added. But from the second century AD there was a trend towards the use of general-purpose military vessels, which could be employed as troop carriers.[34] From the third century AD ship designs were moving towards the typical Byzantine type, with high fore and aft posts, and fixed masts, rowed from deck level; described by Orna-Ornstein of the British Museum as 'similar to a Viking longship'.[35]

The early Byzantine navies of the sixth century were made up of cataphract galleys, called *dromons*, with only one bank of rowers, protected by the decking.[36] The Ostrogothic ships built in response to the Justinianic conquest of Italy were similar.[37] This was a reversion to an older type of vessel, largely due, no doubt, to lack of resources.[38] These *dromons* were very different in size and fighting power to the war-galleys of previous centuries, and this affected naval tactics and strategy.[39] The ships available to Gaiseric, Marcellinus, and Ricimer may well have been closer to this type of vessel than to those of the old imperial navies.

[32] Lewis and Runyan (1985: 11).
[33] Rougé (1961: 135–7). This would be a factor in the ease of the Justinianic reconquest.
[34] Orna-Ornstein (1995: 7). According to Elton (1996: 97–8), late Roman navies consisted of both warships and transports for troops and supplies (with sails only and unable to defend themselves). In the early fifth century AD, up to 5,000 men could be transported (Claudian, *De Bell. Goth.* 418–23; Zosimus, 6, 8, 2). This capacity probably included requisitioned merchant ships.
[35] Orna-Ornstein (1995: 7). This type of vessel reached its greatest size and efficiency in the tenth century AD (Lewis and Runyan (1985: 30–1)).
[36] Procopius, *Wars* III, xi, 15–16.
[37] Procopius, *Wars* VIII, xxii, 17; III, xxiii, 29–38.
[38] Casson (1971: 148) and (1994: 95–6); Bass (1972: 134). The *dromon* relied greatly on speed (the ram was the main offensive weapon) and carried only a small contingent (100–200 men) armed with light weapons.
[39] Rougé (1961: 150).

BIBLIOGRAPHY

ANCIENT WORKS

Acta Agoardi et Agulberti, AASS v: 3–5.

Acta Synhodorum Habitarum Romae a. 499.501.502, ed. Th. Mommsen, *MGHAA* xii: 395–455 (1894).

Additamenta ad Prosper Hauniensis, Continuatio Hauniensis Prosperi (Consularia Italica) ed. Th. Mommsen, *MGHAA* ix, *Chronica Minora*, 1: 298–339 (1892).

Ambrose, St. (of Milan), *Epistolae, Pat. Lat.* xvi: 875–1286.

Ammianus Marcellinus, ed. and trans. J. C. Rolfe, 31 vols. (London/Cambridge, Mass.: 1935–9).

Annales Regni Francorum, ed. F. Kurze, *MGH, Scriptores Rerum Germanicarum in Usum Scholarum Seperatum Editi*, vi (1895).

Annals of Ravenna, ed. B. Bischoff and W. Koehler, *Studi Romagnoli*, iii: 1–17 (1952).

Anonymus Valesianus, ed. Th. Mommsen, *MGHAA* ix, *Chronica Minora*, i: 306–28 (Berlin 1892).

Anonymus Valesianus (Excerpta Valesiana), ed. and trans. J. C. Rolfe, in Ammianus Marcellinus, iii: 506–69 (London/Cambridge, Mass.: 1939).

Auctarium ad Prosperi Epitomae Vaticanae (ad ed. a 455), ed. Th. Mommsen, *MGHAA* ix, *Chronica Minora*, i: 491–3 (1892).

Auctarium ad Prosperi Hauniensis, Continuatio Hauniensis Prosperi (Consularia Italica), ed. Th. Mommsen, *MGHAA* ix, *Chronica Minora*, i: 298–339 (1892).

Augustine, St., *Epistolae, Pat. Lat.* xxxiii: 471–1026.

Ausonius, *Opuscula*, ed. C. Schekl, *MGHAA* v (2) (1883).

——*Ordo Urbium Nobilium*, ed. R. P. H. Green, in *The Works of Ausonius* (Oxford: 1991), 169–73.

Auspicius (of Toul), *Epistola, Versibus Expressa, ad Arbogastem comitem Trevirorum, Pat. Lat.* lci: 1005–8.

Avitus (of Vienne), *Epistulae, Homiliae, Carmina*, ed. R. Peiper, *MGHAA* vi (2): 1–158 (1883).

Basil, St., *Epistulae*, trans. R. J. Deferrari, 4 vols. (London/Cambridge, Mass.: 1950–3).

Candidus, *Fragmenta*, ed. and trans. R. C. Blockley, in *The Fragmentary Classicising Historians of the Later Roman Empire: Eunapius,*

Olympiodorus, Priscus and Malchus, 2 vols., 464–73 (Liverpool: 1981–3).

Cassiodorus, *Chronica ad a 519*, ed. Th. Mommsen, *MGHAA* xi: 109–61 (1894).

——*De Institutione Divinarum Litterarum, Opera Omnia*, Pat. Lat. cxx: 1105–50.

——*Variae*, ed. Th. Mommsen, *MGHAA* xii (1865).

——*Variae*, trans. S. J. B. Barnish (Liverpool: 1992).

Catalogi Regum Francorum Praetermissi, ed. B. Krusch, *MGHSRM* vii (2): 850–55 (1920).

Chronica Gallica a. 452, ed. Th. Mommsen, *MGHAA* ix, *Chronica Minora*, i: 615–62 (1892).

Chronica Gallica a. 511, ed. Th. Mommsen, *MGHAA* ix, *Chronica Minora*, i: 615–66 (1892).

Chronicon Paschale (284–628 AD), trans. M. and M. Whitby (Liverpool: 1989).

Chronicorum Caesaraugustanorum Reliquiae, ed. Th. Mommsen, *MGHAA* xi, *Chronica Minora*, ii: 221–3 (1894).

Claudian, *De Bell. Goth.*, ed. and trans. M. Platnauer, 2 vols. (London/ New York: 1922).

Codex Justinianus, ed. P. Krueger, *Corpus Iuris Civilis*, ii (Berlin: 1877).

Codex Theodosianus, ed. Th. Mommsen and P. M. Meyer (Berlin: 1905).

Codex Theodosianus, ed. and trans. C. Pharr *et al.*, *The Theodosian Code and Novels, Corpus of Roman Law 1 and the Sirmondian Constitutions* (Princeton, NJ: 1952).

Constantius (of Lyons), *Vita Sancti Germani Episcopi Autissiodurensis*, trans. R. Borius, *Vie de Saint Germain d'Auxerre, Sources Chrétiennes*, cxii (Paris: 1965).

Consularia Constantinopolitana, ed. and trans. R. W. Burgess, *The Chronicle of Hydatius and the Consularia Constantinopolitana* (Oxford: 1993).

Damascius, *Vita Isidori Reliquiae*, ed. C. Zintzen (Hildesheim: 1967).

Ennodius, *Epistolae, Carmina, Dictiones Opuscula Alia*, ed. F. Vogel, *MGHAA* vii: 1–326 (1885).

——*Vita Beatissimi Epiphani Episcopi Ticinensis Ecclesiae*, ed. F. Vogel, *MGHAA* vii: 84–109 (1885).

Epistolae Arelatenses genuinae, ed. W. Gundlach, *MGH Epistolae*, iii/1 (1892).

Eugippius, *Epistola ad Paschasium Diaconum*, Pat. Lat. xii: 1167–70 (1863).

——*Vita Sancti Severini*, ed. H. Sauppe, *MGHAA* i (2) (1877).

Evagrius, *Ecclesiastical History 431–594*, trans. E. Walford (London: 1846).

Expositio Totius Mundi et Gentium, ed. and trans. J. Rougé (Paris: 1966).

Fasti Vindobonensis Priores (Consularia Italica), ed. Th. Mommsen, *MGHAA* ix, *Chronica Minora*, i: 274–336 (1892).

Flodoard, *Historia Remensis Ecclesiae*, ed. and trans. M. Lejeune (1854: Reims) repr. in *Revue du Moyen Age Latin* 37 (Jan.–Juin 1981).

Fredegar, *Chronica (Chronicarum Quae Dicuntur Fredagarii Scholastici)*, ed. B. Krusch, *MGHSRM* ii: 215–328 (1888).

Gelasius (Pope), *Epistolae et decreta, Pat. Lat.* lix: 13–140.

George Cedrenus, *Historium Compendium*, ed. I. Bekker *et al.*, 2 vols. (Bonn: 1838–9).

Gildas, *De Excidio et Conquestu Britanniae*, ed. Th. Mommsen, *MGHAA* xiii, *Chronica Minora*, iii: 25–85 (1889).

—— *The Ruin of Britain and other Works*, ed. and trans. M. Winterbottom (London/Chichester: 1978).

Gregory (Pope), *Dialogi (Liber IV)*, ed. U. Moricca (Rome: 1924).

Gregory (of Tours), *De Passione et Virtutibus Sancti Juliani Martyris*, ed. B. Krusch, *MGHSRM* i (2): 562–84 (1885).

—— *De Virtutibus et Miraculis de S. Martini Episcopi*, ed. W. Krusch, *MGHSRM* i (2): 584–661 (1885).

—— *Histoire des Francs, i–v. Text du manuscrit de Corbie*, ed. H. A. Omont (Paris: 1886).

—— *Histoire des Francs. Textes des manuscrits de Corbie et de Bruxelles*, ed. H. A. Omont and G. Collon, 2 vols. (1886–93), republished, ed. R. Poupardin (Paris: 1913).

—— *Historia Francorum*, ed. W. Arndt, *MGHSRM* i (1) (1885).

—— *Historiae Francorum*, 2nd edn., ed. B. Krusch and W. Levison, *MGHSRM* i (1) (1937–51).

—— *History of the Franks*, trans. O. M. Dalton (Oxford: 1927).

—— *History of the Franks*, trans. L. Thorpe (Harmondsworth: 1974).

—— *In Gloria Confessorum*, trans. R. Van Dam, *The Glory of the Confessors* (Liverpool: 1988).

—— *In Gloria Martyrum*, trans. R. Van Dam, *The Glory of the Martyrs* (Liverpool: 1988).

Hilarius (of Arles), *Sermo de Miraculo S. Genesii (Opuscula Dubia)*, *Pat. Lat.* l: 1273–6 (1846).

Hincmar, *Vita Sancti Remigii Episcopi Remensis*, ed. B. Krusch, *MGHSRM* iii: 256–336 (1896).

Hydatius, *Chronica*, ed. and trans. R. W. Burgess, *The Chronicle of Hydatius and the Consularia Constantinopolitana* (Oxford: 1993).

Hydatius, *Chronicon*, ed. Th. Mommsen, *MGHAA* xi: 13–36 (1894).

Isidore (of Seville), *Etymologiarum sive Originum*, ed. W. M. Lindsay (Oxford: 1911).

——*Historia Gothorum Wandalorum Sueborum*, trans. G. Donini and G. B. Ford, *Isidore of Seville's History of the Kings of the Goths, Vandals and Suevi* (Leiden: 1970).

John (of Antioch), *Fragmenta*, ed. and trans. R. C. Blockley, in *The Fragmentary Classicising Historians of the Later Roman Empire: Eunapius, Olympiodorus, Priscus and Malchus*, 2 vols. (Liverpool: 1981–3).

John Lydus, *De Magistratibus Populi Romani*, ed. and trans. A. C. Bandy (Phila.: 1983).

John Malalas, *Chronicon*, trans. E. Jeffreys, M. Jeffreys, R. Scott *et al.* (Melbourne: 1986).

Jordanes, *Gothic History*, trans. C. C. Mierow (New York: 1915, repr. 1960).

——*Jordanis de Origine Actibus Getarum (Getica)*, ed. Th. Mommsen, *MGHAA* v (1): 53–138 (1882).

——*Jordanis de Summa Temporum vel Origine Actibus Gentis Romanorum (Romana)*, ed. Th. Mommsen, *MGHAA* v (1): 1–52 (1882).

Laterculus Imperatorum ad Justinum I, ed. Th. Mommsen, *MGHAA* xiii, *Chronica Minora*, iii: 418–23 (1889).

Laterculus Polemii Silvii, ed. O. Seeck, in his *Notitia Dignitatum*, 254–60 (Berlin: 1876, repr. Frankfurt am Main: 1962).

Laterculus Veronensis, ed. O. Seeck, in his *Notitia Dignitatum*, 248–53 (Berlin: 1876, repr. Frankfurt am Main: 1962).

Leo (Pope), *Epistolae*, trans. C. Lett Feltoe, *The Letters and Sermons of Leo the Great, Bishop of Rome* (Oxford/New York: 1895).

Liber Historiae Francorum, ed. M. Bouquet, *Recueil des historiens des Gaules et de la France*, ii: 542–72 (Paris: 1869).

Liber Historiae Francorum, ed. B. Krusch, *MGHSRM* ii: 215–328 (1888).

Liber Pontificalis, trans. R. Davies, *The Book of the Pontiffs (Liber Pontificalis): The Ancient Biographies of the First Ninety Bishops to AD 715* (Liverpool: 1989).

Malchus, *Fragmenta*, ed. and trans. R. C. Blockley, in *The Fragmentary Classicising Historians of the Later Roman Empire: Eunapius, Olympiodorus, Priscus and Malchus*, 2 vols. (Liverpool: 1981–3).

Marcellinus (*comes*), *Chronicon*, ed. Th. Mommsen, *MGHAA* xi, *Chronica Minora*, ii: 60–104 (1894).

Marius (of Avenches), *Chronica a. 455–581*, ed. Th. Mommsen, *MGHAA* xi, *Chronica Minora*, ii: 225–39 (1894).

Menander (Protector), *Historikon Syngramma*, trans. R. C. Blockley, *The History of Menander the Guardsman* (Liverpool: 1985).

Merobaudes, *Carmina Fragmenta*, ed. and trans. F. M. Clover, 'Flavius Merobaudes: A Translation and Historical Commentary', *Transactions of the American Philological Society*, 61 (1971), 1–78.

Nennius, *Historia Brittonum*, ed. Th. Mommsen, *MGHAA* xiii, *Chronica Minora*, iii: 111–222 (1898).

Nicephorus (Callistus), *Historia Ecclesiastica*, ed. J.-P. Migne, *Patrologiae Cursus Completus: Series Graeca*, 145–7 (Paris: 1865).

Notitia Dignitatum, ed. O. Seeck (Berlin, 1876; repr. Frankfurt am Main: 1962).

Olympiodorus, *Fragmenta*, ed. and trans. R. C. Blockley, in *The Fragmentary Classicising Historians of the Later Roman Empire: Eunapius, Olympiodorus, Priscus and Malchus*, 2 vols. (Liverpool: 1981–3).

Oracle of Baalbek: The Tiburtine Sibyl in Greek Dress, ed. P. J. Alexander (Washington, DC: 1967).

Origio Gentis Langobardorum, ed. G. Waitz, *MGH Scriptores Rerum Langobardicarum et Italicarum*, 1–6 (Hannover: 1964).

Orosius (Paul), *Historiarum Adversum Paganos*, trans. R. J. Deferrari, *The Seven Books of History against the Pagans* (Washington, DC: 1964).

Panegyrici Latini, ed. and trans. E. Galletier, *Panegyriques Latins*, 3 vols. (Paris: 1949–55).

Paschale Campanum (Consularia Italica), ed. Th. Mommsen, *MGHAA* ix, *Chronica Minora*, ii: 305–34 (1892).

Paul (the Deacon), *Historia Langobardorum*, ed. L. Bethmann and G. Waitz, *MGH Scriptores Rerum Langobardicarum et Italicarum*, 12–187 (Hannover: 1878).

——*Historia Romana*, ed. H. Droysen, *MGHAA* ii: 4–224 (1879).

——*Historia Romana*, ed. A. Crivellucci, *Fonti per la storia d'Italia*, li (Rome: 1914).

Paulinus (of Perigueux), *De Vita Sancti Martini, Pat. Lat.* lxi: 1009–72.

Philostorgius, *Historia Ecclesiastica*, ed. J. Bidez, *Die griechischen christlichen Schriftsteller der ersten drei Jahrhundert*, xxi (Leipzig: 1913).

Photius, *Bibliotheca*, ed. and trans. R. Henry, 9 vols. (Paris: 1959–71).

Priscus, *Fragmenta*, ed. and trans. R. C. Blockley, *The Fragmentary Classicising Historians of the Later Roman Empire: Eunapius, Olympiodorus, Priscus and Malchus*, 2 vols. (Liverpool: 1981–3).

Procopius, *The History of the Wars*, ed. and trans. H. B. Dewing, 7 vols. (London/Cambridge, Mass.: 1914–40).

Prosper, *Epitoma Chronicon*, ed. Th. Mommsen, *MGHAA* ix, *Chronica Minora*, i: 341–499 (1892).

Ravennatis anonymi, *Cosmographia*, ed. M. Pinder and G. Parthey (Berlin: 1860).

Remigius (of Reims), *Epistola ad Chlodoveum, Epistolae Austrasicae*, ii, ed. W. Gundlach, *MGH Epistolae Merowingici et Karolini*, iii: 113 (Berlin: 1892).

Sidonius Apollinaris, *Poems and Letters*, ed. and trans. W. B. Anderson, 2 vols. (London/Cambridge, Mass.: 1936–65).

Sixtus III Papa, *Epistolae et Decreta, Pat. Lat* l: 581–618.

Socrates Scholasticus, *Historia Ecclesiastica*, trans. anon., *The History of the Church*, Bohn's Ecclesiastical Library (London: 1884).

Sozomen, *Historia Ecclesiastica*, ed. J. Bidez and G. C. Hansen (Berlin: 1960).

Suda *(Suidas)*, ed. A. Adler, 2 vols. (Leipzig, 1928–38).

Theodorus (Lector), *Epitome Historiae Ecclesiasticae*, ed. G. C. Hansen (Berlin: 1971).

Theophanes, *Chronographia*, ed. B. G. Niebuhr, *Corpus Scriptorum Historiae Byzantinae*, 2 vols. (Bonn: 1839–41).

——*Chronographia, The Chronicle of Theophanes Confessor: Byzantine and Near Eastern History, AD 284–813*, trans. with comm. C. A. Mango and R. Scott (Oxford: 1997).

Vegetius, *Epitoma Rei Militaris*, ed. K. Lang (Leipzig: 1885).

Venantius Fortunatus, *Opera Poetica*, ed. F. Leo, *MGHAA* iv (1) (1881).

Victor (of Tunnunna), *Chronica a. 444–567*, ed. Th. Mommsen, *MGHAA* xi, *Chronica Minora*, ii: 163–206 (1894).

Victor (of Vita), *Historia Persecutionis Africanae Provinciae*, trans. J. Moorhead (Liverpool: 1992).

Vita Aniani Episcopus Aurelianensis, ed. B. Krusch, *MGHSRM* iii: 104–17 (1896).

Vita Aretini, AASS i: 484–5.

Vita Bibiani (Viviani) Episcopi Santonensis, ed. B. Krusch, *MGHSRM* iii: 92–100 (1896).

Vita Dalmatii episcopi Ruteni, ed. B. Krusch, *MGHSRM* iii (Hannover: 1896).

Vita Danielis Stylitae, trans. E. A. S. Dawes and N. H. Baynes, in *Three Byzantine Saints* (Oxford: 1948).

Vita Euspicii Confessore, AASS v: 72–6.

Vita Genovefae Virginis Parisiensis, ed. B. Krusch, *MGHSRM* iii: 204–38 (1896).

Vita S. Lupicini, ed. B. Krusch, *MGHSRM* iii: 143–53 (1896).

318   Bibliography

Zonaras, *Epitome Historiarum*, ed. (in the vita patrum Jurensium) M. E. Pinder and Th. Büttner-Wobst, 3 vols. (Bonn: 1841–97).

Zosimus, *Historia Nova*, trans. R. T. Ridley (Canberra: 1982).

MODERN WORKS

Alexander, P. J. (1967), *The Oracle of Baalbek: The Tiburtine Sibyl in Greek Dress* (Washington, DC).

Alföldy, G. (1974), *Noricum*, trans. A. Birley (London).

Allen, P. (1981), *Evagrius Scholasticus: The Church Historian* (Louvain).

Amory, P. (1997), *People and Identity in Ostrogothic Italy, 489–554* (Cambridge).

Ancièn, B., and Truffeau-Libre, M. (1980), *Soissons Gallo-Romaine: Découvertes anciennes et récentes* (Soissons).

Applebaum, S. (1964), 'The Late Gallo-Roman Rural Pattern in the Light of the Carolingian Cartularies', *Latomus*, 23: 774–87.

Armellini, M. (1942), *Le chiese di Roma dal secolo IV al XIX*, new edn. by C. Cecchelli, 2 vols. (Rome).

Athanassiadi, P. (1993), 'Persecution and Response in Late Paganism: The Evidence of Damascius', *Journal of Hellenic Studies*, 113: 1–29.

Bachrach, B. S. (1967), 'The Alans in Gaul', *Traditio*, 23: 476–89.

——(1968), 'A Note on Alites', *Byzantinische Zeitschrift*, 61: 35.

——(1970), 'Procopius and the Chronology of Clovis' Reign', *Viator*, 1: 21–31.

——(1972), *Merovingian Military Organisation, 481–751* (Minn.).

——(1973), *A History of the Alans in the West* (Minn.).

Bagnall, R. S. *et al.* (1987), *Consuls of the Later Roman Empire* (Atlanta, Ga.).

Barker, E. (1911), 'Italy and the West 410–476', in H. M. Gwatkin and J. P. Whitney (eds.), *Cambridge Medieval History*, i. *The Christian Roman Empire and the Foundation of the Teutonic Kingdoms* (Cambridge), 392–432.

Barnes, T. D. (1975), '*Patricii* under Valentinian III', *Phoenix*, 29: 155–70.

——(1983), 'Late Roman Prosopography: Between Theodosius and Justinian', *Phoenix*, 37: 248–70.

Barnish, S. J. B. (1986), 'Taxation, Land and Barbarian Settlement in the Western Empire', *Papers of the British School at Rome*, 54: 170–95.

——(1988), 'Transformation and Survival in the Western Senatorial Aristocracy *c.* AD 400–700', *Papers of the British School at Rome*, 56: 120–55.

Barnwell, P. S. (1992), *Emperor, Prefects and Kings: The Roman West 395–565* (London).

Bass, G. F. (1972), *A History of Seafaring, based on Underwater Archaeology* (London).

Bayless, W. N. (1976), 'Anti-Germanism in the Age of Stilicho', *Byzantine Studies/Études Byzantines*, 3 (2): 70–6.

Baynes, N. H. (1922), 'A Note on Professor Bury's "History of the Later Roman Empire" ', *Journal of Roman Studies*, 12: 207–29.

——(1929), Review of *La Fin du Monde Antique et le début du Moyen Age*, by F. Lot, *Les Villes du Moyen Age, essai d'histoire économique et sociale*, by H. Pirenne, and *The Social and Economic History of the Roman Empire*, by M. Rostovtzeff, in *Journal of Roman Studies*, 19: 224–35.

——(1955), *Byzantine Studies and Other Essays* (London).

Bloch, M. L. B. (1963), *Mélanges historiques*, 2 vols. (Paris).

——(1966), *French Rural History: An Essay on its Basic Characteristics*, trans. J. Sondheimer (London).

Blockley, R. C. (1981–3), *The Fragmentary Classicising Historians of the Later Roman Empire: Eunapius, Olympiodorus, Priscus and Malchus*, 2 vols. (Liverpool).

——(1992), *East-Roman Foreign Policy: Formation and Conduct from Diocletian to Anastasius* (Leeds).

Böhme, H.-W. (1974), *Germanische Grabfunde des 4 bis 5 Jahrhunderts zwischen unterer Elbe und Loire: Studien zur Chronologie und Bevölkerungsgeschichte* (Munich).

Braudel, F. (1988–90), *The Identity of France*, 2 vols., trans. S. Reynolds (New York).

Breebaart, A. B. (1984), 'Aspects of the Divorce between East and West in the Fourth Century', *Proceedings of the VIIth Congress of the International Federation of Societies of Classical Studies*, 2: 9–22.

British Museum (1922), *A Guide to the Antiquities of Roman Britain* (London).

Bulletino di archaelogia et stočia dalmata, 33 (1910), ed. Fra. X. Bulic.

Bullough, D. A. (1966), 'Urban Change in Early Medieval Italy: the Example of Pavia', *Papers of the British School at Rome*, 34: 82–130.

Burgess, R. W. (1987), 'The Third Regnal Year of Eparchius Avitus: A Reply', *Classical Philology*, 82: 335–45.

——(1992), 'From *Gallia Romana* to *Gallia Gothica*: The View from Spain', in J. F. Drinkwater and H. Elton (eds.), *Fifth-Century Gaul: A Crisis of Identity?* (Cambridge), 19–27.

——(1993), *The Chronicle of Hydatius and the Consularia Constantinopolitana* (Oxford).

Burns, T. S. (1984), *A History of the Ostrogoths* (Bloomington, Ind.).

Bury, J. B. (1886), 'A Note on the Emperor Olybrius', *English Historical Review*, 1: 507–9.

——(1923), *History of the Later Roman Empire, from the Death of Theodosius I to the Death of Justinian*, 2 vols. (London).

Cagiano de Azevedo, M. (1977), 'Northern Italy', in M. W. Barley (ed.), *European Towns: Their Archaeology and Early History* (London), 475–85.

Cambi, N. (1994), 'The Age of Justinian in Croatia', paper given to the Thirteenth International Conference of Early Christian Archaeology, Split/Salona (unpublished).

Cameron, A. D. E. (1970), *Claudian: Poetry and Propaganda at the Court of Honorius* (Oxford).

——(1982), 'Empress and Poet', *Yale Classical Studies*, 27: 217–89.

Cameron, A. M. (1985), *Procopius and the Sixth Century* (London).

Cantarelli, L. (1888–9), 'Intorno ad alcuni prefetti di Roma della serie corsiniana', *Bulletino della commissione archeologica communale di Roma*, 16: 189–203.

Carson, R. A. G., and Kent, J. P. C. (1960), *Late Roman Bronze Coinage A D 324–498* (London).

——(1994), *The Roman Imperial Coinage, x. The Divided Empire and the Fall of the Western Parts A D 395–491* (London).

Casson, L. (1971), *Ships and Seamanship in the Ancient World* (Princeton, NJ).

——(1991), *The Ancient Mariner: Seafarers and Sea Fighters of the Mediterranean in Ancient Times*, 2nd edn. (Princeton, NJ).

——(1994), *Ships and Seafaring in Ancient Times* (London).

Chastagnol, A. (1966), *Le Sénat Romain sous le règne d'Odoacre* (Bonn).

Christie, N. (1991*a*), 'Urban Defence in Later Roman Italy', in E. Herring, R. Whitehouse, and J. Wilkins (eds.), *Papers of the Fourth Conference of Italian Archaeology*, iv (2), *The Archaeology of Power* (London), 185–99.

——(1991*b*), 'The Alps as a Frontier', *Journal of Roman Archaeology*, 4: 410–30.

——(1993), 'Milan as Imperial Capital, and its Hinterland. (Review of *Milano, Capitale dell'impero Romano, 286–402 D.C.* catalogue exhibition Milan Palazzo Reale, 1990)', *Journal of Roman Archaeology*, 6: 485–7.

Christie, N., and Gibson, S. (1988), 'The City Walls of Ravenna', *Papers of the British School at Rome*, 56: 156–97.

Christie, N., and Rushworth, A. (1988), 'Urban Fortification and Strategy in Fifth and Sixth Century Italy: The Case of Terracina', *Journal of Roman Archaeology*, 1: 73–87.

Chuvin, P. (1990), *The Last Pagans*, trans. B. A. Archer (Cambridge, Mass./London).

Clairmont, C. W., Auth, S. H., and von Gonzenbach, V. (1975), *Excavations at Salona, Yugoslavia, 1969–72* (Park Ridge, NJ).

Clover, F. M. (1971), 'Flavius Merobaudes: A Translation and Historical Commentary', *Transactions of the American Philosophical Society*, 61: 1–78.

——(1978), 'The Family and Early Career of Anicius Olybrius', *Historia*, 27: 169–96.

Collins, R. (1991), *Early Medieval Europe, 300–1000* (Basingstoke).

——(1996), 'Fredegar', in R. Collins and C. Straw, *Authors of the Middle Ages: Historical and Religious Writers of the Latin West*, iv (12–13), *Gregory the Great and Fredegar* (Aldershot).

Courtois, C. (1951), 'Auteurs et scribes, remarques sur la Chronique d'Hydace', *Byzantion*, 21: 23–54.

——(1955), *Les Vandales et l'Afrique* (Paris).

Croke, B. (1983), 'AD 476: The Manufacture of a Turning Point', *Chiron*, 13: 81–119.

Croke, B., Jeffreys, E. M., and Scott, R. (1990), *Studies in John Malalas* (Sydney).

Daly, W. M. (1994), 'Clovis: How Barbaric, How Pagan?', *Speculum*, 69 (3–4), 619–64.

Daniel, P., and Heijmans, M. (1992), 'Le Pont romaine d'Arles', *Bulletin Archéologique de Provence*, 21: 97–9.

Demandt, A. (1970), 'Magister Militum', *RE* supp. xii: 553–790 (Stuttgart).

——(1980), 'Der spätrömische Militäradel', *Chiron*, 10: 609–36.

——(1989), *Die Spätantike: römische Geschichte von Diocletian bis Justinian, 284–565 n. Chr.* (Munich).

Demo, Ž. (1988), 'The Mint in Salona: Nepos and Ovida (474–481/2)', in *Studia Numismatica Labacensia Alexandro Jeločnik Oblata Situla*, 26, ed. P. Kos and Ž. Demo, 247–67.

——(1969–79), *La Formation de l'Europe et les invasions barbares* ii. *Le Ve siècle* (Paris).

Demougeot, E. (1951), *De l'Unité à la division de l'empire Romain, 395–410, essai sur le gouvernement impérial* (Paris).

Demouy, P. (1997), *Petite vie de saint Remi* (Paris).

Dill, S. (1926), *Roman Society in Gaul in the Merovingian Age* (London).

Drinkwater, J. F. (1984), 'Peasants and Bagaudae in Roman Gaul', *Classical Views*, 3: 349–71.

—— (1992), 'The Bacaudae of Fifth-Century Gaul', in J. F. Drink-water and H. Elton (eds.), *Fifth-Century Gaul: A Crisis of Identity?* (Cambridge), 208–17.

Dubos, L'Abbé (1734), *Histoire critique de l'établissement de la monarchie francois dans les Gaules*, 3 vols. (Amsterdam).

Duchesne, L. (1894–1915), *Fastes épiscopaux de l'ancienne Gaule*, 3 vols. (Paris).

Duncan, G. L. (1993), 'Coin Circulation in the Danubian and Balkan Provinces of the Roman Empire AD 294–578', *Royal Numismatic Society*, 26 (London).

Dyggve, E. (1951), *History of Salonitan Christianity*, Instituttet for Sammenlignende Kulturforskning (Serie A: Forelesninger), xxi (Oslo).

Elton, H. W. (1990), *Aspects of Defence in Roman Europe, AD 350–500* (Univ. of Oxford D.Phil. thesis).

—— (1992), 'Defence in Fifth-Century Gaul', in J. F. Drinkwater and H. Elton (eds.), *Fifth-Century Gaul: A Crisis of Identity?* (Cambridge), 167–76.

—— (1996), *Warfare in Roman Europe, 350–425* (Oxford).

Ensslin, W. (1925), 'Leo (4)', *RE* xii: 1947–61 (Stuttgart).

—— (1930), 'Maiorianus (1)', *RE* xiv: 584–9 (Stuttgart).

—— (1931), 'Zum Heermeisteramt des spätrömischen Reiches', *Klio*, 24: 102–47, 467–502.

Esmonde-Cleary, A. S., 'The Collapse of a Super-Power: Archaeology and the End of the Roman West', lecture to the Society for the Promotion of Roman Studies, Jan. 1991.

Fanning, S. (1992), 'Emperors and Empires in Fifth-Century Gaul', in J. F. Drinkwater and H. Elton (eds.), *Fifth-Century Gaul: A Crisis of Identity?* (Cambridge), 288–97.

Ferril, A. (1986), *The Fall of the Roman Empire: The Military Explanation* (London).

Friedlaender, J. (1849), *Die Münzen der Vandalen* (Leipzig/Berlin).

—— (1882), 'Die Erwerbungen des Munzkabinets in Jahre 1880', *Zeitschrift für Numismatik*, ix 1–10.

Frye, D. (1990), 'Gundobad, the *Leges Burgundionum* and the Struggle for Sovereignty in Burgundy', *Classica et Mediaevalia*, 41: 199–212.

—— (1992), 'Aegidius, Childeric, Odovacer, and Paul', *Nottingham Medieval Studies*, 36: 1–14.

Galliou, P., and Jones, M. C. E. (1991), *The Bretons* (Oxford).

Gams, P. B. (1886), *Series Episcoporum Ecclesiae Catholicae*, revised edn. 2 vols. (Stuttgart 1982–4).

Gautier, E.-F. (1932), *Genséric, roi des Vandales* (Paris).

Gerberding, R. A. (1987), *The Rise of the Carolingians and the Liber Historiae Francorum* (Oxford).

Gibbon, E. (1897–1900), *The History of the Decline and Fall of the Roman Empire*, ed. J. B. Bury, 7 vols. (London).

Goffart, W. (1980), *Barbarians and Romans, A.D. 418–584: The Techniques of Accommodation* (Princeton, NJ).

—— (1987), 'From *Historiae* to *Historia Francorum* and Back Again: Aspects of the Textual History of Gregory of Tours', in T. F. X. Noble and J. J. Contreni (eds.), *Religion, Culture, and Society in the Early Middle Ages: Studies in Honor of Richard E. Sullivan* (Kalamazoo, Mich.), 55–76.

—— (1988), *The Narrators of Barbarian History A.D. 550–800: Jordanes, Gregory of Tours, Bede, and Paul the Deacon* (Princeton, NJ).

—— (1989), *Rome's Fall and After* (London).

Gordon, C. D. (1960), *The Age of Attila: Fifth-Century Byzantium and the Barbarians* (Ann Arbor, Mich.).

Greene, K. (1986), *The Archaeology of the Roman Economy* (London).

Grierson, P., and Blackburn, M. A. S. (1986), *Medieval European Coinage*, i. *The Early Middle Ages (The Fifth Century to the Tenth Century)* (Cambridge).

Griffe, E. (1964–6), *La Gaule chrétienne à l'époque romaine*, 2nd edn. 3 vols. (Paris).

Halsall, G. (1992), 'The Origins of the Reihengräberzivilisation: Forty Years On', in J. F. Drinkwater and H. Elton (eds.), *Fifth-Century Gaul: A Crisis of Identity?* (Cambridge), 196–207.

Harries, J. D. (1994), *Sidonius Apollinaris and the Fall of Rome AD 407–485* (Oxford).

Haywood, J. (1999), *Dark-Age Naval Power: A Reassessment of Frankish and Anglo-Saxon Seafaring Activity*, 2nd edn. (London).

Heather, P. J. (1991), *Goths and Romans 332–489* (Oxford).

—— (1995), 'The Huns and the End of the Roman Empire in Western Europe', *The English Historical Review*, 110: 4–41.

Heinzelmann, M. (1982), 'Gallische Prospographie (260–527)', *Francia*, 10: 531–43.

—— and Poulin, J. C. (1986), *Les Vies anciennes de sainte Geneviève de Paris: études critiques* (Paris).

Hendy, M. F. (1985), *Studies in the Byzantine Monetary Economy, c.300–1450* (Cambridge).

—— (1988), 'From Public to Private: The Western Barbarian Coinages as a Mirror of the Disintegration of Late Roman State Structures', *Viator*, 19: 29–78.

Hillgarth, J. N. (ed.) (1969), *The Conversion of Western Europe, 350–750* (Englewood Cliffs, NJ).

324 *Bibliography*

——(1986), *Christianity and Paganism, 350–750*, 2nd edn. (Phila., Penn.).

Hodges, R., and Whitehouse, D. (1983), *Mohammed, Charlemagne, and the Origins of Europe: Archaeology and the Pirenne Theory*, (London).

Hodgkin, T. (1880a), *Italy and her Invaders*, i. *376–476: The Visigothic Invasion* (Oxford).

——(1880b), *Italy and her Invaders*, ii. *376–476: The Hunnish Invasion; The Vandal Invasion and the Herulian Mutiny* (Oxford).

——(1885), *Italy and her Invaders*, iii. *476–535: The Ostrogothic Invasion* (Oxford).

Jacobs, A. (1858), *Géographie de Grégoire de Tours, le pagus et l'administration en Gaule* (Paris).

James, E. (1979), 'Cemeteries and the Problem of Frankish Settlement', in Sawyer P. (eds.) *Names, Words, and Graves* (Leeds), 35–89.

——(1982), *The Origins of France: From Clovis to the Capetians, 500–1000* (London).

——(1988), *The Franks* (Oxford).

——(1989), 'The Origins of Barbarian Kingdoms: The Continental Evidence', in S. Bassett (ed.), *The Origins of Anglo-Saxon Kingdoms* (London), 40–52.

Jannet-Vallat, M., Lauxerois, R., and Reynaud, J.-F. (1986), *Vienne (Isère) aux premiers temps chrétiens (Guides archéologiques de la France* xi) (Paris).

Jeffreys, E., Croke, B., and Scott, R. (1990), *Studies in John Malalas* (Sydney).

Johnson, S. (1980), *Later Roman Britain* (London).

Jones, A. H. M. (1962), 'The Constitutional Position of Odoacer and Theoderic', *Journal of Roman Studies*, 52: 126–30.

——(1964), *The Later Roman Empire, 284–602: A Social, Economic and Administrative Survey*, 3 vols. (Oxford).

Jones, A. H. M., Grierson, P., and Crook, J. A. (1957), 'The Authenticity of the Testamentum S. Remigii', *Revue belge de philologie et d'histoire*, 35: 356–73.

Jones, A. H. M., Martindale, J. R., and Morris, J. (1971), *The Prosopography of the Later Roman Empire*, i. *A.D. 260–395* (Cambridge).

Kaegi, W. E., jn. (1968), *Byzantium and the Decline of Rome* (Princeton, NJ).

Kaiser, R. (1973), *Untersuchungen zur Geschichte der Civitas und Diözese Soissons in römischer und merowingischer Zeit* (Bonn).

Kazhdan, A. P., *et al.* (eds.) (1991), *The Oxford Dictionary of Byzantium* (Oxford).

Kelly, J. N. D. (1975), *Jerome: His Life, Writings and Controversies* (London).

Kent, J. P. C. (1966), 'Julius Nepos and the Fall of the Western Empire', in *Corolla Memoriae Erich Swoboda Dedicata* (Graz/Cologne), 146–50.

——(1994), *The Roman Imperial Coinage*, x. *The Divided Empire and the Fall of the Western Parts, AD 395–491* (London).

King, A. (1990), *Roman Gaul and Germany* (London).

King, C. E. (1988), 'Fifth-Century Silver Issues in Gaul', in P. Kos and Ž. Demo (eds.), *Studia Numismatica Labacensia: Alexandro Jeločnik Oblata*, Situla 26 (Ljubljana), 197–212.

——(1992), 'Roman, Local and Barbarian Coinages in Fifth-Century Gaul', in J. F. Drinkwater and H. Elton (eds.), *Fifth-Century Gaul: A Crisis of Identity?* (Cambridge), 184–95.

Kirgan, B. (1994), 'The Late Roman Period on Vis Archipeligo: The Archaeological Evidence', paper given to the Thirteenth International Conference of Early Christian Archaeology, Split/Salona (unpublished).

Krautheimer, R. (1937), *Corpus basilicarum christianarum Romae: Le basiliche cristiane antiche di Roma (sec. IV–IX)*, i. (Rome).

——(1980), *Rome: Profile of a City, 312–1308* (Princeton, NJ).

Krautschick, S. (1986), 'Zwei Aspekte des Jahres 476', *Historia*, 35: 344–71.

Kurth, G. (1893), *Histoire poétique des Mérovingiens* (Paris).

——(1923), *Clovis*, 3rd edn., 2 vols. (Paris).

Lacam, G. (1983), *La Fin de l'empire romain et le monnayage or en Italie 455–493*, 2 vols. (Lucerne).

——(1986), *Ricimer, Leon et Anthemius: le monnayage de Ricimer* (Nice).

——(1988), 'Le Monnayage de Ricimer', in P. Kos and Ž. Demo (eds.), *Studia Numismatica Labacensia: Alexandro Jeločnik Oblata*, Situla 26 (Ljubljana), 219–46.

Latouche, R. (1968), *Caesar to Charlemagne: The Beginnings of France*, trans. J. Nicholson (first pub. as *Gaulois et Francs* (1965)) (London).

Legoux, R. (1993), 'Le Cadre chronologique de Picardie: son application aux autres régions en vue d'une chronologie unifiée et son extension vers le Romain Tardif', *Bulletin de liaison (Association Française d'archéologie Mérovingienne)*, 17: 44.

Lewis, A. R. (1951), *Naval Power and Trade in the Mediterranean, A.D. 500–1100* (Princeton, NJ).

——(1958), *The Northern Seas: Shipping and Commerce in Northern Europe A.D. 300–1100* (Princeton, NJ).

Lewis, A. R., and Runyan, T. J. (1985), *European Naval and Maritime History, 300–1500* (Bloomington, Ind.).

Liebeschuetz, J. H. W. G. (1990), 'Generals, Federates and *Bucellarii* in Roman Armies around A.D. 400', in his *From Diocletian to the Arab Conquest: Change in the Late Roman Empire* (Aldershot), first pub. in *The Defence of the Roman and Byzantine East: Proceedings of a Colloquium held at the University of Sheffield in April 1986*, ed. P. Freeman and D. Kennedy, ii (Oxford, 1986), 463–74.

——(1990), *Barbarians and Bishops: Army, Church, and State in the Age of Arcadius and Chrysostom* (Oxford).

——(1993), 'The End of the Roman Army in the West', in J. Rich and G. Shipley (eds.), *War and Society in the Roman World*, Leicester–Nottingham Studies in Ancient Society, v (London), 265–75.

Longnon, A. (1878), *Géographie de la Gaule au VIe siècle* (Paris).

——(1885–9), *Atlas historique de la France: depuis César jusqu'à nos jours* (Paris).

Lot, F. (1915), 'Les Migrations Saxonnes en Gaule et en Grande-Bretagne du IIIe au Ve siècle', *Revue historique*, 119: 1–40.

——(1930), 'La Conquête du pays d'entre Seine-et-Loire par les francs: la ligue armoricaine et les destinées du Duché du Maine', *Revue historique*, 164/5: 241–53.

Loyen, A. (1942), *Recherches historiques sur les panégyriques de Sidoine Apollinaire* (Paris).

Luzatto, G. (1961), *An Economic History of Italy*, trans. P. Jones (London).

Macadam, A. (1979), *Rome and Environs: Blue Guide*, 2nd. edn. (London).

MacBain, B. (1983), 'Odovacer the Hun?', *Classical Philology*, 78: 323–7.

McDermott, W. C. (1949), *Gregory of Tours: Selections from the Minor Works* (Phila., Penn.).

MacMullen, R. (1966), *Enemies of the Roman Order: Treason, Unrest, and Alienation in the Empire* (Cambridge, Mass.).

McNally, S. (1975), 'Diocletian's Palace: Split in the Middle Ages', *Archaeology*, 28: 248–59.

McNally, S., Marasovič, J., and Marasovič, T. (eds.) (1972–89), *Diocletian's Palace: Site Reports of the American–Yugoslavian Joint Excavations*, 6 vols. (Split).

McNamara, J. A., Halborg, J. E., and Whatley, E. G. (1992), *Sainted Women of the Dark Ages* (Durham, NC/London).

Maenchen-Helfen, O. J. (1946–7) (untitled reply to Reynolds and Lopez), *American Historical Review*, 52 (1): 836–41.

Maenchen-Helfen, O. J. (1973), *The World of the Huns: Studies in their History and Culture* (Berkeley, Ca./London).

Mann, J. C. (1979), 'Power, Force and the Frontiers of the Empire', *Journal of Roman Studies*, 69: 175–83.

Marasović, T. (1982), *Diocletian's Palace*, trans. S. Wild-Bičanić (Beograd).

Marin, J.-Y. (1990), *Attila: les influences danubiennes dans l'ouest de l'Europe au Ve siècle* (Caen).

Martin, M.-M. (1951), *The Making of France: The Origins and Development of the Idea of National Unity*, trans. B. and R. North (London).

Martindale, J. R. (1980), *The Prosopography of the Later Roman Empire*, ii. AD 395–527 (Cambridge).

Martine, F. (1968), *Vie des Pères du Jura* (*Sources chrétiennes*, cxlii) (Paris).

Martroye, F. (1907), *Genséric: la conquête vandale en Afrique et la destruction de l'Empire d'Occident* (Paris).

Mathisen, R. W. (1979), 'Resistance and Reconciliation, Majorian and the Gallic Aristocracy after the Fall of Avitus', *Francia*, 7: 597–627.

—— (1981), 'Avitus, Italy and the East in A.D. 455–456', *Byzantion*, 51: 232–47.

—— (1985), 'The Third Regnal Year of Eparchius Avitus', *Classical Philology*, 80: 326–35.

—— (1989), *Ecclesiastical Factionalism and Religious Controversy in Fifth-Century Gaul* (Washington, DC).

—— (1991), *Studies in the History, Literature and Society of Late Antiquity* (Amsterdam).

—— (1993), *Roman Aristocrats in Barbarian Gaul: Strategies for Survival in an Age of Transition* (Austin, Tex.).

Matthews, J. F. (1975), *Western Aristocracies and Imperial Court, 364–425* (Oxford).

—— (1985), *Political Life and Culture in Late Roman Society* (London).

Max, G. E. (1979), 'Political Intrigue during the Reigns of the Western Roman Emperors Avitus and Majorian', *Historia*, 28: 225–37.

Mazzarino, S. (1942), *Stilicone: La crisi imperiale dopo Teodosio* (Rome).

Meyer, H. (1969), 'Der Regierungsantritt Kaiser Majorians', *Byzantinische Zeitschrift*, 62: 5–12.

Miller, D. H. (1996), 'Frontier Societies and the Transition between Late Antiquity and the Early Middle Ages', in R. W. Mathisen and H. S. Sivan (eds.), *Shifting Frontiers in Late Antiquity* (Aldershot), 158–71.

Mommsen, Th. (1906–9), *Gesammelte Schriften, vi–vii. Philologische Schriften* (Berlin).

Moorhead, J. (1992), *Theoderic in Italy* (Oxford).

Morrison, J., and Williams, T. R. (1968), *Greek Oared Ships, 900–322 B.C.* (Cambridge).

Móscy, A. (1974), *Pannonia and Upper Moesia: A History of the Middle Danube Provinces of the Roman Empire*, trans. S. Frere (London).

Moss, H. St. L. B. (1935), *The Birth of the Middle Ages, 395–814* (Oxford).

Moss, J. R. (1973), 'The Effects of the Policies of Aetius on the History of Western Europe', *Historia*, 22: 711–31.

Muhlburger, S. (1984), 'Heroic Kings and Unruly Generals: The "Copenhagen Continuation" to Prosper Reconsidered', *Florilegium*, 6: 50–95.

——(1990), *The Fifth-Century Chroniclers: Prosper, Hydatius and the Gallic Chronicler of 452* (Leeds).

Muntz, E. (1886), 'The Lost Mosaics of Rome', *American Journal of Archaeology*, 2: 295–313.

Muratori, L. A. (1739), *Novus Thesaurus Veterum Inscriptionum Collectore L. A. Muratorio*, iii (Milan).

Musset, L. (1995), *The Germanic Invasions: The Making of Europe AD 400–600*, 2nd edn., trans. E. and C. James (first pub. as *Les Invasions: Les Vagues Germaniques* (1965)) (London).

Myers, J. N. L. (1986), *The English Settlements* (Oxford).

Nagy, T. (1967), 'Reoccupation of Pannonia from the Huns in 427: Did Jordanes Use the Chronicon of Marcellinus *Comes* at the Writing of the Getica?', *AA* xv: 159–86.

O'Donnell, J. J. (1979), *Cassiodorus* (Berkeley, Calif.).

O'Flynn, J. M. (1983), *Generalissimos of the Western Roman Empire* (Edmonton Alta., Canada).

Oost, S. I. (1968), *Galla Placidia Augusta: A Biographical Essay* (Chicago, Ill.).

——(1970), 'D. N. Libivs Severvs P. F. Avg.', *Classical Philology*, 65: 228–40.

Orna-Ornstein, J. (1995), 'Money for Rome's Naval Secrets', *British Archaeology*, 1: 7.

Palanque, J.-R. (1944), 'Collégialité et partages dans l'empire romain aux IVe et Ve siècles', *Revue des études anciennes*, 46: 47–64, 280–98.

Papini, A. M. (1959), *Ricemero. L'agonia dell'Impero Romano d'Occidente* (Milan).

Pelletier, A. (1974), *Vienne gallo-romaine au Bas-Empire, 275–468 après J.-C.* (Lyons).

Bibliography 329

Pelletier, A. (1982), *Vienne antique: de la conquête romaine aux invasions alamanniques (IIe siècle avant IIIe siècle après J.-C.)* (Roanne).

Percival, J. (1976), *The Roman Villa: An Historical Introduction* (London).

——(1992), 'The Fifth-Century Villa: New Life or Death Postponed?', in J. F. Drinkwater and H. Elton (eds.), *Fifth-Century Gaul: A Crisis of Identity?* (Cambridge), 156–64.

Périn, P., and Feffer, L.-C. (1987), *Les Francs*, 2 vols.; i, P. Périn, *A la conquête de la Gaule*, and ii, L.-C. Feffer, *A l'origine de la France* (Paris).

Perrin, O. (1968), *Les Burgondes, leur histoire, des origines à la fin du premier royaume (534)* (Neuchâtel).

Pirenne, H. (1922), 'Mahomet et Charlemagne', *Revue belge de philologie et d'histoire*, 1: 77–86.

Potter, T. W. (1987), *Roman Italy* (London).

Praga, G. (1993), *History of Dalmatia* (first pub. as *Storia di Dalmazia* (Milan, 1981)) (Pisa).

Reynolds, R. L., and Lopez, R. S. (1946–7), 'Odoacer: German or Hun?', *American Historical Review*, 52: 36–53.

Richardson, L. (1992), *A New Topographical Dictionary of Ancient Rome* (Baltimore, Md: London).

Roblin, M. (1971), *Le Terroir de Paris aux époques gallo-romaine et franque: peuplement et défrichement dans la civitas des Parisii*, 2nd. edn. (Paris).

——(1978), *Le Terroir de l'Oise aux époques gallo-romaine et franque: peuplement, défrichement, environnement* (Paris).

Rouche, M. (1979), *L'Aquitaine des Wisigoths aux Arabes, 418–781: naissance d'une région* (Paris).

Rougé, J. (1961), 'Quelques aspects de la navigation en Méditerranée au Ve siècle et dans la première moitié du VIe siècle', *Cahiers d'histoire*, 6: 129–54.

Salway, P. (1981), *Roman Britain* (Oxford).

Schäferdiek, K. (1983), 'Remigius von Reims', *Zeitschrift für Kirchengeschichte*, 94: 256–78.

Schmidt, L. (1924), 'The Sueves, Alans and Vandals in Spain, 409–429. The Vandal Dominion in Africa 429–533', in H. M. Gwatkin and J. P. Whitney (eds.), *The Cambridge Medieval History*, 2nd edn., i. *The Christian Roman Empire and the Foundation of the Teutonic Kingdoms* (Cambridge), 304–322.

Schönfeld, M. (1965), *Wöterbuch de altgermanischen Personen-und Völkernamen*, 2nd edn. (Darmstadt).

Schwarcz, A. (1995), 'Senatorisch Heerführer im Westgotenreich im 5. Jh.', in F. Vallet and M. Kazanski (eds), *La Noblesse romaine et les chefs barbares du IIIe au VIIe siècle* (Paris).

Scott, L. R. (1976), 'Aspar and the Burden of Barbarian Heritage', *Byzantine Studies*, 3(2): 59–69.

——(1984), 'Antibarbarian Sentiment and the "Barbarian" General in Roman Imperial Service: The Case of Ricimer', *Proceedings of the VIIth Congress of the International Federation of the Societies of Classical Studies*, 2: 23–33.

Seeck, O. (1894), 'Aegidius', *RE* i: 476–7 (Stuttgart).

——(1919), *Regesten der Kaiser und Päpiste für die Jahre 311 bis 476 N. Chr.* (Stuttgart).

——(1920), *Geschichte des Untergangs der antiken Welt*, VI (Berlin).

Sivan, H. (1987), 'On Foederati, Hospitalitas, and the Settlement of the Goths in A.D. 418', *American Journal of Philology*, 108: 759–72.

Smith, W., and Wace, H. (1877–87), *A Dictionary of Christian Biography, Literature, Sects and Doctrines*, 4 vols. (London).

Solari, A. (1938), *Il Rinnovamento dell'impero romano* (Milan).

Stancliffe, C. (1983), *Saint Martin and his Hagiographer: History and Miracle in Sulpicius Severus* (Oxford).

Starr, C. G. (1941), *The Roman Imperial Navy 31 B.C.–A.D. 324* (New York).

——(1989), *The Influence of Sea-Power on Ancient History* (New York/Oxford).

Stein, E. (1914), 'Der Verzicht der Galla Placidia auf die Präfektur Illyricum', *Wiener Studien*, 36: 344–7.

——(1925), 'Untersuchungen zur spätrömischen Verwaltungsgeschichte', *Rheinisches Museum*, 74: 347–94.

——(1928), *Geschichte des spätrömischen Reiches*, i (Vienna).

——(1959), *Histoire du Bas-Empire*, i, trans. and ed. J.-R. Palanque, (Paris).

Steinby, E. M. (1933–9), *Lexicon Topographicum Urbis Romae*, 6 vols. (Rome).

Stevens, C. E. (1933), *Sidonius Apollinaris and his Age* (Oxford).

St-Michel, D. (1979), *Concordance de l'histoire de les Franks de Gregoire de Tours*, 2 vols. (Montreal).

Stroheker, K. F. (1948), *Der Senatorische Adel im spätantiken Gallien* (Tübingen).

Sundwall, J. (1915), *Weströmische Studien* (Berlin).

Tainter, J. A. (1988), *The Collapse of Complex Societies* (Cambridge).

Tessier, G. (1964), *Le Baptême de Clovis* (Paris).

Thévenin, M. (1887), *Textes relatifs aux institutions privées et publiques aux époques mérovingienne et carolinienne* (Paris).

Thierry, A. (1840), *Récits des temps mérovingiens* (Paris).

Thompson, E. A. (1982), *Romans and Barbarians: The Decline of the Western Empire* (Madison, Wis.).

Thompson, E. A. (1984), *Saint Germanus of Auxerre and the End of Roman Britain* (Woodbridge).

Todd, M. (1992), *The Early Germans* (Oxford).

Tomlin, R. (1981), 'The Later Empire AD 200–450', in P. Connolly (ed.), *Greece and Rome at War* (London).

——(1989), 'The Late-Roman Empire', in J. W. Hackett (ed.), *Warfare in the Ancient World* (London).

Treadgold, W. T. (1980), *The Nature of the Bibliotheca of Photius* (Washington, DC).

Twyman, B. L. (1970), 'Aetius and the Aristocracy', *Historia*, 19: 480–503.

Ulrich-Bansa, O. (1949), *Moneta Mediolanensis: 352–498* (Venice).

Van Dam, R. (1985), *Leadership and Community in Late Antique Gaul* (Berkeley, Calif.).

——(1986), 'Paulinus of Périgueux and Perpetuus of Tours', *Francia*, 14: 567–73.

Van Ossel, P. (1992), *Etablissements ruraux de l'antiquité tardive dans le nord de la Gaule* (*Gallia*, supp. 51) (Paris).

Varady, L. (1961), 'New Evidence on some Problems of Late Roman Military Organisation', *Acta Antiqua*, 9: 333–96.

Vasić, M. (1988), 'The Circulation of Bronze Coinage at the End of the Fourth and Beginning of the Fifth Centuries in Moesia Prima and Pannonia Secunda', in P. Kos and Ž. Demo (eds.), *Studia Numismatica Labacensia: Alexandro Jeločnik Oblata*, Situla 26 (Ljubljana), 165–84.

Vassili, L. (1936*a*), 'Il *comes* Agrippino collaboratore di Ricimero', *Athenaeum*, 14: 175–80.

——(1936*b*), 'La Figura di Nepoziano e l'opposizione ricimeriana al governo imperiale di Maggioriano', *Athenaeum*, 14: 56–66.

——(1936*c*), 'Nota cronologica intorno all'elezione di Maggioriano', *Rivista di filologia*, NS 14: 163–9.

——(1936*d*), 'La Strategia di Maggioriano nella spedizione gallico-vandalica', *Rivista di filologia*, NS 14: 296–9.

——(1938*a*), 'La Cultura di Antemio', *Athenaeum*, 16: 38–45.

——(1938*b*), *Il Rinnovamento dell'Impero Romano* (Milan).

——(1939), 'Oreste, ultimo esponente del tradizionalismo romano', *Rivista di filologia*, 17: 261–6.

Wace, H., and Piercy, W. C. (1911), *A Dictionary of Christian Biography and Literature to the End of the Sixth Century A.D.* (London).

Wallace-Hadrill, J. M. (1960), *The Fourth Book of the Chronicle of Fredegar* (London).

——(1962), *The Long-Haired Kings and other Studies in Frankish History* (London).

——(1983), *The Frankish Church* (Oxford).

Ward-Perkins, B. (1984), *From Classical Antiquity to the Middle Ages: Urban Public Building in Northern and Central Italy AD 300–850* (Oxford).

——(2000), 'Specialised Production and Exchange', in A. Cameron, B. Ward-Perkins, and M. Whitby (eds.), *Cambridge Ancient History*, xiv, new edn., 346–91 (Cambridge).

Wes, M. (1967), *Das Ende des Kaisertums im Westen des römischen Reichs* (The Hague).

Whittaker, C. R. (1993), 'Landlords and Warlords in the later Roman Empire', in J. Rich and G. Shipley (eds.), *War and Society in the Roman World*, Leicester–Nottingham Studies in Ancient Society, v (London).

——(1994), *Frontiers of the Roman Empire: A Social and Economic Study* (Baltimore, Md./London).

Wickham, C. (1981), *Early Medieval Italy: Central Power and Local Society 400–1000* (London).

——(1984), 'The Other Transition: From the Ancient World to Feudalism', *Past and Present*, 103: 3–36.

Wightman, E. M. (1970), *Roman Trier and the Treveri* (London).

——(1977), 'The Towns of Gaul with Special Reference to the North-East', in M. W. Barley (ed.), *European Towns: Their Archaeology and Early History*, 303–14 (London).

——(1985), *Galla Belgica* (London).

Wilkes, J. J. (1969), *Dalmatia* (London).

——(1972), 'A Pannonian Refugee of Quality at Salona', *Phoenix*, 26: 377–93.

——(1986), *Diocletian's Palace, Split, Residence of a Retired Roman Emperor* (Sheffield).

Willems, W. J. H. (1986), *Romans and Batavians: A Regional Study in the Dutch Eastern River Area* (Amersfoort).

Williams, S., and Friell, G. (1994), *Theodosius: The Empire at Bay* (London).

Wilson, R. J. A. (1988), 'The Towns of Sicily during the Roman Empire', in *Aufstieg und Niedergang der römischen Welt (Principat)* 22(1) (Berlin/New York), 90–206.

Wolfram, H. (1988), *The History of the Goths* (revised version of the original German edn. of 1979 trans. T. J. Dunlap) (Berkeley, Calif.).

Wood, I. (1994a), *Gregory of Tours* (Bangor).

Wood, I. (1994*b*), *The Merovingian Kingdoms 450–751* (London/New York).

Wormald, P. (1976), 'The Decline of the Western Empire and the Survival of its Aristocracy: Review of J. F. Matthew's *Western Aristocracy and Imperial Court*', *Journal of Roman Studies*, 66: 217–26.

Wozniak, F. E. (1981), 'East Rome, Ravenna and Illyricum 454–536 AD', *Historia*, 30: 351–82.

Zaninović, M. (1977), 'The Economy of Dalmatia', in *Aufstieg und Niedergang der römischen Welt (Principat)* 2(6) (Berlin/New York), 767–809.

Zeiller, J. (1904), 'Les Églises ariennes de Rome à l'époque de la domination gothique', in *Mélanges d'archéologie et d'histoire de l'École Française de Rome*, 24: 17–33.

——(1967), 'Origines chrétiennes dans les provinces danubiennes de l'empire romain', *Studia Historica*, 48 (Rome).

INDEX

Bold numbers denote reference to illustrations.

Index

342 *Index*